R. Cecil DYMALLY

Twisted Circle
TRILOGY

STRONGHOLDS

Copyright © 2015 by R. Ceci Dymally
All rights reserved. No part of this book may be reproduced in any form or by any means without permission in writing from the publisher, except for the inclusion of brief quotations in a review.

Published and Distributed by:
Aaron Alfred Publishing
P. O. Box 361333
Los Angeles, CA 90036

For ordering and additional information:
Visit website: www.twistedcirclenovels.com

This book is a work of fiction. Any references to real people or real places are used fictitiously. Other names, characters, places, and events are products of the author's imagination, and any resemblance to actual events or places or persons, living or dead, is entirely coincidental.

First Printing July, 2015

Cover and Interior Design: Jessica Tilles/TWA Solutions.com

Developmental/Content Editor: Dr. Maxine Thompson/Black Butterfly Press
Copy Editors: Alanna Boutin and Virginia L. Tyson

ISBN: #978-0-692-45079-6

www.twistedcirclenovels.com

Dedication

This book is dedicated to Reno Logan.

His creativity was the catalyst to the development of its menagerie of characters and his steadfast love supported me through the most difficult time in my life (the loss of my mother), which kept me laughing and motivated enough to continue in the writing process. Thank you for all that you poured into me. You are a brilliant enigma! I love and appreciate you!

Special Thanks

First of all I would like to thank my amazing and gifted Agent and Literary Editor, Dr. Maxine Thompson, whose tireless dedication and talent provided me with the tools to bring my manuscript to fruition and make the book so much better. I appreciate your professionalism, your literary genius and your tutelage. You have inspired and encouraged me and I wholeheartedly "Thank you" for all that you have done for me as a writer. You are extraordinary!

Thank you to my copy Editor, Alanna Boutin.

Thank you to my final copy Editor & Proof Reader, Virginia L. Tyson. Your attention to detail impressed me as well as your creative insight and professionalism. You were the icing on the cake. I am very grateful for your timely arrival. You were a gift to me at the right time!

Thank you to my Graphic Designer, Jessica Wright Tilles of TWA Solutions, whose impeccable skills took my ideas and created the book cover that I envisioned. Thank you for your patience and professionalism. You are a class act!

Prologue

August 2014

How come some sins couldn't just be washed away with a hot bath, Rockye wondered as she eased her aching body into a steamy tub laced with scented lavender crystals. Savoring the fragrance, she languidly pulled it deeply into her lungs; her eyes closed and her lips positioned into a pleasant smile. She was now suffering immensely from the results of her personal trainer's earlier upper body workout which left her currently spent and exhausted. She gingerly eased her head back onto the bathtub pillow as much as she could, mindful of the thick towel wrapped around her head so as to not disturb the integrity of her recently flat ironed hairstyle. Getting lost into the soulful harmony of John Legend streaming from her MP3 player resting on a small vanity table near the sink, she slipped into a reflective state.

The peaceful smile painted on her face quickly disappeared as her mind travelled back to a particular event only hours earlier, after she left her trainer. Try as she might, she wanted to block out the memory. As Rockye reminisced, she asked herself, *Why do I do these things? I love my man, but why isn't he enough? What can I do to stop this force that comes over me and calls me to do these vile things?*

"Do you love me?" Andy always asked her.

"Sure, Baby."

Rockye had been seeing her boyfriend, Andy, for over 3 years now, and it was apparent that their love for each other was undeniable. He was everything that she ever dreamed of in a man. Andy was considerate, loving, sexy, thoughtful, attentive, and totally devoted to her. Their lovemaking was exciting and passionate. And despite their racial differences, she found Andy to be extremely compatible with her eclectic temperament. But Rockye, unbeknownst to Andy, harbored a terrible secret. A secret that she never wanted Andy to ever find out about! A terrible secret that she fought every day to control!

Suddenly, she was riddled with guilt from the thoughts of her earlier indiscretion. Rockye reached over and grabbed her Bible, which rested on the back of the commode, and turned carefully to the dog-eared pages of Proverbs 31. Her eyes scanned the pages as it had on countless occasions. She wanted desperately to be this Proverbs 31 woman of the Bible; a capable, intelligent, and virtuous woman, a woman who comforts, encourages, and does her man good as long as there is life within her body.

Pulling the black leather-bound book close to her chest, careful not to let the bottom hit the tepid bathwater, she lifted her eyes to the ceiling and cried out, "O God, help me! Please help me! I need help!" She continued to call out over and over again as the tears welling up in her eyes landed in the fragrant bathwater beneath her. Rockye prayed to God, but the images of her shame from that afternoon suddenly drifted back into the forefront of her mind, playing it back in HD.

After an eventful day of errands, upper body workout, grocery shopping, and a mediocre audition for some cable sitcom in Santa Monica, Rockye glanced down to see her fuel gauge far below the desired empty line.

She needed to refill quickly before she found herself on the side of the road awaiting assistance from AAA. Whirling her car quickly into the Chevron station on Crenshaw and Adams, she bounced out, slid her ATM card into the slot and after the appropriate prompts, inserted the nozzle into her vehicle and stood attentively awaiting for the click indicating that the gas tank was full. There was only one car to her right. She breathed a sigh of relief at the occupant; tall, handsome, slender, chocolate, and dripping with sex appeal. Rockye was relieved because that gas station was known for sinister youths antagonizing its patrons.

He sauntered over to her after she had finished pumping her gas. She felt his eyes studying her frame as she replaced the nozzle in its cradle.

"They call me Merrick. And when I see something I want I go after it! And I want you!" he said with a mischievous smile.

"Oh, yeah? And what about what *I* want?" she teased as her eyes scanned his body from head to toe, settling in on his crotch.

She studied it. He winked. Her lips formed an inviting smile. He moved to the passenger-side window of her vehicle. He joked. She flirted. He reciprocated.

Rockye realized that she was playing with fire. Every fiber of her being was screaming for her to drive off, to just put her foot on the gas pedal and get the hell out of there. But there was this thing that had a hold on her which she was not strong enough to fight. It called her into dark places, into places that she on the surface did not want to go to but could not stop herself, no matter how hard she tried. In this case, some strange man that she had just met at a neighborhood gas station was speaking directly to her erogenous zones, and she couldn't find the strength to pry herself away. She wanted to.

Or did she?

Minutes later, the two were under the freeway, tearing off each other's clothes like wild animals. The sex was wild; he was forceful and confident in his skills and endowment. Afterward, he inserted an embossed business card into her cleavage before speeding off in a black Infiniti. Rockye didn't even look at the business card; she pulled it from her bosom and threw it onto the pavement right next to the abandoned condom wrapper he had thrown out the window only minutes earlier just as soon as he was out of sight. She had no intention of ever seeing him again. She loved her man. She loved Andy!

However, no matter how hard she tried, the demons wouldn't let her go!

Ever since Rockye was old enough to realize that her curvaceous, sensual body could afford her luxuries most women could only dream about, she used it to her advantage to the fullest. She remembered at the early age of 12 that in giving Mr. Clayton, the owner of the corner grocery mart, a peek at her "Kitty Kat" (as she heard it refer to by one of her classmate's grandmothers), it got her many privileges. His peek advanced to a touch, then a taste, and then a poke. These escapades normally were consummated at the Johnsons' abandoned house on the corner of Ninetieth and Avalon.

Afterward, Mister Clayton would give her gifts, money, and compliments. However, one day she realized that she was not doing it only for the things; she actually loved the way her body felt when he played with it, on it, and in it! She craved the orgasms and the feeling of power that was a result of her sexual prowess! She discovered that it turned her on immensely!

Now, while luxuriating in her fragrant bath, she breathed in calm, and as the MP3 player switched from John Legend to Luther Vandross, Rockye took a sip of green tea and sank deeper into the tub. The water funneled through the overflow, causing the draining sound to startle her, and suddenly bringing attention to the fact that the water had cooled down considerably. Stretching forward to turn the hot water on, Rockye thought she heard a thud at the back door.

Pushing the water off, she slightly raised her head to listen intently. Nothing! *Must be the wind,* she thought! Pulling the hot water faucet back on, she eased her head back onto the bath pillow. Moments later... another thud! That wasn't the wind, she thought! Her forehead wrinkled with concern. She continued to listen. Another thud!

Get the hell out of the water and see what that is! the little voice in her head screamed.

Rockye launched out of the tub, quickly covering her wet body with a plush Bellagio bathrobe she commandeered from the 5-star hotel while visiting last summer, and moved with catlike precision toward the back of the house. The thick carpet underneath her wet feet muffled the movement as she neared the back door.

Suddenly a crashing jolt sprang from the front door, causing her heart to race with trepidation!

"Open the damn door, Rockye! NOOW!" Andy ordered.

Rockye's concern propelled to panic! It was Andy, and she knew that tone! That was the *violent* Andy. And when he was violently angry—he was a force not to be reckoned with. Although Andy had never beaten her before in their 3-year relationship, he had put his hands on her enough to give her reason to be somewhat fearful of him when he got angry as a result of him brooding over one of his many issues, coupled with drinking too much alcohol. He was an angry, mean drunk and would not hesitate to take it out on the furniture, windows, and appliances around him.

As a rule, Andy was the epitome of a gentleman: loving, attentive, kind, and affectionate, but when something had him upset, he turned into a beast, and nothing or no one could tame *that* Andy!

Andy adamantly conceded that he wasn't an alcoholic, but when something greatly upset him, he would drink. He was a mean drunk, and on many occasions his violent temper had reared its ugly head at her, causing physiological and emotional bruises.

"I'm not going to say it again, open this damn door NOW!"

Rockye vacillated over whether she would answer the door. She knew with the presence of this angry, inebriated Andy she was going to catch hell. Mustering up all the courage she could, she slowly inched up quietly to the front door and sheepishly responded, "Andy, can you please go away? We can talk tomorrow! Please!"

"Bitch, if you don't open this door . . ."

"Please, Andy! I don't feel like arguing with you tonight!" Her legs felt like Jell-O, causing her to lose balance as she clumsily eased away from the front door.

Now she started to panic. Rockye realized that she had to prepare to run and run fast!

She stumbled to her bedroom, made haste to her closet, and pulled on her burgundy low-rise Juicy sweats and Coach sneakers. She crept back into the living room, her underarms wet from nervous perspiration. Taking air into her lungs was becoming more of a challenge due to anxiety. It was becoming increasingly harder for her to breathe, because she felt on the verge of vomiting from fear!

The heavy footsteps moved to the side of the house near the den. She inched along the wall following the footsteps with her ears with heightened trepidation at each movement.

"You think that I don't know what's going on? I know he's in there hiding like some coward! Tell him to fight for you! He ain't gonna do that! You know why, Rockye? Cause you just some piece of ass to him! He don't give a crap about you!" Andy banged on the side slid door with his fists. "Open this goddamn door!"

"Andy, I swear nobody's here but me!" The pounding in her chest intensified so severely that she believed that she may be having a heart attack!

"Please! Nobody is here! Nobody is in here!" She listened for his response. Nothing! The painfully quiet sounds of the night began to hurt her ears. *Where is he? What's he doing . . . or about to do?* she thought as she held her breath in anticipation.

"Open the door or I will break the damn thing down!" he yelled.

"Andy! Please just go home! Please go home!" Rockye pleaded.

Suddenly a thunderous bang sprang from the back door. The door flew off of its hinges and crashed into her china cabinet just yards away. A demonic roar echoed throughout the house as Andy marched toward her. Rockye turned to run, but Andy was hot on her heels. She felt him grab her by the back of her hair, and with a yank, she went down with a thud.

"Andy, no! Don't! Stop!" she cried out in horror as she sank deeper into an abyss of pain.

Chapter One

One Year Earlier
☞ *Rockye Haynes* ☜

*T*he guilty harbor their own secrets and endure their own punishment in silence.

"You sucked!" she shouted out loud to herself, socking the leather steering wheel with a fully clenched right hand. The thickness of the traffic greatly added to her frustration as she anxiously navigated out of the CBS studio's parking lot on Beverly Blvd. The sweltering sun of the August afternoon was causing her meticulously applied MAC makeup to liquefy down her face, leaving a trail of unsightly streaks.

Rockye left the audition for a Taco Bell audition, feeling terribly distraught while fighting back a wall of angry tears. Angry not only because of her poor performance but the knowledge that that poor audition would ensure her that she would not get a call-back, only a complaint to her booking agent. Why did she have such a poor performance? Rockye had essentially forgotten all of her two lines, as well as missed every single cue. What an idiot!

Those producers had to conclude that she was an amateur, and not a very good one at that! What kind of person can't even remember *two* simple lines? All she had to do was open her mouth, bite a Doritos Locos Taco, wipe her mouth, and then roll her eyes back as though it was the most delicious thing she'd ever tasted while cooing out two lines. *What a dumb ass I am!* she thought. Was she really a dumb ass or was it just the guilt from the earlier indiscretion? Apparently it weighed so heavily on her mind, causing her to be remiss from even being able to find a sliver of focus in order to sell the Super Crunchy Taco made with premium seasoned beef, crisp lettuce, and real cheddar cheese, in a shell made from Nacho Cheese Doritos Chips.

Moments earlier, while hurrying out of Stage 15 at the CBS Studio from the audition, the leg of her nylon snagged on a nail protruding from the doorway as she quickly slid out of the massive warehouse roll up door. Damn! Shit! Now her leg was throbbing. The nail must have nicked her leg as well. She gingerly slid her left hand down the length of her leg to find a tender wet spot a couple inches above her ankle. Great! What else was going to happen to her today? She felt wretched and believed that whatever bad thing that happened to her today, she deserved every bit of it! The guilt became consuming!

The traffic on Fairfax was abnormally slow for midday, midweek traffic with impatient drivers honking their horns as traffic lights turned from green to red repeatedly without any movement. In the distance, sirens blared, sounding increasingly closer as the hovering August heat began to greatly affect her temperament in a not-so-positive way. She was once again experiencing that claustrophobic feeling. Like she was going to implode if she didn't get some relief—right away!

As the thickness cleared, the object of the cluster fuck was a nasty accident where she witnessed a white-haired lady lying sprawled out on the sidewalk with paramedics urgently moving about her. Rockye said a prayer for the lady and in that moment she felt the presence of her Higher Power. She felt God! And at that moment she knew she needed to get to church to make her confession. Rockye needed absolution—and she needed it right away.

Rockye had been attending St. Patrick's Catholic Church ever since she was a young child of eight. The altar, the pews, and the lighted candles in the vestibule always gave her immense comfort and peace; it was the first place she always went to find solace. Once tucked inside the confessional, Rockye slid the little wooden door of the window that afforded her the opportunity to share with the priest and confess her scandalous sin. Once again, she was here feeling horrible after throwing her morals to the wind and looking for the priest to wipe her sins away and make her feel better. She wanted to feel clean again.

"Bless me, Father; for I have sinned. It has been 2 weeks since my last confession." It was always the same she thought as she poured out the *Readers Digest* PG13 version of her sin to the priest. Answering the urging of her overactive libido, Rockye submitted to and satisfied the primal cry of her ravenous body. She didn't merely want to but *needed* to scratch the itch; heed the call, respond to the burning desire. Her body desperately craved to be mounted, pounded, and climaxed! This longing innately burned within her so much that it seemed to forcibly overtake her. At the moment when this sensation permeated her mind, body, and soul, she didn't have the power to fight it but to fall into it, into the spell and the promise for satiation that it ensured. Afterward, she was always burning with remorse, remorse from compromising her body, putting herself in dangerous situations. Not only was she morally breaking her commitment to Andy, she was betraying and being unfaithful to the only man who ever really loved her. As she adjusted her buttocks on the hard wooden seat, she confessed, seeking forgiveness from the priest. Rockye allowed her mind to revisit the reason for her confession.

Last night, at the recording session of her demo CD, "Just listen to me," she performed a song she had written about a girl, who, ironically, is pleading with her husband not to leave her because she was caught cheating on him with his brother. That evening the chemistry between her and her producer, T Max, felt immensely strong, like a current that hung in the air during a winter storm. This combined energy between the two was responsible for propelling her to a whole other level of creative genius. The notes that emanated from her vocal cords were surreal.

About 20 minutes after the session was over all of the crew had quickly vanished, except for Rockye, the producer, T Max, and the janitor who faded into the background polishing the hardwood floors. She could feel T Max's licentious eyes tracing her movements as she slid on a multi-colored crocheted shawl over a form-fitting yellow wife beater T-shirt which held her form like a second skin. Rockye could sense the sexual energy emanating through his pores, which fuelled her more than she cared to admit.

"Rock, you laid it down tonight! Where the hell did you pull that shit from, I don't know," he commented.

"It was you, T. You brought that shit out of me. You have a way of making me feel so invincible! I feel so uninhibited; I feel like I have no limitations. You make me feel like I can do anything, and that shit just turns me the hell on!" she teased seductively.

"You turn me on!" T Max said, easing up behind her and cupping her firm breasts with his massive hands.

"T, you should stop!" Rockye moaned, half-meaning it.

He ignored her weak rejection, and instead, grabbed her hand and placed it on his engorged crotch. She squeezed it. He groaned.

Next, he unzipped his pants and released "Big Max," as T Max often referred to his penis.

Rockye gasped at the sight. "Damn, T, I didn't know that you was packin' like that!"

"Now that you do, what ya gonna do 'bout it?" His head tilted to the right as he slid his pink tongue across the smooth curvature of his symmetrical lips.

Seconds before grabbing his penis with both hands, Rockye hesitated slightly, as the image of her man, Andy, briefly flashed across her mind.

"What's wrong, girl? Too much for ya?" he teased.

Then just as quickly as it came, the face of her man of 3 years just vanished. His wide set darting eyes, his thick eyebrows that rose slightly when he was perplexed about something, his thin upper lip and wide full bottom lip that kissed and teased her full lips with such passion; his sexy full moustache, sometimes spilling into a light beard, his smooth vanilla-toned skinned that burned so easily when exposed too long to the sun, his spiky dark brown hair full of gel and the 1 carat diamond earring she bought him on their first-year anniversary which decorated his left lobe—vanished—was gone—poof!

"Never too much!" Rockye breathlessly mouthed, simultaneously plunging her tongue down his open mouth to the depth of his hot throat.

T Max ripped the shawl and wife beater right off her body in one full motion. In reciprocity, she tore off his shirt so quickly that all six buttons scattered to the floor beneath them.

Things were so dangerously erotic that they didn't even see that the night janitor had eased up behind the door, his narrow-set, voyeur-transfixed eyes on their salacious behavior. He laid down his mop, rolled out his penis from the dusty dungarees, and pleasured himself. Nothing like a live porn show right in front of you!

In that instant the only thing that concerned Rockye was chasing the climax that her body craved and tweaked for. The need for breathless intercourse—sucking, thrusting, mounting, exploding, and vigorous activity overrode all sensibilities. No one or nothing at that moment mattered for she was chasing that orgasm, and she would get it at all costs—nothing other than an intense explosion, a voluminous climax and the release of the fire in her body would satisfy her. At that time, nothing else mattered!

Now there she was at church, confessing to the priest and dealing with the aftermath of a guilty conscience.

Rockye Haynes grew up in the Jordan Downs projects in Los Angeles where everything she learned about life came with a great deal of calculated sexual manipulation. She was a product of a welfare system West Indian mother from Trinidad and an African American father, who abandoned them seconds after finding out that the woman he had been having casual sex with outside of his marriage was pregnant.

Soon after hitting puberty, it didn't take Rockye long to learn that her large, sultry, almond-shaped eyes, pouty, curvilinear lips coupled with her cocoa-brown skin highlighted by her West Indian red undertones and 38-24-40 measurements, if used correctly, would award her opportunities and benefits that her female counterparts could only dream about.

Rockye was an exotic-looking beauty. Carrying her 132 pounds on a 5 foot 7½ inch frame proportionately, Rock, affectionately called by her friends, would complement her wavy mid back-length hair with extravagant bejeweled hair ornaments and her body with designer form-fitting fashion. If her beauty, gregarious personality, or uninhibited style of dress didn't call attention to her, the amazing sounds that emanated from her vocal cords would cause anyone to stand up and take notice. Rockye was a truly gifted singer, and as most men labelled her, "drop-dead gorgeous."

After many unsuccessful years of dating black men, Rockye investigated other races, and eventually settled on Andy, a Caucasian who had slightly favored Matthew McConaughey, carrying an ample amount of black swagger. He was so vastly different from the black men she was used to going out with. Instead of hard, controlling, and inflexible, she found Andy loving, attentive, easy to please, and agreeable. His lovemaking, while not pounding headboards like she was used to, was satisfying and extremely unselfish. He loved on her body for hours before he even took to getting himself pleasure.

Growing up without a father, Rockye wasn't sure exactly how a man should behave. As a result, she cultivated a lot of insecurities and inadequacies. She didn't know why she did a lot of the things that she did; she just knew that it satisfied something in her for the moment. Meeting strange men, exchanging sexual overtures provided a thrill like nothing else in her life could. Rockye loved sex for the mere pleasure of it, and she returned to it over and over again at every opportunity that presented itself.

Conversely, afterward, she was utterly appalled and disgusted with herself and her careless actions. Rockye constantly prayed for healing. She prayed that she could stop before it was too late. God help her if Andy ever found out!

"Bless me, Father, for I have sinned. It has been 2 weeks since my last confession. I had sex again with a strange man! I didn't even know him and I just ... I just did it! I did it again!" Rockye confessed to Father Maloney at St. Patrick's Catholic Church.

"... and also pray 10 Hail Mary's. And may God be with you, my child!" the priest concluded after briefly counseling her before closing the little window that allowed her access to his holiness for a few precious minutes during confession. Making the sign of the cross, Rockye rushed to the altar to do the penance given by the priest for absolution.

Two days later, Rockye rushed to an appointment with a holistic doctor, Dr. Tong. He was known for his unconventional treatments with sexual addictions. She was desperate to do whatever it took to rid herself of this monkey on her back. Dr. Tong's office was clear across town and traffic was thick on the

Santa Monica Freeway. She heard that his treatment was a bit unorthodox, but in her desperate need to find a solution to her addiction, she was willing to try just about anything.

Rockye had been having illicit sex with strange men ever since she discovered the pleasures it rendered after the first experience she had with Mr. Clayton, the owner of the neighborhood corner market at the age of 12. And after he helped her discover the pleasures of the many erogenous zones on her body and how to master them, there was no turning back. But after falling in love with Andy, so many times she felt appalled by her behavior afterward and the excessive need for sex and desperately wanted to get help.

As she entered the underground garage of the medical building, she reached into her purse and discarded the extra condoms she stored for her encounters. She tossed them at the receptacle, but they landed on the outer rim. Rockye couldn't even do that right! Dumb ass!

The doctor's quaint office smelled like a mixture of herbs, incense, and musk. Dr. Tong was a small man with an odd, offensive odor emanating from his person. She held her breath as he talked. His mouth smelled like stale ass.

"That smells awful! You expect me to drink that foul-smelling stuff?" Rockye complained as the Korean homeopathic physician poured a sludgy brown-colored brew into a tiny china cup. After their brief consultation, he ushered her into a tiny room no bigger than an apartment closet which barely held an exam table, a folding chair, and a stool. He pointed to the metal folding chair.

"Sit."

From the cabinets above which overflowed with tiny drawers full of various exotic herbs and plants, he proceeded to produce an admixture of the contents of several drawers into a steeping pot of water that smelled of vinegar. After 10 minutes of brewing, he handed her the cup of the smelly concoction.

"You must drink now!"

Her face wrinkled up instantly from the strong bitter taste as the mixture landed on her tongue. Halfway through the swig she asked, "Is this really necessary, Dr. Tong?"

"Drink! Drink all now!"

After finishing the putrid brew, the doctor summoned her onto the examination table.

"Take all off," he gestured to her lower extremities. "Lay down! Open legs!"

He proceeded to rub a sticky substance onto her abdomen, inner thighs, and pubic area.

Immediately following, he lit a series of candles and started chanting. Intermittently, he pulled in a mouth full of liquid from a canteen on a small table behind him and spit it all over her.

"Open leg! Wide!"

Next, he inserted a cold, plastic-textured tube into her vagina. His chants became louder and quicker as his strokes of the cold, textured tube fell in line with the beat.

He sucked in more liquid from the canteen and continued to spit on her over and over.

Rockye wanted to ask him what all that shit had to do with helping her overcome her addiction with sex. She had read an article about Dr. Tong and his revolutionary procedures in the treatment of sexual perversion. And that was why she was subjecting herself to this craziness. She was desperate to find out why her body craved the physical attention of men when she had a wonderful man at home who loved and adored the ground she walked on!

Rockye needed to kill the inner demons driving her to this aberrant sexual behavior. Those demons called her into dark places and dangerous, risqué situations. She had finally found a good man and didn't want to lose him. She would try anything, including this weird Korean man spitting some liquid all over her while inserting some cold, plastic-textured tube into her vagina.

Forty-five minutes and $175 later, he instructed her to go into the bathroom.

"Wash now! Cleanse your body, inside too!" He pointed to her vagina.

"Next 3 weeks you come back. We do again!" He turned and left, leaving Rockye feeling absolutely ridiculous and duped out of $175. Dr. Tong took her money once, but it would not happen again. She would not be insane enough to return to this foolishness.

As she washed the sticky substance from her body, all Rockye could think about was that there wasn't anything that she wouldn't do to kill the insatiable appetite burgeoning within her. She would try anything to kill it . . . before it killed her.

Chapter Two

~ Keno Hunter ~

"Faster . . . faster . . . right there . . . ohhhh, I'm comin'! I'm comin'!" Her eyes rolled back into her head as her oversized frame violently shook beneath him. As his partner reached multiple orgasms, which the French called "*les petites morts,*" she really looked as though she had died each time she shuddered to a climax.

Long, rough, and penetrating were his thrusts. Her screams vibrated off the mauve-colored walls, creating a symphony of voice, banging headboards, and squeaky bed frame.

When he heard his partner's last ecstatic scream, Keno breathed a huge sigh of relief. *The job is over!* he thought. Finally, she'd achieved her last orgasm! Keno elongated his over 6 foot frame onto the substantial oversized mattress and stretched catlike. Vigorously stroking the deep caverns of her vagina in and out, intermittingly, slowly alternating from side to side had left Keno physically spent. She took a lot of exertion, for her 57-year-old body, which showed obvious signs of aging, had long lost its elasticity from its younger days. Due to the strenuous sexual activity, a nagging cramp crept in on Keno's left butt cheek.

A few more hours of witty banter and he would be able to get the hell out of here. His job will have been done for the day! Having sex with Sharon was a task he dreaded, but the benefits for sure outweighed the agony of the chore.

After falling back heavily onto the California king-sized bed, he flexed his buttock, hoping to quickly relieve the intense spasm while indiscreetly wiping off the sweat on his face on the 1,800 thread count cream-colored Egyptian cotton sheets.

"You enjoyed that?" Keno asked, not really giving a damn about the answer.

The bloated woman beside him rolled over to face him, smiled her yellow smile, and then said, "Cupcake, I needed that! I have been thinking about that all day long!" Her close-set eyes quickly started to survey the 800-square foot master bedroom.

". . . get my purse for me, will ya?"

Easing his bare feet onto the heated jade bedroom floor, Keno quickly located the oversized Louis Vuitton satchel she routinely carried tucked in the corner of the room near the chaise lounge. Picking it up, he presented it to her with quickness. He knew from the request that she was having a nicotine fit and the quicker she was able to pull in a drag of the stick, the happier she'd be.

The view of Wilshire Blvd. from her floor-to-ceiling bedroom windows called Keno to fantasize about rolling back to his Culver City condo in the new Mercedes CL 500 Sharon had purchased for him only 2 months prior.

The sunset painted the sky with a sequence of colors that resembled a luminous abstract painting. The yellow grew brighter and denser, and then began to fade into a deep orange that spread freely across the sky, the orange spewing higher and higher, left to right, right to left. It appeared the sun was screaming, "Check me out!"

"Thanks, Cupcake!" the middle-aged woman responded as Keno handed her off the Louis Vuitton satchel. She pulled out a pack of half-emptied Benson & Hedges, as well as a 24k gold cigarette lighter with the initials SNF engraved on the front.

She was Sharon Nicole Faraday of the Chicago "Faradays." Her family's dynasty was one of three generations of International

Builders. She was a multimillionaire many times over! Sharon was a woman who loved her cigarettes, her liquor, and the pleasures of younger men—preferably 25 years to 30 years her junior.

"I'm going to have to watch out for you, babe! You may put me in the hospital yet with moves like that!" the slightly gray-haired, 57-year-old Caucasian heiress teased. She attempted to laugh, but her smoker's hack disabled her from doing so.

"Get me a glass of water, Cupcake, will ya?"

Inwardly, Keno cringed. He detested the nickname. He padded to the kitchen and secured a cold bottle of Fiji water from the refrigerator and handed it off to her as she readjusted her half-naked body against one of the many oversized pillows resting at the head of the bed.

"Come over here and snuggle with me. Lay with me for a while! Don't get up so quick!"

Before he could take the first dreaded step in her direction, one of her many business cell phones started to sing. He was familiar with the tune, Claude Debussy's "Clair de Lune."

"Sharon Faraday here," she announced with confidence after sharply depressing the talk button.

"Is everyone involved already logged onto the Web conferencing station? I will not wait one moment for any latecomers like last week."

He knew it was her overseas office on the line because of the lateness of the hour and by the condescending tone in which Sharon spoke. Immediately ignoring him, after grabbing the singing phone, Sharon suited up with her deliberate business voice, draped the top sheet around her wide bottom, and headed toward her tastefully decorated office. He could hear her delegating and barking orders.

"I need all projections for the Bangkok Project e-mailed to me immediately before we even begin."

By the tone in her voice, Keno knew that she would be on that phone call for quite some time. *So much for being able to get the hell out of here soon!* Another damn Web conference meeting! And by the looks of it, he would have to wait a few more hours until she was off the phone before he could secure his weekly allowance and get the hell out of there. *Damn!* he screamed in his head.

After turning on the ceiling fan, Keno stretched out his muscular 6 foot 4 inch frame diagonally across the bed, closed his eyes, and reviewed his plight.

Keno Hunter was a 33-year-old high school dropout with a lengthy prison record. His inability to get and hold a job was largely due to his unwillingness to work for pittance when he could generate considerably more money performing a crime or securing the affections of a wealthy, older female. As he lay comfortably in the plush feather poster bed of his paramour, he contemplated his bone of contention. Keno was in love with someone else; not his usual "rich-what-can-she-do-for-me type," but a much-younger "I-am-broke-and-struggling" type. This woman who loved him with all that she had, a woman that provided him with the unconditional love and acceptance that he had always craved since childhood, was the only woman his heart truly connected with, the only woman he really wanted to be with. However, in spite of his love for her, he was not willing to give up Sharon and all of the benefits that she provided him with. Nobody was worth that sacrifice—not love, not anything!

This someone special was Deidre Griffin, Dee Dee for short. She was a 22-year-old college student with more heart than money. She was broke and of no help to him, other than emotional support. Keno scoffed. That and a dollar could not even buy him a cup of coffee. And although he loved Dee Dee very much, his love for money and financial security was significantly more substantial.

As he lay there in Sharon's bed, pondering what he would do for the next few hours before she came back to bed, he drifted off to sleep as the soothing breeze from the ceiling fan above danced lightly across his naked frame.

Keno pretended to be asleep as Sharon hovered over him, watching his chest rise and fall as he lay sprawled across her bed; the Italian imported comforter wedged tightly between his legs. Kneeling beside the bed she whispered, "You are one beautiful man! You have no idea how much pleasure you give me!" she said as she massaged her stimulated groin with one hand and with the other rubbed his round, firm derrière.

"Cupcake, as long as you continue to satisfy me, you will be well taken care of. But God will not be able to help you if you fuck over me though!" She kissed and fondled his ass as she stood above him pleasuring herself.

Although Keno played asleep, he knew that the enormity of his now limp man-tool dangling over his left leg excited her immensely, causing her vagina to immediately become wet at the sight. He knew Sharon and what she liked. She stood looking down at his body as she masturbated. Ten minutes later, she panted and let out an audible groan from her orgasm. He increased his breathing so she would continue to believe that he was asleep. Eventually, he heard her leave the room and when she returned, Sharon placed two large overstuffed shopping bags on the chaise lounge next to the glass wall, overlooking Wilshire Blvd. His left eye peeked from beside the feathered pillow. He knew that those packages contained the very things that Keno had been hinting about for some time. Sharon also inserted a wad of what looked like $100 bills within the billfold of his wallet she retrieved from his sweatpants. *A little pocket money for me*, he thought. It was just enough to do a few things, but not enough so that he might feel too independent. Alongside his driver's license was her platinum Master Card and Visa Master money debit card she had given him months earlier.

Sharon was leaving no stone unturned. Regardless of their nearly 25-year-age difference, Keno knew that she thought that no other woman could do for him what she could do for him. That was her edge!

He rolled over allowing his manhood to come in full view of her hungry eyes.

"Damn, you are one fine-ass hunk of a man!"

He opened his eyes, no longer pretending to be asleep. "Hey, beautiful, you off the phone?"

She didn't reply; instead, she dropped her robe to the ground and navigated her heavy frame over to the bed, positioning her vagina on top of his face.

Time for me to get back to work, he thought. He closed his eyes and thought about the Mercedes she just bought him and the gifts awaiting him over on the chaise lounge. Thinking about that was all the foreplay he needed. His penis rose up like a cobra, and he was ready to handle his business.

Chapter Three

~ Bailey Levine ~

Have you ever loved someone so hard that you did things that sickened you to your core just to get their love and approval?

Bailey's answer to that question was Chance!

Her private cell phone sang "We belong together" by Mariah Carey. It was him! Although she held a master's degree in economics, owned 12 pieces of property, was the founder and sole owner of Levine Realty, a successful, top-ranked real estate brokerage firm in Southern California, her stomach catapulted into somersaults every time she heard that ring tone. It was a combination of trepidation and exhilaration!

She had fallen under Chance Lewis's spell over 3 years ago. He came into her life like a whirlwind; quick, dramatic, and disastrous. His 6 foot 3 inch frame held a proportioned sexy, muscular physique. His eyes were expressively large, bright, and enticing. His smile was ample, mesmerizing, and inviting. He wasn't particularly handsome, but there was something about him—an intangible "something" that Bailey couldn't define but nonetheless invaded her spirit and had her hopelessly consumed.

Chance was never particularly nice to her. He never took her out on dates, nor spent any quality time with her. He never promised her anything, nor made any authentic pledges of love. Instead, he lied to her and kept her at arm's length, emotionally and physically. Including their sexual trysts, he only used her body for his selfish pleasures. He always contacted her when he wanted to have sex, and afterward, he would vanish from her world, leaving her feeling hollow and soiled.

But regardless of how Chance treated her, when Bailey was with him, she felt that she was exactly where she was supposed to be. He never did anything that made her feel important or special; however, just being in the general vicinity of his essence made her happy. Bailey didn't understand the hold that this man had on her. She didn't understand why a man who mistreated her could conversely make her feel so happy. Her emotions danced between elation and despair. Whenever she anticipated their get-togethers, she was overjoyed; but conversely, after leaving him, the disappointment and hurt she experienced sent her too often spiraling into a state of depression, frustration, and confusion.

She slowly raised the phone to her ear as her heart pounded intensely within her chest and apprehensively pressed the TALK button. "Bailey Levine!" she announced.

"Do you miss Daddy?" His sexy baritone voice echoed through the phone.

"Hello, Chance." She forced a dry edge in her voice.

"Don't act like you ain't glad to hear my voice, babe."

Bailey didn't respond; just grunted.

"Aw right . . . be like that! What ya doin' tonight? I got a surprise for you, babe!"

"Chance . . . I told you I'm not going to do that stuff anymore."

"Come on, babe. You know you miss Daddy. Nobody does it for you like me! Have you forgotten how good it is?" His voice was low and breathy.

In front of her staff and clients, Bailey was a confident, self-assured woman with answers and solutions appearing quickly on the tip of her tongue; however, with Chance, she was a cowardly, scared little girl, constantly compromising herself for the hope of his approval, which she never got! She had acted this way for years, and it was only recently that she decided to put an end to it. Six months ago, Bailey firmly pledged to no longer subject herself to his narcissistic requests and sexually deviant demands!

"I told you that I needed some space!" Bailey timidly responded.

"Come on, babe... You know you want to see me. Don't you miss me, babe?"

"I gotta go!" Beginning to lose her resolve and taking notice of the fierce heart pounding within her chest, she started to vacillate. Bailey pictured his long, curly eyelashes, his full lips that turned to a point in the middle, and the way his round, full derrière sat high on his backside. She realized how desperately she missed his kisses, his jokes, his arms that held her like nobody else ever had, his stiff, long, thick di—

"I gotta go!" Bailey jolted herself from the spell.

"Hey, babe... don't you love me anymore?" he whined.

Gripping the phone closely to her ear, she uttered no response. She wanted to say, "Hell yes, I love you. I miss you so much. I can't breathe without you. I need you, baby!"

"Do you love me?" his sexy voice repeated through the phone.

"How I feel about you is not the problem! You know what the problem is, Chance? Let's talk about the *real* problem!"

"Damn, girl, why you always got to be naggin' all the damn time?"

"I just don't understand why I can't come to your house. We have been seeing each other for 3 years and you never let me come to your house! Why can't I come to your house, Chance?"

"I told you, my roommate doesn't like strange people in his house. He had a bad experience before, so he doesn't want any strangers all up in his space. If I had you come over it would just cause problems for me, and I don't need more problems in my life right now! One day I will be able to afford my own place, and then you can come over then."

"You have been saying that for 3 years, Chance! Why haven't you been able to afford your own place in 3 years?"

"Look, Bailey, you know that I am busting my ass to make this music thing happen! I got this deal working with Paramount Records, and any day now it could all happen for me!" he lied.

"Okay, then, why don't you ever take me out? We never go anywhere," she sniffled.

"You know I don't do the public thing! I like it to be just you and me. I am *not* into crowds! I don't know how many times I need to tell you that!" he lied again.

"So what you are saying is that we are never going to go out and do anything? Is that what you are saying to me?"

"Look, babe, I got something for us to do right now. I got the huge, stiff pipe in my pants, and you and I can work on relieving some of his tension. You want something to do—*that's* what we can do!" he chuckled.

"Damn you, Chance . . ." She depressed the END button, quickly stuffing the cell phone into the lower left-hand side of her desk drawer. She was tired of the lies, the games, and the disappointments.

It continued to play "We Belong Together" as he persistently dialed her number. Bailey had to admit that Chance was extremely persistent when he wanted something. She reopened the drawer, retrieved the phone, and stared at it. There flashing over and over was his picture. Chance . . . sporting his favorite navy-blue Nike baseball cap, cocked to the side, smiled at her with that knowing look in his eyes that always made her weak on impact.

The memories rushed in as she continued to stare at his flashing picture on her cell phone's face.

Bailey reminisced.

It had been a cold, rainy December late night, days before Christmas, not more than a year ago. His call that night led her to believe that he had a Christmas gift for her. Excited, she rushed out from the warmth and safety of her home to meet him, hopeful of a new beginning. They met in the lower level of a deserted parking lot at the Westside Pavilion in Los Angeles. The location was his suggestion, and although she was apprehensive, she relented.

Chance had never bought her a gift before and the anticipation of one gave her immense expectation for the possibilities that just maybe he had a change of heart toward her and was finally ready to treat her the way she had always wanted . . . with love and adoration. Her hopes were quickly dashed several minutes after arriving to find no gift at all, only Chance—and another man leaning against his car with a big red bow on the strange man's nakedness, and Chance grinning from ear to ear as though he had just presented to her a fantasy come true.

"Come on, babe . . . Do it like I like it! You know what to do." He pushed her head down onto the groin of the unfamiliar man.

"Yeah, girl, I have been waiting for this all day! I heard that you got mad skills! Show me what you got!" His hand cupped the back of her head and shoved it onto his fully erect, waiting penis; his prickly bush overgrown from lack of maintenance scratched her face.

"Chance, I really don't want to do this!" She was trying to remove the blindfold he'd secured on her just moments earlier.

"Babe, do this for Daddy. You know how much it turns me on. I love to watch you! Come on, do this for Daddy!" he coaxed.

She started to cry. She didn't want to do it.

He leaned forward and whispered into her ear, "Don't embarrass me in front of this guy! I ain't gonna go out like some punk! Do the damn thing! And do it like I like it!" He pushed her head further down into the lap of the thick-legged man in front of her whose genitals reeked of Aloe Vera. She wanted to vomit at the stench.

"Come on, girl, give Daddy a show!" he instructed as her rhythm slowed.

As the tears escaped through the tightly secured blindfold and rested on the ground beneath her, Bailey continued to move her gaped mouth up and down on this stranger's shaft with reckless abandon until he spilled forward a large amount of thick semen into her mouth. It was bitter and held the fragrance of absinthe.

After it was over and the two men conversed, she huddled in the corner watching the man who had just emptied himself in her mouth, and Bailey asked herself, "Why am I once again performing oral sex on a man I don't know in order to make the man that I love, love me back?" Bailey had been performing sex acts on men for Chance every bit of the 3 years of their relationship. He would mostly watch. Hardly participate. Occasionally, she would free herself from the blindfold to discover Chance standing at a distance watching, cheering, all the while pleasuring himself.

Calling herself back to the present, she pushed the END button, and turned her cell phone completely off. As she stared off into the distance, Bailey wondered exactly how long it would take until the sound of his voice no longer held that addicting effect on her.

The buzz of productivity hung in the air at Levine Realty as its employees moved deliberately about the office in efforts to reach the high expectations set forth by the 31-year-old owner, Bailey Levine.

Levine Realty was the second-largest independent real estate firm in Southern California; a ranking that the owner was determined to change as expeditiously as possible to become the #1 real estate firm in Southern California.

Bailey twirled a burgundy Mont Blanc pen within her French-tipped right hand as her assistant, Mandy, updated her on the events of the busy workday ahead.

"Okay, who is the first client on our list today?"

"Maggie and Paul Jones. It seems that there were many offers on the Raintree property. We submitted the best offer we could and should have the final counter by midmorning tomorrow."

"Does it look like their offer will be accepted?" Bailey queried as her eyes maintained their hypnotic gaze into space, a habit she had acquired her last years at UCLA during the endless drowning lectures from the stoic professors.

"In speaking to the seller's agent, it doesn't look so good for them. So just in case, I have scheduled other properties to show the Joneses Saturday if their offer is not accepted." Mandy waited for Bailey's nod of approval before continuing.

"Okay, then, keep me posted. What about the Longs?"

"The Longs are refusing to fix anything from the buyers' request for repairs. They are becoming really difficult." Mandy handed her boss the form detailing the client's repair requests.

"The buyers are not asking for much to be done. Just to replace the heating and air-conditioning filters and to replace the sliding door screens." Bailey eyed Mandy with a frustrated look.

"I'll go by there tomorrow and see what's really going on. They are holding out for some reason, and I hope that it is not one of Sid's agents trying to steal one of my clients again!" Bailey handed Mandy back the form.

Mandy remained silent as did most of her employees when the name of Sid Shultz was mentioned. Sid Shultz's Real Estate was #1, and Bailey desperately wanted to buy him out, therefore making her agency #1—a dream she was diligently working at turning into a reality.

"Anything else?" Bailey scanned her appointment book for the morning. She had many calls to make.

"One more thing. The Gonzales family called and wants to list their house."

"Give it to Felicia. She will be happy to have her first listing." Felicia was a newly hired, extremely ambitious, highly motivated dark-skinned African American girl in her mid-20s. Bailey hired her because she exhibited every characteristic that she herself wished she had possessed. Felicia was a confidant, self-assured, determined young lady who knew who she was, what she wanted, and was not afraid to go after it.

Bailey Levine, a product of a Jewish-European father and an African American mother, was constantly struggling with her identity. Physically, she inherited her father's chiseled nose, his light eyes, straight hair and light skin; basically, she was told that she "looked white." However, everything about her on the inside was African American . . . from her love of African American literature and history down to the powerful connection she had with her Southern roots given to her by her strong-willed Valdosta, Georgia-born mother. Although she looked Caucasian on the exterior, the core of Bailey felt African American!

Being constantly mistaken for white had become an extremely unsettling issue for Bailey. Internally, she continuously battled with feelings of inadequacy, and little by little, it was imploding within her, resulting in shadows of rejection, bitterness, and depression in her day-to-day life.

"They only want you!" Mandy announced.

"Okay, confirm the appointment and check with Felicia. I will take her with me and have her co-list it."

Felicia had only been hired about 5 months prior. Even though she had only a few months' experience, Bailey saw her raw talent and burgeoning desire for success. The fact of the matter was that when Bailey looked at Felicia she felt that she was looking at her black self. She felt that Felicia was what she would look like if she looked black, and that in itself gave her a great sense of comfort and belonging!

"Anything else?"

"I think that we pretty much covered everything for now," Mandy concluded.

"Okay, then, please close my door when you leave. I don't want to be disturbed."

Mandy marched out, leaving Bailey feeling anxious and unsettled.

She leaned back into her leather chair, palms of her hands cradling the back of her head. Then she reached into her drawer and pulled out her cell phone. After turning it on, she scrolled to his photo.

What was it about Chance that imprisoned her very soul? What was it about him that enslaved her, tormenting her spirit? Why couldn't she extricate herself from his treacherous hold? He was a toxic person, and being with him was like being addicted to crack.

Chapter Four

☞ Keno Hunter ☜

Keno adjusted the Raymond Weil Toccata watch that Sharon had just given him. It had a stainless steel, 18k gold-plated bracelet with a mother-of-pearl dial. He snapped it onto his right wrist and salivated over how expensive it was, for he had never before owned a watch over $79. He had his eye on it for several weeks and anticipated that it would be just a matter of time before Sharon made a gift of it to him after his all-too-many-subtle hints.

Satisfying her overzealous sexual appetite had seemed sometimes too much for him to bear, but today, as he looked at the $1,200 timepiece and the various packages spread before him, he felt that maybe it wasn't so bad after all. Keno knew that he could not afford to buy any of these things on his own. He had neither the money nor the means. So until he could provide for himself, he would do whatever it took to keep Sharon happy. Because if she was happy, he would get everything he wanted but couldn't afford to pay for on his own, at least not yet!

When he eventually awoke from his second round of attending to her uncustomary nymphomaniac needs, he found her gone but the remnants of her gratitude left behind: packages, a card, and a Post-it note with Sharon's signature lipstick kiss on it resting on the chaise lounge adjacent to the bed. Beaming like a child on Christmas morning, he propped himself up on her decorative pillows in bed to begin tearing away at the packages. In them he had found the watch Raymond Weil watch, a 64 GB iPad, an iPhone, a couple of cashmere sweaters, a pair of

Versace men's lace-up dress shoes, and a diamond pinky ring consisting of two rows of brilliant diamonds totaling about 20. It was incredibly gorgeous!

Opening the card last, it read:

Cupcake, you make me feel like a teenager again! I love you! Sharon

The Post-it read, *Had to go to the office! You were sleeping so peacefully. Didn't want to wake you! Dinner tonight? Kisses, Sharon*

Noticing the time as he glanced at his new Raymond Weil, he picked up the house phone and dialed the private line of Sharon's Beverly Hills office. It was kissing noon; the time she was usually rounding off her ten a.m. staff meeting. Obviously anticipating his call, Sharon picked up on the first ring.

"Cupcake!" Her voice was noticeably pleased to hear his.

"Sharon, you shouldn't have!" he lied. If she hadn't, he wouldn't be there.

"It's just a little token of my love for you."

"I love the ring and the watch! You spoil me!"

"You deserve it, Cupcake."

He flinched at the name. He detested that damn nickname.

"I just called because I wanted to tell you that I was leaving. Last night and this morning were great, babe!" he lied again.

"Will I see you for dinner later?" she pleaded, obviously dick whipped.

"Sure will!" He grimaced. Keno hated having to prostitute himself to Sharon for the sake of the monetary benefits that she provided. He really didn't care for her as a person, but what he did care for was the money and success the relationship provided him.

"I love—"

He hung up before she could finish the sentence, pretending not to hear her.

Keno picked up his cell phone, which was always turned to silent while he was with Sharon, and scrolled down the screen. Twenty-one missed calls. All of them from the same phone number. He would wait until he got into his car before returning the call.

He took a quick hot shower, redressed in the Nike sweats he had come over in the night before, and made a beeline to the subterranean garage of Sharon's multimillion-dollar Wilshire high-rise condominium complex. He had to return those missed calls quickly before all hell broke loose. The valet had his car sitting off to the side as if he knew Keno was on his way down.

Earlier that morning, Sharon instructed the valet of her multimillion-dollar Beverly Hills condo complex to have the CL550 she leased for Keno only a few months earlier to be washed, waxed, and filled up with gas.

He inconspicuously slid a $20 bill into the awaiting palm of the envious valet and plopped down in the leather seat.

His black CL 550 had a glass-shine finish. Sharon was a class act! She knew exactly what she was doing! She left no stone unturned. Money in his pocket, he glanced at the packages in the backseat, a grip of gifts, and an impeccably shined and gassed up vehicle.

Cruising the Miracle Mile via Wilshire Blvd., Keno passed the El Rey Theatre and His & Her Hair Goods where a lot of women got their hair extension supplies. As he made a right off of Wilshire onto La Brea across from the Bank of America, he picked up his cell phone and hit speed dial #3.

"Where have you been, Keno? I've been calling you all night!" a high-pitched female voice broke through the phone lines.

"You know I'm out hustling, Dee Dee! You know that I'm out busting my ass to get my chips." He lied. Keno had to keep up the charade. Dee Dee could never know that he was cheating on her with Sharon for money and all of the benefits it provided him. His car, his town house, his clothes, jewelry, and not to mention all of the money he used to pay his, as well as some of her bills. He didn't particularly like lying to the woman that he loved, but it was a necessary evil.

"Why couldn't you call me back?" she asked.

"Look, baby, when I'm out here hustling, I gotta watch my back for Five-O. I'm not thinking about calling nobody."

"I just don't understand how you can be so busy that you can't call me back. That sounds like the excuse of a man who is seeing another woman! Are you seeing another woman, Keno? Why can't you just tell me the truth? I can feel that you're lying to me! I'm tired of being alone all the time, and I'm tired of you disappearing and telling me these bullshit stories! Why can't you just be honest with me and tell me the truth?" Dee Dee fumed.

"Look, baby, trust me, I ain't with no other woman. I don't have to be! I got you, and you are more than five of the hottest women put together. You know that I love you and only you! So why don't you just stop trippin'? It's all about me getting paid. Not being with other women! If I really wanted another woman I could have one, but I want you and only you!"

She softened. "Baby, I just don't understand where you go! Why do you disappear all the time? Why can't I—"

"Honey, can you please stop the 20 questions! I told you that I'm out hustling! And that's it! Stop sitting around creating all these crazy-ass scenarios in your head! I'm not doing shit but getting my chips, so stop trippin' with me!"

Dee Dee started crying. "I hear what you're saying, Keno, but I just know something is going on! I feel it!"

Keno hated to hear his woman crying, but what could he do? He had to do what he had to do. And as much as he loved his girlfriend of 4 years, she was one broke bitch! She would be in college for another year, and the part-time billing job she had was not cutting it. Dee Dee was a good woman, and he would do the best he could to keep her in his life for she provided the unconditional love that he yearned, but, on the other hand, he would not allow her, or anyone else, to jeopardize him getting paid.

It was hard for a brotha with a record! If people knew how many robberies and home break-ins he had done, they wouldn't believe him. Well over 200 at least! After his sixth arrest, he vowed to find another way to get paid; hence, his skill in wooing lonely, older women to fall in love with his charming alter ego. However, as quiet as it was kept, most times, he really longed to have a life of normalcy. Keno often meditated on how nice it would be to have a 9-to-5 job, a bunch of kids meeting him at the door when he came home after an 8-hour day of work, and Dee Dee barefoot and pregnant in the kitchen, cooking his favorite meals and servicing his every need. He wouldn't mind being the breadwinner, marrying Dee Dee, and providing a stable home so that he could have the type of family he had never enjoyed as a child. However, Keno felt that was just wishful thinking because nobody would ever hire a black man with a rap sheet as long as his. So with that in mind, he would do what he had to do until he could do for himself. He would service Sharon until he got enough resources to start his own business! Although he never shared it with anyone, Keno harbored the lofty desire of having his own security company. Lord knows he was an expert at breaking and entering. Every time he burglarized a home, he looked for the signs that made that home an obvious target. His dream would be to take those skills and parlay it into a business that would empower people to no longer be sitting prey.

He halted the playback reels of his wannabe life to deal with the present.

"Sweetheart, stop crying! You know that I love you! Hey, I got an idea. Why don't you put on that red dress that I bought you last week? I'm going to take you out!"

"I don't want to go out!" she whimpered. "I just want to be with you, I just want you!"

"You got me then, baby! I'll be over soon!" He adjusted the earpiece of his cell phone. Every time he hit La Brea near the 10 Freeway, the connection got scratchy.

"Keno, are you there?"

"Yes, baby?" He pushed through the annoyance he felt from the static connection.

"Please don't hurt me! I'm asking you to tell me the truth. If you are dealing with other females, please just tell me! Let me know. Don't lie to me. Please just tell me!"

"Honey, I don't know how many times I gotta tell you that all I'm doin' is out hustling every night, trying to make my money. I am not dealing with any other women, okay?"

"Really?"

"Yes, baby! It's just you! Just you!"

"Okay, baby. I'm sorry. I'll try to stop trippin'," she conceded.

"Good! That's my girl. Now go and put on that red dress I bought for you and put your hair up the way I like it with the one curl falling on your face."

She giggled.

"I'll be there in a couple of hours. We'll go do something special, okay?"

"Okay, baby," Dee Dee cooed.

"I love you, girl!"

"I love you too! See you in a couple of hours."

Keno hung up his cell phone and noticed that Sharon had called him twice. He turned it off and rested his foot on the gas pedal, heading home. It was getting more difficult by the day to juggle two women. Dee Dee was not as sharp as Sharon, but she, nonetheless, was starting to put two and two together and ask too many questions. Questions that he could not answer! It was getting increasingly harder to keep her close to his heart while simultaneously at arm's length in relation to his day-to-day personal activities. It was a good thing that they did not live together because he would for sure not be able to juggle such deception with Dee Dee so close under foot.

But what was a brotha to do with no high school diploma and two felonies on his record? He had glimmers of hope that one day he'd settle down with just Dee Dee, but the reality was, his desire to have money and success overrode his fleeting need for a normal life. He already had two strikes on his record. One more strike and he was gone for life, so he knew he had to stay below the police radar. This was easy money.

So what was a brotha to do?

Chapter Five

☞ Rockye Haynes ☜

Desire for sex carries with it an uncontrollable energy; it pulls with it an obligation of satiation. It's addictive. It can be exploitative, irresponsible, emotionally distant, secretive, and unsafe. It has no limits. Sex allows you to have power over someone. Sometimes it requires a double life. It can compromise your values, and it sometimes causes you to feel shameful—a guilty pleasure!

Speaking of guilt, why was she not feeling guilty at all? She was in a committed relationship and cheating on the man that she loved; feeling no guilt whatsoever. Well, maybe she did feel some type of guilt. She felt guilty for not feeling guilty, if that made sense. Is there something wrong with me because I feel no guilt? she pondered.

Lying bottomless on the backseat of a compact sports car with her legs spread-eagle, Rockye allowed the sexy hunk of meat to serve her up a healthy dose of his stiff third leg. Her thighs burned as she held them opened wide enough to allow him easy access to the visceral pounding he afflicted into her cavity with reckless abandon. It was very carnal, rather savage like, in fact. She searched herself to see what she was feeling.

She was excited, anticipating an explosive orgasm while her heart pounded. Desirous and simultaneously apprehensive, nervous and disconcerting . . . but no guilt whatsoever!

He pushed into her harder. Real hard—almost too hard! What was he trying to prove by punishing her vagina as he did? It didn't hurt, but it was vulgar and abrasive, to say the least. Why was she allowing him to punish her Kitty Kat? At the thought of the animalistic pounding of this wilder beast she started to search her mind again. Did she enjoy this vaginal torture? How did she feel about this abject pounding? She was trying to feel something. What was she trying to feel? She was trying to feel some semblance of who she was as a person.

Who was she? She was a borderline sex pervert who engaged in abject sexual escapades. That was who she had become!

It was strange because oftentimes during her random sexual escapades, she turned her body off to the indifferent thrusting her body experienced to think about what she was feeling and who this woman was engaging in random, detached sex with strangers. During these times, she'd detach physically while searching for the meaning of it all; it was surreal because she was looking for a connection mentally. It all was so crazy and somewhat psychotic. It was at this point that it seemed as though her body automatically turned itself off. A familiar act she realized when she wouldn't, or couldn't, cope with something malevolent.

She surveyed her surroundings. Her legs were held open by the bucket seats of a small sports car. Its leather interior rendered a cold stiffness underneath her. The tiny windows were fogged up with their breathy pants and the temperature arising from inside. The man-meat straddled the center console clumsily as he spent a concerted effort to balance himself while continuing his rhythmic dance into her cavern of sex. His groaning was barbaric and annoyingly distracting. *Shut up!* she yelled in her head at each deafening vocal output.

"Oh, baby! It's so good! Is it as good to you? OOOOOOOOOO! OOOOOOOO!"

This fool kept yelling OOOOOOOOOO! Did he know how damn ridiculous he sounded? Whatever possessed her to take his inappropriate flirting at the gym to the parking lot and subsequently to having sex with him in the back of his car? It seemed like a good idea at the time. Rockye wanted to have a fierce orgasm, one that wasn't attached to any emotion; only mere carnal lust.

They eyed each other in the back of the gym throughout her 90 minutes' workout routine. He wasn't particularly handsome, but he had a six-pack that was to die for. His ass was pronounced within his off-the-shelf sweatpants. He had really big feet and hands. This caused her imagination to go wild as she salaciously studied him at each rise and fall of the free weights. He benched-pressed what looked like 240 and with little effort, it seemed. That turned her on!

His ding-dong slung back and forth within his loose-fitting sports attire. He was riding commando. She found the obvious size of his dong tremendously erotic. Their foreplay in the gym was hot and obvious. So she was not surprised that he followed her out of the gym when she left.

"Where ya goin' so fast?" He eased up next to her as she quickly strode out to the parking lot.

"Home!"

"Can I come with?"

"I don't know you like that!" she teased.

"Well, how about us getting to know each other? We can change that really quick!"

"What you got in mind?" Her nipples were getting hard at the thought of what was to come.

"Whatever you want!"

"Where you parked?" she asked.

"Right over there, near the back of the building."

She followed him to a small burgundy sports car. He opened the passenger's door and let her in. Then he sauntered over to the driver's side and hopped in. By the time his butt hit the bucket seat of the driver's side; she had disrobed from her workout pants and underwear and was massaging her clit.

"Damn, baby!"

"What did you say about us getting to know each other?" She smiled a wicked smile.

With an awkward familiarity, he reached over and fingered her until she came. She had to admit that he had skills with his fingers. Her orgasm was strong, but her vagina still throbbed to be filled. She slid into the small backseat and opened her legs wide for his entry.

"Let's see what you got!" she prodded.

"Oh, baby, you are some kinda special!" He wrestled to remove his gym pants, which revealed a supersized penis that was expanding by the moment.

"What you going to do with that?"

"Give you the ride of your life, baby!" He plunged into her. The girth of it satisfied her on impact.

She closed her eyes and got lost in the depravity of it all. Fucking a stranger in a parking lot with absolutely no attachment to his feelings was in itself her aim, but the thoughts of how he would pleasure her body heightened the addiction.

Rockye didn't understand what came over her at these times. It was as if she was two different people. What troubled her mostly was the lack of concern prior to and during the act that she had no remorse or shame for cheating on her boyfriend or for the danger that she had put herself into by having random sex with strange men without the use of a condom many times.

Why did she do it? Why did it pleasure her so? Why didn't she get the same pleasure from her boyfriend, a man that loved her so much? Why couldn't he be enough? Why wasn't he enough?

At moments like this, her reason and intellect signed out and her vagina took over. She wanted to get lost in the feeling of being ravaged. She wanted the release that only a fierce orgasm brought and the wickedness of the random sex of a man far detached from her heart, a man who was just an instrument for her pleasure! Nothing else. His welfare afterward was not a concern to her at all. She didn't give a crap if he lived or died. Only that he pleased her at the moment. Her only concern was the rise and fall that only a fierce orgasm would provide!

Rockye had hoped that the therapy sessions at The Circle would aid her into understanding this perverted behavior and subsequently allow her to extricate herself from such misguided behavior. She had tried so many things to cure herself of this deviant behavior, but nothing had worked so far. Most of the times after it was all over, she felt guilty as all get-out, but during the act, she felt nothing for anyone other than the anticipation and excitement of the pending release.

She turned her body back on as his rigorous plunging was beginning to meet up with her G-spot. The intensity was swelling, and her body grew hot at the impending release. He caught wind that she was on the verge of an orgasm, and his rhythm increased.

"Come on, baby, come for me! Let it goooooo!"

And she did just that. She let it go! It was a rather large, enveloping release! She felt light-headed afterward and slightly dizzy. Seconds afterward, he came again as well.

"OOOOOOOOOOO! OOOOOOOOOOO!"

Oh, my goodness. Shut the fuck up! she screamed in her head. The very sound of the ape screaming OOOOOOOOO made her va-jay-jay dry up instantly! She positioned herself to the left of him after he had released, found his T-shirt, wiped herself off, and slid on her pants. She couldn't find her panties. She didn't care because all she wanted to do was get the hell away from this baboon.

"I gotta go!" Her hand was flipping open the car door.

"Hey, wait! How about your phone number?"

She sucked her teeth. "Are you kidding me?"

"I'd like to see you again."

"Come on now. Let's not mistake this for more than what it is—a mere fuck!"

The coolness hit the inside of the car as she swung the door open.

"Well, at least tell me your name." Rockye heard him yell from across the parking lot.

She kept marching until she reached her car. After climbing in, she started it up and sped out of the parking lot into the oncoming traffic with a smile on her face and satiation between her legs. Suddenly she felt like someone was following her, and she glanced in her rearview mirror. A chill raced down her spine, and the smile left her face. Was Andy following her? she wondered.

Chapter Six

～ Bailey Levine ～

"Hi, Daddy!" Bailey's face lit up when she saw her father's face peeking out from over the morning newspaper. After kissing her father on the forehead, she then turned in an obligatory gesture to her mother.

"What smells so good, Mother?"

"Bacon and eggs. Your father has been insisting that I also make pancakes," Marjorie scoffed. "He really needs to lose a few pounds!"

Bailey's father winked at his daughter as she sat down adjacent to him at the kitchen table.

"How's your blood pressure?" Bailey noticed that her father's face appeared flush.

"Too damn high!" Marjorie interrupted. "He doesn't know when to push back from the damn table. One day he'll have a massive stroke, and then I'll be left to take care of him as he lies in bed a damn vegetable!"

"Calm down, Marjorie." He turned to his daughter. "It isn't that bad, baby girl. You know your mother just likes to exaggerate. I just have to watch what I eat and get a little more exercise."

This morning she was looking forward to Sunday morning breakfast with her father, the only man she trusted, for she desperately needed advice from him on how to handle this situation with Chance. Her mother, on the other hand, was another source of exasperation. They never had a close mother-daughter relationship; it had always been strained, combative, and expressly volatile. She basically was a bitch in Prada!

The sweet smell of hickory-smoked bacon had greeted Bailey when she eased open the front door of her parents' two-story brick Hancock Park home. It was the third Sunday of the month; the morning of the Levine's monthly scheduled breakfast which, for the past 30 years, was an established family custom. This was a tradition that had never been broken by Bailey—ever! No matter what she had going on in her life, she was always there every third Sunday for breakfast. It wasn't so much that she desired to be there, but rather the prevailing abject fear of her mother's wrath if she wasn't!

The only bright spot during those arduous family gatherings was that Bailey got to spend some quality time with her father. Her mother, on the other hand, was always a major source of her trepidation. It was a strained relationship, to put it mildly. Her mother was that big bad dragon of most childhood dreams. From as early as she could remember, her mother was an abrasive disciplinarian, critiquing instead of encouraging, accusing instead of complimenting, condemning instead of praising, disdaining instead of admiring. No matter what accomplishment or success she reached, it was never acknowledged by her mother. She was always in the backdrop, shooting poisoned arrows with her words, criticisms, and constant disapproval.

Bailey reflected on a time in junior high where she had been the youngest recipient of a first-place trophy for the regional spelling bee! She beat out over 500 kids. She was praised, congratulated, and recognized by all—except her mother, who brandished a criticism that annihilated the moment. *"That dress made you look cheap."* That's all the bitch had to say. All of that studying, all of that hard work, and to have it all summed up that way devastated her and absolutely ruined *her* moment! She hated her mother for months afterward because of that statement!

Her mother allowed the skillet to hit the bottom of the sink with a thud. She muttered something derogatory under her breath. Bailey's mother, Marjorie Levine, was a middle-aged, darker-skinned beauty. Her hair was coarse and dark, her skin smooth and shiny, her breasts full and her waist small, which accented her full, round derrière. Physically, she was a natural African American beauty, but her personality held its share of bitterness, resentment, and a healthy dose of anger; anger for which Bailey could never identify its origin no matter how hard she tried.

A woman who should have been grateful because of the immense abundance of blessings in her life had instead fashioned a disposition of a scorned, unhappy old woman.

"What's going on with my beautiful daughter?" Her father diverted the subject.

"Things are good," she muttered as she watched her mother spooning a generous portion of her signature scrambled eggs consisting of bell peppers, green onions, cottage cheese, fried okra, and bacon into a serving bowl and placing it in the center of the table.

"If there is one thing that I know for certain in this world it is when my daughter is not telling me the truth." He reached over and stroked her hand. "What's up, sweetie? Is it work?"

Her father's eyebrows rose from concern. Bailey's mother poured the bacon fat from the cast-iron skillet into the bacon grease cup she kept on the stove, and then removed the bacon nestled on folded paper towels which absorbed the extra grease onto a serving dish before joining her family at the table.

"Work is work! But I do have a problem . . . with . . . with Chance!" she confessed.

"Tell me about it, baby girl!" her father encouraged. Her mother remained silent, which, according to history, Bailey knew to be a bad sign. The hairs on the back of her neck began to rise. It was the calm before the storm.

"He won't leave me alone. He keeps calling." Bailey started to feel itchy, something that happened frequently when she became nervous. Her mother's presence always had that effect on her. She felt sweat beginning to form on the back of her neck and under her arms.

Marjorie intentionally dropped the serving spoon onto the table, causing a startling noise.

"What is it, sweetie?" Her father's eyes softened with concern.

"Well, it's kinda hard to get out. I am . . . am . . ." Bailey struggled for the words.

"I knew it! I knew it! I knew that you were going to mess around and get your ass fucking pregnant! Douglas, I told you that this was going to happen! Everything that we did, all of the sacrifices we've made to give you the best opportunities in the world, and what do you go and do with it? You get knocked up with the first no-good thug that gave you the time of day! What the hell is wrong with you, Bailey! Do you *really* think so little of yourself? I wouldn't have even let that thug pick up my trash, much less climb up inside of me and create a bastard!"

"Marjorie! Stop it right now! That's enough! Let the girl talk!" Her father reached out and stroked his daughter's arm. "We are a family! What happens to Bailey happens to us as well!" her father passively remarked.

"Bullshit! I'll be damned if I accept a thug's bastard! I've worked too hard in my life to give HER every opportunity I didn't have!" Marjorie's eyes turned cold as she shifted her attention to her husband.

"It's your fault, Douglas! You coddled her too damn much! What she needed more of was a belt to her fast-tailed ass. You wanted to talk things over with her! I should have never listened to you! I knew I should have followed my mind and beat the slut right out of her the first time I saw it."

"STOP! STOP! RIGHT NOW!" Bailey jumped up from the kitchen table so quickly the coffeepot tumbled to the floor, spilling the dark, hot beverage all over her mother's recently polished kitchen floor.

"What the hell is wrong with you, Mother? I try to talk to you about something that's bothering me and look at what happens!" Bailey belted.

"Girl, you'd better watch who you're talking to like that! I'm your mother, and you'd better show me respect!"

"Respect?! You never show *me* any respect! You talk to me like I have an ass for a face, like my ability to feel was severed with the umbilical cord. I have feelings, and I deserve respect! You have no right to talk to me that way!" Bailey felt heat quickly rise up within her.

"*Right?* I will talk to you any damn way I please. I have a right to do anything I fucking want to do to you because I brought you into this world! You want me to respect you? Ha! Who the hell do you think you are to tell me that I should give YOU respect? I don't have to give you anything! I gave you *life!* That's all you get from me. And I'll be damned if I'll raise a bastard in this house! Go ask that thug you laid up with to give you respect! You ought to be thanking God that I'm not pushing this knife through you right now . . . ending your life and that damn bastard's!" Her mother held a position of attack, a kitchen knife secured in her right hand while her head and neck jutted forward in front of her chest.

Bailey lunged toward her mother. Douglas sprang from his seat just in time to grab his daughter's hands before they found their way around his wife's throat. Bailey's body trembled, her heart racing as she began to hyperventilate, the extra oxygen causing her slight dizziness. Bright red rage coursed through her brain and, in that instant, all that she wanted was to see her mother lying in a still, bloody heap in the middle of the kitchen floor—dead!

"Marjorie! Bailey! Stop it right now!" Douglas positioned himself between them.

"Let's just sit down and talk this out! We're a family! Not barbarians. Now let's sit down and talk this over!" he attempted to reason.

Bailey glared at her father. She loved her father so much, but when it came to his wife, Marjorie, he was a weak excuse of a man. Too many times to remember when she was growing up, Bailey prayed for her father to stand up to her mother, to take control and put an end to her judgmental comments and cruel criticisms. Her mother was always so verbally abusive toward Bailey, and for the life of her she didn't have a clue as to why. Although she fed her, clothed her, and nurtured her like most mothers did, it seemed that the core of her hated her very own daughter. Was it possible to love and hate a person at the same time? Countless hours of reflection concluded no concrete reasons why her mother's behavior was so formidable!

One day my dad will defend me! she continuously hoped. Today was the day it finally hit her. She finally realized that that day would never ever come! Her father would always protect her mother, never her! If anybody was to stand up for her, it would have to be her! Only her!

"Daddy, you stop it! Why don't you stand up and be a man! Why do you let her talk to you crazy and treat me like I'm a reject from some foster home? I have always hoped that you would one day man up and tell her to stop talking to me like she does and treating me so cruel. But you never did! You continue to take up for her! WHY? Do you know what that has done to me? DO YOU?" Bailey threw her hands up in defeat.

"Daddy, I hate you for being so weak!"

Bailey frantically searched the kitchen for her keys.

"A father is supposed to look out for his daughter; he is supposed to be the example by which all other men coming afterward would have to live up to. Some example you turned out to be. No wonder my love life is a fucking mess! No wonder I gravitate toward the wrong type of men!!! It's because of YOU! YOU ARE SO DAMN WEAK!"

Bailey finally found her keys. "I hate the two of you! Daddy, you allowed this woman to treat me like shit most of my life and never said anything! Mother, you call me a tramp, a slut, and whore! How *dare* you talk to me that way."

"I will talk to you—"

"SHUT UP! You listen to me now! You won't have to worry about talking to me ever again. Since you are so disappointed in me, well . . . hear this! As of this day forward, you don't have a fucking daughter anymore!"

Douglas held his wife back who was struggling to get free, swinging the kitchen knife and swearing.

"And by the way, I'M NOT PREGNANT! I just wanted some advice about how to deal with Chance—that's all!" Bailey scooped up her purse and headed for the front door. The morning air still held an obvious chill in it, and as she hurriedly descended the steps of the house, she heard her mother cussing and yelling from the porch behind her. She didn't care anymore. She didn't even look back. SHE WAS DONE WITH BOTH OF THEM!

Bailey trembled as she inserted her keys into the ignition and sped recklessly out into the street toward the guard gate. As she passed the puzzled-looking guard, she glanced down to see her cell phone was illuminated. She pulled over and noticed that she had 22 missed calls from Chance.

She hit his speed dial number and within seconds his agitated voice was on the other end.

"Where have you been? I've been calling you!" His voice was raised and cutting.

"I was with—"

He cut her off. "Whatever, Bailey! I don't really care what the hell you were doing! When I call you, just pick up the damn phone! If I call you, I need you for something, and I don't want to have to keep calling you back to back. When you see my number, just pick up the damn phone!"

"But, Chance . . ." she whimpered. Why did she love a man that was so abrasive and utterly oblivious to her pain, in this moment or any other?

"*But Chance my ass!* When I call you, you need to answer your phone! I don't care what you are doing or who the hell you are with. You need to pick up the damn phone! Do you understand me?"

She remained silent, afraid to give him the wrong answer! She was terrified to provoke him even further.

"Do you fucking hear me?"

"Yes. It will not happen again!" she conceded.

After a few seconds of uncomfortable silence, she timidly asked. "You called me over and over. Is there something wrong?" Her voice was barely above a whisper. Although she had told herself that she was done with Chance, he was one of the few sources of solace that she had in her life right now. Although he was a real asshole, there was something about him that always soothed her! And for that reason she found it hard to excommunicate him from her life entirely.

"Yeah! My car is in the shop, and I need money to get it out! I'll give it back to you when my money is wired from Germany."

Chance was always asking her for money. He always had some deal falling through and was constantly in a state of financial desperation. Bailey realized that he was using her for her massive bank account, but to her, it was a small price to pay for the minuscule amount of happiness that she experienced from the union.

"You told me that last time when I paid your rent. When is your money coming from Germany?"

"Look! You are either gonna help me or not! I ain't got time for all these bullshit-ass questions. You either love me enough to help me or you don't! It's that simple!"

Bailey tried desperately to think. She had lent him so much money, and she was really tired of being his bank, but she also wanted to show him that she that she loved him and would never abandon him in his time of need. She was inadvertently giving him what she needed! Unconditional love!

"So do you love me or what?"

"I love you, Chance, you know I do! I'll get you the money."

"Okay, *that's* what I am talking about! So how soon can you meet up with me?"

"How much do you need, Chance?"

"Only $5,500..."

Bailey drove to her office, tears streaming down her face, and her hands shaking as she tightly gripped the steering wheel. In an indiscriminate location in her office was a wall safe where she kept $50,000 for emergencies. She would get the money that Chance needed and take it to him.

She had just told her parents that she hated them and never wanted to see them again, and now she was on her way to give a man that could care less about her almost $6,000 because she wanted him in her life! She knew that something was terribly wrong with this picture, and although he was an unhealthy obsession, she *had* to do this.

Chapter Seven

~ Keno Hunter ~

Sweetheart, Zach's company is hiring for its West L.A. branch. They are doing interviews next week, and he said that if you just came down, he could get you a job!" Her face beamed with excitement.

"Dee Dee, you know that they ain't gonna hire no ex-con! It'll be a waste of my damn time. The same shit always happen! I'm not gonna put myself through that crap again!"

"It's not like that this time, baby! Zach says that if you just show up, he'll hire you! You won't have to go through none of that stuff like before! He said that he would take care of everything!" She eased up next to him, wrapping her mocha-colored arms lovingly around his waist.

"Besides, baby, it kills me to see you go out every day hustling, not really knowing if you'll get caught!" Dee Dee nestled herself within his chest as he stood easily 6 inches taller than her within the doorway of the clustered kitchen containing more items than the space allowed.

Keno made a sigh of defeat, allowing himself to drink in the probability of a legitimate gig. If he could really get a job then he could finally settle down with Dee Dee and lead a normal life. Could this be a dream come true, or was it just wishful thinking?

"Baby, I know that finding a job with your record is hard! I've seen you go through it! It breaks my heart to see the disappointment on your face after one of those interviews, but this is going to be different. I promise! Zack is going to make sure that you get into the management training program and the best part is that you will be making a lot of money!" Dee Dee handed Keno a white piece of paper with the description of the job that he would be applying for with the salary range written in bold letters across the top. "STARTING SALARY RANGE $75,000–$125,000."

"No shit!" He grinned when his eyes caught the numbers in bold black print.

"And it has medical, dental, vision, and a 401K. Check this out!"

Keno studied the threefold brochure she just handed him. "It looks like they also have profit sharing!" she continued.

"By this time next week, you should be in the manager training program at Papercom!"

She kissed him on his chest, just above his partially exposed 6-pack.

"Just maybe it will be different this time!" he hoped.

Keno had 9 months left of probation on the latest conviction of burglary from a Best Buy in Culver City. With the assistance of a stocking clerk, he loaded over $15,000 worth of appliances, flat-screen televisions, and media equipment in the back of a rented U-Haul. It wasn't until he had passed Sepulveda and Washington that the cops rushed him and ushered the large U-Haul truck into the tight Johnnie's Pastrami parking lot on Sepulveda Blvd. He had been set up by a Best Buy employee and as a result, got convicted of grand theft. Over the last 5 years, Keno had attempted at least a dozen times to find a reputable job but because of his criminal record, the doors were always slammed in his face.

He studied the excitement in her face as she excitedly talked about their future, and strangely enough, it turned him on immensely. He found his manhood growing and the throbbing heightened his sexual prowess beyond control. Dee Dee wasn't really a good looking woman. In fact, her eyes didn't quite fit her face, and her nose was rather disproportionate. Her pear-shaped body evidenced that she ate too much high-calorie foods. It allowed the weight to land unfavorably on her hips.

Regardless of her physical imperfections, the light from her inner being is what resonates and permeates so that you only see the glorious *beauty of her spirit. No other woman he'd known had ever possessed such a quality. He found that immensely sexy and provocative! At the thought, his lips found hers and within moments, the two were pinned up against the doorway, Keno vigorously stroked her insides with his massive erection until audible screams signaling the onset of her climax echoed throughout the tiny apartment.*

After resurfacing from an evening at Sharon's lavish condominium, he made up with Dee Dee and reprogrammed her impressionable mind to believe his web of lies and to trust him without reserve. Keno had to admit that although he loved the fringe benefits of his paramour, it didn't compare one bit to the possibility of acquiring the American dream with the woman he loved by his side.

Tucked away in the tiny confines of her Leimert Park apartment, Dee Dee convinced him of a better life together. The visual that she painted from the loquacious banter excited him immensely. That morning he was in Sharon's bed serving her up with hyperboles and attentive sex, and that evening, with Dee Dee, allowing her to sell him the American dream and believing that he could have what so many took for granted and what he wanted so desperately to have but deduced at times was unattainable for *HIM*.

Smiling at the memory, Keno adjusted his ass from left butt cheek to right on the metal chair, anxiously awaiting his name being called amongst all of the stuck-up suits in the room at his Papercom interview. He looked anxiously around for Zach . . . Where was he?

Could he earn enough income, live with the woman who truly loved him for who he really was, and own a home with a white picket fence full of his own kids? Was it possible for him? Although most days he was extremely confident in his plan to manipulate Sharon long enough to secure enough money and resources to be able to one day pull off attaining independence of her and perhaps start a business, nonetheless, he had rare moments when he began to doubt himself as the fear of his inadequacies began to creep in. It was in those moments that he entertained what he deemed what one day could be possible—impossible!

As a youth, his mother didn't bake cookies for the nonexistent Boy Scout troop he always wanted to be a part of; there was not a father to take him fishing; no siblings to play a wholesome childhood game with; and no nice house with a backyard, green grass, and unconditional love to greet him when he came home from a horrendous day in the public school system. In those moments of reflection he hovered optimistically with the possibility of it becoming a reality with Dee Dee; a house full of their children and all the trappings of that perfect family that he never had but always wanted. On those rare occasions he allowed Dee Dee's dreams to become his own.

Sometimes someone else's belief in you will have to be enough until your own belief in yourself kicks in. And in those moments of hopeful expectation, he allowed her dreams to become his reality.

The hardness of the metal chair was slowly numbing his right ass cheek. Keno closely surveyed the applicants; all dressed up in their best suits, white shirts, and complementary ties. He would have never imagined himself amongst this group of straitlaced do-right white boys in a million years had it not been for his girlfriend, Dee Dee. Her cousin, Zachary, was one of the recruiters for Papercom, the West Coast division. That night, she excitedly convinced him that just maybe he could have the unattainable!

"Keno Hunter," a gray-haired, stocky Caucasian man finally called his name from the doorway of a large conference room.

Keno's face wrinkled with concern. *Where is Zach?* he asked himself again.

"Have a seat, Mr. Hunter." The man ushered him in, pointing to a chair adjacent to his; all the while never taking his eyes off the stack of applications he was nervously rummaging through in his hand.

"How are you today . . . Keno, is it?" the man said with his eyes glancing up periodically as he fumbled through the many applications.

"Yes, it is! I am fine, Mr.—"

"Sorry about that. Thomas Kempfer." He extended his hand for a brief, impersonal handshake.

Keno cleared his throat, "Umm, Mr. Kempfer, is Zachary Johnson here today?"

"He's in our Northern California office. We had a tremendous response to our recruiting, and he was much-needed there." He lifted his eyes just long enough to wrinkle his forehead in annoyance at the sun filtering in through the blinds of the conference room. Moving his seat slightly to the right, he escaped the invasion of the sun by a couple of centimeters.

"You know, Zach? Did you go to college with him?" he asked.

"No."

"Oh! What college did you attend, Mr. Hunter?" he asked, his head slightly tilted to the left in inquisition.

"I didn't!" he firmly replied. "I didn't go to college." Keno dropped out of school at 13, approximately 20 years ago. He was diagnosed with ADD and found it virtually impossible to keep up with the rest of the class. Children with attention deficit disorders had difficulty focusing on tasks or paying attention for extended periods of time.

"Oh!" Mr. Kempfer continued to shuffle through the applications, obviously searching for something.

"Did you go to high school locally?"

"Mr. Kempfer, may I ask you why you are asking me questions that I already answered on my application?"

"I am so embarrassed, Mr. Hunter! But it appears that your application is missing. It is probably with one of the other managers." Conceding, he, instead, leaned back into his seat and commenced with the interview.

"Why don't you just tell me about yourself, Mr. Hunter?"

"Call me Keno," he said, forcing a half smile.

"Keno ... never heard that name before. What's the origin?" Mr. Kempfer asked while inadvertently returning to the stack of applications.

"Don't know the origin ... All I know is that my mom liked Pokeno."

"Named after a card game, huh? I like the game myself." Mr. Kempfer droned on about how he was the Pokeno champion in college.

Keno began to feel a rush of ease suddenly wash over him. He knew that he had a natural gift of gab, and if there was one thing that he could do with finesse like no one else, it would be his ability to effectively communicate, so he encouraged the mundane topic about the man's college days.

Forty-nine minutes later, he had Mr. Kempfer laughing and eating out of the palm of his hands.

"You are exactly what Papercom needs, Keno! You will be an excellent addition to our team! What I am going to do is put you down for our next orientation." He looked at the calendar.

"It's scheduled for 2 weeks from Monday. I believe that is the 18th. Does that work for you?"

Keno was bursting inside! He had never been so happy! Finally he would get a chance to go legit; something that he thought was out of the realm of possibility. He couldn't wait to tell Dee Dee that he got the job. Finally he would be able to totally dedicate himself to her and get out of that unsavory relationship with Sharon. He didn't love Sharon; he was just with her for the benefits that she provided. But now with this job, he would be able to carry his own weight and make a decent life for himself.

"That is *perfect* for me!" He picked up his smart phone strategically placed beside his Mercedes-Benz key and entered the date into the calendar section.

"By the way, Keno, you never did tell me how you know Zachary. Did you go to Loyola High with him?"

"Yeah, I did!" Overconfident with himself, he lied.

"It's a great school. It has the finest science department in all of Southern California!"

"Yeah, and not to mention the finest honeys in all of Southern California too!" He joked.

"Excuse me?" Mr. Kempfer stiffened up.

"The girls there are fine!" He looked over his shoulder playfully. "Just don't tell my girlfriend that I said that!"

Mr. Kempfer bristled up. "Mr. Hunter, I'm afraid that this isn't going to be a good fit after all. I appreciate you coming in. Good luck to you!" He stood up and opened the door.

Bewildered, Keno stood in the middle of the room with his mouth agape. What the fuck just happened?

"Excuse me, Mr. Kempfer. Just moments ago I had the job! What happened?"

"For your information, Mr. Hunter, Loyola is an all-boys preparatory school. There aren't any girls in attendance there. Never has been! If you had really attended the school, you would have known that!" He held the door open wider. "We don't hire liars! Have a good day, Mr. Hunter!"

Dazed and deflated, Keno made his way out the front door and back down to the underground parking lot of the 26-story office building of 5454 Wilshire. Exiting the elevator in the dimly lit garage, he sat on a bench just left of the elevator and stared into space in utter disbelief.

His dreams were once again destroyed! Just moments ago he felt that he had finally climbed the last precipice and stood on the summit of attaining his dreams—and out of nowhere it all fucking disappeared!

Keno convinced himself that it had to be because of his criminal record. He was an ex-con and nobody would ever hire an ex-con! Ever! The thought that he had told a blatant lie and got caught never crossed his mind for a second.

To hell with them all! he decided. He didn't need no penny-ante job no way! If he applied himself he could make more money with his fucking brain in 1 week than most of those suits make in a year. He didn't need that damn job, and in that instant he decided that he didn't need Sharon either. Fuck 'em all! Keno knew that if he put his mind to it and performed the right crime, it would pay him just as much as those suits made in one year. So fuck 'em all! It was time to suck it up and do what he did best . . . Take somebody else's shit and make it his.

Keno bristled up, snatched his cell phone from his jacket, and dialed his old neighborhood buddy Jimmy. As a child, Keno was raised on a cul-de-sac in a little section of South Los Angeles called Watts. He lost his father when he was 8. His father got shot as he slept off a drunken bender while in his car on Manchester and Broadway Street. Mistaken identity they said!

After his father's murder, his mother, Claritha, married again when he was 14 to a truck driver who was, in all reality, pretty decent to Keno the short time that he was around. His stepfather, Hank, had a gregarious personality and possessed quite the way with women.

Shortly after the marriage, Claritha threw him out due to too many issues of infidelity. During the less-than-2-year marriage, Keno learned a lot about women from his stepfather, specifically how to manipulate them. Hank was a master at getting a woman to do whatever he wanted her to do, and liked every minute of it! He was a virtuoso with his tongue and could own women in a matter of minutes with the strategic way he pulled together words.

He never told his mother, but Keno would ride along with Hank when he'd skip school. During those days and afternoons, in between his deliveries, he would witness Hank's pit stops to young and old women alike, expressing various hard-luck stories and walking away with wads of cash from the naïve women. Keno learned from his stepfather how to create a plausible story and deliver it in a way that would render an optimum financial payoff.

Shortly after his stepfather Hank left, Keno met Jimmy at the age of 16, a neighborhood juvenile delinquent, and became fast friends after they witnessed a neighborhood liquor store robbery. They were amazed at how easy it was to acquire money so quickly. Days after the robbery, the very men who robbed the store paraded around with the money that they had just stolen in that same neighborhood liquor store. It seemed to the boys an easy way to get some cash with little-to-no consequences! Ever since then they were the culprits of many petty robberies in the neighborhood, particularly home burglaries.

Although over the last few years they didn't hang out with each other as much as they did as juveniles, they still had an unbroken bond of brotherhood. No matter how infrequent, when they did speak it was like they had just talked to each other only moments before. The last time he had spoken to Jimmy was about 4 months ago.

"What's up, man?"

"Everythang is everythang!" Jimmy responded with a comfortable familiarity.

"Hey, Jimmy, you still working part-time for that manufacturing company?"

"Naw, man, got laid off a couple months ago!"

"Wanna make some money?" Keno asked, already knowing the answer.

Keno knew when Jimmy heard those words; it meant to get your gun and let's go rob somebody.

"Hell, yeah, man, a brotha's tired of being broke. What ya got?"

"Meet me at the IHOP on Wilshire in about an hour."

"Word up, man . . . I'll be there!"

"A'ight."

"Hey, Keno? What happened to that old rich chick you was banging? She dumped you or what?"

Keno hung up the phone, pretending not to hear Jimmy. He knew exactly that he was hinting at the fact that she had dumped him and that's why he was calling him to perform a crime . . . because he was broke. He didn't feel like explaining himself. He needed to take his manhood back. And robbing someone always empowered him! It made him feel like a real man! And right about now he *needed* to feel like a real man.

Chapter Eight

⁓ Bailey Levine ⁓

"*The problem is not that most men are assholes. The problem is that most women put up with those assholes.*"

All the asshole said was "*Thanks, babe!*"

No hug! No "I love you." No "You're the best for saving my ass!" Absolutely no spectacular notice of appreciation!

He just retrieved the envelope from her hand through the driver-side door of her car window and grunted as he lasciviously tugged on his fly.

She watched him saunter back over to a blue Audi and hop into the passenger side. She squinted to see the driver. It was an attractive brown-skinned young woman with a healthy abundance of hair cascading down her head; it screamed *really cheap weave!* Bailey watched him disappear as the driver merged into traffic. She watched the car fade out of sight, along with her money!

Bailey was livid after she left her parents' house, and now, coupled with the anger she felt from her diminishing bank account for an unappreciative jerk, she now felt like a buffoon. She had just given Chance almost $6,000 and watched him drive off with some other bitch! What the fuck was wrong with her? Why was she such an idiot when it came to him? And then there were her parents. Why did her mother hate her so much? Why was her father such a weak excuse of a man when it came to his wife?

Feelings of remorse began to overtake her as she contemplated the answers, so much so that Bailey pulled over to the side of the road and through the intermittent dry heaving crying bursts, called her best friend, Rockye.

She picked up on the first ring.

"I hate the bitch! I wish she was dead!" she hollered into the phone.

"Awwww, shit! What the hell happened now?"

"She is the meanest woman on the fucking face of the earth. I hate her!"

"Calm down, girl, and tell me what the hell happened!"

"We had a huge fight. My mother thought that I was pregnant by Chance and started saying all of these horrible things to me as my dad did nothing to stop her! He just sat there and let her say awful things to me. Why does she hate me so much? What did I ever do to her for her to despise me so much?" Bailey sobbed uncontrollably.

"Pregnant?"

"It's a long story. I just don't know what to do right now! I stormed out of the house and told them that they didn't have a daughter anymore! I told them that they didn't have to worry about seeing me ever again, and, Rockye, I fucking meant it! I don't care if I ever see either of them ever again!"

"You don't mean that! You're just upset! For heaven's sake, Bailey, they are your parents; you just can't make a call like that!"

"I do mean it. I don't care if they dry up and die right now!"

"Look, girl, just calm your ass down and drive over to my house! We can have a few drinks and sort this out! Nothing is as bad as it seems. Where the hell are you anyway?"

"A few blocks from my office. I'm parked on the side of the road talking to you!"

"I knew something had to be wrong for you to be calling me on Levine Sunday Breakfast Morning. Look, just drive your ass over to my place. I'll take care of the rest! Okay?"

"Okay!" Bailey depressed the button ending the call, turned up the stereo, and sobbed all the way over to her best friend's house.

The next morning Bailey found herself back in familiar territory, a position that always empowered her; negotiating a real estate transaction with a couple whose net worth crowned in the billions. She loved the art of the deal, and she loved bartering the details of covenant partnerships. This was a dimension of her life that grounded her and gave her a tremendous sense of self-worth. This confident, self-assured side of Bailey was a far cry from the weak, self-critical, insecure Bailey of the day before dealing with her parents and Chance.

The situation with her parents brought her dejection, and coupled with Chance who always made her feel worthless, aided to enhance her doldrums. Conversely, negotiating a real estate deal always made her feel invincible and restored the balance in her life. She *needed* to do this! She *needed* to feel like she was worthy of living!

"Six point five percent," she answered their question with confidence.

Bailey was positioned at the head of the oversized dining table of the three-story mansion of Jillian and Theodore Taylor in Beverly Hills discussing listing their fifteen million-dollar property with her agency, Levine Realty.

"Really? Other agents quoted us 4 percent!"

"Mr. and Mrs. Taylor, I believe that people get what they pay for!" Pulling out the listing agreement, Bailey turned it to face them. At the bottom of the contract was displayed their names typed under the seller's line.

"Mrs. Taylor, I look around at the sumptuous furnishings in your home as well as the inestimable artwork on your wall that frames it so nicely and I recognize that I am in the presence of a woman who understands quality and believes that she deserves nothing but the best. Am I correct?"

The sophisticated Mrs. Taylor, elegantly dressed in Dior and Chanel, nodded approval.

"Mr. Taylor, when I drove up, the one thing that stood out to me the most was the exquisitely paved stoned driveway that frames your home so nicely. If my memory serves me correctly, you got the premium package, didn't you?"

His left eye brow rose slightly in confusion over the question. "Well, yes, we did purchase the premium package."

"For a brief moment, I worked with Stone Wood Pavers in their marketing department. I helped revamp the components of each package for optimum marketability, so that is why I have knowledge of all the home improvement packages that Stone Wood provides."

"I believe that the package you purchased was the most expensive driveway paving package that the company offered. Am I correct?"

His face positioned an agreement.

"It is apparent that the two of you spared no expense because you appreciate quality and understand value." She raised the half-filled glass of water to her perfectly painted lips and took a slow sip before continuing. This was a negotiation strategy she learned to keep the clients pulled in to the conversation.

"I command top dollar because I know my value!"

Bailey's prospective new clients, the Taylors, were wealthy, a classic representation of old money. She detested dealing with these types of clients; they carried around with them a huge sense of entitlement. They had no problem paying an exorbitant amount of money for some tangible thing that they considered valuable, but would squeeze every penny of a dime when it came to paying for the services of others. In other words, they were opposed to being generous to the hired help.

She took another slow pull from the water glass before continuing.

"I work for nothing less than 6½ percent commission. My staff is exemplary, my successes are my advertisement, and my negotiating skills are formidable. I give the best and get exceptional results! Always!"

They were disconcerted by the confident realtor's retort as evidenced by the nervous squirming in their chairs.

"And as I said before, looking around your lovely home, it is quite obvious that you surround yourself with quality. Since you surround yourself with the best, shouldn't I assume that you would not want the same in a Realtor?"

They both nodded in unison.

"Great, then I'm glad that we are on the same page!" She repositioned the listing agreement directly in front of them.

"Mr. Taylor, I need for you to put your signature of approval here! Mrs. Taylor here!"

After getting all of the paperwork signed, Bailey leaned back into the dining-room table's high-backed chair, lifted the glass of water again, and pulled in a victory sip. She smiled a confident smile to herself before continuing.

"Now, let's go over my 30-day marketing plan to get your home sold!"

Thirty-five minutes later, Bailey was closing up her briefcase with all the appropriate paperwork completed. She was pleased with herself, for this tough East Coast-born and -raised couple was indeed a force to be reckoned with.

"Thank you, Bailey. We are confident that we have the right agent to sell our home!" Mrs. Taylor beamed.

"Yes, indeed, you should have seen what we had to choose from," Mr. Taylor confided.

"We just don't want to work with those Mexicans or coloreds."

"Excuse me?" Bailey responded as her entire body stiffened at his racist comment.

"We had this Mexican man come over earlier in the week, and yesterday, this colored girl came by trying to convince us to let her sell our house. She was very nice, but I just don't want a colored person selling our house and knowing all of our business!" Mrs. Taylor continued.

"Well, Jillian, we don't have to worry about that now. We got one of us!" Mr. Taylor expressed while simultaneously savoring in the distinct scent from the Cuban cigar he had just retrieved from a humidor. His eyes focused on the Star of David hanging from around Bailey's neck; a gift from her father on her eighteenth birthday.

Bailey's body went instantly hot. She couldn't believe her ears. Here it was happening to her again!

The little voice inside of her started screaming... "*You fucking racist bastards! How dare you say that shit to me? I am one of those 'colored people'! Who the hell do you think you that are?*" She wanted to spit in their faces, tear up the paperwork, and run out of that huge house full of prejudiced aristocrats! She wanted to tell them that she was a "*colored girl.*" Yes, she did! But instead, she did as she always did... swallowed the disdain with her saliva.

Being mistaken for white was commonplace for Bailey, and to correct or admonish the culprit caused her so much anxiety that she opted to just ignore it. Instead of correcting them and scolding them for their insulting words of bigotry, she just held her tongue, allowing it to implode within her. Bailey knew that one day she would stand up and admonish the bigots, but today would not be the day! Today, she would, once again, retreat within herself as a tortoise within its shell.

"Mr. and Mrs. Taylor, my assistant will be in contact with you Thursday to schedule our crew to come and shoot footage for the virtual tour. If you should have any further questions, just give us a call!"

Bailey wouldn't look them in the eye; instead, she issued them an obligatory handshake and ushered herself abruptly from the opulent two-story Beverly Hills palatial mansion without as much as a word of disapproval or correction.

She got into her black-on-black S600 Mercedes, turned on the seat warmer, and leaned into the comfortable leather seat for a relaxing ride home. In efforts to squelch the rising rage burgeoning within her, she turned on her stereo and settled on a Jonathan Butler CD. Halfway home as her labored breathing subsided she reached down to retrieve her cell phone to dial Chance. She had not spoken to him since he met her and got the money from her. Every time she called him over the last few days, it always went directly to his voice mail. And today was no different. It went directly to voice mail. Bailey cranked up the volume of her Bose surround sound stereo.

She thought about Chance. Was she a fool for loving him? Why was she so unlovable? Why did she so desperately love someone that apparently didn't give a damn about her at all? Why did she miss him so desperately right now, knowing that he had scammed her out of money and was most likely spending it on another woman?

She thought about her parents. Why did her mother always treat her like she didn't like her . . . hell—hate her? Why was she always so angry with her? What had she done as a child to warrant such contempt from her? Why was her father so weak when it came to her mother? Why did he always sit back and allow her to treat her with so much indignation? Was it because she looked white; not at all like her mother?

She thought about herself. Why did she feel so out of sorts all the time; like she didn't really belong to the human race?

Why did she feel like an alien when she looked at herself in the mirror? She didn't feel white or black. She felt removed from the reflection in the mirror. What was she? White? Black? Why did she identify more with blacks? Why did she look so apparently white? Not even a hint of her maternal African American heritage.

Most of her life was spent in the disconsolate environment of an indignant mother, and people with an aversion to the black race. Right now she wished she were dead! Bailey felt like the most miserable person on the face of the earth!

The tears gushed forth, leaving a trail of the salty questions down her cheek.

Why? Why? Why?

Chapter Nine

≈Keno Hunter≈

Flaming with humiliation, Keno carried his bruised and battered ego out of the parking lot of the 5454 Wilshire Building and plopped down in the driver's-side leather seat of his Benz. He had been teetering on the edge of surrendering to felonious activity for quite a while now. Because of the domineering nature of his paramour and the "you can be anything you set your mind to" pressure from his girl Dee Dee, Keno longed for the ability to be self-sustaining, to be able to meet his own needs without cowering down to Sharon for resources that he needed to maintain the life he felt he deserved. He detested the fact that he couldn't provide for himself without jumping through the hoops of his ringmaster, Sharon. He compromised his self-respect every time he lay down in bed with Sharon because of what she could provide and how she enhanced his lifestyle.

Once again, Dee Dee had awakened the hope of attaining the American dream, a dream that he had relegated to the realm of impossibility. She convinced him that it was possible for an ex-con to have a six-figure job; a house of his own filled with kids, and all the trappings of an upper middle-class household. However, that was all squashed when he was once again dismissed because of his prison record after his interview with that idiot from Papercom. Keno was angry at himself for succumbing to the possibilities of a better life . . . a life that was no longer attainable for an ex-con. He was a black man with a criminal record, no education, and no marketable skills. The only thing he felt that he was good at was giving a woman multiple orgasms and performing robberies. That he could do with his eyes closed.

However, at the moment, he desperately needed to get his swagger back. He needed to rid the chains that restricted him to the prison cell of his paramour as well as its roommate of inadequacy because every time he looked into his girlfriend's eyes he felt less than a man. He felt incompetent and unworthy. Keno had had enough, and today was the day that he was determined to snatch his manhood back.

"Keno, that was like taking candy from a baby!" Jimmy remarked to his childhood buddy riding shotgun in the passenger seat. They were cruising eastbound on Venice Blvd. leaving the parking lot of a jeweler who was transporting a sizable amount of diamonds and precious stones from his store contained within a black satchel. They rolled up on him so quick that the man didn't even have time enough to react. The look of shock on his face evidenced his consternation.

The smell of tire rubber hung in the air as Keno flung opened the passenger door.

He pointed the .22 in the face of a Middle Eastern man who appeared to be in his late 60s as evidenced by the deep lines in his face and dusty gray, thinning hair. The oversized dark brown suit he wore hung awkwardly on his frail body.

"Don't try to be a fucking superhero. Just drop the bag on the ground and step back. Slowly!" Keno screamed at him as the gun jetted out from his side.

The man looked wide-eyed at the gun, then swiftly around him, appearing to be considering his alternatives.

"I could put a bullet in you if you prefer, asshole, or you can put the bag down now!"

The man relented and placed the satchel slowly on the ground, intertwined his fingers, and put them on top of his head as he retreated cautiously as though saying, "*Go ahead. I will be no trouble.*"

Brandishing a .22 Magnum; Keno bent down and snatched the satchel, turned, and retreated back into the car. Jimmy slammed his foot down on the accelerator, and they sped off to a nearby alley where they switched cars and transferred the jewels into a protective sack and funneled them into the radiator opening of a white Mazda which was nestled against a back wall. Jimmy had rented the car from Rent-a-Wreck the night before with fake ID under the alias of Michael Johnson.

Without words between the two, Keno and Jimmy quickly changed into the clothes he had placed in a duffle bag. They replaced the all-black attire with jeans and a white polo shirt. Keno peeled off the beanie, gloves, shades, fake sideburns, mustache, and thick eyebrows he used as a disguise and tossed them into the backseat of the black sedan they used to commit the crime, along with the gun. Since Jimmy was behind the wheel of the car, his disguise consisted only of wraparound shades to hide his eyes and eyebrows, a black unmarked baseball cap, black shirt, and slacks. Taking the gloves, black shirt, pants, beanie, and shades, he also threw everything into the car, and then, without missing a beat, Jimmy unscrewed the top of a gasoline canister he had in the backseat, allowing its contents to spill onto the floor. Pulling out a disposable lighter, he flicked it, lit a piece of paper, and threw it into the vehicle. The car, on cue as if in a James Bond film, within moments, went up in flames.

Five minutes later, they were cruising down through Venice as though nothing had happened.

"That was smooth as china silk!" Keno replied. "Did you tell Stack where to meet us?"

"Yeah!" Jimmy glanced at his watch. "He's probably there right now, waiting for us."

"With all of that beautiful cash!" Keno beamed.

"And just think that yesterday this time we was some broke-ass fools!"

"Not anymore." They fist pounded each other.

"Hey, that old man was too damn calm considering he just lost over $500,000 worth of jewels," Jimmy stated.

"By the way he acted, this was for sure not the first time he had been robbed!"

"What a fucked-up business to be in!"

"Don't worry about his ass. He got insurance, for sure! He will probably report that much more was stolen anyway. Believe me, in the end, he will make out better off."

"How much ya think we gonna get from Stack? I know that he is the best fence for this type of merchandise."

Keno shifted in the passenger seat. "Between 40–50 percent of its value."

"Whatcha gonna do with your part?"

"I don't know what I'm going to do, but I do know what I am *not* going to do, and that is deal with Sharon anymore. Just the thought of not having to climb up on that wore-out old body and bang it until she has reached her exhaustion in climaxes is a fucking joy for me."

"So how are you going to end it?"

"Move and disconnect my phone!"

"What about the car? You gonna give it back?"

"She ain't getting shit back! I'm counting it as well deserved hazard pay!"

They laughed in unison.

"What about you, man? How are you going to spend your cheddar? Probably take your daughter shopping first, huh?"

"You know it, man! My baby comes first! Life means nothing to me without her. Just thinking about the look on her face when

I take her to the mall and tell her to get anything she wants ... makes all this shit worth it. Also, I've been wanting to start a car detailing business."

"Well, Jimmy, now that you have the money there ain't nothing stopping you, is there?"

"Not a damn thing! Whatcha gonna do about your girl? You gonna tell her how you got this money?"

"Fuck no, man! You never tell a woman no shit like this! Friend today, enemy tomorrow. This is the kinda shit that they will hold over your head, and when they are beefin' with you, next thing you know it, they are calling the cops on you just because they mad at your ass."

"You think your girl is that kind of woman?" Jimmy's face wrinkled in disbelief as he eyed Keno. "She is such a down girl. She has been with you through so much shit. I wouldn't believe she would ever do anything to hurt you. Besides, that chick is in love with your ass!"

"Maybe so, but I am not going to take any chances with my life like that! Women trip out so much you never know what they will do. As much as I love Dee Dee, I will not give her that kind of ammunition."

"I never thought I would have heard something like that come out of your mouth about her. But you live and learn." Jimmy shook his head and took a quick left onto Overland Boulevard.

"However, I am going to get us a place to live together. She has been bugging me about that for years. I can't wait to see the expression on her face when I give her the keys to our new place. She can finally move out of that dingy apartment, and we can start living like a real couple ... without Sharon in the picture."

Jimmy opened his mouth to respond, but his face suddenly tensed up as he caught sight of flashing lights in the rearview mirror.

"Fuck!" he called out.

"What?" Keno sat up, concern resting on his chocolate-toned face.

"Five-O!"

"Shit!" Keno put his seat belt on.

"I think they are running our plates!" Jimmy started perspiring.

"So let them run it. We ain't speeding or doing anything wrong! Don't do anything crazy! Just keep talking to me like nothing is wrong. Act natural!"

"Too late! They're pulling us over!" Jimmy hollered. "I can't go to jail, man. My daughter needs me! I can't go back to the pen!" Jimmy shouted as his foot slammed on the gas pedal. The wheels screeched as he pulled off.

The siren started blaring from the police car accelerating behind them. A voice boomed over the bullhorn. "Pull over! Pull the car over NOW!"

Jimmy raced the engine, leaping ahead of the traffic. "What the fuck are ya doin', man?" Keno bristled up. "Just pull the fucking car over!"

"I can't get caught! I am not going back to the pen!"

"Jimmy, just pull the fucking car over! Who's to say they will search the car and find the stuff stashed inside the radiator? Now we are evading the police. These fuckers don't play with car chases. So just pull the fuck over!" Keno urged, pounding his fist on the dashboard.

"Keno, I got some warrants on my ass. I can't go back to jail and leave my daughter!"

"What the fuck! Are you kiddin' me, man? Aw…shit!" Keno hollered back. A handful of scenarios danced across his brain of what could happen to them within the next few minutes, all of which ended them up in jail. But why did he have to be so cynical? The jewels were very secure in the radiator. Besides, the car was not stolen, and they had no evidence on them in reference to the robbery. All he had to do was get Jimmy calm enough to pull the car over.

"Look, man just pull the car over. I would rather us go to jail for a minute then getting shot from trying to outrun the cops." He tried to reason with Jimmy with a voice breathy from fear.

Keno held onto the dashboard with his right hand and with the left he braced himself on the armrest as he angled his head to see the police trying to keep up as Jimmy sped recklessly over speed bumps through the neighborhood of Palms to evade them.

"Come on, man. Just pull the car over."

"I ain't tryin' to hear that, Keno. I can't get caught. If you don't want to have your head go through the fucking windshield, I would hold the fuck on. I'm about to lose these fuckers." Jimmy punched the accelerator to almost 100 mph, barreling down the streets of West L.A. as he sped through amber and red lights.

Taking a curb at a high rate of speed, Jimmy, angling the car, made a sharp right on a residential neighborhood side street, sending the car airborne, subsequently losing control of the steering and smashing into the tail of a white Ford Explorer parked car in a driveway.

"Run, man!" Jimmy shouted as he quickly extracted himself from the driver's side and headed up through some foliage near a community park. Keno scooted out the passenger's side of the car, jetting out through the backyard while keeping his head tucked low.

"Hold it!" two cops shouted as they finally slammed up behind the car that they just abandoned. The fat one angled his pudgy body out of the car and headed in the direction of Jimmy.

The short, stocky officer took off looking for Keno, but Keno had already struck out in the opposite direction of Jimmy, out of sight and huddling quietly behind a garage until he no longer heard the officer's footsteps. Luckily, there were no neighbors around.

This all seemed like a bad dream to Keno. Just moments before, they were cruising down the street discussing what they would be doing with the money from the jewels they had just stolen from a Middle Eastern jeweler. And now everything felt so surreal as he set out on foot to evade the police as his childhood buddy sprinted in the opposite direction.

He felt his heart thudding within his hollow chest and heard his breathing getting louder as his eyes scanned the area for any evidence of police. He didn't see any. It appeared that they all went in the direction of Jimmy.

With what seemed like a clear shot to escape, Keno took off running. A couple hundred yards ahead he boarded an abandoned skateboard, possibly left in the front yard by some teenager. He was not a skateboarder, but this day it was as if he was a veteran on the thing. He navigated it with expertise, his left foot on the board and the right pushing him to a high rate of speed; the wind slapped his face as the adrenaline in his body pumped. As he rounded the corner of the block, in the distance he heard multiple gunshots.

"Oh shit!" he hollered out loud, fearing the worst. Could Jimmy have been shot and now was lying bleeding and dying in the street?

He thought he heard someone holler. Could it have been Jimmy? Or was it his imagination?

He wanted desperately to turn around and go make sure that his friend was okay; instead, he kept his eyes in front of him and pushed forward at a record-breaking speed on that skateboard.

In his gut he knew Jimmy was hit!

Just hours earlier, Keno called his friend out of the comfort of his home with his daughter. Called him out to perform a crime and possibly lose his life!

He thought about the jewels in the radiator of the rented car. They would for sure impound it. Can't very well walk up to the rental car agency and ask for a car that was used in a robbery! His mind was whirling about with reproof of his ingrained tendency to conceive the worst.

He just knew that Jimmy was lying shot and bloody in the street. Dying alone! And the person responsible for that ominous position was running away like a fucking coward!

"You are a fucking coward, Keno!" he hurled at himself. "What kind of person abandons his friend like an animal to die in the street? This was your idea. You did this to him! You killed your friend."

Guilt engulfed him.

The sound of helicopters startled him back to reality. He had to get somewhere safe and get there quickly. But where would he go? As much as he didn't want to, he knew that there was only one place that he could go.

He felt in his heart that Jimmy was dead. He felt that he was probably lying shot and bloody in the street. And he was the coward responsible for it.

Chapter Ten

～ The Circle ～

The room was ablaze with pre-therapy session chatter as Jango, The Circle leader and facilitator, stood in the doorway, watching the interaction of its members' every detail, especially the one woman, who, when she spoke, everything around him ceased to register because bells and whistles went off, just as her mellifluous words hit him in his hungry, wanting heart. It was a stealthy movement of a man harboring a hard-on for one Bailey Levine.

Four years ago, two college buddies, Jango Cunningham and Tyler Jimenez, started the psychotherapy group called "*The Circle.*" Jango and Tyler met at UCLA in their sophomore year and quickly formed a fast friendship. After graduating college, Jango became a social worker in the inner city of Los Angeles, and Tyler went into law school and subsequently became a Beverly Hills corporate attorney. Well into the first decade of their careers, Jango had a burning desire to provide a resource of help for the many Angelenos that danced with the infinite challenges that hindered them from leading lives free from debilitating addictions. Jango brought the concept to his college buddy; Tyler embraced the idea due to the lack of personal fulfillment from his own career. From concept to inception was no more than 6 months.

Minutes before everyone arrived, he positioned himself in an obscure alcove above the room to ogle his secret love interest, as well as to view the other members of the Tuesday afternoon group to get an idea of what issues were prevalent in their lives so as to properly navigate the topics for an optimum session.

Jango typically led the sessions with religious overtones against the desire of his partner due to his strong belief in God. However, at the insistence of his partner, he did incorporate a lot of basic psychotherapy techniques.

"What's up, gurl?" Rockye greeted Bailey, tugging at the too-tight pair of Baby Phat jeans just before positioning herself to sit so as to conceal the yellow laced G-string rising up from underneath. Her ensemble was completed by a white wife beater strategically torn at the cleavage for ample exposure, and ankle-length, brown, fur-trimmed boots.

"Hey, Rock!" Bailey pushed forward in her seat and patted Rockye on the knee. "What took you so long? I thought we were supposed to meet 30 minutes before group?"

"Traffic was a bitch! I'm stressed the hell out!" Rockye complained as she stood up again, pulling her thong from out between her butt cheeks just before plopping back down in the folding chair to Bailey's left, causing it to wobble on impact.

Bailey pulled back, appearing to scan her group mate with investigative eyes.

"You sure don't look like it! Looks like you got it all together today! When did you get your hair done?" It appeared that the tone in her voice evidenced suspicion of her friend's truth telling. Bailey had expressed her opinion on many occasions that Rockye was all too familiar with the art of subterfuge!

Patting her curly tresses and smoothing down the sides behind her ears with her right hand, Rockye replied, "It does look good, doesn't it? That chick I told you about in Pasadena sure can work magic, huh? She has the Midas touch!"

Bailey pulled out her cell phone. "Give me her phone number. I'll call her so that she can do my hair!"

Rockye snickered. "What the hell do you need her number for? You got that white girl hair. All you need to do is wash it, blow dry it, and go!"

Jango smiled at the comment. He had to admit that she had hair that appeared to be wash and wear. He dreamed many a night of inhaling the sweet aroma of whatever she used in her hair, for the fragrance hung in the air moments after she left the spot she usually sat in. He would stand there long after the sessions were over just basking in the delicious smells that hung in the air of the area she sat in during the therapy sessions.

Bailey blew a burst of air from her nose in response to the comment. Jango could tell that such remarks regarding her biracial features annoyed his darling Bailey immensely, especially coming from a person that she considered her friend. Jango wondered why she kept making them because Rockye was well aware of how much those off-the-cuff remarks bothered Bailey.

It grieved Jango's spirit every time he became aware of anything that caused his darling Bailey any type of uncomfortable feelings. If he had it his way, he would keep her in a bubble of protection against any unfavorable interactions with anyone.

The object of his heart, Bailey, had built a successful life for herself despite the unsavory relationship that she had with her parents. The trappings of her carefully orchestrated career were quite substantial: a 4,500 square foot home, a $125,000 vehicle, a thriving multimillion-dollar real estate brokerage company, an extensive wardrobe of designer labels, sizeable savings in the bank, just to name a few. But underneath all of Bailey's professional successes lay a personal life resembling that of a scrambled jigsaw puzzle.

She planned hard, and she worked long hours. But the confident demeanor she wore on top of her suits camouflaged the raging war of self-recriminations that erupted within her daily. Jango knew everything about her. He paid close attention to her every move and conducted many investigations on her. Some may have called his investigation into her private life unsavory;

however, he deemed it a necessary evil to keep her safe, especially potentially safe from herself. He loved her that much. At least, that is what he told himself to justify his actions.

Typically, after a 12-hour workday, she sat in her office alone with only the echo from the business of the day earlier, lost within her own self-condemnation. He knew that Bailey longed for the love and approval of her mother, but conversely harbored an intense hatred and disdain for her as well. This was the origin of all of her issues. He knew that the anger and resentment she experienced was so debilitating that most days she fought immense depression. She admitted in group once that it was at the height of one of those moments that she desperately needed some help which sparked the investigation that led her to finding and joining this group.

"Hey, look, what do you think she's done this time?" Rockye commented on Lynette who had just sauntered in and made a beeline over to the coffeepot.

Lynette Castle was a 27-year-old affluent narcissist, who, by any other person's opinion, was perfection promenading around in a 6-foot tall, 130-pound frame. Her long blond tresses, perfect Colgate smile, and blue-green-colored eyes had everyone hypnotized when they looked at her. However, according to Lynette's reasoning, she believed herself a walking mess. The statuesque beauty found her body utterly appalling, therefore squandering tens of thousands of dollars trying to correct what she felt Mother Nature deprived her of by frequenting plastic surgeons on the regular. It was due to the urgent requests of one of her doctors which led her to The Circle, for he made it abundantly clear that she was addicted to plastic surgery and gravely needed help.

"Come on, Rock! Why do you always have to talk about her like that? We are all here because in some way or another we have freaking issues. We are all in the same boat! The only difference between us and her is that she wears her issues on the outside."

"What . . . eveeerrrr! I still think that she is a friggin' nut job!" Rockye stood up and placed both hands on her narrow hips. "I'm gonna go get a donut. You want a Krispy Kreme too? Girl, you know you do!"

"No, thanks, I ate a big lunch!"

Jango watched Bailey eye her friend as she sashayed away after rearranging her wife beater over her too-tight jeans.

Rockye Haynes had an insanely spectacular body with a firm apple-bottom ass, tiny waist, and ample cleavage which she always had harnessed high upon her chest. Her perfectly formed Coke-bottle figure, she always told everyone, was her ticket into parties, functions . . . the rather exclusive club that most women only dreamt about. In spite of how beautiful or shapely she was, Rockye grew up with a tremendous inferiority complex due, in part, to her absentee father, and she spent a great deal of time and energy sleeping with men to gain acceptance and approval.

Unknowingly, she was desperately trying to gain from other men what she felt she didn't get from her father. After almost getting hit by a drunk driver while parked on the shoulder of a freeway as she was having sex with a city worker, who'd she'd never seen before, she deduced that unless she got help she may one day end up dead, or even worse, wishing she was dead because she had AIDS from having sex with countless random strangers at whim. That revelation is what finally brought her to The Circle and became the springboard to the women's friendship.

Jango noticed Keno standing in the doorway. Keno Hunter was the live wire in the Tuesday afternoon group. A high school dropout with a prison record, Keno vacillated between doing what was decent and right or self indulgent, but ultimately, he always succumbed to what was best for his narcissistic character.

He never bridled his tongue and impulsively spoke whatever was on his mind. Ironically, even though he used women, committed crimes, and was an avid liar, the very core of him really wanted a normal life. In group sessions, he was an animated character, always controlling and dominating the sessions too much of the time.

While watching Keno as he indulged in an animated conversation on his cell phone, Jango had to admit that he had an enormous amount of swagger, and it was noticeably obvious why so many women found him appealing. His silk shirt hugged his muscular form, which rested slightly above his lower extremity, highlighting the fact that the man was very familiar with the gym.

Removing his glasses, Jango closed his eyes, rubbing for some relief from the strain that the day of reading reports brought. He didn't want to hold envy for such an obvious opportunist regardless of what appeared on the surface.

His eyes left Keno and refocused back to the object of his affections as she sat beautifully in the foldout chair perusing her cell phone. He closed his eyes and got lost within the sound and smell of his daydream of the two of them walking by the ocean, the breeze gently kissing their faces, and the sun resting on their backs as the softness of her delicate hand rested within his. He savored the thought, hovering over a state of satiation and nirvana. That was, until the sound of the alarm on his watch called him back to reality. It was time to start. He put a bookmark on that fantasy for him to pick up again at the next opportunity that arose.

"Okay, group, how did last week go for you?" Jango's eyes surveyed the crowd after everyone settled down once they took notice of Jango's presence at the head of the room, his eyes finally locking in on Bailey. He nodded at her.

"Bailey, why don't we start with you?" The words flowed off of his tongue as it caused his heart to skip at an erratic pace.

She smiled an uncomfortable smile and proceeded to talk.

"I had it out with my mother again! This time I really blew up." She paused.

"Tell us what happened," Jango urged.

"I finally realized that the relationship I always wanted with my mother is never ever going to happen! You simply can't make someone value who you are! I have spent my entire life trying to please my mother, trying to get her approval! All I ever wanted her to do was acknowledge any one of my many accomplishments! Graduating high school at 16 with a 4.5 GPA, or any type of acknowledgment for winning every contest that I ever entered! What about buying my first home at 23 or opening and running my own brokerage firm by the age of 22? You would think that she would have been proud of me! But no! All she ever does is criticize me! And for the life of me, I don't know what the hell I ever did to that woman!" She took a deep breath before continuing. The words appeared to come pouring forth so effortlessly.

"But last night it hit me. I see things so much clearer now!"

"What is it that you see clearer, Bailey?" Jango asked.

"I see that my mother is who she is. I can't change her! It's not her that has to change but me! I'm the one that has to change! I'm the one who sees the problem, not her. She may never see where she is wrong! For that fact, she may never feel that she has ever done anything wrong to me! I'm the one whose stomach is tied up in knots, not hers!"

"I know exactly what you mean! I feel the same way!" Carlos chimed in.

Carlos Alvarez, a dark-haired Enrique Iglesias look-alike, was grappling with accepting his homosexuality. His dark, smoldering eyes, thick eyebrows, and keen handsome features were hidden within his pensive demeanor, and he had an intense fear that his father would discover his secret. This secret kept him in a constant state of anxiety.

Carlos constantly trolled the Internet daily, and while surfing the 'net one afternoon just before leaving work, he ran across an ad for this group. He left work and popped in to check them out and had been coming ever since, off and on, for almost 2 years now.

"My dad hit my little brother yesterday! Slammed him up against the wall in the kitchen and told him to stop acting like some little sissy because he got hit in the head with a baseball at practice and started crying," Carlos continued.

"I realized then that my dad feels that a man should act a certain way, and any other behavior is weak and contemptible. I am so afraid of what he will do when he finds out that I am gay! I agree with you, Bailey. My dad is who he is, and nothing I can say, think, feel, or do will ever change that! I guess that it's me who will have to change!"

Bailey reached over and with empathy, lightly stroked Carlos's left arm.

"So I know *exactly* what you mean, Bailey!" Carlos concluded.

"What the fuck is all that supposed to mean! Sometimes you guys act so damn weak! To hell with them! People go around making judgments on people all the time, not knowing the whole damn story about shit! They take one look at someone and immediately form a fucked-up opinion about them!" Keno interjected with fury.

"That's not true! I don't believe that," Lynette responded.

"Are you fucking *kidding* me? What do you think people think about you when they see you, Lynette? What do you think goes on in their mind the first time they see you walking down the street, or entering a room, or coming out of your house to get into your car, *huh*?" Keno barked.

"Well, I hope that they say that there is one hot chick with a really great tan," she joked.

"Oh, so you think that this is some funny shit! The one thing I know about you, Lynette, is that you keep your head in the damn sand. You don't like to face shit! Look at you right now! You come in here today with a wafer-thin white sundress on. Hell, I can see your nipples. Those high heels you have on are so high you almost tripped twice! Between those overpowering perfumes you drowned yourself in, the two cans of hairspray you used to puff out your hair, and all that damn makeup on your face, you look like some kind of a clown! You are a *joke*! Hell, I will just say it: You look like a fuckin' hooker. A well paid hooker, but still a damn hooker!"

"Keno!" Jango motioned for him to put the brakes on.

"Look, Jango, I'm just keeping it real. She says that she doesn't believe that people make negative judgments just looking at someone. I'm just pointing out the real to her."

"If you asked everyone else here in the room, they would agree with me. We all know that Lynette is a smart chick, but she looks like a hooker, plain and simple!"

Lynette turned to Bailey. "Do you agree with Keno, Bailey? I trust that you will tell me the truth!"

Bailey looked helplessly at Jango for guidance.

"Remember our pledge we took to always be honest with one another," Jango urged her.

Bailey swallowed before speaking.

"You are a beautiful girl, Lynette, but you could stand to make a few changes in your attire."

"Be fucking *real* with her, Bailey! Sugarcoating shit is not what we come here for, and you know it! Stop bullshitting her!" Keno urged.

"Lynette, it is not so much about what others say about you that you should take to heart because, goodness knows, things aren't always as they appear. What ultimately matters is what you feel about yourself when you look in the mirror and really look deep inside of yourself for the answers. The answers are always inside of us!" Carlos said.

"What kind of bullshit is that? That is *not* what really matters! She is here because she feels fucked up inside! That is why we are *all* here! Look at her! She is one fine-ass bitch who thinks that she needs a bigger this, a smaller that, a newer this. That shit is crazy! On the outside, the bitch is fine, but inside, she is all fucked up! So save that bullshit. Help her out by giving her the real and not some patronizing bullshit," Keno said.

"People do judge, Lynette! Keno is right! And to tell you the truth, you do look like a well dressed call girl," Rockye added.

Lynette winced.

"What are you feeling right now, Lynette?" Jango asked.

She didn't response, just shrugged her shoulders.

"Lynette, 80 percent of success is just showing up! You can't grow or heal if you don't face and deal with your feelings! You are safe here, so go ahead. It's okay."

"I see people look at me and they are always judging me! I feel the stares and hear the comments when people think I'm not listening. It hurts like hell! So many times I wish I was invisible. I wish I could stop all of the criticisms, the comments and the looks of judgment. Hell, I can't blame people because I am hideous! When I look in the mirror, the sight of myself makes me ill." Lynette started sobbing.

Carlos got up to hug Lynette.

"Don't! Sit down!" Jango ordered.

"The one thing that I have tried to stress to you guys all the time is that in the midst of this journey of self-discovery is that you must find your own voice. Own up to your own feelings! I say this to you guys all the time, you can't let someone else's opinion of you become your own! Lynette, I gave you an assignment last week. How did you do on it?" Jango asked.

"It was kinda hard," Lynette forced out through some newly forming tears.

"Did you do it?"

Lynette's eyes darted around the room showing a hint of embarrassment.

"Yes!"

"Tell us what it was."

"To ask a few friends to pick three words that best described me," she answered.

"What did you find out?" Jango pushed.

She stiffened up.

"You are safe here, Lynette," Jango reassured.

She removed a folded up piece of paper from her purse. After slowly unfolding it, she read.

"I first called my ex-boyfriend, Thomas. His answer was '*scared, insecure,* and *delusional.*'" Lynette looked around the room before continuing. "My girlfriend Dana from college said, '*self-absorbed, troubled,* and *confused.*' My cousin Bobby said, '*beautiful, crazy,* and *funny.*' My stepmom said, '*private, opinionated,* and *unsettled.*' My dad said, '*spoiled, immature,* and *self-centered.*' I asked one more person. I went out on a date last week with a guy that I have known all of 2 weeks, and he had the audacity to say, '*sexy, wild,* and *freaky!*'"

Her eyes met Jango.

"I think what he said hurt me the most."

"Why?" Jango asked.

"Because he didn't really see the real me!"

"Oh, he saw the real you all right!" Keno added. "That's exactly what I was talking about. If you hang all of your laundry out on the clothesline for everyone to see, what else do you expect?"

Her eyebrows rose at Keno in disapproval.

"Does everything that comes up have to come out of that sewer mouth of yours?" Bailey fumed.

"I'm just telling the damn truth. It's not my fault that she looks like a fucking walking advertisement for—"

"That's enough, Keno! Lynette, please tell us what part 2 of the exercise was."

"To write down how I felt about what was said about me and if I agreed or disagreed."

"You are in a safe space to share…go ahead."

Lynette couldn't speak from the tears that began to flow.

"I don't know about any of you, but that stuff they said would have made me real mad! It's okay to tell us about how you felt, Lynette," Rockye urged.

"I felt like such a loser! After thinking about it I just wanted to be anybody *but* me." She paused all of 30 seconds while gingerly dabbing her tearstained face with her index fingers. "It made me feel so bad that I picked up the phone to make an appointment with my doctor," Lynette concluded, breaking the silence.

"You called your doctor, the plastic surgeon?"

"Yes! I didn't want to be me anymore! So I figured that I would have him change me into anybody else but me. But I changed my mind, and I didn't make the appointment. I just hung up the phone!"

"Why did you change your mind, Lynette?" Jango probed.

"Your voice came into my head saying, *'Someone else's opinion of you doesn't have to be your opinion of yourself.'* So I went to my bathroom mirror and said 10 times, I am not what others think of me but what I think of myself!"

"And what do you think of yourself now?"

"I am a work in progress, and who I was or who I am is not who I will be!"

"Very good! What was the lesson that you came away with?" Jango asked.

"I learned that I am going to stop caring about what other people think of me."

"Like you did tonight?" Keno remarked sarcastically.

She glared at him. "I know that I am still struggling with it, but the good thing is that I am aware of it and that is half the battle, right, Jango?" Lynette managed a faint smile.

"I'm proud of you, Lynette. Good job!" Jango turned to face the group. "Does anyone have anything to add? Any comments for Lynette?"

"Lose the tramp clothes and trade in your ho heels for some low heels," Keno joked.

Bailey shot him a look of disdain before responding.

"I, for one, am proud of you for being able to hold it together after those remarks. It is not easy to hear what others think of you and digest it the way you did."

"Hey, you guys have it all wrong! I say if it looks like a duck and walks like a duck, hell, it *is* a duck! What were some of the words that were used to describe her: self-absorbed, troubled, crazy, unsettled, spoiled, immature, self-centered! Hell, I say that you should concentrate on the fact that the people who've known you the longest thinks these things about you. There is some truth in all of that, and you need to deal with it and not dismiss it so easily! That kind of thinking is not going to get you anywhere! You need to address that shit!" Rockye commented.

"That is the next step, Rockye. Right now, give the girl credit for successfully getting through the first step!" Carlos defended. "We have to take baby steps!"

"Says who? I don't believe in baby steps!" Rockye insisted.

"So, Ms. Perfect, what progress did you have since our last meeting?" Lynette asked.

"We are not talking about me now! We're talking about *you*!" Rockye then turned to Jango.

"Just what I thought! It's not so easy being in the hot seat, is it?" Lynette retorted.

"How did last week go for you, Rockye?" Jango inquired.

"It was shit! I'm just going to be honest and say that I am still having sex with anyone that I feel like it with. I am trying everything that I can think of to stop, and not a damn thing is working. So as far as I am concerned, you can just go to the next person because my shit is still the same! All fucked up! No changes here!" Rockye folded her arms defiantly across her chest, signaling that she was unwilling to discuss it any further.

Jango eyed Rockye for a while; his slightly raised left brow indicated that he would revisit the conversation with her in private. He had seen that look many times before when she behaved in much the same manner in past sessions and in every instant he later cornered her after group and scheduled a private session. So for the moment he'd let it go, turning his attention toward Bailey.

"Very well then." Turning to Bailey, he continued. "Bailey, can you tell everyone what your assignment was last week?"

"Uhhhhh, yeah! You asked me to write down half a dozen things that I admired most about my mother." She pulled out her day planner from under the chair, flipped to a middle page, and removed a Post-it note.

"And?"

"It was a struggle just to get three!"

"Why was that?" Jango asked.

"Because as I was searching my mind for the memories, instead of remembering happy times, all I could think about were the arguments, criticisms, and disappointing experiences. It made me crazy! My anger had me cursing my mother and father. I think that may have led up to the blowup I had with her this week."

"Can you tell us the three things that you did come up with?" Jango urged.

Bailey inhaled. ". . . a strong conviction in what she believes in; her ability to not take no for an answer, and her skill to get people to do things her way!"

"What did you learn from that exercise, Bailey?"

"I don't know what I learned, but I do know that I truly have a lot of hatred for my mother! I hate the fact that she never listened to me, that she always thought the worst of me, and that she always showed me more anger and disappointment than maternal love. She always made me feel like I was always some big fucking mistake and obligation that she never wanted. I hate her because she hates me. I also learned that I have tremendous disrespect for my dad because he allowed my mother to treat me so badly and never did anything at all about it!" Bailey confessed.

"So much hate inside of that beautiful heart!" Carlos commented.

"I don't blame her. Her mother is a bitch!" Keno added.

"Come on, Keno, that was uncalled for. You don't know what is going on in her mother's head!" Lynette commented.

"Look, I'm just telling the fucking truth. Her mother is some piece of work! What kind of woman does some of the stuff her mother did to their own fucking child? That is straight-up foul!"

"Aren't you the pot calling the kettle black?" Rockye commented.

"Yeah, look at what you're doing to your own girlfriend! You're cheating on her with that old chick! Should *you* be the one to pass judgment?" Lynette added.

"I take care of my girl! She's got my love, and I take care of her!" Keno defended.

". . . by sleeping around on her and lying to her about it? Is *that* how you take care of her?" Rockye asked.

"She is not hurt by any of it! I handle mine as a man," Keno roared.

"So you don't feel what you are doing is wrong?" Carlos asked.

"My girl is struggling financially! She's barely able to make ends meet, and between her tuition for school and her rent, she's always a few dollars short from being flat broke. I need some help! And whoever or whatever can help me out, it's fair game. I need money, and I do what I gotta do to get it. I'm not asking her for a damn dime, so how is that hurting her? As a matter of fact, I help *her* out by giving her money!" Keno reasoned.

"Are you out of your mind? You can't really justify what you're doing by passing the blame on her lack of financial resources to help you. That's ridiculous!" Bailey fumed.

"I ain't passing no blame on nobody! I'm doing what I need to do to survive out here in this fucking crazy-ass world." Keno turned to fully face Bailey. "You can't possible understand my situation. You are not a black man with a prison record."

"No, I may not be black man with a prison record, but what I am is sick and tired of you using that excuse for all of the wrong things that you do! You didn't have to drop out of school and start robbing people. That was *your* choice! Now you use that as an excuse for all of the bad things you do! That is total BS!" Bailey continued.

". . . to hell with you, Miss Stick-Up-The-Ass! You don't know me!" Keno retorted.

The clock sang indicating that the time was up.

"Okay, time is up for tonight!" Jango looked around the room before continuing. "I want you all to remember something . . .

People don't always remember what you say or what you do, but they will always remember how you make them feel! I want you to think about how the people in your lives make you feel. Don't concentrate on what they say as much as how what they say makes you feel." He stood up in the middle of the room.

"Nothing is more important than how you feel and think about yourself. A high opinion about you is the only thing that matters. Understand that when you truly love yourself you won't make mountains out of molehills from what people say about you or to you. When you like yourself more, when your opinion of yourself goes up, then you will not need validation from others. You will become less needy, and your inner life becomes much less of an emotional roller coaster. Sometimes your own worst enemy is you!

"By raising your self-esteem you'll feel more deserving of good things in life. You will be less likely to self-sabotage yourself. In this, you will be more stable and able to handle tough times that come your way.

"So for this week's assignment I want you to concentrate on stopping your inner critic. A good place to start with raising your self-esteem is by learning how to handle and replace the voice of your own inner critic. When this inner voice whispers destructive thoughts in your mind, you don't have to accept these thoughts. At this point, what you need to do is change how you view yourself. One way to do this is simply to say *Stop!* whenever the critic pipes up in your mind. As the inner critic says something in your mind, shout *STOP!* Then refocus your thoughts to something more constructive."

Jango moved over to the side of the room closest to Lynette before continuing.

"I want each of you to write down three things daily that you can appreciate about yourself. Write down your answers every evening in a paper journal. I say to keep a journal because you can read through all the answers to get a good self-esteem boost and change in perspective on days when you need it the most. Bring your journal next session."

He turned to Carlos. "Before we disassemble, can you close us out with the pledge?"

"Everyone, stand up, please. Let's all say it together," Carlos directed.

"I pledge to be a positive person and a positive influence on my family, friends, and community. I promise to share more smiles, laughter, encouragement, and joy with those around me. I vow to stay positive in the face of negativity. When I am surrounded by pessimism I will choose optimism. When I feel fear I will choose faith. When I want to hate I will choose to love. When I am faced with challenges I will look for opportunities to learn and grow. When I am faced with adversity I will find strength. When I experience a setback I will be resilient. With vision, hope, and faith, I will never give up and will always move forward toward my destiny. I believe my best days are ahead of me. I believe I am here for a reason and my purpose is greater than my challenges. So today and every day I will be positive and strive to make a positive impact on the world. And so it is!"

After Carlos ended the pledge, Jango added, "Have a blessed rest of the week and may the favor of God go before you changing rules, regulations, and policies for your ultimate good in Jesus' name."

After everyone was dismissed, Jango made a beeline over to Rockye to make a follow-up appointment with her as he always did when she shut down in midsession. He navigated her through a barrage of feelings until she became calm enough to commit to a date for a private session. Jango comforted Rockye with seasoned words of knowledge while his eyes hovered in the direction of his secret lover, counting the minutes until everyone had left and he could go and sit in the seat she occupied and indulge in the delicious aromas that permeated the air around where she sat. He grew excited with anticipation at the thought of him picking up where he left off from his earlier fantasy of Bailey once everyone had gone as Rockye's voice echoed in the distance.

He had it bad. Jango was hopelessly in love with Bailey Levine, his patient. He knew that ethically, this was wrong, but he couldn't help obsessing over her. He had no idea what he was going to do.

Chapter Eleven

~ Andy Reynolds ~

The nightmare might have awakened you, but it's the content that keeps you awake!

"Get the hell out of here! Get out of grown folks' business!" she yelled with a drunken slur while simultaneously instructing the men to continue.

"Don't stop, baby! Don't mind him! He's gone... See, he's gone!"

Andy bolted up in bed, his body totally drenched in sweat. His heart raced at an accelerated pace as his body violently reacted to another damn recurring nightmare. It had been months since the last one, and up until tonight he had convinced himself they were tapering off.

Andre Reynolds, a 38-year-old marketing executive for a local ad firm, had been having recurring nightmares ever since he was 10 years old. It had been months, and he breathed a sigh of relief every morning when he realized he had not had one. But this morning they started up again and that fact pissed him the hell off. Andy hated his past, he hated where he came from, who he came from, and the hold it had on his present.

He pulled himself out of bed and made his way to the bathroom. The reflection in the mirror alarmed him; his eyes resembled a wild animal's with bloodshot streaks; his hair stood disheveled on his head, and his skin appeared colorless and dingy. The cold water he splashed on his face while refreshing carried no release from his anxiety.

Andy sat on the toilet, hoping that emptying his bowels would give him the relief he so desperately needed. It was always the same dream, over and over again.

Andy was about 10 years old, and one terribly cold Chicago winter night, after awakening with a tremendous urge to pee, he groggily got out of bed and stumbled toward the bathroom. As he rounded the corner through the hallway cluttered with old magazines, newspapers, and empty plastic containers, which led to the only bathroom in the small two-bedroom trailer where he resided with his mother and two older sisters, the young boy stopped cold in his tracks as he caught sight of his mother having sex with two men. He searched the faces of the men to determine if one of them was his mother's regular boyfriend, Mack. Nope! They were much younger! The shocking scene of his mother doggie style with one man pumping her wildly, and the other man stroking her mouth with his appendage petrified him as a child. What child should have to wake up to that shit?

She was pleading for more and asking the man kneeling over her to push it deeper into her mouth. The sounds escaping from his mom's throat scared him. Initially, before his eyes found focus he thought that those men were hurting his mother, but after a few minutes he discovered that she was asking—no pleading—for them to keep going.

Andy became paralyzed as he watched. He didn't recall how long he stood frozen in the doorway, but eventually his mother caught sight of his small frame and screamed at him to get out of the house. When he didn't move quick enough she threw an empty Michelob beer bottle in his direction, missing him by only a few centimeters.

"Get the hell out of here! Get out of grown folks' business!" she yelled with a drunken slur while simultaneously instructing the men to continue.

"Don't stop, baby! Don't mind him! He's gone . . . See, he's gone!"

"I ain't paying for no damn peep show!" one of the men grumbled.

"Don't worry! He's gone! He's gone!" his mother reassured, as she continued in her lewd acts of debauchery.

Distraught, the little boy ran out into the night and slept in the backseat of their broken-down La Sabre. His cries didn't drown out *the sounds of his mother's sexual clamoring, which remained in the recesses of his head to this very day. That nightmare was one of many that tortured him regularly.*

For Andy, that was his introduction to the immoral, detestable behavior he was convinced that most women engaged in with men. By the time he left home at 16, his two older sisters, Cynthia, 18, and Patricia 19, were sucking and fucking any man within the tri-county area who offered them a pack of cigarettes, a meal, or a few dollars. Patricia, his oldest sister, had five children by five different men by the time she was 25. Andy developed a built-in mechanism of disgust for all women exhibiting promiscuous behavior, which, in his book, made up the greater percentage of females.

Andy wasn't able to expel anything through his anus. He felt plugged up. He didn't know if he was constipated again or just too stressed to shit.

After sitting there for about 20 minutes, his right leg began to fall asleep, so he inevitably decided to get off of the toilet.

The toilet paper felt harsh against his skin as he cleaned himself. As the warm water rinsed the foaming soap from his hands, he stared at himself in the mirror and reflected on the last encounter he had with his girlfriend earlier that afternoon. The memory flashed across his mind in vivid detail.

Rockye had swung by his house after her dance rehearsal. Or so she said! Although her disposition was jovial and effervescent, there was this undercurrent of deception that made him uneasy.

"Is that what you wore today?" he said, noticing how crisp her outfit was, and the fresh clean scent sitting on her skin.

"Yeah, why?" she called from the kitchen, her head buried inside the refrigerator.

"What time did rehearsal end?"

"Not too long ago!" She lied.

She sat down on the couch, two Diet Cokes secure within each hand.

"Brought you a soda, baby!" She kissed him on the forehead, the faint smell of jasmine dancing around her.

Andy tasted the bitter taste of distrust on his tongue. His narrowing eyes consciously squinted at her in doubt. Rockye moved to the floor in front of the television and started tinkering with the DVD player.

"I got this movie for you, honey." She inserted the DVD and sat back down on the couch next to him.

Andy reached over and pulled her to him. She giggled, unaware of his intentions.

"Take your clothes off!" he demanded.

"I want to watch this movie, baby!"

"Take your clothes off!" Andy firmly repeated.

"Damn, baby! When you want some pussy, you don't play, do you?"

"Just take your clothes off!"

"Okay . . . just let me go to the bathroom and freshen up!" She lifted her firm, round derrière from the couch.

"No! Sit down! I am not going to ask you again!"

Andy yanked her towards him, and with one full motion, pulled her pants down below her knees and inserted a couple of fingers into her vagina.

"What the hell are you doing, Andy?" Rockye screamed while vigorously attempting to pull away.

"I want some pussy now!" he insisted, holding her down on the couch.

"Let me go to the bathroom first." She fought to get free.

He didn't answer. Instead, he plunged his face between her legs, groping for her clit. She squirmed. He persisted.

"No, baby, I just came from dance. Let me take a shower first!" She managed to break free.

It was okay because he had discovered all he needed to know.

He no longer insisted. Andy wasn't after sex; he was after answers to his nagging suspicions.

His mouth tasted a recently washed vaginal area, smelling fresh of jasmine and not of perspiration and musk from a *so-called* earlier dance rehearsal.

Rockye sprang up and raced to the bathroom. He heard the shower come on and the toilet flush.

Sitting perfectly still on the couch, Andy felt an uncontrollable anger bubbling up within him.

Ten minutes later, Rockye emerged from the bathroom, wrapped in a white towel.

"I'm all yours, baby! Fresh and clean! Do what you want with me!" she teased, attempting to hide her uneasiness.

Andy continued to stare into space.

"Oh, you want me to go to work, huh?" She tugged at his pants as she lowered her head into his lap.

He pushed her away.

"Where were you tonight, Rockye?" His stare was cold and accusatory.

"What are you talking about, Andy? I told you where I was!" She sat up.

"At rehearsal?" he repeated.

"Yes!" she insisted.

"Did you just leave rehearsal and come straight over to my house?"

"I already told you that! What the hell is wrong with you?"

Rockye got up, but Andy pulled her back down onto the couch. The towel separated from her body as Andy hastily spread her legs and thrust his erection deep within her.

She hollered for him to stop, but Andy had to see if her pussy felt different. After a few strokes he pulled out!

It did!

"Slut! Whore!" He got up and slammed his fist into the wall.

"What the fuck is your problem Andy?!" Rockye yelled as she fumbled to cover up her nakedness with the towel Andy had just ripped from her damp body.

He felt in his gut that she had been with another man, and the fact that her pussy felt different was all the proof he needed to confirm his suspicions. Andy wanted to bust up something. It felt good to sock the wall, but it didn't satisfy him. He wanted to put his fist through her entire grill, right in her pride-and-joy face angling to bust up all her perfectly white teeth. He wanted to, but instead, he just got up, put on his coat and left the apartment as Rockye echoed obscenities from the doorway through the courtyard. He didn't care! He had to leave because staying would produce an outcome that would be irreparable.

Now as Andy moved from the bathroom back to his bed, he stretched out and tried to force himself back to sleep. Once in bed, it hit him that possibly the earlier incident with Rockye might have triggered the recurring nightmares about his mother.

After some time, unable to return to sleep, Andy reached over into the nightstand and pulled out his trusty friend, Mr. Jack Daniels.

"Hello, Jack! I really need you now!" He tilted the bottle and allowed the liquid to guzzle down his dry throat. He coughed, wiping the overflow with the back of his hand that laced his narrow chin. When the alcohol began to take effect he suddenly felt a deep desire to speak with his mother. He needed to get answers to the many questions that had been plaguing him for so many years!

Looking at the clock, he deduced the lateness of the hour in Chicago but decided to call anyway.

It had been about 16 weeks since his last attempt to call his mother. He apprehensively dialed her number. After about four rings, he abruptly slammed the receiver back down into its cradle and retrieved the half-empty alcohol bottle from the floor near the couch, tilting it full back into his waiting mouth until he emptied the contents completely.

The tempestuous rage brewing within him was what he was trying to nullify with every swig of alcohol.

With each burning sip, a little of him succumbed to the intoxicant, and eventually he passed out, snoring loudly.

Chapter Twelve

⁓ Rockye Haynes ⁓

God saw her getting tired and a cure was not to be, so He put his arms around her and said come home to me.
Her mother was dying!

Propped up in the hospital bed, Hazel's emaciated body struggled to pull in what she could through the oxygen mask into her slowly failing lungs. Rockye clenched her mom's hand tightly as she watched her frail 65-year-old body begin to shut down organ by organ. Her 5 foot 11 inch frame had dwindled to 78 pounds. The smell of sickness permeated the room; it was a stench that would forever be etched within her mind. Her mom's 4-year battle with lung cancer was only minutes away from concluding.

While stroking her brittle, thinned hair, Rockye sang the soothing words of "Amazing Grace" softly into her left ear, which seemed to render her mother some degree of comfort. That was at least what she told herself.

The nurse came in to adjust the expiring woman's flow of oxygen as the degree of difficulty she was now facing in breathing became more obvious.

As the clock kissed 3 p.m., Hazel Haynes stared out of the window of her hospital room, eyes transfixed on some seemingly peaceful scene as evidenced by the sudden change in the luminous expression exhibited on her face. She smiled an obvious smile of joy, and then took her last earthly breath, simultaneously emanating an audible gurgling gasp before her body became void of any form of life.

"I can't believe another year has gone by!" Rockye whispered to herself as her watery eyes traced her mother's name-engraved marble placard which adorned the square where her body lay buried some three coffins high as she reflected on that day, her mother's last day of life. It was now 5 years since her mother's death, and it still tore her heart out just as much as it did that day she watched her mother expire.

It would have been her mom's seventieth birthday, and Rockye stood at the foot of her grave at the Inglewood Cemetery in reflection, as she did every year. It had become a ritual to visit her grave every Mother's Day and birthday. You would think it would get easier, but it didn't.

Her mother had been a proud woman, a woman that never complained but worked tirelessly to put food on the table and provide the best quality life she could for her family in spite of being a refugee without a husband. Rockye never knew her father because he vanished shortly after finding out that Hazel was 2 months pregnant. Although it was obvious that Rockye's mom loved her by the selfless acts that only mothers do, she was never privy to actually hearing her mother utter the words "I love you" to her, ever! Can you imagine never hearing your mother tell you that she loved you? But in discussing this, her "sore spot" with different people who were the fourth or fifth generation removed from slavery, many said their mothers didn't tell them they loved them either. Their love was evidenced by them never running off in the face of hardship and deprivation. That was their way of saying "I love you!"

Her mind lingered on the thought as she became aware of someone's presence a few rows down. She glanced over casually. A tall bald man probably in his mid-40s shot a glance back in her direction. She looked away. He looked away. She shot another peek in his direction. His eyes danced back in her direction after he saw her look away. The exchange of eye tennis was titillating to Rockye.

He smiled as he caught her eye. She reciprocated with a coquettish grin. He winked. She swiveled her hips turning her back toward him, aware that the full view of her round apple bottom would be pleasing to his sight. He placed a set of red roses inside of a vase on the vault that held his loved one about two squares up. She watched out of the corner of her eye as his eyes gazed in the distance in front of him. His eyes transfixed on the square while his large hands cupped his head as though he had a headache. Rockye wondered who this bald stranger had come to visit. Seizing the opportunity to pounce on her prey, she moved over to the bench a few yards away and slowly eased down, crossing her legs erotically. She wore 5-inch heels, Skinny Jeans, and a white V-necked tee. She eased her shades on and leaned her head down, so as to survey him without notice.

The fair skinned fellow was rather short but impeccably dressed, sporting a shiny bald head and a thin mustache. Her clitoris began to tingle, and her female parts began to juice up at the thought of him inside of her. She cleared her throat. He looked in her direction. Lowering the Coach shades off her eyes, she cut her hazel eyes in his direction indicating an invitation to come over. He looked around, quickly observing his surroundings, then sauntered over and sat uncomfortably close to her. She smelled the day on his stale breath.

"Husband?" He nodded at the tombs in front.

"Mother," she corrected.

"Mother?" she asked him.

"Wife."

They sat in silence before Rockye brazenly elongated her right arm within his lap and cupped his crotch firmly. He winced and gasped simultaneously but didn't stop her. Unzipping his pants, she pulled out his sex and began stroking the shaft with long, quick pulls, bringing it to full erection. He leaned his head back and enjoyed the appetizer. Breathless and fully aroused, he navigated her into the crypt two floors down. She held her breath as the sickening aroma of what seemed like decaying corpses, road kill, rotten eggs, and toe jam, all wrapped in one, slapped her across the face. No matter how foul the smell, it didn't stop him from pulling her pants down and mounting her eagerly from behind. It was a quick plunge without an ounce of concern for her comfort. His thrusts were jetting and sharp; at times seemingly begrudging strokes. She attempted to look back but his palm thrust her back into a T-position until his strokes brought both of them to a voluminous climax.

He pulled off his socks and quickly wiped his penis off before scrambling to put on the rest of his clothes. Then he gave her a dry stare before motioning to leave.

"I'm sorry for your loss," he threw from over his shoulder as he made his way up the stairs two at a time until he was out of sight.

She could still feel him inside of her as she climbed back up the stairs and rested on the bench adjacent to her mother. Looking around she determined the bald guy was long gone. She walked over to the vault where he had placed the red roses. It read, *LaTonya Duncan. Loving daughter, mother, and wife. I love you, LaTonya, Charles.*

She slid down the wall as her legs gave way. His name was Charles. He loved his wife. She did it again. Once again being unfaithful and having sex with a stranger for the mere thrill of the explosion and now here she was feeling like shit as the image of her man, Andy, who loved her, drifted into her thoughts.

⇝

"Can you meet me for coffee?" she bawled into the phone. Rockye's face was stained with tears, her body heaving with uncontrollable sobs.

"What's wrong? Where are you?" Bailey responded with obvious concern in her tone.

"I just need my best friend," Rockye continued to sob.

"I know, honey; it's your mom's birthday today. You've been to the cemetery?"

Rockye told her yes. She allowed Bailey to believe that she was upset because of her mother, but it was really because of what she had done. Once again, she'd had random sex with a stranger. In fact, she'd had unprotected sex, as dangerous and reckless as that was, in this day and age of rampant HIV. What was *wrong* with her? How come she couldn't control this demon?

Her best friend agreed to leave her office early and meet her right away. That gave Rockye some degree of comfort. She knew that Bailey loved her unconditionally, and right now, she needed that kind of love.

Now, as she sat across the table for two in the Brentwood Border's Bookstore coffee shop from Bailey, her heart ached with remorse. She wanted desperately to confess about what she had just done with the bald man at the cemetery and have her friend say the right words to give her guilty heart some comfort. However, no words would come. She couldn't bring herself to confess, so the two sat looking out into the distance at the darkening late-day sky in an awkward silence.

"So you went to your Mom's grave today?" Bailey prodded, breaking the silence.

"Yeah, I did!" She paused before continuing. "It was so hard, Bailey. Why does it still hurt so badly?"

Bailey shrugged.

"I still pick up the telephone at least once a week to call her." Rockye glanced off into the distance as her mind rewound one of the hundreds of videotapes in her collection of maternal memorabilia.

"I remember the last Thanksgiving we had together. My mom and I both woke up at 5 a.m. to put the turkey in the oven. It was weird. It was like both of our internal alarm clocks went off at the same exact time.

"After stuffing the turkey, we sat down at the kitchen table, drank coffee, and just watched the news as we had for over 20 years." Rockye wrapped her long arms around herself and slowly inhaled the memory before continuing.

"What I wouldn't give right now to just be at that kitchen table with her just one more time! To see her hands as they mixed the ingredients in her famous sweet potato pies. What I wouldn't give to taste her over salted collard greens just one more time!" She turned to face Bailey, and studied her friend's face colored with casual interest.

"You are so lucky, Bailey! You can still see your mother, talk to her, and taste her food and—"

"Speak for yourself, Rockye! Just because you feel that kind of love for your mother doesn't mean that I do! My mother is nothing like your mother was! My mother is a bitch, and believe me, if I never saw her again, it would be just fine with me!" Bailey cut her off.

"Don't say that! You know, Bailey, I didn't have a perfect mother. So many times I cursed her because of her ignorance and bad choices. My mom did things to me that I thought I would never—" She paused in reflection. "—never forgive her for! But somehow all of that became so irrelevant when she died. After she died it was like this veil of resentment suddenly lifted from my heart." Rockye cleared her throat before continuing.

"Somehow those things that I was angry about all of those years didn't seem to matter anymore! It wasn't that important that she wasn't there for most of my childhood functions, or encouraged me to keep going when I felt so fucked up as a teenager that I just wanted to take my life, or when I got pregnant at 15 and she dragged me down to the clinic to get an abortion against my wishes, or even when she locked me out of the house all night after I missed my curfew by ten minutes."

Rockye shifted in her seat and continued.

"Shortly after my mom died, I was listening to some talk show one day on the radio and some lady was complaining about how unfair her aunt was to her growing up after her mother died, and how her aunt favored her natural daughter over her and her younger brother. I started to get angry all over again with my mom for all of the things that she didn't do. But then, the radio host said something that changed my perspective totally. She said that maybe her aunt may have been unfair or favored her natural child over her and her brother, but at least she was not put in a foster home. The host told her that at least her aunt kept her in her home and did the best that she could! She told her to find the gratitude in that!

"That put everything into perspective for me! I may not have had a storybook family, but at least my mom didn't put me in a foster home, she didn't leave me or walk away from the responsibility of raising me like so many other mothers could have done when my dad got ghost. Young mothers today are throwing their babies away in trash cans because they don't want them ... but my mom didn't do that to me!"

"Come on, Rockye! You can't compare the two! Throw your child away in a trash can or treat them like shit! In some cases, maybe the former would be preferable!"

"You can't mean that, Bailey! I can see how much resentment you have for your mother. All that hatred is weighing you down. That hurt and anger will eventually turn you into a bitter person. Bitter people live sour lives. You got to forgive your mother!

Where there is life, there is hope! Your mother is alive and breathing, so there is still hope!" Rockye preached.

"I don't want to work it out with her! I don't care if she lives or dies!"

"BAILEY! You take that back right now! You don't mean that!"

"Look, Rockye! You have no idea what my mother is like. All of my life I have dealt with her critical, harsh abuse while my father sat by allowing her to demoralize, disrespect, and dehumanize me time and time again. You may have a few bad memories about your mother doing some hurtful things to you, but for me, it runs fucking deeper! She could take her last breath today and I wouldn't give a shit!"

"I understand what you're saying. I am not saying that I don't have shit inside of me that hurts like hell. As a matter of fact it still fucks me up that my own mother had never in my whole life ever told me that she loved me. I never heard those words come out of her mouth. Do you know the kind of pain and insecurities that can give a girl growing up? I always wondered what the hell was wrong with me that my own mother didn't love me enough to say she loved me. Do you know what she would say when I would ask her if she loved me?" Rockye's eyebrows rose at the question.

Bailey's head tilted in wait.

"I go to work every day, I buy you shoes when I don't buy them for myself. Food is on the table every night, and the lights are always on when you hit the switch. If that ain't love I don't know what is." Rockye shook her head. "What kind of shitty answer is that? It would have taken way less effort to just say 'I love you!'"

Bailey shrugged.

Rockye shook her head in distress. She looked past Bailey, through the ceiling-high windows of the Borders Book Store in Brentwood into the night sky. Bailey seemed distant and she didn't seem to be listening to what Rockye was saying.

Adjusting her firm ass on the hard wooden bench, Rockye noticed her cell phone message light blinking. Forcing her mind back to the present she remembered that she had neglected to return Andy's calls. He called her several times throughout the day, and although her intent was to call him back, the events of the day took precedence, leaving him again neglected as she did all too many times.

Excusing herself and walking over to a secluded corner of the bookstore, she called her boyfriend back.

"Hi, baby!" She inserted a cooing sound into her voice.

"Where the hell have you been? I've been calling you all day, Rockye. What the fuck is going on?" His bark blasted through the receiver.

"I went to the cemetery today," she meekly responded.

"Who did you go with? How long were you there? Was there anybody there with you?" he interrogated.

"No, honey, I was there all by myself." She started to sob so as to throw him off his rant. "It has been a really hard day for me, Andy. I miss her so much."

"So where are you now? What have you been doing all day that you couldn't pick up the phone when I called you?"

"Baby, it's not a good time for me right now! Can we talk about it later? I just need my 'zone of silence' now." This "zone of silence" was used when Rockye needed some alone time from the world. After reading the phrase in a book years ago, it fast became her terminology when she wanted people to leave her the hell alone. Not really being able to dictate such harsh commands, she adopted the phrase "zone of silence" instead.

"Where are you now? Who are you with? What have you been doing all day? Why did it take you so long to call me back? I find it crazy that you are always—"

She pressed the end button on her phone. "Fuck!" This is the part about having a significant other that she hated. This accountability shit was for the birds. Andy was always on her ass like in that old saying, "like white on rice," and because she was not always on the up and up, she had to maintain an allure of distance many times. Later, she would tell him that her battery died. She always kept a dead battery in her car and would insert it into her phone right before seeing him. He always checked, his eye of suspicion arching up at her when he attempted to verify her story by trying to turn it on. Rockye knew that he didn't believe her, but up until now he couldn't prove shit!

She returned to her friend Bailey sipping on a hot tea, dismissed Andy from her thoughts until later, and redirected their earlier conversation to conversation about their plans for visiting the spa the next day. Bailey excitedly outlined their itinerary for the various spa treatments.

Rockye desperately tried to pay attention to Bailey's words, but the tingling in her groin was heightening by the moment. Her female parts began to juice up, accelerating the urge for release. It was hard because her clit was swelling at the very thought of an explosive release. The sad thing was she didn't care if she had sex with a complete stranger or with her boyfriend, Andy. She just wanted to get her nut.

Chapter Thirteen

⁘ Bailey Levine ⁘

At the intersection of lonely thoughts and desperate actions, we must remember that we chose that path.

"I've been calling and calling you!" Bailey uncharacteristically bellowed into the phone.

It had been 2 weeks, 4 days, and 12 hours since she had given him almost $6,000.

He appeared as impertinently as he disappeared. Chance was the ultimate enigma, and perhaps she would never really know the secrets that he harbored, but, nevertheless, she was always chasing that elusive stranger or any fragment about him. She wanted any wisp she could get to help unravel the mystery that had such an addictive effect on the very essence of her.

He interrupted her tirade with amorous words that placated her frustration, which stemmed from his disappearance. Within minutes, she had once again become double minded and agreed to meet up with him at his request. She quickly penned the address he recited and rushed out the door with excited titillating anticipation.

He lulled her with seductive words, and she complied with his audacious requests! And now she was rushing anxiously to once again be in his presence.

She felt the burn on her calves as she completed climbing the fourth floor. The stench of urine rose up from the corners of the floor as she hit the seventh floor. Jazz music greeted her through the slightly opened double doors of the address of the apartment where Chance had invited her to meet him.

He was mysterious as usual with where he had been over the past few weeks. Every time she asked him where he'd been, he diverted the attention to some surprise he had for her. He led her to believe that she was meeting him at his very own apartment. Because she wanted to believe in their future together, she persuaded herself to believe that finally they could have a normal relationship, one without secrets or lack of trust. Maybe he had used some of the money that she had given him to get his own apartment so that they could finally be in a real committed relationship together. She hated that she had never been invited to where he lived before this time. They always met at some friend's house. Maybe now he was finally ready to settle down with her. Her heart pounded with anticipation!

After closing the front door behind her, a loud commotion alerted her from what seemed to be the kitchen.

"I'm here!" She breathed deeply from her lungs.

"Oh, snap! You finally made it, baaa bee!" His head peeped out from the kitchen for a quick second. "You look so sexxxyy!" Once he finally emerged, his devilishly sparkling eyes and charismatic smile caused her to revisit a few of the many reasons why she was so utterly captivated by him. He held in his hands a bottle of wine and two burgundy-colored wineglasses.

His lips firmly pressed up against hers while his tongue sharply pushed its way into her mouth.

"Hold up!" Bailey pushed back.

"Come on, girl, you know you missed Daddy!" After securing the contents in his hands on the coffee table, he reached for her once again, grabbing her ass with full force.

"I said hold up! I am not a fucking piece of meat!"

"Maybe not, but I am sure a hungry animal for your sweet pussy!" he joked.

"Look! We need to talk!"

"Damn, girl, do you always gotta bring that fuckin' drama everywhere you go?" he snapped.

Bailey moved to the oversized couch and plopped down on it so loud the leather clapped. "You can't say 'Hi, how ya doing?' or something like that before you pounce all over me like some just-released convict from prison?"

"You know you wanted to see me. You missed Daddy, didn't you?" Leaning against the edge of the couch he tilted his head staring at her with conceit. "You know you missed all this!" He grabbed his crotch and salaciously tugged at it.

"Where the hell have you been? I've been calling you for weeks!" She sounded pathetic.

"I had to go to New York to meet with these guys from Entertainment Negotiations about funding for my next project." He uncorked the wine and poured it carefully into the wineglasses.

"You couldn't call me and tell me that you were going out of town?"

"I was busy from the time I got off the plane until the time I got back on the plane to come home!" His cheek twitched, an indication that he was lying.

"So you are trying to tell me that you couldn't pick up the phone once and call me back?"

"Damn. Bailey, do I get into your shit when you are busy doing your thing? So get off my back!"

She retreated. He handed her the glass of wine. She sipped it. Looking around she commented on the apartment.

"This is your new apartment?" She noticed that it looked nothing like him, and it sure didn't look like a place that someone had recently moved into. Dust was settled in a thick layer on most of the surfaces.

"No, this is my buddy A. J.'s place. He's out of town, and he gave me the key in case I wanted to get freaky with my girl." He wiggled his tongue in a vulgar gesture in her direction.

"So let me get this straight; you called me up here to just have sex with me?" She bristled up.

"Come on, babe, you know you wanted to see me! You wanted to be with Daddy, so I just found us a place to have a little privacy."

He took a stand in front of her. "So, what? Do you want to argue or fuck? I ain't got time for the first one!"

Tears started to form in her hazel eyes. Chastising herself, Bailey wished she hadn't answered his call earlier; however, the loneliness sometimes got so unbearable that she agreed to things that she knew she shouldn't just so as not to be alone.

After leaving Rockye earlier that afternoon and coming home to an empty house with no promise of any later activity, Bailey begin scrolling through her address book looking for some companionship for the evening, which she eventually settled on trying once again to get a hold of Chance. She called and again it went to voice mail. She cursed at the phone and eventually gave into the idea of a lonely evening in front of the television, but within minutes he had called her back.

One looking at Bailey would assume that she had a full social calendar because of her beauty, intellect, and success, but the reality was that other than business and The Circle, she was a consummate loner. She didn't have any friends other than Rockye. Nobody really liked her; hell, she didn't even like herself!

Bailey stared him down, her eyes holding his gaze. She wanted to get up and run out of that apartment but the emptiness in her gut was unbearable, so she just sat there and convinced herself that maybe today he would give her what she wanted. Just maybe today he would love her the way she needed to be loved.

Bailey met Chance one afternoon as she was leaving a business meeting at the Courtyard Marriott in Sherman Oaks. He swept up as she was exiting the hotel in his silver and black Camaro fashioned with high-profile tires and blaring loud rap music. The limousine-tinted driver-side window lowered to reveal his full smile and deep dimples. He asked her out several times. Each time she said no, but after the fifth time she acquiesced and within the week they had their first intimate encounter in the bathroom of one of his friend's houses. Unbeknownst to her at the time, his friend was in the shower enjoying the show. That was the beginning of the sordid, perverted, sexual relationship between the two of them.

"It just would be nice if you could at least ask me how I'm doing. How was my day and put your arms around me for a minute. You know, like you care or something!" Bailey knew she sounded vulnerable and desperate.

"So you want a 'Leave It to Beaver' moment, huh?" he joked.

Her eyes threw out a cold retort.

"Okay! Shit, I guess that ain't like asking for a Bentley or somethin'!"

Chance scooted over to her, wrapped his arms around her, and patronized her. "How was your day, dear? Was there a lot of traffic today?"

"Fuck you, Chance!" She quickly pulled away in disgust.

"Hopefully, you will!" He laughed a sinister laugh while cupping his penis with his right hand.

Why couldn't he just love her? Why couldn't he just see how amazing she was? What was wrong with her that he just couldn't see that she was worthy? Bailey thought to herself.

"Look, Bailey, we could do this thing that you like to do. This back-and-forth shit, or we could just do what you came over here for! You know that is what you *really* want! That's why you're here, looking all fine and shit with your tits hanging out. You got your sexy ass poured into them True Religion jeans, makeup banging, and shit! If you didn't want this—" He unzipped his jeans, reached in, and pulled out his hugely endowed manhood, "—would you be here looking so damn sexy?" He reached over and grabbed her crotch.

"I bet your pussy is dripping wet right now, ain't it?" His tongue slowly dragged across his ample lips.

"Stop it, Chance!" she protested.

He pulled at her BeBe top, stretching it out of shape. "Bailey, take that shit off! You know I like to see you naked."

Bailey could see his enormous penis standing at attention through his fly. A full erection! Chance's sex was amazing, and Bailey was indeed addicted. *Isn't this what you came over here for?* she asked herself. *You knew that the two of you would not be playing board games.*

"Suck Daddy's big dick!" His large hands forced her head into his lap.

Bailey initially resisted, but as she had so many times over the last couple of years, eventually she succumbed to the request.

His moans encouraged her to suck faster, swallow more, and rotate her hands in unison until his screams echoed his satiation.

"Come here, girl." With one sweeping motion, he lifted her up and ushered her into the bedroom, throwing her atop a California king. The comforter smelled musty and felt slick and oily.

"Get on your knees!"

Bailey struggled to get her Jimmy Choos off before slipping off her Skinny Jeans. She heard him mutter something.

"What you say?" She threw over her shoulder while he roughly positioned her on all fours.

"Nothing. You know the position that I like!" He positioned her right and left leg to a point that formed a nice arch in her back. Bailey heard something rustle behind her that disturbed her. It felt like another presence was in the room.

"Chance, what's going on?" She tried to turn her head to see what was going on behind her, but he grabbed her head, jamming it down into the folds of the musty comforter.

"You know how I like it, babe. Don't mess this up for me!" he whispered into her ear.

Bailey struggled to get free. She knew exactly what was happening, and she couldn't blame anybody but herself. Chance hadn't changed a bit. What made her think that he would suddenly and miraculously be a loving, tender, kind lover was beyond her.

"No, Chance, I don't want to! Stop!" Bailey struggled to get free.

"I thought you told me she wanted to be fucked by two guys. What's up, man?" Bailey heard a strange voice.

"Hold up," Chance tossed the guy with a throaty deep voice.

"Come on, babe, you know how I like it! Don't disappoint me. This is so good to me! You are the only woman that can share this with me. Don't ruin this for me! Take it like a big girl! You want Daddy happy, don't you?" Chance said while continuing to hold Bailey's face down on the bed.

As the guy with the throaty voice plunged deep inside of her, Chance continued to encourage him, while simultaneously feeding Bailey manipulative lies and false pledges of love.

"Give it to her, man. She likes it hard!" Chance kept saying over and over to the stranger.

"Damn, girl, you know exactly what I like! You are fucking incredible! Yeah, just like that! Give it all to him!" At each plunge, stroke, and pounding from the strange guy, Chance followed it up with more disingenuous declarations.

As she had for so many years, she turned off her body to the wills of the foreign men invading her body and focused on the kind, loving words she wanted to hear from Chance. She needed desperately to hear somebody tell her that they loved her and make her feel special. Although this was not her ideal choice, it was better than the emptiness that consumed her. If for only a few minutes, Bailey convinced herself that she was important and that somebody really cared about her.

The stranger plunged deeper into her vagina until he howled out his climax and fell instantly to her side. Chance immediately climbed in after him, thrashing his fully erect penis within the walls of her soppy cavity until his sticky liquid exploded within her.

Afterward, Bailey lay there, their voices as a backdrop to her sorrow, and their spillage draining slowly from her. The smell of the mixture of semen was repugnant.

She cried softly to herself, feeling emptier than when she arrived. What had made her succumb to his sick, twisted, sex games? This wasn't the first time, so she should've known better. She knew she deserved better, but unfortunately, he was like a drug for her; once she started, she couldn't resist him. She was addicted to him. This wasn't the first time Chance had brought a strange man into their bed. Why did she subject herself to this type of abuse? What the hell was wrong with her?

Chapter Fourteen

⁓ Keno Hunter ⁓

You can make a bad decision and find yourself plummeting in a downward spiral. At that point, you can give up or you can find someone that can get you out of it.

"Okay, what the hell is wrong with you? You have been draggin' your ass around here for the past 3 days now! What the fuck's going on?" Sharon called Keno on his uncharacteristically morose disposition. She loomed over him; face grimaced with *"I have had enough of this bullshit!"*

Keno had been hiding out at her Wilshire condominium, the Carlyle, since the shooting. And even though he felt miserably guilty and terrified at the thought of finding out the outcome of his childhood friend Jimmy, he nevertheless allowed himself to enjoy all the creature comforts of her multimillion-dollar residence.

He had turned off his cell phone and hadn't been home or in contact with anyone since the robbery. Although the thought of Dee Dee going out of her mind with worry about his whereabouts perturbed him, he still hadn't pulled from his funk long enough to call her. He was so weak emotionally, he couldn't even figure out what he was going to say to her.

"I just got thangs on my mind, Sharon, that's all!" He shot the sharp comment to Sharon as he glanced up from the scrambled eggs and diced ham he had been tossing around on his plate. One of the many privileges of residing with Sharon was the full-time French chef, Pascale, who prepared all of the meals. She was a small woman who spoke broken English, but nonetheless, cooked her ass off! Sharon spared no expense for the things that she wanted, and a top-rated chef was one of them, as evidenced by the extra pounds she transported around on her stout frame.

The furrow of her brow suggested to him that she had grown exasperated of his sullen, withdrawn behavior. Keno knew that eventually he'd have to tell her about what was going on, so he might as well get it over with. His life was in total shambles now, and he couldn't take any more risks in losing the only resource he had going for himself right at this point.

"Sharon, I ummmm..." His voice was slightly above a whisper as he cradled his head in his hands, rubbing intermittently from his eyes to the back of his head in surrender.

Sharon tilted her head in response.

"...there is something I need to tell you!" Keno felt his heart racing with dread at her reaction. Would she throw him out on his ass? Would she yell and scream at what a dumb ass he was for his actions? What would she do? Although his heart pounded with anxiety, he took a deep breath and prepared himself to confess.

"I'm listening," she answered curtly.

"The other night my friend Jimmy and I ... ummm ... We committed a robbery." *There, he finally said it!* It was out there hanging in the air like a fragrant fart! He eyed her timidly before continuing. Her faced showed no trace of emotion.

"We robbed a jeweler." Her face held no expression. "Afterward, we got pulled over by the police. Jimmy tried to outrun the cops, but we ended up crashing into a car. After the crash, we jumped out of the car and took off running in different directions. I heard shots fired!" His eyes never left Sharon's face, which still held a placid expression.

"It all happened so fast. After I heard gunshots, I stopped and was about to turn around and go back, but I panicked and kept running!" He cradled his head in his hands again before continuing.

"What kind of a friend keeps running when his buddy gets shot?" Keno asked Sharon. Reeling with guilt, he peered at her from between his fingers as he squeezed his head tighter.

Sharon rested her freshly manicured hand on his shoulder, an uncharacteristically gentle gesture. A long, contained breath escaped her throat before she responded.

"The kind of friend that knows it will do him no good to get his ass shot either!" Sharon reasoned.

"Jimmy would have never left me behind like that, Sharon! He would have—"

"—he would have done what? Come back and take a chance at getting shot and killed as well? Is *that* what he would have done? Is *that* what you are telling me? I don't think so!" Sharon released her hand from his shoulder and moved quickly over to the bar and poured herself a double shot of bourbon.

"You have absolutely no idea what the hell he would have done in your position."

"I just keep thinking that because of me his daughter is probably without a father now! It's my fault! I feel so horrible! I just totally screwed up my life with one stupid decision! Look at what I did to my friend—I got him killed! I have really fucked up this time!" Keno whimpered.

Sharon's voice finally rose, laced with agitation. "I see that you want to play the victim here. Okay, fine! But let me tell you this. Yes, you did fuck up! That was one of the dumbest things that you could have done, and then to come to my house and make me an accomplice to your fucking crime! You are an idiot! This is not something that I would have ever expected of you, Keno! You have everything you could ask for right here. Just look around. Whatever you wanted, I could have given it to you! But instead of asking, you go and do something so utterly ridiculously idiotic!" She padded back over to the bar to replenish her drink.

"I don't know what to say other than I am just so damn disappointed in you. I guess I gave you far more credit than you deserved." She sighed a long resolute breath.

"I'm so sorry that I disappointed you! I just wanted to be able to get my own money so that I could contribute to things around here," he lied. He knew he was only concerned with himself. "I get tired of taking money from you. I hate taking and taking and taking. I want to be able to buy something nice for you with my own money. Not being able to take you to really nice restaurants and pick up the check myself really bothers me! It really fucks with my head every time they hand you the bill, as though it ain't even a possibility that I could pay it. It's fucking humiliating! I hate it!"

She moved closer to him and leaned into him. Tenderly, almost motherly . . . Just the way he had hoped. Sometimes women were so damn predictable. They always needed a lost cause, someone to fix, someone to nurture, some creature to bring back to life! Women are so malleable!

Sharon softened.

"I appreciate that you want to contribute, but you have to admit that you went to the fucking extreme here! A robbery, Keno! Ever thought about a job?"

They laughed at the irony, for she knew his plight in that area. The mood lightened.

"What about my friend? He's probably dead because of me!"

Sharon stiffened at the comment. "Go ahead and blame yourself if you want, but remember that this friend of yours made up his own mind to do what he did, knowing full well the possible consequences! He knew exactly what he was doing. Let me ask you something. Did you force him?"

Keno shook his head.

"Was this his first robbery?" Sharon asked.

"No!" he answered. "But I left him, probably shot and dying in the streets all alone!"

"Don't be so melodramatic! But let me ask you this, what if it had been you that was shot, are you 100 percent sure that he would have turned around and put himself in imminent danger to see about you?" she continued.

After additional thought Keno answered, "No! No, I'm not 100 percent sure!"

She sat next to him, the smell of bourbon coming off her breath.

"Do you know anything about what happened to him?"

"I don't know, Sharon, that's the thing that's killing me! I don't know if Jimmy is alive or dead! I'm afraid that he's dead, and if he is, it will be all my fault!" he whimpered.

"Is that why you have been camped out over here in this funky mood?"

"Yeah! I didn't know what to do. I'm afraid to death that Jimmy is dead!"

"Well, isn't that about a bitch move! You are telling me that you are afraid to find out the truth? You have been hiding here the entire time because you are *afraid* to hear the fucking truth?" Sharon sharply turned on him.

It wasn't until he heard her say it out loud that he realized how cowardly he sounded.

"What's your friend's full name?" she asked as she picked up her cell phone.

"James. James William Johnson."

Sharon dialed the number of a longtime friend, Judge Jeremiah Spencer. He was her "go-to" person every time she needed a favor in the court system. A huge yearly contribution to his favorite charity, The Prostate Cancer Foundation, had made him putty in her hands for he had been diagnosed with prostate cancer and the organization was paramount to his recovery.

Halfway through the conversation, Sharon left the room and without so much of a word to him, traversed into the bathroom. Suddenly the sound of the multi-jets of the massive marbled shower drowned out any chance of Keno overhearing the contents of the conversation. He sat there, his gut churning, his bowels tight, his breath shallow, and his fists clenched in anticipation. Would his childhood friend be dead? Did they discover the jewels in the radiator? Did Jimmy tell them that Keno was the accomplice? A myriad of questions jetted through his mind! He prayed. He paced. And he worried!

Fifteen minutes later, Sharon marched back into the dining room.

"Get your butt up and go take a shower! Your friend Mr. Johnson is incarcerated at the Twin Towers for probation violation and evading the police. He suffered a superficial wound and is fine. His arraignment is in 18 days."

"Did he . . . Did he say anything about me? Did they find the jewels?" He held his breath waiting for a response that could change his life forever.

"No, they didn't even connect you two to the robbery at all! And your friend never mentioned you!"

"Thank God! Thank you, Sha—" He lunged up to hug her.

She backed away. "I said GO take a shower! Afterward, we need to get a few things straight!" Her face was tight now; humorless; taciturn.

Keno knew that tone all too well. He had heard that very same stern voice when she was fed up with her employees. Shit was about to hit the fan. He would need the comfort that the shower would provide before he faced her wrath. He felt that

Sharon was about to give him a significant chiding, a rebuke that would leave its marks behind, much like that of a childhood whipping from one's parents as a youth!

Sharon Nicole Faraday was a strong, successful, wealthy Caucasian woman who always dealt with things head-on. She didn't run away from any challenge. Instead, she faced them boldly with a confident defiance. Keno knew that the object of her aggravation now was his cowardly behavior, his carelessness, and mostly, the lack of forethought that his actions could possibly implicate her as an accomplice. He knew Sharon was angry, but she'd never been this mad at him before. He'd seen her go off on her employees, so he knew she didn't play. He knew he was about to get it and get it good!

The soothing stream of hot water from the multi-jets comforted Keno's tense body. The water's pelts satiated the knots of stress in his joints. However, there was still that dull ache in his heart that hadn't gone away. It was just hidden, secured within the many folds of his fear but now it was beginning to surface, tugging and gnawing at him. This time, the subject of his anxiety wasn't for his buddy Jimmy but his woman, Dee Dee. He knew that across town within her tiny one-bedroom apartment, she was worried sick about him. They had a practice of speaking a couple of times a day, and when he wasn't held up within the luxurious confines of his paramour, he consistently took her calls immediately.

By now he was sure that the word had traveled back to her about Jimmy's plight and Dee Dee knew Keno well enough to know that he would have been riding shotgun with his childhood friend. Regardless of how well Dee Dee may have known her boyfriend, she didn't know him well enough to know why he hadn't called.

Standing there in the opulence of Sharon's marbled shower as the multi-jets tickled and teased his manhood, Keno wrestled with his guilt, and even though he felt lower than pond scum, he cupped his oversized penis within his hand and pulled and tugged on it until its white creamy substance spewed out all over the rim of the soap dish. Regardless of how badly he felt about neglecting his girlfriend, it didn't stop him from pleasuring himself. He needed the relief. He needed to feel like a man again, that is, before he headed back into the living room to deal with Sharon and the major ass whipping that he was sure he was about to receive.

Bend over and take it like a man, he told himself as he stepped out of the shower, bracing himself for what was to come.

Chapter Fifteen

~ Andy Reynolds ~

"Today I will adapt new habits and new thinking!" Andy kept repeating over and over his newfound affirmation. "My woman is a good, decent woman! She loves me! She isn't like the others! She is a decent woman! She would never cheat on me! She has never cheated on me! She is a good and decent woman! She isn't like the others! She has never cheated on me! She is a good and decent woman."

This was their standard Friday night date night, and Andy was going over these words like a mantra to try to assuage his suspicions. He shook his head. How can it be that love can feel so good at times, and at other times, felt like a knife going in and out of your heart in rhythm? Love can hurt so much sometimes that it leaves you in a depth of misery so much larger than the high of the happiness that it initially gave you!

His girlfriend would be there any minute now. It was their standard Friday date night, and he vowed to put aside his trust issues and just love on his woman without prejudice for the night. Andy made a commitment to put aside his doubts, adopting the adage "If you want better, do better!" Insanity is doing the same things over and over again and expecting different results, he kept telling himself. He had so much apprehension about his girlfriend, and the lack of trust was the catalyst in their sometimes turbulent relationship. But as he considered the alternative of being without her, he realized that he had to really try hard to forget his reservations and give it 100 percent to make it work.

Andy loved his girlfriend with the intensity of an inferno. As a matter of fact, never in his wildest dreams did he ever think that a woman could generate these types of feelings out of him.

Andy contemplated this as he loaded the bootleg DVD of *American Gangster* into his wall-length eight-speaker entertainment unit. Then he sat back down on the couch awaiting the arrival of his girlfriend, Rockye. As his eyes scanned his apartment, a smile signifying approval of the exceptional job he had done cleaning the place warmed his face. Everything was in place, the candles were lit, and the Stouffer's lasagna was warming up in the oven with less than 30 minutes to go.

He desperately wanted to stop the insanity that caused so much of the drama in their relationship and adopt new habits and attitudes toward Rockye. He was afraid if he kept pushing Rockye, he would push her away, and he really didn't want that. He didn't want to be left alone, for it seemed like most of his life he felt alone.

He heard the front door open as her massive collection of keys acted as a doorbell, confirming that it was his woman entering his apartment as he continued to chant his mantra.

"Hey, honey. Something sure smells good!" Rockye shouted from the hallway.

Andy took a deep breath, adjusted the tulips on the table, and cheerfully greeted his girlfriend. "You can do this! You can do this! She is the woman that you love, and she is as good as you tell yourself that she is."

"Wow, look at you!" His eyes bugged out of his head at the sight of her skintight, flesh-colored, one-piece bodysuit. Although the little man in his pants screamed approval, his entire body stiffened with disapproval. She looked like a hooker, plain and simple!

"You like?" She turned around several times for his viewing pleasure.

"Uh, well—" He moved closer to her, grabbing her, and squeezed her ass firmly before releasing. Rockye's tight, hourglass dancer's body was perfectly painted by the flesh-toned bodysuit she wore which was accented by a low waist belt, a three-layered row of crystal necklaces, and ankle-high boots.

"Did you just come from home?" he asked, trying desperately to fight back the suspicion.

"No, I met a friend of mine from high school, Natalie. You remember the chick who was my roommate for a few years?"

"I guess . . ." he replied, not really remembering who she was talking about but distracted by her indecorous attire.

"Well, she wanted me to meet her fiancé. Did I tell you they got engaged last week? At first I thought she just wanted to ask me to be a bridesmaid at the wedding, but come to find out all she wanted to do was to show off her big fat-ass rock."

She moved over to the small refrigerator near the wet bar and grabbed two bottles of Smart Water.

"Want some water? I can't say that I blame her. That motherfucker was huge!" She handed Andy the bottle which he didn't take, and she eventually set it on the coffee table next to him. "Here, honey!"

"What did you do before you met Natalie?" His eyebrows furrowed as he glanced at the water bottle resting on the coffee table without a coaster. He was anything but thirsty and highly annoyed that she had placed the water bottle down on the table without a coaster. It would most likely leave a ring!

"Got my car washed, got my shoes from the repair guy, oh yeah, and I got you this!" Pulling a tiny Nordstrom's box from her oversized Coach purse, Rockye handed it to Andy with a wide, sexy smile.

Andy received the box with apprehension, because it was not like her to give him gifts for no reason at all. "What's the occasion? It's not my birthday."

"No occasion, a just-because gift!"

"You bought me a gift just-because? Why?" His faint smile dissipated. His suspicion started to brew once again. What was she trying to make up for by buying him this gift? he asked himself. His mind danced with the idea that she did this because she was guilty of something. He just knew it!

"Come on, Andy. Don't ruin the fun! Open it!" Rockye nudged the box in his hand.

With one single pull, the package was opened, revealing a black onyx money clip which he had admired in a Nordstrom's catalog just weeks ago.

"Sweetie! You remembered!" He was touched. Putting the box on the dining-room table, his arms secured her curvaceous body next to him.

"I can't believe you remembered that I wanted that money clip!"

"So I take it that I did good?" She kissed him sensuously on the lips.

What a thoughtful thing to do he told himself. It touched him that she remembered that he coveted the money clip while flipping through the magazine, and actually went out and got it for him. What a wonderful gesture! How could he have doubted her? What a fool he was! He looked at her face, and the doubt and distrust suddenly melted away.

"You did really good! Thanks! I love it!" Andy took the money clip to his bedroom and placed it on top of the chest of drawers next to his wallet.

Andy was moved by her thoughtfulness. He desperately attempted to hold on to that positive thought, but upon entering the living room, the issue of her unsavory attire revived itself once again as he caught sight of her ample ass as she bent over to pick up something off the floor. The scene that kept playing in his mind was one of her walking around all over town with men gawking at her sexy body, and her grinning and lapping it up! He had to shake his head to rid himself of the jealous thoughts. She couldn't help it if she had a sexy body.

"You got *American Gangster*! You know I love me some Denzel!" Rockye said as she studied the back cover of the DVD jacket.

As Andy watched her flit around the room, the voices in his head kept telling him that she was not to be trusted. It yelled at him, "*Be warned of someone bearing gifts for no reason at all.*" It probably was an attempt to appease the guilt she felt for some indiscretion of hers. *Cheating bitch!* he thought.

"Look, Rockye, we need to talk!"

"What?" she responded while continuing to study the DVD jacket.

"I don't like you wearing stuff like that when I am not with you."

"Fuck, Andy, not that shit again! You are *always* in my ass about what I wear!"

"Rockye, that's the damn problem! So is everybody else—in your ass with what you wear. Why do you have to show off every fucking thing you got?" Andy argued.

"It's my damn body! And quite frankly, I work really hard for this body, and if I want to show it off, shit, I *am* going to do just that! The last time I looked you were not my father or my damn husband!"

"And you sure won't get a damn husband dressing like a fucking slut!" he judged.

"Oh really?! Is *that* what you think? You think that somebody wouldn't want all of *this*?" Rockye gestured her hands over her curvaceous form settling on her plump, firm ass.

"No man is going to marry a slut!"

"Just keep thinking that shit if you want and one day you will find yourself sitting here all by your damn self!" she threatened.

Andy felt the heat rise up to his neck. His hands involuntarily began to ball up into tight fists. His upper lip started quivering with anxiety.

He wanted to sock her in the face, quiet that loud, disrespectful mouth that didn't know when to shut the fuck up! He looked at her, and all he saw was red. He saw his mother, his sisters, his money-grubbing baby mama, and all the lies and deceitful acts of women everywhere who betray the trust of their men. He wanted to get vengeance for all of the men who were hurt by conniving women with hidden agendas of deceit. By just driving his fist into her face, he would be making amends for millions of men across the world. He slowly raised his fist to meet it with her face, but the mantra echoed so loudly in his head he put it down.

Today I will adapt new habits and new thinking! Andy repeated over and over in his head trying to change his angry thoughts.

"Rockye, I love you! I don't want you walking around showing everyone what is mine! A man doesn't want a woman who is a walking advertisement for someone to fuck!"

She didn't respond, just stood in the hallway with stubborn pride as her anchor.

"What do you want me to do? How should I feel when I see you looking like this? You're out there walking around with all your business exposed for everyone to see. That is supposed to be *my* ass; *my* breasts, *my* pussy, and you do what? Put it out there like it's available for everyone! How am I supposed to feel about that? Tell me, how the hell am I supposed to feel about that?"

"I don't know how you are supposed to feel, but I am just tired of you acting like my damn father all the time! You are *not* my damn father!"

"That's the damn problem! You didn't have a father, and that's why your dumb ass acts like you do!"

"Fuck you, Andy! You didn't have to go there!"

He knew that he had crossed a boundary, but so did she, and although he wanted to reduce her smug ass to pieces, he realized that that father comment was below the belt. The fact that her father had left her mother soon after she found out she was pregnant was a huge sore spot to Rockye. He regretted throwing it in her face, but the alternative was putting his hands on her. He wanted to hurt her, and this blow would not leave any bruises, at least not physical ones.

She started cursing and hurling expletives about his family at him.

He knew that to keep playing verbal war with her would only escalate to the physical so with that realization he just turned and walked into the bathroom. Every fiber in his body wanted desperately to slam his fists into her face and choke the shit out of her disrespectful loudmouthed ass.

He didn't want to reason with her, he wanted to put his hands on her and have her plead for her fucking life. But instead, he retreated into the bathroom, biting his lower lip with fierce anger burgeoning inside him! Somehow, he was able to control himself—this time, at least. He had never hit her before, but he didn't know how long he could hold out from letting this demon inside of him break out.

Chapter Sixteen

~ Keno Hunter ~

*S*trategy: *advancing one's agenda through the skillful art of subterfuge.*

Keno's salacious derrière perched within eye level of his sugar mama as he dried off in silence, paying particular attention to his feet. Strategically bending over, he'd hoped that the sight of his round, tight ass would minimize the degree of her annoyance. Leaning over, he carefully swiped the towel slowly up and down his legs. The sweeping motion was deliberate and calculating, with each pull he anticipated her agitation diminishing.

Although the bathroom was slightly steamy from Keno's shower, it still didn't stop Sharon from applying her makeup at the dressing table nestled in the corner. The long sweeping lines of black mascara she applied gave her face an alert look. Although gravity had played havoc on her face, the meticulously applied coloring from the MAC makeup she painted on gave her a more vibrant appearance.

Not pulling her eyes away from his calculated moves of enticing her with the dance of the towel over his virile form, it appeared Sharon relished the sight in her lascivious ruminations. She let out a long breath before speaking, which resembled the sound of a release from the top of a pressure valve.

"Keno, do you know why I keep you in my life, in my bed?"

Deciding that making a joke at that moment would agitate the situation, he decided to be direct.

"The sex?"

She chuckled at the answer before continuing. It appeared as though she were contemplating a response of humor but ultimately chose the contrary! Her mood was noticeably somber and humorless.

"I don't like weak men, Keno! The men that I've had in my life prior to you eventually proved to be spineless jellyfish; weak little pussies! Other than the sex, they ended up serving me absolutely no purpose. I grew tired of them after the orgasms subsided."

She paused in reflection before continuing, a smile washing over her face.

"But when I met you, your cavalier attitude and unwillingness to accommodate my constant demands was a huge turn-on. There was this ethereal swagger about you! You were certainly different than anyone I'd ever been with before. I watched you own a room when you walked into it. I fell in love with that confident, 'I don't give a shit' attitude! You showed me that there were still strong young men in this world that didn't need a woman to lead them around with the proverbial ring in the nose. And even though you had not come into your own success, I knew that with the right support you would find your way," Sharon confessed.

Keno sat on the edge of the sink after securing the towel around his narrow waist.

"However this, this *indiscretion* for lack of a better word, gives me reason for great concern. I have a future in mind for you, for us. I am not a woman who believes in wasting my time, but after this robbery, I am now questioning the man that I thought you were. Robbery? Come on now. Was that the *best* you could do? What the hell were you thinking? And to make it worse, you come over here and hide out like some coward, like some weak, pathetic little man, like a punk-ass bitch!

"I'm going to tell you this only one time. Are you listening?" She waited for his nod before continuing.

"I am not a woman to be fucked with, Keno! I have not gotten to where I am today making bad decisions or allowing people around me who don't use the damn brains God gave them!

"Weakness is not a trait I admire in a man. You cannot be with me if you continue to behave like a weak, punk-ass bitch!" Sharon leaned in to Keno so close he caught sight of the creases in her face hidden slightly behind her recently applied foundation.

"Look around. Does it look like I want for anything?"

"Nawww," he eked out.

"Do you realize that whatever I have, you have as well?"

He eyed her sheepishly before answering.

"All this is yours, Sharon, not mine! This is *your* shit, not *mine*! I need to find a way to get my own shit!"

Keno's retort appeared to have softened Sharon's castigating tone.

"And you will, Cupcake, but in the meantime, in the lean times, we are a team, and what is mine is yours. You don't have to go out and commit crimes! All you have to do is let me know what is going on. I will help you. You don't ever have to worry about a thing as long as I am on your side!"

Keno eased over to her and cupped her face within his hands. "You are a good woman, Sharon! I don't deserve you!" He kissed her tenderly on the mouth, partly manipulative but mostly out of a momentary genuine affection for her benevolent heart.

"Do you love me, Keno?" Her eyes sought for a yes.

"I do love you, Sharon," he lied. What else could he say in that moment? No, bitch, I don't . . . I just love what you can do for me. Not!

"Then it doesn't matter if you think you deserve me or not. We love each other, and we need to look out for each other and realize that the decisions we make affect both of us."

She moved closer to him. He straddled her body between his legs as he leaned up against the marble basin.

"The man that intrigued me when we first met, bring him back! This spineless, impetuous little bitch, lose that mothafucka!

He's lethal to both of us. We will not make it together with those types of stupid-ass decisions, do you hear me?"

He nodded as he gazed hungrily into her eyes. That look he purposefully gave her was his Kryptonite for it calmed her immediately and started the furnace that was her sex. He took the liberty and started seducing her slowly, beginning with small sweeping kisses down her neck, allowing his right middle finger to dance delicately across her plump clit. She groaned a seasoned, throaty sound. Throwing her head back, it appeared that she allowed her body to succumb to the ecstasy. His fingers brought her back and forth from the brink of explosion, driving her wild with passion. Suddenly, he pressed her firmly up against the wall and plunged his thick apparatus deep within the caverns of her extended walls, push and pulling it in and out until she yelled an explosive orgasm. Her face reflected immense pleasure. The wetness of her vagina echoed her euphoria as the afterglow softened her earlier harsh demeanor.

"This is precisely why I keep you around. You make my body feel young. You awaken these feelings, these sensations, and these orgasms within me that I have never experienced before in my life. I am not a spring chicken, but you make me feel like one." She reached down to grab his slightly deflated penis. "And I never knew that, that something like this could give me so much pleasure. And after the sex is all over, you make me laugh. Keno, you always make me feel special! And that is why you are in my life, in my bed!"

He held her gaze until she suddenly became aware of the time.

Glancing down at her watch, she extricated herself suddenly from the intimate moment. "I have to get out of here; I have a board meeting in less than one hour." She swung around in thought before exiting the room.

"But remember this, Keno. Straighten up your shit! Don't ever do any shit like this ever again, because if you do, I will be done with you so quick it will make your head spin! I will *not* have you fuck up my life! Understand?"

"Loud and clear!" he winked at her.

Her face stiffened with intensity of her seriousness.

"Okay! Okay, I hear you, and you will never have to worry about me doing no stupid shit like that ever again!"

"Good! Because I would hate for you to ever become a distant memory."

She repositioned herself between his legs again. "Keno, I have never been fucked so well in my life!" She secured his man-tool within her hands, yanking it slightly too rough. "And I expect to get plenty of it when I come home tonight! How about an early dinner, and then we can have dessert in bed all night long!" She winked.

"I can't wait!" He grimaced at the thought as she turned to leave.

"I'll see you tonight then!"

"Great!" Before exiting the bathroom, she swung around again and concluded, "Twelve left, twenty-eight right, two left!"

"What's that?"

"The combination to the bedroom wall safe. Take what you need. I never want to hear that you robbed anyone ever again!" The sound of her heels on the hardwood floors echoed throughout the condo as she scudded to the front door and left.

Keno thought to himself as he let out a huge sigh of relief. *You pulled your ass out of that fire, and what a hell of a fire it was! You are one fucking lucky bastard to pull that shit off with that crazy bitch.* He mentally patted himself on the back as he realized how he maneuvered a narrow escape from being homeless, penniless, and minus one rich, generous paramour.

Keno dressed himself quickly, making a mental note of all the things that he had to do before Sharon returned to the condo later on that evening. Put some money on Jimmy's books, pay some bills, spend a good amount of Sharon's money, and, of course, smooth things over with Dee Dee. This was not a meeting that he was looking forward to at all!

He zipped up the Abercrombie & Fitch navy-blue hoodie before marching over to Sharon's wall safe. Twelve left, twenty-eight right, two left, and with ease it sprang open. With his right hand he eased it open to catch the view of its contents. To the left were three stacks of $100 bills; behind them were various sizes of brown envelopes stacked on top of each other. In the middle were at least 20 black velvet jewelry boxes, and on the right side was the object that called him to stand at attention. *"Well, I'll be damn!"* he thought. It was a gun!

Sharon had a gun! That bitch had a gun! He should have known that she would be packing. He took mental note as he peeled off fifty $100 bills from the stack. *Hazard pay,* he thought! Hazard pay for dealing with this dried up, old lecherous bitch, stealing his youth and manhood. *I should have taken ten thousand. She has more money than she can burn.* He was the one who needed the money. As far as he could see, fair exchange was no robbery.

Chapter Seventeen

~ Andy Reynolds ~

Compromising doesn't mean that you are wrong and someone else is right. It only means that you value your relationship more than your ego.

"Andy, do you remember when we first met?" Rockye, sitting at the kitchen table in his apartment, turned to face him. Her question startled him out of the trance he was in. He swallowed back his rage.

"Yeah, of course."

"Do you remember the first thing that you said to me?"

Andy walked over and sat opposite her.

"Didn't I ask you for your phone number or something?"

Rockye interrupted, "No! You told me that I was the most beautiful girl you had ever seen!"

He chuckled, "Boy, was that original? You must have thought that I was an idiot or something."

"It was corny, but it made me feel good." Rockye smiled a soft smile. "Do you remember what I was wearing?"

"It was a purple dress with a slit up the back and some sexy-ass black high heels that showed off your gorgeous legs."

"What was it about me that you were attracted to first?"

"Your tight, round ass!" he answered without hesitation.

"Do you remember what I was wearing on our first date?"

"You had on this black slinky short dress with a pair of black high-heel boots!"

"What was the name of that girl you were seeing when you met me?"

"I don't know! Who cares?" His face showed confusion at the questions.

"Shelly! That was her name!" Rockye remembered.

"Okay, whatever, Shelly, then! Where the hell is this going?" Annoyance was beginning to rise up his collar.

"How long had you been seeing her?"

"About 8 or 9 months. Why?"

"Last question. I know that you were seeing both of us at the same time. What made you decide to get with me instead of her?"

"Well—"

"Be honest!" Rockye insisted.

"It was most definitively your body, and the sexy way you made love!" he confessed.

"Exactly. Shelly was replaced because of my body and my sexiness! Do you think that you would have given me the time of day when you first saw me if I was dressed in baggy sweats, a baseball cap, and flip-flops?"

"Well—"

"Be honest, Andy!"

"Probably not!"

"Okay, if it wasn't for what I was wearing, you and I would not be together today, right?"

"Maybe not," Andy surrendered. "And the point is . . .?"

"The point is that I was dressing like this when you met me. I'm just being true to who I am, regardless if I have a man or not. I'm a free spirit, and I'm expressing who I am by how I dress. That's all!"

"So what are you saying? That I'm going to have to accept the fact that my woman still dresses like a whore?" Andy became angry.

Rockye eyed him sharply.

"That was unnecessary! I apologize for that but—"

"Look, I know what I am doing. I know that the clothes that I put on makes people look at me. I know this! But I have been dressing this way for as long as I can remember. I like the attention, Andy! It makes me feel beautiful, special, and quite frankly, I need it and crave it!"

"It's not *people*, Rockye, it's men. Men stare at you, and woman just think that you are a cheap tramp. You are a walking advertisement! Did you forget that you are not a single woman anymore? Isn't the attention that I pay you enough? Why do you need more?"

"It should be enough, Andy! It should be! But it isn't!"

They sat in silence for about 10 minutes before Rockye continued.

"Baby, I do understand your point. I am who I am, but I will try to do better! I will really try! I can't say that I will change overnight, but I will try to be more selective of what I wear when I am not with you! Okay?"

"That's a start," Andy conceded. He hugged his girlfriend.

"Because it really is all about *'progress, not perfection,'* right?" Rockye added.

"Progress not perfection!" Andy repeated as he embraced his woman in his long, muscular arms. He no longer wanted to put his fist through her face any more, but looking at how her body filled out that jumpsuit, he did want to get so deep up in her that he would forget that this was a subject that would rear its ugly head again ... and again! He couldn't get over how conflicted he felt. On the one hand, he wanted to jump her bones and bang her back out, but on the other, he wanted to put her in a capsule so no other man could look at her. How come she couldn't dress more conservatively?

Andy shook his head. *I guess they were right. You can take the person out of the ghetto, but not the ghetto out of the person.*

Chapter Eighteen

~ Bailey Levine ~

Bailey lay in bed, feeling empty. She didn't feel like getting out of bed to face another day of work. The only thing that she had going for herself at this point in her life was her real estate brokerage firm. It was the only thing that validated her. Without the firm, she believed that she had no other reason for living. That was Bailey's reality. She had no children, no husband, no real friends to talk about, and no family. All she had was her company. And propelling it to #1 was her life's purpose, and it consumed most of her waking moments. She spent most of her free time formulating ways to strengthen her company, and subsequently positioning herself to take advantage of the first opportunity to seize Sid's company at the first signs of vulnerability.

That is where Robert Mercer came in.

Robert Mercer stood all of 5 feet 5 inches tall in a black Brooks Brothers suit complemented by an emerald-green striped shirt and tie. His hair was a dirty blond, which set off his deep blue narrow eyes. Bailey had heard much about this business acquisition negotiator, and aside from his height, everything she heard was true to fact. He was much shorter than she was told.

Bailey had decided a year ago that she wanted to be a dominant force in the Southern California real estate market. Since then, she had been successful at acquiring four independent real estate firms, bringing hers to number two. However, she needed the assistance of an expert negotiator to acquire Shultz Realty which would instantly propel her to the #1 largest independent Real Estate Agency in Southern California.

The rumors were that after the industry leader, Sid Shultz's, second heart attack, he finally reconciled with the fact of selling his company. That was the moment Bailey began to strategize on how she would be able to acquire his company for herself. After much inquiry she was told of Robert Mercer and his unprecedented successes with many company acquisitions and mergers. She conversed with him on the telephone on several occasions, and subsequently decided that he would fly from his home base city of Seattle to Los Angeles to formalize their partnership and solidify the specifics of the merger.

After speaking with him, she indeed found Robert Mercer to be an astute businessman with a sharp wit and a tremendous aptitude for successful business mergers.

"My sources tell me that Sid is all but ready to pull the plug any day now," Bailey informed Robert who sat across the table from her, eyeing the detailed reports he was given on Shultz Realty. Sid Shultz had started his real estate company over 35 years ago, and now, as he entered his late seventies, his health began to fail, as well as his interest in the business. His repeated attempts to turn the company over to his son, Mylar, met with disaster. The immature 40-year-old wanted to run with women, play rock music, and smoke pot.

"Twenty-five percent of his realtors have gone to ReMax," Robert announced from behind the reports.

"And more will follow because of their generous commission structure and benefit package," Bailey added.

"Well, that's something we are going to have to contend with if we are to win the majority over here." Robert spoke with slight concern.

"Glad you brought that up." Bailey hit the intercom on her phone.

"Mandy, tell Felicia to come in now."

She turned confidently to Robert Mercer. "I have the solution!"

Robert studied her from across the desk, smiled, and said, "My plane doesn't leave until 11:00 tonight. How about an early dinner after the meeting?"

"I would love that!" Bailey sounded too eager.

"It will give me a chance to get to know you better!" he flirted.

"I have to warn you, it is *not* good to mix business with pleasure!" she flirted back.

"When I'm doing business, I'm doing business. When it comes to pleasure, I separate myself from the business. I would hope that you could do the same." His smile was sexy and reassuring.

"Dinner it is!" Bailey was dying for some male company, and Robert Mercer would indeed be a charming, engaging dinner companion. And the best part was that she wouldn't be expected to pay, like with Chance whose pockets were always empty!

Felicia softly knocked on the door, announcing her arrival before entering.

"Robert, this is my assistant, Felicia. Felicia this is Robert Mercer."

Felicia held out her hand. Robert glanced up at the girl before reluctantly shaking her hand.

"It's nice to meet you, Mr. Mercer." Felicia was met with a dismissive response.

Felicia handed Robert a bound copy of a proposal. He gave her a pointed look.

"We have drafted a comprehensive package that not only matches everything that ReMax offers its agents, but incorporates an unparalleled bonus structure," Bailey added.

"Our commission structure is a three-tier system. If you will turn to page 17, Mr. Mercer, you can follow along," Felicia instructed.

"Tell him about the program we have for the clients!" Bailey added.

"Oh yes, we are offering them a 15 percent rebate at each closed transaction, and a 20 percent rebate if they use our in-house resources, such as escrow, title, inspection, and loans."

"We have worked it out where we have an undeniable win-win situation for the both client and the agent!" Bailey concluded.

Skimming the proposal, he shook his head before responding. "Sounds like you have worked up a formidable package. It's now left up to me to put the winning pieces together to get Sid to pull the trigger."

He took his glasses off and laid them down on the table before pulling out his Samsung Galaxy Note.

"I have scheduled a meeting with Sid for next Tuesday, the 17th, at 11:00 a.m. How does that look for you, Bailey?"

"Wow, you had that much faith in us?" Bailey asked.

"You have a reputation yourself." He smiled.

Bailey turned to Felicia, "Make sure you clear both of our calendars for Tuesday the 17th."

"I'll take care of it!" Felicia said as she made a note of the date on her legal pad.

"Thank you, Felicia. Excellent job!"

"That's what I am here for!" She turned to Mr. Mercer. "It was nice to meet you, Mr. Mercer, and I look forward to seeing you on the 17th."

He didn't look up from the report but instead grunted his response. "Ah yes!"

Moments after Felicia left the room Robert said, "I think that it would be a better idea if you would have that girl out front come instead of her."

"Excuse me?"

"It would look better if that other girl came instead of her," Robert repeated.

"What would look better?" Bailey said with disbelief in her voice.

"Come on now, Bailey, you know what I mean."

"You mean it would look better to have a blond white girl accompany me, instead of a black girl wearing braids. Is *that* what you meant?"

"To be frank, yes!" Robert confirmed. "I don't want to show any signs of incompetency within our infrastructure." He began to place his papers within his leather briefcase.

"So what you are saying to me is that black people are incompetent?" she fumed.

"No, what I am saying is bring the white girl and leave the black one in the office. *That* is what I am saying, nothing more and nothing less!" His voice showed annoyance.

"I didn't know that I was dealing with a bigot!" Bailey rose from her massive oak desk.

"There is an objective here, and positioning is key!" he argued.

"And having blacks in your camp puts you in a position to lose?"

"Look, Bailey, why are you making such a big deal of this? You act like I have personally insulted you!"

She became quiet, letting her silence confirm his statement.

His right eyebrow rose in query.

"Yes, Robert, you *have* insulted me. *I* am black!"

"What? But you—"

"Don't look black! I am though! And I will not leave my assistant behind because she is black." She walked over to him. "And if you have a problem with me being black, then we need to extinguish this partnership right now."

Robert's body stiffened up. "Bailey, I didn't know! It was not my intent to offend you!"

Glancing at his watch, he moved toward the door. "Oh my! Look at the time! I just remembered an appointment I have in

L.A. We'll have to do dinner another time. I'll touch base with you when I get back to Seattle." He opened her office door. "And again, I didn't mean—"

"Save it, Robert!" she stopped him.

"I'll call you when I get back to Seattle!" He quickly exited her office, but an odious fragrance of bigotry lingered behind him.

Bailey lay her head on the desk. It felt heavy and started to throb. *What a bastard! What an absolute bastard*, she thought. The anger was rising up within her resembling water quickly hitting the boiling point. It was exasperating and always all around her; the bigotry! Because she looked white, people openly criticized her race right to her face. No shame, no restraint!

⁓

Hours later the emptiness of the office started closing in on her as the ticking of the wall clock seemed to get louder at each movement. Everyone had gone home for the day and she was all alone in the office. Dreading going home to be alone again yet another night, even though she owned a beautiful home with all the creature comforts, Bailey was desperately lonely. She contemplated calling Chance.

Perhaps they could go to the movies or out to dinner. After tossing the idea around in her head for about 10 minutes, Bailey picked up her land line and dialed Chance. The melody of the rings on the other end caused her to reflect on their last meeting. Shame started to bubble up in her gut, and as quickly as the thought popped into her head, she slammed the phone back onto its cradle; the reality of what she was about to do came crashing down on her.

"Come on, girl! Stop it! You are better than that!" she said aloud to herself.

Packing up her briefcase, Bailey decided to go home and take a long bubble bath, drink a glass of Merlot, and curl up in bed with a good book.

After locking the front door of her office, her cell phone rang. It was from a blocked number. Hoping it was Rockye, she picked up immediately. She had called Rockye earlier in the day and left a message for her to call when she was free from her acting class that evening.

"I tried calling you back on your office line, but it kept going to voice mail."

Shit, it was Chance!

"Bailey, are you there?" he asked.

"Yeah, Chance. I'm here. What's going on?" she asked curtly.

"I was just thinking about you when you called me. Daddy misses you, girl!"

"Oh, really?" Boy, did she regret that earlier impulse call.

"What are you doing? Why don't we hook up? A few of my buddies are on their way over, and we can have some fun! I feel real freaky tonight."

Bailey interrupted. "Chance, I got an important call coming through. I gotta go."

"Just come on ov—"

She hung up on him midsentence, and then switched her cell phone to the off position. "Fuck you, Chance! Fuck you! I have had all I can take with assholes today. All I can take!"

Perhaps standing up to Robert today had given her some backbone. Suddenly she knew that she should stand up for herself with Chance too.

Yes, she should have resisted the unwelcoming sex from his friends, but she hadn't. The less she set boundaries, the more pieces of her died inside. She shook her head. What was it about her that made her feel so damn unworthy of good treatment?

Chapter Nineteen

～ The Circle ～

Jango's eye was jammed in between the crack of the slightly opened office door that led to the room where the Tuesday group had assembled. Suddenly he felt a tap on his shoulder. "Boo!" Tyler teased.

Jango jumped with a start.

"You got it bad, man!" Tyler eased up behind his partner, startling him.

"You shouldn't sneak up on people like that!" Jango fumed.

Little did Tyler know but Jango spent long hours in his apartment thinking about Bailey; he meditated on how soft her skin would feel up against his as they lay naked under the sheets as well as anticipating how her sensuous lips would taste pressed up firmly against his. The one thing that he knew was taboo, he had gone and done. Jango had fallen for one of his patients. He chastised himself for ever thinking those forbidden thoughts, but nevertheless, he couldn't help himself. He was falling deeper and deeper in love with her.

"Why don't you just tell her how you feel about her?"

"You know that I can't do that!" Jango mouthed as he secretly tossed around the idea of pursuing a relationship with Bailey.

Jango bristled up, grabbed his notebook, and headed out of the door. "I can't, Tyler!" he called from over his back.

"You mean you *won't!*" Tyler responded, but it was too late. Jango was out of earshot.

～

"Hello, everyone! Good to see all of you!" Jango welcomed everyone as he entered the room. His eyes zigzagged about the room, eventually settling in on Bailey sandwiched in between Rockye and Carlos. She wore crème-colored linen slacks, a short-sleeved fuchsia shirt, and her French-tipped toes displayed beautifully within open-toed flat sandals.

"You might have noticed that Lynette is not here. There was a family emergency, so she will not be joining us today! Let's keep her in our thoughts and prayers." He didn't share with them the fact that she had encountered some complications during a recent cosmetic surgery and was hospitalized as a result. If Lynette wanted them to know, then she would tell them.

Keno smirked out loud, "She's probably out getting a tummy tuck or something!"

"I will not have that kind of talk from you, Keno!"

"I was just joking around, Jango. Didn't mean nothing by it!" Keno said with a grimace on his lips.

Surveying the room at a glance, Jango settled on Bailey who was sitting directly in front of him with her arms and legs crossed.

"Picking up from our last session, I want to start off by talking about conscious living, actually being more present in your own lives. I don't want you to close your eyes anymore to your life, wondering how things might be in 10 years. I want you to be smarter moving forward. Take the time to study your current existence to monitor how well you're doing now. I want you to look more closely at your thoughts, behavior, and interaction with others.

"If you come at life from fear and separation, you have no reason to expect anything but fear and separation in return. I want you to seek to increase your strengths and decrease your weaknesses. You no longer need to seek satisfaction in things outside yourself or in the completion of yourselves from others.

"You are who you are, not who you might one day be. Your life is what it is, not what it might someday be. You must remember that your life has purpose. The benefit of a life lived with purpose is that aimless living ends when you operate in your purpose. A person caught in a cycle of purposelessness tends to jump from one thing to another in search of meaning. This deception, associated with a fast-paced, busy lifestyle, creates an illusion that progress is occurring, when all along, a person most likely is just moving around in circles."

"So what are you saying? We need to focus?" Keno interrupted.

"Yes, that is exactly what I am saying. You need to start living a life of laser-beam focus. The more you distance yourself from aimless living, the closer you come to living a life directed toward fulfillment. What I want you to do is just be aware of *what* you are doing and *why* you are doing a thing, moment by moment. This is laser-beam focus.

"At this point as we move forward. I want everyone to keep that in mind, okay?"

"I guess!" Carlos agreed.

"Now, let's get started by summing up the last couple of weeks in a few words. Let's start with you, Bailey. What were the last few weeks like for you?" Jango's head swooned every time he looked into her hazel eyes.

"A few words, huh? Okay, let's see. That would be frustrating, disappointing, and infuriating."

"Okay. Okay," Jango responded as he scribbled her response in his notebook.

Looking around the room he then settled on Keno.

"Keno, you!"

"Fucked up! Fucked up! Fucked up!"

"Briefly tell us what was so 'F' about it."

Keno's eye flashed. "I hate not being in control! I am my own man, but when I can't be in control, I feel the heat rise up within me, my heart starts beating fast, and I get so frustrated that it feels like I'm about to explode." His breath quickened as he talked. "I feel like lashing out. I get so mad—I could kill somebody!"

"I see. We'll talk later about where the rage is coming from." Keno eased back into his seat.

Turning to Carlos he continued. "Carlos, what about you?"

"Jango, I have this crazy feeling. It's like the feeling you get when an airplane takes off. Your heart is racing, and you get really nervous as the plane goes higher and higher into the clouds. Then comes the turbulence, and then the fear and anxiety starts to kick in. I have that feeling when I think about my father finding out about my homosexuality!"

"Fear of the unknown." Jango nodded as he noted Carlos's comment. He then turned to Rockye.

"Rockye, what about you?"

Her eyes looked up with the openness that one sees in people with nothing to hide.

"I feel terrified!" She paused before continuing, lost in thought. "I just can't seem to run fast enough away from it. It's there when I wake up, when I go to sleep, and all throughout the day. Everywhere I go, it's there! I simply can't get away from it!" Rockye rambled as she starting tearing up.

Jango passed her a box of Kleenex.

"You can't get away from what exactly?" he questioned.

"My past! It is always hanging on, really tight and not letting me go!" Rockye continued to softly sob. "I can't run fast enough away from it!"

"Why do you want to run away from your past, Rockye?"

"Because it's ugly, dark, and shameful!"

"How many of you want to run away from your past?" Jango asked.

All expressed agreement in some form or another.

"The family we were raised in is usually a microcosm of the world that you have created for yourself. Whether your childhood was good or bad, it lives in your cells. It laid down tracks of thought and thus behavior that has run your lives for decades.

"By now from the time you have spent in this group, you guys have collected some very important clues about yourself. The next step is to discover what they mean now. Our personal issues began in childhood, and we soon must come to realize that only by facing these issues head-on can we escape their consequences.

"If you were appreciated as a child—you attract people in your life that appreciate you. If unappreciated—then you attract people who don't appreciate you. Subconsciously, you are drawn to individuals and situations that mirror the drama of your childhood. We must therefore heal the inner child. Only after healing that inner child that we used to be can the adult of who we want to be emerge."

"How the hell do we do that?" Rockye asked.

"Okay, let's try this exercise. Imagine that there is a huge hole right here in the middle of the room, surrounded by dirt. What would you want to bury in that hole about your childhood . . . about your past?" Jango asked.

"I would bury the things that I have done with men. This hunger for things I shouldn't want! Hurt that is so deep within me that the roots are fused within my very marrow and bone! Selfish, indiscriminate behavior! Selfish desires that I fulfilled! Half of me! I would bury about half of me!" Rockye confessed.

"I know what she means!" Keno added.

"I can relate to that. If I could only get away from my fucking past, not only leave that shit behind but forget it altogether so I wouldn't even know the kind of shit that I was capable of doing, I would do it in a heartbeat!"

"Give me an example." Jango's eyes danced between Rockye and Keno.

"I keep hurting people that I truly love because the selfish part of me will not be inconvenienced or uncomfortable. I don't do the right thing. I do the easy thing; that is, what is easy for me! And as a result, I cause major destruction all around me." Keno sighed before continuing. "I would bury that that part of me, that inconsiderate bastard who only thinks of himself," he confessed.

After a few moments of silence, Jango turned to Rockye. Her solemn face rose to meet his.

"I have these urges; it's like those vampires in the movies who crave blood. I have these cravings for a release, a massive, explosive release. This sensation overwhelms me; it just takes over me and the next thing I know is that I am with some stranger somewhere doing things that make me feel really good at the time and then like . . . like shit afterward."

"Rockye, what do you think triggers you? What is going on in your head right before that all happens?" Jango queried.

"She wants some dick up inside her! That's what she's thinking!" Keno jetted.

Rockye eyed him before speaking.

"Well, you probably think that I am going say something like I am looking for the feelings of being loved or accepted, something like I never felt valued as a child so I am seeking it through men, but the simple fact is the only thing that is going on in my mind at the time is the anticipation of a mind-numbing explosive orgasm. So I guess Mr. Asshole is right." She looked at Keno with that last comment.

"I knew it! She is a straight-up freak!" Keno exclaimed.

Jango eyed a reprimand.

"Fuck you, Keno!" Then she turned to Jango to continue. "It's simple. I just crave that feeling of the release. I am not trying to get some lost love that I didn't get from my father! I just want the explosion, that's all!" Rockye folded her arms across her chest, a signature move to indicate that she had concluded.

Jango nodded his head at her response, and after logging it in his notebook, he then turned to Keno.

"Keno, what goes on in your mind right before you engage in your destructive behavior? Does a part of you want to stop yourself at the time?" he asked.

"Not exactly. I know that I'm being an asshole. I realize that my behavior is bad and that it's destructive. I just think more of myself than anyone else. I know exactly what I'm doing. I know that the shit I am doing is wrong, but fuck, sometimes it's the only alternative that I have at the time. My ass is drowning so much in my own fucked-up circumstances; I just do what I gotta do! That's all there is to it! I'm only thinking about me!"

"Fucking narcissist!" Rockye retorted.

Keno rebuffed her, then turned to Jango to finish answering the question.

"I act selfishly and cowardly, but later I look back on it and I do think about what I did, but the crazy thing about it is if I was in that same situation again, I would still only think of myself and I would do the same exact thing all over again!" Keno concluded.

"Wow, that's crazy! You would really do the same thing all over again?" Bailey commented.

"Sure the fuck would!"

"Look, guys, you know that you can make a decision to release the drama of your childhood by redefining who you belong to. You are products of your parents, but who is that exactly? Is it your mortal parents or our immortal parents? Your earthly parents may have raised you, but they are not who created you or who programmed into you your purpose for being. God is your true parent. Ephesians 2 says that God is rich in mercy because of His great love He has for us, even when we are dead in our trespasses," Jango said.

Jango stopped momentarily for he remembered Tyler cautioning him about using The Circle as a religious platform. He decided to retreat and go in another direction.

"Rockye and Keno, I want you to know that whatever the errors of your past are, they belong to the past and they are NOT YOU! You don't have to be that coward, Keno! You can make a decision today to be brave and accountable. Rockye, you can stop doing those ugly, shameful things. You can just decide to not let your past be your present or your future."

"It ain't that damn simple, Jango! How do you expect us to just stop? That shit you saying ain't realistic at all!" Keno retorted.

Jango stood to address the group. "Look at it this way. Take a lemon cake, for example. A lemon cake is comprised of many things; milk, eggs, flavoring, flour, icing, water, oil, etc. Each component stands on its own; however, when you put them all together, they become a lemon cake.

"So it is the same with your past. Each experience stands on its own. You are not one single experience; you are the sum of all of your experiences, not just the bad.

"You have to identify each component for what it is. Get to know it. Get intimate with it and realize that each one of those components has its own flavor, consistency, and texture. But when you put them into the mixing bowl, what comes out is the sum total of all of the components."

"Jango, sometimes you make me crazy with the way you talk. Why can't you just talk normal so a simple person like me can understand what the hell you are talking about—instead of using some damn cake story? Give us an example that we can relate to," Keno barked.

"Very well then. In your youth you formed issues that have now become a part of you like a second skin. However, it is now time to slay them. It is now time for a major commitment to heal our childhood wounds. There will be no victory without this childhood healing. We can heal if we are honest with ourselves about what those issues are, and then take 100 percent responsibility for them.

"A wound that might have been inflicted on you years ago by someone has turned into a character defect that is all yours now. We project responsibility for a dysfunction outside of ourselves. Wherever we got this childhood wound from, its healing lies within us now and therefore you will continue to trigger this wound until it's healed."

"So when are you going to tell us how to heal them?" Rockye asked.

"In your case, Rockye, your mother's neglect of you when you were growing up, the abandonment of your father when you were only an infant, the lack of acknowledgment of your talents, your beauty, and so much more makes up who you are today. It is all of these things that make up Rockye—not just one of them.

"Your past has left a mark on you! That mark, along with the traits that you possess now and are developing, is the sum total of who you are today. Your past is a part of you, but it is not all of you! You don't have to continue that destructive behavior! You have to say STOP, even if you have to fake it until you make it.

"You start the healing process by identifying that your childhood issues don't have to be your adult issues. You single them out and you focus, day by day, moment by moment, that you will not let it have a hold on you any longer!"

"I have tried everything, Jango, but I just can't stop no matter what!"

"I'm getting ahead of myself here, but I will address what Rockye just said by talking about volition. Volition is a series of continuous, unceasing determinations until it produces a much-craved result." Jango continued, noting the look of confusion on everyone's faces.

"Let me break it down this way. A **wish** implies a helpless desire of the mind. A **desire** is a stronger wish followed by fitful efforts to manifest itself into action. An **intention** or a **determination** is a strong desire expressed very forcefully once or twice through action for the accomplishment of a certain purpose. Such a determination is often discouraged after one or several unsuccessful efforts. Which lead us to **volition**, the ultimate series of actions, continuous and unceasing until the result is accomplished."

Turning to Rockye, he said, "A person of volition never stops repeating conscious acts of determination to achieve what they want. They never stop until it is accomplished. In short, volition is the truest use of willpower. It opens up the door of limitless possibilities for success.

"With a determined direction of action and through force by a developed, consciously exercised willpower, we can accomplish so many things that otherwise may be considered impossible! Therefore, a strong will creates strength, a strong will is never stifled, and a strong will always finds a way!"

"How do we get this volitional will?" Rockye asked.

"Let's talk specifically. Give me an example of when you would need to exercise a strong will," Jango said.

"Well, when I'm in a situation when the temptation to get something is so great that I just have to have it right then or I feel that I will burst. At that moment what do I do? How do I tap into this volitional will you talk about?" Rockye asked.

"You mentioned temptation. Temptation is a delusive . . . a compelling, conflicting, joy-expecting thought which should be used to pursue happiness-making truth and not misery-producing mistakes. At that moment you feel tempted, you feel that the end result will be satisfying, delicious, and beneficial, but in the end, it fools you. While sometimes the benefit may be fleeting moments of fulfillment, it renders more misery, more heartache, and more damage to your psyche than it renders anything positive."

"You never answered the question. How do we tap into this volition you are talking about?" Keno interrupted.

"Before you can tap into anything you have to realize that you cannot do anything by yourself. You have to contact God first! By contacting God first, you harness your will and activity to the right goal. By itself, our human will is limited by the circumstances of the body and boundaries and the physical universe, but God's will has no boundaries; it works in all things all the time. After calling on God, He will then give you the strength to accomplish your undertaking."

Bailey's voice arose strongly from within the midst.

"Overcoming a temptation is not that simple, Jango. There are so many emotions that override everything. It's almost impossible to stop, and what you say, contact God, well, then, what? Wait for Him to give you strength? Most of the time, Jango, things happen so fast that you don't have time to think or rationalize. If that were the case, we would not make half of the mistakes that we make as human beings!"

"Yeah, Jango, you make it sound so simple. Most of the time we do things because we are trying to fill a hole that is so deep and empty inside of us. We are just pulling at anything we can to put inside of that hole so that we don't feel so lonely or so invisible. We are looking to find love, someone to understand us, to care for us, or to make us feel like we matter in this crazy world!" Carlos chimed in.

"That's right! We don't stop to think about shit! Things happen, you act on it, and *bam*, afterward you realize what you have done, and by that time, it's too late and you realize that you have created a fucked-up situation for yourself," Keno added.

"I agree with them, Jango. When I'm at the crossroads of most of my indiscretions, I can't imagine myself having the ability to stop, call on God, and wait for Him to give me strength. That just sounds so unrealistic to me," Rockye said.

"To get absolute control over these crossroad moments, as you say, and for destroying prenatal and postnatal root causes of failure, you must exercise your will in every undertaking of your life until it shakes off its mortal delusion of limited human will and becomes the all-powerful divine will. This divine will is not something you acquire—you already possess it. It is just a matter of harnessing it for yourself!" Jango explained.

"Sometimes I don't think that you live here on this planet, Jango! At times you are right on the money, and then there are times like this when I think you don't understand what the hell we are going through. I don't think that you really understand our pain!" Keno added.

"Let me sum it up by telling you about the story of two frogs," Jango continued.

"Awwww..." The group groaned in unison.

"Hey, just give me a second. I think you'll understand what I'm talking about after you hear the story. Okay?" he encouraged.

"Go ahead," Keno spoke for the crowd.

"There were these two frogs, a big one and a little one, hopping along, and they saw a barrel of milk. Looking for something to get into, they decided to jump into the barrel. After a while of swimming around in the barrel of milk, they got tired and decided they wanted to get out. However, they couldn't jump out of the barrel.

"Eventually after repeated tries, the big frog decided it was no use. That there was no way out and that he was going to die. So he gave up and drowned."

"What the hell kind of story is that?" Keno stated with a furrowed brow.

Jango continued, ignoring the comment. "The little frog, however, thought to himself that to give up meant he would meet the same fate as his friend, death. So he continued swimming faster and faster. He kept saying to himself, *'I will not cease trying—as long as there is life, there is hope!'*

"Intoxicated with determination, the little frog kept his incessant paddling until the milk turned to butter and he leaped to freedom. The moral of the story is that the little frog decided to keep going because the only other option was death. He then developed an incessant action until he became successful. I want you all to remember that when you are out there living your lives, coming across difficult situations and formidable temptations, that as long as there is life, there is hope. Remember the frog, remember that you have to reach for a higher power for strength, to overcome your temptations, and to be ultimately successful and become victorious over those childhood issues. The how you will do it in each situation will come to you after you realize you cannot do it without God. Once you realize that, you will then surrender yourself to Him."

The buzzer indicating that the session was over went off about 3 minutes earlier but everyone waited for Jango to finish his point. Now that he had, they started to gather their things, anxious to exit. It was apparent by everyone's response that today wasn't at the top of the list of his best sessions.

After a hasty departure, Jango found himself all alone in the middle of the room. This was definitely unusual because The Tuesday afternoon group normally lingered for at least 15 minutes to chat amongst themselves. Today they were anxious to get the hell out of there.

"Didn't end too well, huh?" Tyler said from the front of the room.

"You heard," Jango responded, folding up the chairs.

"I sure did! I keep telling you not everybody will identify with those stories and that God thing. You got to stick with the agenda, Jango!" Tyler warned.

"God is the only way to real healing! I believe that with every part of me, and one day they will see it, too," he insisted.

"I don't agree, Jango. We are here to help these people find a way to manage their lives, to get a handle on things, and not to convert them to religion!" Tyler insisted.

"Tyler, there is nothing without God! We are nothing without His grace, His love, His mercy, and His power. It's hard for me to give hope to people without putting God right smack in the middle of it!"

"You are off base, man! As I told you before I don't agree with it at all!" Tyler picked up his book bag and headed for the door. "I'm going home. I'll see you tomorrow."

"Later, Tyler!" Jango folded up the last chair and headed for the office to turn off the lights and get his briefcase.

Reentering the front room again, a looming figure startled him. After focusing his eyes, he realized it was Tyler.

"You scared the shit out of me, man! I thought you left!" Jango said.

"I came back because I just wanted to tell you that even though I was teasing you earlier about stepping to Bailey, you need to put yourself in check when it comes to your feelings for her. You are responsible for her progress, and a personal relationship outside of this group is totally inappropriate. And all joking aside, you know it too! I hope that you can exercise that same philosophy of volitional will on yourself that you talked about in group today." Tyler turned to leave.

Tyler's words still echoed in Jango's head as he headed to his car. It was cold outside. Jango pulled his jacket collar high up around his neck to keep the night hawk at bay. He maneuvered his way into his vehicle, with Tyler's words echoing in his head. Yet he still had romantic hopes of Bailey burning in his heart. Feeling conflicted, he felt torn as to what he should do. Should he or should he not pursue a relationship with Bailey outside The Circle?

In The Circle, he was a therapist, and he would give the best guidance that he could, however when it came to the matters of his heart, he didn't know what he was going to do. He hadn't a clue.

Chapter Twenty

～ Rockye Haynes ～

Would you continue to do wrong if you knew with certainty that you would never be caught?

"I think Andy has been following me!" Rockye confessed to Bailey, as they luxuriated on the heated jade floor of the Olympic Spa. Simultaneously, Rockye rolled her eyes at the women's cackling at a pitch inappropriate for the setting. Some people just didn't know to use inside voices. They both felt relaxed after the most incredible Goddess spa treatment; a combination of massage and scrubbing the body of dead skin tissue, concluding with a rinse of warmed coconut milk.

"I knew it! I just knew that this was going to happen eventually!" Bailey turned her head slightly to face her friend, adjusting the foam pillow to comfortably support her neck.

"The other day I saw him on Wilshire while I was leaving the Beauty Supply Store! He was in a Ford Explorer. I remember thinking, why was he in that car instead of his own. At first I thought it was just a coincidence but shortly after that I spotted him again. Then he called me on my cell and started asking me all kinds of questions about where I was and where I was going. I knew at that point that he was for sure following me."

"What did you do?"

"After it became obvious that he was in a frame of mind to argue, I got angry and just hung the phone up on his ass!"

"What happened then? Did he keep following you?"

"I don't think so. I just kept driving down Wilshire for about 4 or 5 miles and at some point he must have turned off because when I looked back I didn't see him!"

"I got to ask you this, Rockye. Did he see you doing anything?" Bailey eyed her friend in query. Rockye knew exactly what Bailey was talking about for she had said to her on many occasions, *"Rockye, you got to stop with all these men!"*

"No! I was just running errands and stuff! But if he has been following me at other times, I don't know what he may have seen. I don't think he has seen anything though because he can't hold water if his life depended on it. If he saw anything, I would know it by now!"

"Rockye, you know how he is! You are playing with a loaded gun! If you can't stop yourself, just get out of that relationship before somebody gets hurt! And I don't mean him either!" Bailey sat up, propping her back against the wall.

"I know! But I love him so much! I don't want to be without him!"

"You love him, huh? Then why can't you just keep your damn legs shut? Why can't you realize that you have a wonderful man, a man who loves the shit out of you, and just do what you are supposed to do, instead of fucking every Tom, Dick, and Harry that comes along?" Bailey fumed.

"You, of all people in this world know why. Why are you judging me like that? You know what my problem is. You are there in our therapy sessions when I pour my heart out about this monkey on my back! You know how hard this is for me." Rockye started to cry.

Bailey's tone softened. "I'm sorry. I guess sometimes I just wish I had a man in my life who loved me as much as your Andy loves you. I have never had what you have! I'm sorry for what I said!" Bailey rubbed her friend's arm tenderly as a gesture of apology.

"I guess I just get jealous sometimes. Forgive me! I know how hard this is for you! I see you trying!" Bailey sympathized.

"I AM trying! I am! Really I am. Don't you think I would stop if I could? I can't! I try and try and try! But this thing, it just takes me over and before I know it, there I am with some strange guy, giving him all I got and taking every inch he can give!" Rockye confessed.

The door opened, bringing in a gust of cool air, and along with it a petite, wafer-thin Korean girl. She adjusted her naked untoweled body onto the hot jade floor. The two girls temporarily ceased their conversation, returning to their leisurely position of before.

They remained quiet until the Korean girl exited, allowing another cool gust of air to enter in behind her.

"Rockye, what's the difference between them?" Bailey asked with obvious apprehension in her voice.

"The difference between who?"

"Black men and white men. What's the difference? I've only been with black men. Your boyfriend is white, and you are always having sex with mostly black men. Why? What is the difference?"

"Well—um, I don't know. I never thought about it as a black or white thing. Let me see. I guess the white men I've been with were just more attentive. Their lovemaking was tender and selfless. Andy makes love to me with such tenderness, and when he holds me in his arms, I feel the love he has for me in his soft, gentle kisses, his slow licking, lapping, and sucking. I feel it when he slow strokes me, allowing all parts of my body to wake up in unison. I feel his love when he takes the time to wake up all of my erogenous zones with his tongue. And not just my vaginal area, if you know what I mean."

"Girl, you crazy!"

"I don't know, I guess it's just more sensual!"

"And with black men?"

"Black men totally make my body come alive! They own my pussy and for those minutes that we are together within that raw savage like exchange I can escape my own crazy shit with each pound. I feel like there is nothing else on this planet except for the orgasm we are chasing. Every part of my body tingles like electrical exposed wires. I feel raw and powerful! I can do whatever my uninhibited self wants to do in the attempt to get that orgasm! Whatever the hell I want!"

"Wow that sounds—"

"Crazy!" Rockye finished. "I know that it doesn't make any sense. I know!"

"I'm afraid for you, Rockye! I don't want anything to happen to you! And if Andy ever found out—" Bailey's face was painted with immense concern.

"I can appreciate where you're coming from, girl, but I'm not worried about Andy. He would never hurt me! He would be angry and all, but he would never lift a finger to hurt me because he loves me too much!" Rockye expressed with solid confidence.

Bailey's stomach let out a loud growl. "I sure hope so, Rockye. I sure hope so!"

"Believe me, girl; I know my man, and he would never lift a finger to hurt me—ever!

"Now let's take a break and get some sushi from the kitchen. Your stomach is making all kinds of noises." Rockye got up, heading to the spa's restaurant as Bailey quickly followed in tow.

*

Rockye downed her third grape drink. She loved those delicious grape drinks that held peeled green baby grapes lingering at the bottom. Besides the incredible full-Korean body scrubs that exfoliated the skin, or the aromatic seaweed body shampoo and warm mineral pools that released the day's tensions, the natural-formed oxygen stone room that detoxified and moistened the body, or the jade steam sauna, the attached Korean restaurant containing authentic delicious Korean dishes was what she anticipated the most when she frequented the quaint Asian retreat.

While savoring the explosive combination of flavors dancing around in her mouth, she realized that she had monopolized most of the conversation, so she quickly turned it to her friend.

"What's going on with you?" Rockye said, plopping a slice of sushi into her mouth.

"I want to ask you a question and please be honest with me."

"Shoot!"

"What is wrong with me? Why I can't find a good man? What is so wrong with me that my mother hates me so much? Why can't I get proper respect from my clients? I feel like no matter what I do, how many successes I have in my life, I still don't measure up. Why aren't I ever enough?" Bailey rambled.

"*One* question?" she joked.

"I know. I am really some piece of work, aren't I?"

"Let me say this—it seems to me that you care entirely too much about what other people think about you. And to top it off, you don't even think too much about yourself!" Rockye answered.

Bailey bristled up in defense.

"Before you go and get mad hear me out!" Rockye took a sip of the seaweed soup, allowing the slippery green matter to slide down her throat. She didn't particularly care for the taste, but the healing properties of the soup were reason enough for her to force it down.

"You are always talking about what your mom thinks, about what those bigoted clients of yours think. Who the fuck cares what they think? And then you deal with that loser ex-boyfriend of yours, Chance, and you keep waiting for him to love you and turn into this man that is kind, considerate, loving, and committed—when the truth is that he is a pervert who is not worth shit!"

"Ouch!"

"Just hear me out. I look at you, and I see this extraordinarily beautiful, talented, successful woman; a woman that is doing more harm to yourself than your mom, you're ex-boyfriend, or your business associates—combined. You are your own worst enemy, Bailey! Look, sweetie, people will say what they want, but it's you who will choose to believe or reject what they say about you!

"Your question shouldn't be what is wrong with you but what is wrong with what you think about yourself. I don't think that there is anything wrong with you. I think you need to change what you think about yourself!" Rockye answered.

"I hear what you're saying, but all I want is for someone to love me. I want to be loved like Andy loves you! It's so hard, and sometimes I just feel like giving up!"

"I know that it's hard, girl, but you are one of the toughest people I know. And if anyone can do it, it's you! You can do it! I know you can!" Rockye reached across the table and stroked her friend's forearm.

Rockye could see the torment in her friend's eyes, and although she tried her best to make Bailey feel better, she knew that her best friend had some serious challenges to overcome and now was not the time or place to attempt it. That's what therapy was for. That's why they went to group! The truth of the matter was . . . They both were really fucked up, although in vastly different ways. As Rockye attempted to console her friend, a burning desire began festering within her groin once more! It slowing percolated initially until the throbbing in her clitoris had a vigorous heartbeat of its own.

At the earliest opportunity Rockye excused herself to go to the bathroom in the quaint spa. Her body ached for a release, and while she would not be able to leave the premises to find a worthy opponent because her friend was in tow, she would attempt some sort of release on her own.

"Excuse me for a moment; I gotta go to the bathroom," she called out from over her shoulder as she abruptly propelled herself up from the tiny table in the modest eatery.

She sat on the commode, legs agape with her middle finger rapidly sliding up and down her swollen clitoris falling in step with her breathless beat. Inserting her left three fingers inside of her vagina intermittently, she prodded and flicked herself with her right hand until she climaxed and exploded, releasing a watery substance from her genitals. Although her body released some tension with the orgasm, she was not completely satisfied.

Her body ached for a pounding, forceful, deep penetration that only the savage pull and toss a man could provide. Masturbation just didn't get it.

Rockye reentered the restaurant and signaled for Bailey to meet her in the oxygen rock room after she'd finished her meal. She needed some quiet time to sort out the war going on inside her head. Ninety percent of the times that room was empty, and she should be able get the much-needed quiet for which she usually came to the Korean spa for.

After layering the bamboo floor with towels, she removed the spa-issued robe and positioned her naked body next to the wall furthest from the door.

Rockye languished and contemplated her plight. Why was she this way? How did she get so out of control? Did she realize how much danger she put herself into by escaping to sequestered places with men she didn't know, and all for the sake of a climax? She meditated as she followed her breath to relaxation.

On the surface she looked perfectly normal, healthy, and sane. Some would even say in total control of her life, but day by day she dealt with spirits of lust, fornication, masturbation, and perversion. These spirits commanded her to throw caution to the wind and serve them. It took authority over her thoughts and navigated her mind and body to follow it to satiation.

Several minutes of silence followed before Bailey's voice echoed within the room. Lost in thought she hadn't heard her friend enter.

"You all right? You left the restaurant so abruptly—"

"I'm good. I just needed some time to think."

"About?"

She didn't respond to the question but remained silent as she continued with the mental gymnastics that tormented her very soul.

Why didn't my mother ever tell me that she loved me? Why am I such a slut, and why am I jeopardizing the best relationship that I ever had in my life, risking it by having sex with men I don't even know?

Chapter Twenty-One

~ Andy Reynolds ~

*I*nfidelity does not come from a lack of love—it comes from a lack of respect.

"I'm gonna catch her ass today!" Andy hollered out loud as he fell a comfortable distance of four car lengths behind Rockye while maneuvering down North La Brea, making a quick left on Wilshire Blvd. Andy suspected that his girlfriend of 3 years was cheating on him, and it nagged on his brain so much that it was getting increasingly difficult for him to function at work.

The cramped quarters of his buddy's Ford Explorer Sport provided him an extremely uncomfortable ride compared to his Range Rover which had ample leg room for his long frame.

She pulled into the post office. Andy slowed and eased the mini SUV into the parking lot adjacent to the post office on Detroit and Wilshire, then quickly slid out to secure an adequate hiding place from being discovered by her. Part of him was feeling like a punk, sneaking around trying to catch some woman in the act of cheating. No bitch was worth all this clandestine behavior—no bitch! Why didn't he just leave her ass? Why had he resorted to sneaking around like some crazy person in hopes to catch her in the act? What would he do if he actually caught her cheating? He couldn't imagine it turning out too well. I mean, really, what would he do?

The cool Tuesday afternoon breeze quickly cut him through the silk shirt he was wearing. The only regret he had for the day was leaving his jacket behind in his Range Rover when he switched cars with his neighbor, Todd. Todd was all too eager to upgrade his vehicle for the day. A new Range Rover for a 9-year-old Ford Explorer Sport! A no-brainer! His arm was sporting chill bumps as he made his way over to a recycle bin and ducked behind it; again, he thought as he rubbed his arm for warmth, is this bitch really worth all of this?

Andy's eyes followed her entering The Hair Shop, the beauty supply store, and then a quick beeline back to her vehicle illegally parked in the red zone due to limited parking.

Picking up his cell he called her as he got back into the Ford Explorer.

"Hey, baby, where you at?" he asked with a suspicious and accusatory tone.

"I'm leaving the beauty supply store," Rockye answered. "Where are you?"

"What are you doing?" He ignored her question.

"Errands," she answered, obviously hiding her agitation. Andy knew that she hated when he switched places with his doppelgänger. When he was in this emotional state it was impossible to reassure him of his insecurities, and frankly, he knew that she had grown exhausted from the effort.

"Where are you now?" he continued.

"I am driving down Wilshire Blvd; headed to my therapy group."

"And then where are you going?"

"I have a Pilates class afterward," she answered.

"The one in Culver Circty or Brentwood?"

"Brentwood."

"Who are you meeting there?" Andy demanded.

"I am not meeting anybody there! What is going on with you? Damn!"

"I just got this feeling, this feeling that something is going on!" he replied.

"Andy, you gotta stop this shit! I keep telling you that nothing is going on."

"Who do you know in this Pilates class or in that psycho group you go to all the time?" he questioned.

"Who do I know? What kind of question is that? I know everybody in the class; after all, I have been going to this class for months and as for my group, if it wasn't for my group, I wouldn't be able to deal with your crazy ass!"

"I really ain't worried about the crazies in that group anyway." He paused before continuing. "How many men are in that Pilates class?"

"What the fuck is wrong with you? You think that I'm just gonna make out with men in my Pilates class? That's scandalous! What kind of woman does foul shit like that?"

"What kind indeed?"

"Andy, I don't know what you want from me. I love you, and I am with *you*, not some guy in my Pilates class or anywhere else, for that matter!"

"I will end all of this if you just take a lie detector test."

"Not that again! Andy, I told you before and I am telling you again . . . I am not going down to no police station to take a lie detector test."

"We don't need the police. I found a private agency right here in L.A. not too far from my house. Meet me there when you are done, and we will put an end to this right now!"

"This is getting ridiculous, Andy! I gotta go. Hell, you need to pull yourself together. I can't deal with this shit now. I'll talk to you later." She hung up the phone before he had time to respond.

Andy threw his phone into the passenger seat.

"Lying bitch! I am going to catch you one of these days!" he vowed. And maybe today would be the day after all.

Suddenly he decided to play detective and drive to her house. Rockye wouldn't be home for hours, which would give him plenty of time to look for some evidence of her infidelity. He believed that he would find something at her house because he knew within the marrow of his bones that she was hiding something ... or someone, and he wouldn't stop until he found out who it was.

Chapter Twenty-Two

☙ Bailey Levine ☙

Have you ever considered that your own mind was sabotaging your path to happiness?

On her way home from the office that evening, Bailey decided that she would drive down her parents' street. She desperately missed her father, and, yes, in spite of everything, she missed her mother as well. The moon was full that evening and against the dark night sky its ominous backdrop left Bailey feeling melancholy.

It had been over 3 weeks since she had spoken to her parents after the big blow up in the kitchen during the last Sunday family breakfast, and although she was still hurt by the fracas, her heart ached for her dad and, to her surprise, even her mother's criticisms.

Driving up to the entrance of her parents' gated community in Hancock Park, the guard, recognizing her, waved her in.

She smiled an acknowledgment to him as she eased her car slowly inside the gate. Turning off her headlights so as not to call attention to herself, Bailey cruised down her parents' street easing to a halt two houses adjacent to their two-story Mediterranean.

Most of the upstairs lights were off in the impressive mini mansion. The only light on in the spacious five-bedroom, 6,000 square foot house was a table lamp in the living room. Bailey parked, got out of the car, and crept up to the house, nestling herself between two mulberry bushes that framed the oversized picture window of the living room to get a bird's-eye view.

Crouched down underneath the window, she caught a clear view into the dimly lit home of the Levines. Snuggled up on the couch adjacent to a dwindling fire were her parents. Her mother appeared to be asleep in her husband's lap, and her father, bifocals perched on the tip of his narrow nose, was engrossed within a large green leather-bound book. Bailey knew that book very well—it was a volume of Shakespeare, his favorite. How odd! Her mother was lying in her father's lap with a blanket covering her legs. In all of her life she had never seen such a sight!

As long as she could remember, her mother had never lain in her father's lap while he read! Bailey inched up closer to get a better look at her mother. As her eyes narrowed in, they confirmed that her mother was indeed sleeping. Bailey glanced at her watch. Something was not right! It was not even 8 p.m.

Why was her mother sleeping at that hour? Bailey's eyes surveyed what little else she could see of the rest of the house in spite of the darkness. Everything else looked normal.

She observed her father's face holding signs of fatigue and exhaustion as he carefully turned the pages with a deliberate smoothness so as not to awaken his sleeping wife. Something was wrong. Bailey could sense it!

Dashing swiftly back to her car, she retrieved her cell from the passenger's seat and dialed her parents' home number. Despite the fact that her body tensed with apprehension, she forced a smile on her face and awaited her father's voice on the other end of the telephone.

After four rings, the answering machine picked up. She hung up and redialed. No answer! Voice mail! What the hell was going on? Sliding her cell phone into her jacket pocket, she made her way back across the street to the house once again. Securing herself underneath the picture window, she found her parents still in the same position. She pulled out her cell from her pocket again and hit redial.

As the house phone rang, Douglas tilted his head slightly in acknowledgment but didn't move one inch. Instead, he eased his head down, kissed the forehead of his sleeping wife, and continued reading. She redialed again, and when the answering machine picked up this time, she called out to her father.

"Dad, it's me, Bailey. Are you there? Dad, if you are there, please pick up the phone!"

Again he tilted his head slightly, but he didn't budge. No movement. Nothing!

Immediately anger bubbled up within Bailey. She understood perfectly well what was going on. They didn't want to speak to her. They had written her off just like they did her older brother, Edbart. On too many occasions to count, Bailey watched her mother ignore Edbart's phone calls and discard his unread letters into the trash as her father stood pensively by, never once intervening.

Edbart, her older brother, was ostracized from the family about 5 years ago when he decided that he wanted to defy his mother's wishes to finish grad school. The one thing that you didn't do in the Levine household was defy Marjorie Levine. And Edbart did it with gusto!

Her brother was extremely intelligent, sharp, and gifted in all areas of finance. Throughout his undergraduate years at USC, he interned with a small investment company and because of his innovative ideas and concepts, the company propelled expeditiously to global success. Marjorie was adamant about him securing his master's in business and subsequently implanting himself into a prestigious firm, but Edbart had aspirations to enjoy his life for a few years, traveling the world. Something Marjorie Levine was not a proponent of! He defied her, she disowned him, and he disappeared! From her parents' lives as well as hers!

Angry tears started to collect within her large hazel eyes as she raced back to her car and got in.

"Fuck both of you! Since you don't care about me, I don't care what happens to you either! You can both die and rot in hell for all I care!"

On the quiet street of Las Palmas Avenue in Hancock Park at twenty past eight in the evening, the sound of screeching tires could be heard clearly off in the distance as she sped off into the night as pearl-shaped tears flowed down her flushed cheeks.

Chapter Twenty-Three

☞ Keno Hunter ☜

The best laid plans often go astray.

Keno was on his way home mentally preparing himself for a performance of a lifetime; an elaborate lie to Dee Dee to cover up the reason for his disappearance for the last week.

He cruised all the way down Overland Avenue to his Culver City apartment, playing Sade and rehearsing what he would say to his girlfriend Diedre about why he was MIA for so many days. In about half an hour, the time that it took for him to drive from Sharon's Wilshire penthouse condominium to his Culver City apartment, he felt that he had conjured up the perfect excuse for his absence. He'd been MIA for almost a week.

He would tell Dee Dee that he had been arrested on a mistaken identity and isolated until the police determined that they had arrested the wrong man. His elaborate story would include the police's mistreatment, how they threw him in solitary confinement, taking his phone and not allowing him to make any phone calls. He would stress that he couldn't call her because they had taken his phone and he didn't remember her phone number by heart. He had to wait until he got home to call her because his cell phone had died while in jail. Keno knew that it sounded farfetched, but he would give Dee Dee his famous bedroom eyes, hypnotic sexy voice, and mesmerizing smile, which would cause her eventually to succumb to his charm. Then, like the icing on the cake, he would bed her and it would be all over!

Before calling Dee Dee, he wanted to chill out for a moment on his couch and mentally prepare for the performance. Keno didn't like lying to his woman, but he had absolutely no choice in the matter. As wonderful as Diedre was, she was not in the position to help him out financially, and Keno needed a lot of help at this point in his life. Knowing that his girlfriend of 6 years loved him and supported him emotionally was wonderful, but the one thing that she didn't possess at that moment was the one thing that he needed most to survive! Money, and plenty of it!

Her sweet round face flashed across his mind as he waited for the electric gate to open at his apartment complex's entrance. Staring off into the distance, he thought about how much he really loved Dee Dee and how empty his world would be without her.

His girlfriend wasn't the most personable woman, or the most attractive, nor did she even have the best body. In fact, she was pudgy and had homely features, but what made her irresistible was her unique ability to make him feel loved, adored, and accepted. She showed him immense adoration, making him feel like the most important man in the whole world. Although he didn't think she was aware of this, but every time Keno walked into the room, Dee Dee's face would light up like a Christmas tree. It was the best feeling in the world to see someone's true love for you evidenced on their face. Dee Dee's love made him feel like he really mattered to someone . . . a feeling he never really had in his life from any woman—not even his own mother who was by no means a horrible mother. She was just unavailable because she worked all the time to keep food on the table.

Beep! Beep! A car horn honked behind him, arousing Keno back from his distant thoughts.

After easing his Mercedes into the underground garage to his back stall located up against the stairway, Keno backed in slowly for an easy future exit.

"Damn!" he called out to himself, remembering that he had things in the trunk. Because he had backed in, he would not be able to pop his trunk to retrieve his duffle bag due to the close quarters.

"Fuck it! I'll get it later," he concluded as he pulled his jacket and water bottle from the passenger seat. Michael Jackson's song "Beat It" made its way into his head, and he hummed it loudly while climbing the outside stairs to his apartment.

Positioning his keys to fit into his apartment keyhole, Keno felt a familiar presence behind him.

"You sure are in a damn good mood!"

Keno quickly turned around to find Dee Dee slumped down against the doorway of his neighbor's apartment, her hair askew and her clothes rumpled. Her eyes were bloodshot, and white crusted sleep formed in the corner of them.

"Dee Dee, baby!" he said, startled by her presence.

"Don't Dee Dee baby me! Where the hell have you been? I have been worried sick about you! I thought something horrible happened to you! I called everybody, and nobody has seen your ass for days! I imagined the worst and when I didn't hear from you I came over here! Since yesterday I have been here waiting for your ass—trying to get into your apartment and here you come—walking up, humming and shit! Where the hell have *you* been? What the fuck is going on?" Foam frothed in the corner of her mouth as she ranted.

"Come on inside! You must be freezing!" Keno managed to finally get the front door to his apartment open even though his hands were shaking from nervousness. Then he stood aside signaling for her to enter first.

She paused before walking past him, confusion coloring her round face. Once inside she insisted again on answers. It was obvious that her range of emotions vacillated between anger to inquisition.

"Calm down, baby! I'll explain everything to you! Just sit down and let me get you warm!" Keno pleaded.

He flicked the switch of the heater's thermostat to the on position and set the temperature to high.

She reluctantly rested against the wall adjacent to the heater as she silently stared at him. He nervously leaned on the couch in front of her.

"I heard what happened to Jimmy! La Tanya called me and told me he got shot, and that you were with him! We called the police station and the hospitals and nobody knew anything about you! Where have you been, Keno? Where the hell is your cell phone?"

"In my pocket! It's dead!" he lied.

"I have been calling and calling you. I filled up your voice mail with messages! You didn't check your messages?" She asked, her face twisted with frustration.

He looked away into the distance, uncertain of what to say. So much for the rehearsed speech!

"I don't understand why you haven't called me! Where have you been, Keno? Where?"

"Just trying to get my head together! It has been a rough couple of days. You can't begin to understand what I've been through!" he defended.

"You didn't answer my question. Where have you been?" she insisted.

"Everywhere and nowhere!" Keno placed his head in his lap, his mind trying to recall his rehearsed speech which now seemed inappropriate.

"Me and Jimmy was out hustling and thangs, and, baby, it just got out of control. The cops rolled up on us, and then bullets just started to fly and shit. I panicked, and the next thing I know was—"

"I asked you where you've been. I am not stupid! Who is she?" she demanded.

"Why is it that you always think that I am with another woman?"

"I am not an idiot, Keno; there is absolutely no reason for you to not have called me unless you were with another woman! None! So just tell me who she is. Tell me!" She uncharacteristically screamed hysterically at the top of her lungs.

"There is no other woman! I can't give you a name of someone who doesn't exist! I am not seeing anybody else! You are the only woman in my life! I swear! I swear! I just had one of the most fucked-up experiences in my life, and I panicked. I panicked and got drunk, so drunk that I didn't want to wake up and face what I had done. So I kept drinking and drinking!" he lied.

"Keno, that doesn't even make sense! You don't even drink! You hate the taste of alcohol! That doesn't even sound like something that you would do!"

"Well, whether it sounds like it or not, that's what happened! If you don't believe it, that's on you!" Keno went into the bathroom and turned on the shower. He had to quickly divert the attention away from himself.

"You can believe me or not! That's up to you! I told you what happened, and there is nothing more to the story than that!" Keno yelled from the bathroom as he pulled off his shirt.

Dee Dee followed him into the bathroom and with an almost hypnotic voice asked, "I am going to ask you only one more time, and this time I suggest that you tell me the truth! Where have you been?"

Diedre was relentless, and Keno knew that he had to do something drastic to change the direction of this conversation in order to protect himself from any further inquisition.

He picked up the Listerine bottle and hurled it into the bathroom vanity mirror, breaking it into many tiny pieces. Shards of glass sprang forward and bounced off his chest and stomach.

Even though distress was written within her bloodshot eyes, she didn't move a muscle.

"I fucking told you what happened! You are the kind of bitch that keeps on a man until he breaks. If your man tells you that some shit went down the way it did, you need to fucking believe it! Who the fuck wants to be interrogated like some child? I told you that it was one of the worst times in my life and that I got drunk! That was it and nothing more! So fucking stop with the damn nagging!"

She continued to follow him with her eyes. The frown on her wide lips parted slightly to respond. She sat down slowly on the commode before speaking.

"I have loved you for a long time, Keno! I have been there for you for over 6 years, and we've slept in my car for 2 months when we had no place to live! I have given you the last $10 to my name. I have bailed you out of jail, wrote you in jail, and even sent you money in jail. I have stayed in to watch movies on TV instead of going out because you had no money. I have used toilet tissue because I didn't have enough money for tampons, just so I could give you gas money to go out and look for a job. I have eaten crackers and sardines because I was saving money to pay the light bill. I have worn the same clothes over and over without buying new ones because I bought you a suit to wear to an interview. I spend many nights at home alone because you tell me that you are out hustling to make a dollar.

"Did I complain? Did I get mad because you moved out of our house to this—this—incredible place without me? You told me that you moved because you needed to get a better image for business, but where is the business? Did I even get a key?

No! Did I even complain about it? No! As many times as I have given you money and gone without and you walk around here with expensive watches, jewelry, and things, and you think that I am some stupid dumb bitch that don't know what the hell is going on."

She stood and inched up right next to him, so close that he could smell the stale tart of her breath.

"I have my flaws, and one of them was loving you too hard! Loving you so much that I stopped loving me! I stopped loving me, Keno, when I handed you my last $10 and walked around hungry with my stomach growling! I stopped loving me when I continued to always put you first and let my own needs go unattended!

"You have treated me without consideration for years, and the worst part about it is that I let you! I *let* you!" She picked up her purse which was sitting in the middle of the floor, threw it over her right shoulder, and marched toward the front door.

"Wait—"

"I can't believe that in all those days you didn't once pick up the telephone and call me! Whoever you were with was the woman you wanted to be with!"

"Let me explain—"

She paused. "I have been a fool! No matter what lie you try to tell me, we both know that you are seeing somebody else! And whoever she is, she has a lot of money!"

She opened the front door.

"You really hurt me, Keno! Nobody could have ever told me that it would have ended like this! I thought we had something special! Good-bye, Keno!"

Dee Dee walked out of the front door and moved quickly toward the stairs that led to the entryway of his apartment complex.

Keno watched the woman that he loved walk out of his life.
"Do something you idiot!" he heard in his brain.
"Baby, stop! Please don't leave! I love you! I'll make everything right, I promise!" He padded up to her.
"So you want to make everything right?" she asked with a newfound determination in her eyes.
"Yes! I will do anything to make it right," he promised.
"Then answer this question for me."
He raised his eyebrow, apprehensive of the question.
"Were you with another woman?" Her eyes locked with his.
He shuffled.
"Tell me the truth! You owe me that much."
He had nowhere else to go but to tell the truth. He had to take his chance and tell her that he didn't love Sharon. He had to tell her that she was the only woman that he ever loved. He had to tell her that he was doing it only for the money and the opportunities. He had to tell her that he hated every minute of it and instead wished that he was within her arms instead of Sharon's.
She would understand, Keno told himself in the quick moments it took him to convince himself to make the confession.
"Yes!" He spoke above a whisper. He didn't know why he told the truth. Maybe this therapy thing was working. All he knew was that he was desperate to keep the best thing in his life from walking away and walking out of his life forever.
"I knew it!" She breathed in a sigh of confirmation. A pleasant smile instantly washed over her round face.
"I knew that I wasn't crazy! A woman knows when her man's spirit has taken up with some other woman!" She moved into Keno, lightly touching his face.
"Thank you for telling me the truth! I really mean that! Thank you!" Her smile appeared forgiving.

"Dee Dee, I am so sorry. I—"

She interrupted him. "Do you know, Keno, why Jesus never said that He was sorry?" She didn't wait for an answer. "—because He never did anything to be sorry for! When you truly love somebody, Keno, you don't do things that will hurt that person you love. Real love means never having to say that you are sorry because you don't do anything to be sorry for!"

She kissed him on his left cheek.

"Good-bye, Keno!"

Keno watched her descend the stairs. He searched his brain for something clever enough to say that would change her mind from walking down those stairs and out of his life. Something that would make her turn around and run back into his arms. Keno knew that he was guilty as sin, and deep down he felt that nothing he could say or do at that moment would change her mind in the least! He could kick himself for not using his original plan of telling her he was in jail. He now regretted telling her the truth; he should have stuck with the lie.

From the stairs of his apartment building, Keno watched his girlfriend of 6 years navigate her Nissan Sentra through the busy intersection and out of sight.

He just stood there realizing that he could have stopped Dee Dee if he really wanted to. He knew the words to say, but it would mean giving up Sharon and all of the things that she brought to the table. He was not ready to go back to where he was before Sharon: broke, hungry, and struggling. He really loved Dee Dee, but he loved what Sharon could do for him much more. So much for fucking love, just give me some money. He pulled out the hundred-dollar bills he had retrieved from Sharon's safe. Running his fingers over the slick bills, he turned his attention away from what he lost to the thought of what he would buy for himself to kill the pain of losing the woman whom he truly loved.

Chapter Twenty-Four

~ Andy Reynolds ~

Jealousy is the relative of insanity.

As Andy entered Rockye's house through an open bathroom window, he heard the noise of all her personal hygiene products falling to the floor. She had entirely too many damn candles, hair products, and lotions on the sink. He lowered himself through the window and landed on the counter, sending all of the various products crashing to the floor.

Surveying her bathroom, he noticed that she had quotations taped on the mirror and the walls. Andy thought to himself how cluttered her bathroom was. He hurried and picked back up her products and put them back in place.

Rockye had an odd habit of taping quotes on pieces of paper to the walls around her. One quotation in particular over the sink mirror caught his eye.

Wisdom isn't seeing what's in your face but recognizing what is about to come!

As he stared at it pondering its meaning, his eyes slipped away from the sheet of paper taped above the mirror to his reflection. He eyed himself, and in doing so noticed the knot near his right temple was slightly larger than yesterday. It had grown to the size of a dime. Sliding his right index finger across it, he felt the hardness at the touch. The growth appeared every time he was stressed or worried about something over a long period of time.

Why was it getting bigger? His casual thought turned from concern to worry! As he considered the possibilities of a brain tumor, the singing of the house phone catapulted him back to the present.

"This is Rockye! Leave a message at the beep. I'll get back to you when I can, and remember, life is what you make it!"

Beeeeeeep.

"Hey, sexy, it's me. Black. I need to see you! You got my number. Call me! Later!"

Beeeeeep.

Instantly, Andy's head started throbbing. It seemed that the knot on his temple suddenly had a pulse of its own.

Who the hell was Black? Andy walked over to her answering machine, watching the blinking light like it was going to answer his question.

The ringing of his cell phone startled him.

It was Marcella! He started to hit the IGNORE button sending her to voice mail, but he was angry and this would afford him the opportunity to divert some of that anger to his baby's mama. That bitch always wanted something. Although he was not in the mood to deal with her baby mama drama bullshit right now, he nevertheless right swiped his phone open.

He'd never told Rockye about the baby, and he had no intentions to. He never gave Marcella or that damn baby a second thought until she called. This was another secret that he kept from his girlfriend. He would do everything within his power to keep Marcella and that kid away from his precious girlfriend. Rockye was the main reason he had made arrangements to send Marcella a check monthly, to keep her out of his hair. In spite of the check, every now and then, the bitch popped up on the surface!

"This is Andy—"

"Andy, this is Marcella. I need to talk to you!" The high-pitched female voice on the other end pushed up Andy's anger to double digits. Marcella always had a negative effect on him.

"What is it? I'm not trying to hear any bullshit right now!"

"Andy. It's the baby! She's really sick. She kept me up all night last night crying. I thought it was like the other time, colicky or something, but then she started shaking and shit. I called 911 and—"

"Get to the point. Why the hell do you have to always go around the damn block to tell a goddamn story? What is it? What do you want?" Andy barked.

"Your kid is in the hospital with some sort of a virus!" she finally spat out.

"Where are you now?"

"I'm at home. I came home to change my clothes." Marcella's voice began to quiver. "Andy." She took a pregnant pause. "She looks so, so small and scared in that big hospital bed. I'm so afraid that—"

Andy quickly cut her off. "Marcella, let me get something straight! The kid is in the hospital and you come home to change your damn clothes? You gotta be kidding me! What do you want me to do about it?" Andy's voice was coated with contempt. He had verbally contested his paternity of the kid too many times to count. But Marcella was relentless! Her unwavering insistence sometimes caused him to entertain the thought that he quite possibly may be that baby's father. Still he didn't do a DNA test because if it was his he would have to attest for the years of his paternal neglect.

"You son of a bitch! Your child is in the damn hospital! Don't you even care?" she yelled into the telephone.

"Look! If you got your fat ass out of the hospital to go home and change your clothes, then it ain't that damn serious! The kid has a little fever, and a cough or something and you call and waste my damn time. Kids get sick! If you spent more time taking care of her instead of watching TV and feeding your fat ass the way a real mother is supposed to do then maybe she wouldn't be in the damn hospital!"

"To hell with you! I just thought that you would want to know that your kid was in the hospital fighting for her life," Marcella shouted.

"You are such a damn drama queen, Marcella!" he retaliated. "You seem to have forgotten that I told you when we was fucking around that I didn't want no kids with you. You knew where I stood! But you decided that you was gonna do whatever the hell you wanted to anyway! You bitches always got some plan up your sleeve! You're always lying, cheating, scheming, or using a man for something!"

"You are one cold-ass bas—"

Andy's mind briefly reminisced back to his many tumultuous years growing up with his mother and sisters. So many times he would watch all of them tricking and lying to men to get one thing or another.

Andy interrupted. "All of you bitches ain't shit! Look, I made it clear that I didn't want a baby with you! Hell, I even gave you money to get an abortion. But, no, you decided to have it anyway! So deal! Stop calling me! I give you money every damn month, and that's all I'm going to do! I don't want to have nothin' to do with you or that baby! Hell, she don't even look like me! That little bitch probably ain't even my kid anyway!"

"I can't believe you!" Marcella hollered into the telephone.

"If I were you, Marcella, I'd take the money I give you every month and leave me the hell alone!" Andy ended the conversation by pushing the END button on his cell phone.

"Low-down dirty bitches! All of them!" he shouted out loud as he thought about his skank of a mother, trash of a baby mama, and tramp of a girlfriend. He flung the phone onto the desk as he revisited the origin of his anger. It was time the cheating bitch got caught! *Enough with the bullshit!* he thought. He had business to handle! He had to find out who this Black was!

After a few minutes of picking through the papers on her desk only to find nothing, his cell rang once again. He glanced at the caller ID before flipping it open. It was his buddy, Campo.

"What's up, A?" Campo asked.

"Fucking pissed the hell off right now, that's what's up!" he barked.

"What's going on?"

"You won't believe this shit, man! I'm at my girl's house and some fucka leaves a message on her machine! I know she's cheating on me! I can feel it!"

"What did he say? Did you finally find the proof you been looking for?"

"Naw, man! Nothing solid, but I'm about to get something real soon. I feel it!" Andy sat down and started rummaging through her file cabinets. He studied its contents, paying particular attention to receipts, little slips of paper, and business cards.

He started pouring through everything, looking for any shred of evidence.

The one thing that Andy hated most in the world was a lying, cheating bitch! He had no concrete proof, but he had a gut feeling and eventually he would catch her!

He couldn't talk to Campo right now; he had to get back to the task of finding out who this Black was. He was fighting angry at the familiarity of his tone on her voice mail and would turn her fucking house upside down to find proof that she was fucking around with him.

"Gotta go, man. I got to handle this business. I'll call you back later!"

"Don't get caught, man. Watch your back!"

"I am not the one who should be worrying about getting caught! That bitch's days are numbered."

Chapter Twenty-Five

~ Rockye Haynes ~

The allure of the forbidden contains a mysterious charm.
She swerved her car dangerously fast into the underground parking of the Century City Mall off Santa Monica Blvd., taking the curves with reckless abandon. *Was that him?* she asked herself as her eyes continued to nervously survey the cars around her. Feelings of paranoia were her bedfellow of late. She was seeing Andy everywhere she went, or so she thought; at the car wash, the grocery store, the bank, even coming out of the nail salon. The other day when she came home, she could have sworn that someone had been in her house.

She wasn't a neat person by any means. As a matter of fact, if you entered her home, you would believe a bunch of college students lived there. Dirty dishes in the sink, underwear all over, dust forming on shelves, and clothes piled up in almost every corner. It was a mess! But regardless of the mess, she knew where everything was and could have sworn that things had been moved or tossed around.

Come on, girl, you are just feeling massive guilt! Andy couldn't be still following you, could he? They had their share of disagreements, but he wasn't some sort of a psychopath, she thought.

Brushing it off, she assured herself that she was just imagining things! Just because she saw him following her one time, it doesn't mean Andy was always following her. Rockye shook the thought from her head, and proceeded across the parking lot to the escalator that would take her into her favorite store. She desperately needed a shopping fix!

As she neared the entrance of Bloomingdale's, she discovered a massive crowd of young girls screaming and losing their damn minds. She asked a hysterical teenage girl what was going on. "Taylor Lautner is here!" she answered breathlessly. That was the actor from the Twilight franchise.

Damn! Can't go in there now! Looking around she decided to go to Sephora to purchase her favorite Philosophy Amazing Grace Whipped Body Crème, for she was almost out.

Their eyes instantly locked as she entered the fragrance section.

The heavy frown on his full lips quickly turned upward as he caught sight of the curvaceous, sexy, almond-eyed beauty fashioning a navy-blue thigh-length Marc Jacobs dress with red ankle wrapped Jimmy Choo sandals. Her jet-black hair wavy from the recently applied gel was parted neatly down the middle and rested on her bare shoulders. She trailed the counter until she ended up hovering in his area.

He arose as she neared him. Aggressive and deliberate were his words, and movements.

He was medium height, about five seven or eight, his broad facial features and blue-black skin indicated that he was most likely of African descent.

It would have been best for her to leave, remembering that she was in a committed relationship with a wonderful man. She should have raced out of that store as fast as her legs could carry her, regardless of the 4-inch high heels that she was sporting; but that would mean that she didn't get to indulge in something verboten.

Quickly stepping in front of her with confidence, he held an expression on his face of determination like an African warrior.

"They call me 'Black,' and I will not let you leave this store until I get your telephone number!"

Pulling out his cell phone, he instructed her to do the same. "What is your cell number?" he demanded.

Rockye knew that move; it had been tried on her many times before. They would take her cell phone and call their own cell number, and naturally, afterward, her number would be displayed on their phone. Realizing that Andy could possibly find out, she lied about not having a cell phone. Since Andy had become extremely suspicious recently, it would be the dumbest thing in the world to give this guy her cell number. She would get his.

"Don't have a cell…don't believe in them?" she lied.

"Then what is your home number?" he demanded.

Damn, he was not taking no for an answer. Rockye couldn't resist his sexy, enigmatic persona and gave him her home number instantly. He quickly punched the numbers into his cell.

The sharply dressed stranger twisted his head up to face her, leaned into her personal space, and asked her name. He smelled of imported cologne and family money. Lots of family money!

"What's your name?"

"Rockye."

He undressed her with his haughty eyes. A shiver blazed up and down her spine. He was crazy sexy, a dark sexy—a dangerous sexy, and Rockye found his blue-black skin and dazzling white teeth erotic.

"I need to see you again!" He looked around before leaning deeper into her space. "You are by far the sexiest woman I have ever seen. I need to see you again!"

Rockye inhaled the look of lust painted on his dark, chiseled face. She was lost for words, but her body was crying out for satiation once again. His raw male energy had her in a heightened state of sexuality.

No, stop… Think of your man at home! Andy loves you! He is the one you should be giving your body to. He is the one who you should be getting all hot and bothered over. Just walk away. Turn around and walk away! You can stop this right now . . . You don't have to do this.

She entertained—and quickly dismissed—some of the advice Jango told her in therapy. She didn't want to do what was right; she wanted to do what felt good. Her moral compass had gone askew again.

Her pussy spoke for her. "What ya doing now? Why wait?" she flirted.

He looked around as though he was on the lookout for someone.

She threw caution to the wind. She didn't care if he waiting for his woman, wife, or girlfriend. So what? Rockye wasn't looking for a man, she already had one. All she wanted was for him to put it down on her like a man who'd recently been released from prison, and then get on with his life. Nothing more . . .

A younger African woman spotted him and was expeditiously making her way over in their direction. By the look of annoyance on her face, it had to be his girlfriend for he didn't have a ring on his finger. Observing this, he bristled up, ran his fingers across his wooly dark hair, and pivoted to leave.

"I will be in touch!" And with that he was gone, leaving behind the essence of his charisma. She heard someone say that charisma was something that makes you stare at a person and keep staring. And this Black had plenty of it.

☙

A couple days later he called. His name, Apunda "Black" Nwosu. He'd informed her when he called her one evening at her home that his family owned several diamond mines in Angola, Ghana, Tanzania, and Botswana. He came from privilege and wealth as she deduced from their first meeting.

She watched as he drove up in a black-on-white Maybach Landaulet. Tossing the keys to the valet, he maneuvered into the lobby of the Ritz in Marina Del Rey with the confident stride of a lion. He owned the walkway as a model owns the runway. He slid into the seat next to her at the bar.

"Hello, sexy."

"Hi, yourself." Her grin was large and inviting.

"The usual, sir?" the bartender queried.

"No, tonight, give me a Louis XIII." He was referring to Louis XIII de Rémy Martin cognac. Rockye had heard of rappers such as T-Pain sing of "Louie Tres," and it runs about $150 a shot in most bars.

The bartender set two shots in front of him.

He shot a glance over to his companion. "What you drinking?"

"I'm good. Still nursing this white wine."

"Bring her one too."

"Presumptuous, aren't you?"

"Trust me, you are going to need it!"

"Really? What makes you think—"

"Let's cut the small talk. You want me, and I want you! We don't need to play games here. You are one of the sexiest women I have seen in a long time. I wanted you the moment I laid eyes on you. If my instincts are correct, your body is burning for mine as I am for yours. And if you came here for the same reason that I did, we should finish our drinks and get down to business." He held her gaze without a blink as he put back one shot of Rémy.

"No small talk?"

"That type of foreplay is not necessary. Unless I was mistaken you *need* me inside of you as much as I need to be inside of you." He raised the second shot and downed it before continuing. "Am I wrong?" His dark eyes penetrated to her soul, sending a formidable chill throughout her.

"Am I wrong?" he repeated within her silence.

"Nnnnnnno! You are right!"

He gestured to her drink. "Okay, then, drink up, and let's make it happen!"

She quickly emptied her glass of wine as well as the shot of Rémy and followed him to the pool area of the Ritz. They settled in a secluded section in the back area under a canopy by the pool. No words were exchanged. He glared at her. Tucked away under that canopy, Black slammed her down on the chaise lounge, his hands quickly locating, and then ripping off her G-string.

She gasped with excitement.

"You are fucking sexy!" Black grunted as the brown in his eyes turned instantly void of emotion.

"Uggggghhhh!" Rockye grunted as he pushed her legs apart and inserted himself with a single blunt thrust.

"Take it! You will take all I give you!" he spoke in her ear as his right hand tugged at her hair.

It hurt! He was pulling at it with fervor.

"You're hurting me! Take it easy, will ya!" Rockye pleaded.

"Shut up!" he voiced as his thrusts became faster and deeper.

Her head was hurting from the pulling, but the pleasure that he was giving her pussy offset it all. So it was true what they said about the African men being hung. He was huge. She screamed as she hit her fourth orgasm, which fueled him to increase the speed of the thrusts. The wildness in his eyes was animalistic. Rockye had never seen such cold detachment in anyone's eyes ever before. He pumped, prodded, and thrust in her until the dark, deafening howl he let out as he climaxed could be heard in the lobby she was sure.

Falling off of her after his climax, a shiver of guilt suddenly overwhelmed her. Rockye had to get the hell out of there. What had she done? Why did she once again give in to the calling of her sex? She felt miserable, and the guilt was eating her up once again! She looked around and suddenly felt cheap. Why didn't she at least demand that they got a room? He fucked her in a cabana near the pool. What kind of trick was she? She felt disgusting and had to leave his presence immediately.

She abruptly excused herself to go to the bathroom, and after washing up with about six of their starched white hand towels, she slipped out the front door to the street. She left her car at the Coffee Bean some five blocks away and walked over for she didn't want to pay the valet fee.

Walking down the street she lambasted herself. She didn't even use condoms with this guy. Shivers ran up her spine as she thought of the interlude. This "Black" guy was too dark for her! Thank God, he didn't have her cell number. She knew that she would never see him again. Although he was creepy and dark, the intensity of his fuck she would never forget!

As she walked back to her car, she thought about the question that Bailey asked her in reference to the difference between black and white men. In her opinion, the difference between their lovemaking was that white men sucked, kissed, and caressed while black men, fucked, pulled, grinded, and were animalistic raw and rough. She had to face it. She loved getting her back blown out. She loved how thuggish some of the brothers were. But at the same time, she also loved Andy! She was in a quandary. She didn't want to give up either the sexual experiences with strangers or her long-term relationship with Andy. What was a girl to do?

⁓

She cried all the way home. Guilt had unnerved her and was running coarsely through every inch of her body. Her heart beat faster and faster. She went from crying to laughing hysterically at herself.

"You got demons inside of you! Get out of me, damn it! Get out!" she screamed over and over until her voice became hoarse.

Placing her white prayer cloth on the hardwood floor in the den, she knelt down to pray. Folding her hands, Rockye raised her eyes to the ceiling to pray in spite of the clamor going on in her head, making it hard for her to concentrate.

"Lord, help me with this twisted, lustful desire in my heart. I come to you now and ask for help. It seems like every day of my life I am overwhelmed with sexual temptation. Everywhere I go. Please help strengthen me to walk away from it instead of running to it.

"Please forgive me for having sex with strange men. Forgive me for being unfaithful to Andy. I know I should not be committing fornication with these men, not even with Andy, but, Lord, I need help. Deliver me. Give me the strength that I need to resist and run away for I can't do it by myself. Hear my prayer, Lord, Amen."

Rockye fell asleep on the floor for she had worn herself out crying, and when she woke up hours later, her cell registered 29 missed calls from Andy. Her heart immediately started racing. Andy would be seething angry. Not answering her phone was a huge bone of contention between the two. He wouldn't believe that she was asleep alone at home all this time. The fear of his anger sent her reeling with anxiety. Her heart began palpitating again. She knew her disappearance created this trouble. She also knew that her sex addiction created a lot of dissension in their relationship because she was taking more and more chances. She looked at the phone as she contemplated what *lie* she would tell him now about her disappearance.

Would she ever catch a break?

Chapter Twenty-Six

~ Andy Reynolds ~

"I have never met a woman in my life who had so many orgasms back to back as you!" Andy said as he looked down at Rockye.

"Are you complaining?"

"Hell no! It seems as if you crave for a release just as much as most men!"

"It is what it is, that's all I can say. A girl's gotta get hers."

Andy stretched out in his California king-sized bed totally spent from the last 3 hours of lovemaking. Rockye's sexual appetite just did it for him; so much so that it had been the reason he was faithful the entire 3 years. His penis was now deflated from giving his woman well over 10 orgasms. The covers were strewn about the room, and various items once located neatly on the bedside nightstand, including a large bottle of uncapped Evian, spilled onto the floor giving his bedroom that UN-kept look.

As Rockye positioned her silky naked body in the standard after-sex spoon position, signaling to him the cuddling portion of their session, Andy drank in the beauty of their opposite skin tones. Her smooth, cocoa skin against his ruddy, hairy body was one of the many things that turned him on. She was the first African American woman he had ever dated. Even though the diversity of their curves and beauty, as well as the confidence they exuded in their own skin, was something he always admired about black women, he never once thought about dating one of them. He was a backwoods white boy who grew up miles away from any black people as a child. It wasn't until he came to Los Angeles in his 20s that he started really interacting with them and realized that they were just like most people.

When he first arrived in L.A. he had a propensity for blondes, then redheads, and then back to blondes. He then concluded that his preference was blondes; that was, until he met Rockye. She was strikingly beautiful and exuded a sex appeal that captivated him body and soul. He relentlessly pursued her until she agreed to go out with him. At first, he thought his interest was purely sexual, but soon he realized that there was something utterly different and special about this ebony beauty, and he just had to have her.

Andy recalled their first date. She sat down on the stool next to him at the California Pizza Kitchen on Ventura Blvd. in Tarzana waiting for their order of a Chopped BBQ Chicken Salad with extra, extra avocado to arrive. Andy remembered her emphasis on "extra" when ordering avocado. He took a mental note that she really likes avocado.

After placing their order, Rockye acknowledged his hungry eyes with a generous smile and a sexy wink. The sexual tension was so thick that they didn't even make it to dessert. Not much more than an hour after they sat down in the restaurant to eat, his date was back in his car giving him the most mind-blowing fellatio he had ever experienced in his life. Her mouth swallowed him so deep that his member felt the heat in the back of her throat. Damn, that was so hot!

Even though he enjoyed her sexual prowess, that night Andy labeled her a sleazy tramp! After all, what female would go to the vehicle of some man less than an hour after meeting on a first date to engage in oral sex? Only a tramp, slut, whore would do such a thing! He labeled her a "*One-Time Sally*" and decided that after that night he would lose her phone number. However, the mojo that she put on him that night had him coming back time after time again for more, and more, and more! He simply couldn't get enough!

Andy was whipped. And although he came back primarily for the Kitty Kat, he eventually discovered that he enjoyed everything about her. The obvious, of course, the way she looked, her sex, of course, was off the chain, but it was the little things like her laugh, her enthusiasm about life, and her eternal optimism and, of course, the way she paid attention to his needs and laughed at all his jokes that hooked him. And then one day he messed around and fell in love, which was far from his intention!

Regardless of his feelings about her morality, after that first date, the two were inseparable and spent the majority of their free time together, carrying on like teenagers well into the early-morning hours talking, having sex, and learning all about each other. It was then after spending so much time with Rockye that he realized that skin color was not the barrier he originally thought that it would be. It seemed to him that this stunning African American female was far more suited for him than most of the blond, blue-eyed waifs he was used to dating. Ever since then, Andy pursued Rockye until she relented to dating him exclusively.

Andy slid his hand up and down her back, enjoying the silkiness of her creamy skin.

She purred.

"That feels niiiiiiiiice!"

His hands continued the length of her body, paying particular attention to her firm, round, plump sitting-high-up-in-the-air ass that called him like a fresh baked apple pie sitting on a windowsill to cool.

He slapped it. He loved the sound of her firm ass when his hand met it with the right force.

"You better not start nothing you can't finish, baby."

"Oh, I think you know that I can take care of business!"

"Without a doubt, baby, you sure left your mark on my va-jay-jay tonight!"

They shared a laugh.

"Turn around and look at me, baby," he instructed Rockye with a sexy bass in his voice.

She eased her body over, positioning herself eye to eye with him. She giggled.

"What?" he asked with a toothy smile.

"Your hair, it's all porky-piney!"

"Yeah, it's that new mousse I just bought!" His choppy, short, dirty-blond strands stood to attention on his head, giving him a slight psychotic look.

He ran his long, narrow fingers through it in an attempt to tame the locks.

Rockye giggled more.

"Just leave it! You're making it worse! Besides, it turns me on when you look all caveman and shit!"

He started to tickle her.

"Caveman, huh? I got your caveman."

Roaring with laughter, her words became choppy and winded.

"Stttooopp, babeee! I wiiiill dooooo anything youuuuu wwwwwant. Just stooooop! Can notttt taaaaaake it! Stopppppppppp!"

They both ended up on the floor, his hands following her body at each attempt to get away. Andy loved tickling Rockye, watching her get wild and uncontrollable in attempts to break free from his mischievous fingers.

"You will do anything I want, huh?" he repeated.

"Yeeeeesssss! Anything! Jussssst stooooop tickliiiiiin' meeeeeeeee!"

He stopped! They both repositioned themselves back onto the bed. Sitting up against the headboard, he looked deep into her brown eyes, his smile slightly crocked from suddenly turning serious.

"I want to have a baby with you! Hell, not one but a whole bunch of kids. Let's make us some babies!" Andy stated, his eyes narrowed from intensity.

"What?" Rockye wrapped a blanket around her naked body, suddenly aware of the chill hanging in the air.

"You want to have babies with me? What? Where did all of this come from? You want to have babies now?"

Andy realized that he had totally caught her off guard.

"Why not? I will find the perfect place for us to live to raise us some kids!" His excitement filled the room.

"So let me get this straight, you not only want to have children with me, but you also want us to move in together?"

"Well, not in that order, but yeah!"

"We have never talked about living together before. Where did all of this suddenly come from?"

"It just hit me right now. Sitting here with you now made me realize that I want you to have my kids. I want to come home to you every night. I want to have a family with you!"

"Haven't you forgotten something?" Rockye asked. "Something extremely important!"

He wrinkled his brow in query.

"Marriage!" She abruptly threw the word out there in front of him. The word hung out there all naked and exposed.

"Oh, uh, marriage! I guess we can get married!" he conceded with reluctance.

"Oh! Yeah, you *guess* we can get married!" Rockye repeated with sarcasm. "What kind of bullshit response was that? You *guess* we can get married?"

"I just figured that we could take it one step at a time. First we would move in together, and then get pregnant, and then see how things go. Why should we be in such a hurry to get married? Everything will work out how it's supposed to be in due time."

"Are you fucking crazy? Do you hear yourself? What you are saying to me is that you want to shack up with me and have kids, but that you have to think about marrying me? Are you out of your damn mind?" Rockye fumed.

"Baby, that is not what I said! I—I—just want us to take it slow, that's all!"

"Okay, so the darkie is okay to fuck and have babies with but not good enough to marry! So next, I guess you will want me to call you Mr. Charlie and serve your damn food with a bandanna on my head and an apron around my waist?"

"That's not what I said, and you know it, Rock!" Andy responded in an attempt to defend himself. "You know that I don't feel that way about you! I never have!"

"You could have fooled me!"

"I have never ever called you that 'N' word, and I don't like it when you say it! I love you, and all I want to do is have a family with you!" Andy attempted to kiss her hand.

She pulled back.

"We can get married one day, I promise! Just give me a little time to get used to the idea. I want to get you the perfect ring and plan an incredible proposal and—!" he lied.

"Don't do me any favors, Andy! Trust me. We can stay just like we are for a long time. I am just fine being your sex toy. No need to have any babies or get married!" Rockye got up and walked toward the bathroom, but before entering she turned around and added,

"This dude told me when I first started hanging out with you not to get too hooked on you because a white man will fuck a black woman, but he will never marry her. I thought at the time that he was just hatin', but now I see that he was right on point."

Andy eased off the bed and walked over to Rockye. "I have never treated you like a black woman, whatever *that* means, but like *my* woman, the woman that I love and need in my life. It's just that marriage is a big step, and I want to make sure that I'm ready! That's all I'm saying!"

"Like having a baby *isn't* a big step? Wow! And I thought I knew you!" She ran into the bathroom and slammed the door.

He heard the water from the sink faucet come on. Andy knew that she had probably turned it on in efforts to hide her crying. It was a practice she always did when she went into the bathroom to take a dump; she turned on the sink to hide the sound of the feces hitting the water in the toilet bowl.

Andy wanted so desperately to open the bathroom door and tell Rockye that he would marry her. He wanted to tell her that everything that she just said was not true. He wanted to tell her that he would marry her tomorrow . . . but he couldn't. He couldn't because what that dude said about him not marrying a black woman had some truth to it! Although he didn't spend time contemplating the issue, he always knew that the differences between their two cultures were for sure a problem for him at times. Marriage was so permanent, and he felt comfortable if he had an exit strategy. Being married provided no exit strategy, at least not an uncomplicated one.

At second thought, it did appear that he really did have serious trepidation about marrying Rockye, a black woman! Especially a black woman who would suck his dick within hours of their first date!

Listening to the muffled sobs of his girlfriend crying in the bathroom a few feet away tugged at his heart, but regardless of how he felt, he now knew that this white boy would not be marrying that black woman anytime soon!

Chapter Twenty-Seven

~ Bailey Levine ~

One of the most painful things in life is losing yourself in the process of loving someone too much, and forgetting that you are special too."

Bailey was thinking about what she'd learned in group as Felicia strolled into the conference room, her micro braids pulled back neatly behind her ears, leaving a few braids dangling, decorating her oval face.

Bailey studied the happy bob in her gait, the pleasant smile that illuminated her face, and the assured confidence that spilled forth from her aura.

"Something wrong, Miss Bailey?" Felicia caught her boss eyeing her in a dubious manner.

Pulling herself from the trance, she asked, "How do you do it, Felicia? How do you always make things seem so easy, so effortless? Are you always as happy as you look?"

"Wow! I didn't expect that!" She was taken aback by her boss's comment.

"I'm sorry, I don't mean to pry. It's just that you are always so self-confident, so secure in who you are. I admire that! Have you always been that way?"

"Well, as a matter of fact, I haven't! My mother died when I was young, and my father . . . Well, I never knew who he really was. When my mother died, I was raised by various relatives until I turned 18."

"And when you turned 18?"

"I set out into the world on my own with two pairs of shoes, a coat, and three dresses. I didn't have much, but what I did have was a strong desire to come to Los Angeles and find the man of my dreams. You know, the ones in all the magazines, TV shows, and fairy tales. A handsome, rich man who loved me so hard that he would literally ball up and die if I was not around! Crazy, huh?"

"Where did you come here from?"

"Tucson, Arizona."

"Did you ever find him?"

"Him?"

"The handsome, rich man who loved you so hard that he would literally ball up and die if you were not around?"

Felicia chuckled as she heard it repeated from Bailey's mouth. It sounded so stupid.

"No, I didn't! What I did find were plenty of men who manipulated me, used me, and broke my heart with their black book of lies. I think I ran into all the disingenuous men in Los Angeles!"

"What happened?"

"Well, let's suffice it to say that I almost became homeless behind this guy who said that he loved me and wanted us to move in together. He said that he wanted to get married and to have children with me. He said that he found a cute apartment for us in North Hollywood and we could go in together to pay for the first and last month's rent. I believed him and gave him all the money that I had for the deposit on that apartment." She paused to reflect. "I gave him the money three o'clock on a Tuesday . . . I never saw him ever again, nor my two thousand dollars."

"You're kidding me?"

"And the worst part was that I had to leave the little studio that I did live in. I didn't have any money to pay rent because my gullible butt had given him all my money, so at that point I lived in my car for 2 months until I could afford to get another place."

"I am so sorry!"

"Oh, no need to be sorry! Adversity causes a person to reflect, and I sure got a healthy dose of adversity. Do you know what I learned? I learned that we plant the seeds in our lives for our own successes or failures. In the Bible, Jesus teaches about the parable of the sower. I will never forget the effect that it had on me when I first heard it. Ummmmm . . . Let me see how it goes. It talked about a man sowing seed and as he sowed, some seeds fell on rocky places, where they did not have much soil; and immediately they sprang up because they had no depth of soil. When the sun rose, they were scorched and because they had no root, they withered away. Others fell among the thorns, and the thorns came and choked them out. And others fell on the good soil and yielded a crop, some a hundredfold, some sixty, and some thirty. In other words, good fruit will be brought forth in good soil.

"When I heard that, I realized that I had to spend my time pouring into things and people that would yield me a crop of hundredfold, and I couldn't do that if I spent time with people that raped me for all that was good and decent about me. I had to reconsider where I spent my time, money, attention, and love. We really are only as great as the people we surround ourselves with, so at that point I decided to be brave enough to let go of all that stuff that was bringing me down."

"That was so profound from someone so young."

"Life has also taught me that I had to learn to first love me before I could love anyone else. I found out that I had to find out what love looked like by loving me first. I didn't know what love looked like because it was always a stranger in my household."

"What does love look like?"

Felicia smiled. "It is not about what it looks like, rather more like what it feels like. Love makes you feel good. It makes you feel happy! It makes you feel whole, invincible, beautiful, special, and comfortable with yourself. It is really a good feeling! Love, Miss Bailey, makes you feel good!"

"So what you are saying is that love is a good feeling?"

"That's what I think anyway."

"So conversely, if something makes you feel bad about yourself, then that is not love?"

"That's how I see it."

"Thank you for sharing that with me. That gives me something to think about!"

"I notice things with you. I mean, I can see that you are dealing with some heavy things. Although I don't say much, it is obvious that you are dealing with some not-so-good things in your life. I want you to know that you are much stronger than you give yourself credit for, Miss Bailey. In time you will see, I promise you!" Felicia smiled one of her confident smiles.

Bailey loved how Felicia always made her feel so special! It was interesting this thought about love as a feeling because Felicia always made her feel good every time she was around her. At that moment she wanted to share with her all of her family issues and hurts and pains from Chance. She knew that Felicia would say the right words of encouragement to help her make sense of it all. She wanted to, but she didn't. This was work, and Felicia was an employee. That was a line she refused to cross. She would meditate on her words of wisdom later on, but for now it was time to get back to work.

Seated at the opposite end of the six-seat conference table, Bailey glanced up from over the residential purchase agreement of the clients Steve and Angie Whitehouse and thanked Felicia for her morning vanilla latte and the wonderful words of encouragement before taking on her signature work voice.

"You're welcome. Anytime!"

"Okay, so let's get to work... Who do we have on our agenda this morning?"

"We have a full-price offer on the Whitehouse property." She eyed the contract in front of her. Bailey perused it carefully before speaking.

"It looks like the offer on the Whitehouse property is a good offer, but let's see if we can orchestrate a higher price for them." Bailey flipped through her Rolodex and instructed Felicia after pulling in a sip of the latte, "Take this number down. 555-2990. Call Marc and tell him to send me over an offer for 15 percent more. Then we will counter the buyers. Who are they again?" Bailey looked at the first page of the contract. "—the Rodgers family, and get them to increase their offer and remove these silly cosmetic requests, and close the window on the escrow period. Forty-five days, my ass!"

Felicia looked up in confusion.

Reading the expression on her face, Bailey clarified. "Marc is independent Broker, and a good friend of mine. He will write me an offer on the property on behalf of one of his clients who has seen the property. I will tell my sellers of the other offers and send back a counter, and voilà, the Rodgers will increase their offer by 15 percent, remove these silly conditions, and close the escrow period. We will accept the offer, and the deal will be in escrow within days!"

"But how do you know that the Rodgers will up their offer by 15 percent, and why 15 percent? Why not 25 percent?"

"The first rule in sales, Felicia, is to know your prospects. I always place recording equipment in the kitchen of each property that I have listed. It is turned on 15 to 30 minutes before the property is shown, and I instruct the agents to lead the prospects to the kitchen where coffee and pastries are laid out for them. They sit down, drink coffee, eat pastries, and within seconds they begin divulging what they like and don't like about the property. The notes here say that Mrs. Rodgers loved the Olympic-sized pool! She fell in love also with the backyard and that is why we will get 15 percent more! And as for the increase of 15 percent, I saw their approval letter, and they are approved for one million five hundred thousand dollars. And at one million three, 15 percent will have them kissing one million five!"

"Wow, that is brilliant! I would never have thought of that!" Felicia complimented.

Ignoring her comment, she continued, "Now, who is next? Ahh! The Winslows. It looks like the sale price is still priced too damn high."

"I spoke with them last night, and they are not budging on the price at all. They say that they are the only ones on their block who has a house for sale, and they believe that they can get it."

"From what I can tell, there are no other listings within a two-block radius, right?" Bailey asked.

"Actually there is one pocket listing from Keller Williams on the block to the north of them," Felicia noted.

"At what price?"

"One million one," Felicia said.

"Okay, this is what we are going to do." She grabbed her Rolodex again. "Call Jake Kite and tell him to get 3 For Sale by Owner clients within a two-block radius for between one million and one million one. Have them put up the signs, wrap the garage doors, and do open houses this weekend. That will get the Winslow's to drop their price pronto. By next week they will do whatever we tell them to do, and we can finally get that house sold!" Bailey explained.

Felicia looked perplexed.

"Jake is on my payroll. I have trained him to convince a home owner to put their home on the market through a 'For Sale by

Owner' program. The packet that we created shows them how much money they can make selling their property without an agent. Jakes tells them if he cannot do all of the things that he promised to help them sell their house, then we will go away in 14 days at no cost to them. We then place signs, wrap their garage door with a 'For Sale by Owner' advertisement, place elaborate flyers with the lower pricing, and do dramatic open houses; all of this to call attention to our clients to reduce their price because of the newfound competition. They get a dose of reality, and then all of sudden they are pliable for us to work with. Within 2 weeks the property is usually in escrow and the 'For Sale by Owner' stuff goes away!" Bailey clarified.

"Woooooow! That is amazing! And it works?" Felicia asked.

"There is always a first time for everything! But so far it has!"

Bailey's phone alarm went off.

"Oh, Felicia, we'll have to finish this later. I have a conference call with Robert Mercer in 30 minutes and I need to get prepared."

Felicia glanced at Bailey's calendar.

"Don't forget you are having lunch with Rockye at the Strand at one thirty."

"Okay, got it!"

Bailey thought to herself as she watched Felicia leave her office that it really felt good to be recognized for her skills and talents. So often her well planned strategies went without acknowledgment, other than the results which was success. Nonetheless, it felt really good to have another human being recognize the process! It is amazing how someone calling attention to something that you do well can make you feel so on top of the world!

As she perused the documents for her conference call with Robert, her mind reflected on the earlier conversation with Felicia about her definition of love.

"Love makes you feel happy, whole, invincible, beautiful, special, and comfortable with yourself. It's a really good feeling!"

She thought about Chance. He didn't make her feel happy, whole, and invincible or any of those things; neither did her parents. Did that mean that her parents didn't really love her? She knew for sure that Chance didn't, but could it be true that her parents never really loved her? What was wrong with her? How come she never felt love? Bailey longed for the answers. She decided that she was definitely going to stay in her therapy group. That place was her only saving grace!

Chapter Twenty-Eight

~ The Circle ~

Typically in group therapy, approximately 6–10 individuals meet face-to-face with a trained group therapist. During The Circle sessions, members decide what they want to talk about.

When people come into a group and interact freely with other group members, they usually recreate those difficulties that brought them to group therapy in the first place.

The purpose is to give these individuals a safe and comfortable place where they can work out problems and emotional issues. Hopefully, these patients gain insight into their own thoughts and behavior as well as offer suggestions and support to the others in The Circle. But conversely, when one or more of the members are in a pungent funk, they all become knotted together in that funk.

That particular day, Lynette applied soft, pink lip gloss to her taut lips and squirmed nervously within the metal seat of the folding chair. Everyone had arrived and settled within their seats, each carrying various levels of toxicity as they awaited the session to begin.

Carlos robotically acknowledged Lynette from across the room with a half wave. Lynette responded in kind with what appeared to be a newly bleached, forced smile, frustration painted on her forehead.

After calling The Tuesday afternoon group to assembly, Keno recited the pledge. Jango positioned himself at the helm, concern apparent across his face at the demeanor of the group.

"Some gloomy faces today!" he remarked. "It looks like you guys appear to be in a bad place today. Am I right?"

Everyone remained quiet.

"I want to share something with you guys."

They grunted in unison.

"Just hear me out! When I was 18, I let the opinions of my peers influence a lot of the decisions that I made, so much so that it steered me away from things I strongly believed in. I realize now, that this was a foolish way to live, especially when I consider that nearly all of those people whose opinions I cared so much about are no longer a part of my life now. I want you guys to not let the opinion of others stand in the way of your hopes and dreams. What people think about you isn't important. What *is* important is how you feel about yourself."

Jango eyed Lynette and noticed the look of irritation etched across her face.

"Lynette, what's going on with you?" Jango asked.

"I keep asking myself, why am I really doing this? I just think that I don't really want to be here!" she confessed.

"Why don't you want to be here?" he queried.

"Because I don't belong here! I am not one of—" She looked around the room.

"I am not like everybody here!" Lynette cleared her throat. "There is nothing wrong with me! I really don't need to be here!"

"Why don't you feel like you need to be here?" Jango pursued.

"Honestly, I am not getting much out of these sessions, that's why! I feel like it's a waste of my time!"

"Does anyone else feel like they are wasting their time, as well?" Jango asked.

"I wouldn't go that far, but I am frustrated as hell. It's just taking too damn long!" Rockye confessed.

"How I see it, Jango, is that I think we bullshit each other too much in here! In order to get to the core of our shit, we need to get real with it! We need to just put it out there and not sugarcoat the shit! We need to get raw with it! You sugarcoat shit too much sometimes with these stories!" Keno contributed.

"What are your thoughts about it, Bailey?" Jango directed the question toward her.

Bailey's eyes widened. He knew that she was uncomfortable with being put on the spot.

"I guess I feel a little frustrated as well. It seems like I can't see the progress sometimes. I'm just so tired of dealing with these same issues. I get tired of the fight, but I don't necessarily agree with Lynette. I don't feel coming here is a waste of time."

"Keno said let's be raw with it! I really don't always feel like being raw, but in the end, I know that this is what I really need to do! Sometimes it does seem like we are going around in circles; it seems like we are moving at this comfortable pace. I think that we need to shake it up a bit and get really raw like Keno said," Carlos chimed in.

Jango's eyes danced amongst the five.

"I just think we need a bit of a change! We need to spice things up!" Rockye added.

"Okay, very well then." Jango got up from his chair and stood erect.

"Let's shake it up a bit then. Keno, I'm going to let you do just that! Come on up here and take my place today! Let's get raw!"

"Are you fuckin' kiddin' me?" Keno enthusiastically replied.

"You up for it?"

"Hell, yea! I got this!" Keno eagerly sat in Jango's chair.

"Okay." His wide smile turned serious as he stroked his chin with his right hand in contemplation.

"I know that we are more than just a twisted circle of crazies, so let's solve some fucking problems today! Here's a question for all of ya! Think about the last few weeks. Think about the things that happened to you." He allowed the silence to encourage reflection.

"Now out of everything that happened, what was the most fucked-up thing that happened to you?" His eyes floated from face to face in query before he continued.

"And after you answer the question, next own up to your part in it. Let's talk about how you played a part in your own disaster."

Silence hung in the room like the smell of burnt microwave popcorn.

"Come on, guys, lay it out." His eyes settled on Carlos.

"I-I-uhhhhhh," Carlos stuttered, too uncomfortable to proceed.

Keno looked around the room to unresponsive faces.

"Fuckin' pussies! I'll go first then." He cleared his throat before continuing. "My girl Dee Dee found out that I was cheatin' on her, and she left my ass! For good!" Keno said, hanging his head between his legs in shame.

"Good for her!" Bailey remarked.

Keno looked up and eyed her before continuing. "I fucked around on her and lost her! Plain and simple! I brought this shit on myself because I made the choice to put my selfish-ass needs ahead of my woman! I have nobody else to blame but me! So now I just have to suck it up and deal with the shit I caused! It was my actions! It was my selfishness that caused the woman that I loved to leave my ass! I got nobody to blame but myself!" Keno then turned back to fully face Carlos.

"Your turn."

Carlos said, "Last week, I went to this gay bar hoping to run into the guy I met online. From the moment I got there, I was not real comfortable in that place. I should have left right then, but I didn't. After a while I saw Pablo in the corner with some dude. He got angry with me when I tried to talk to him and insulted me in front of everybody. I was so devastated that I just ran out of the bar! I was really a mess." He paused trying to catch his breath.

"I went outside all fucked up, and there was this guy standing up against the wall smoking a cigarette. He saw how messed up I was and asked me if I wanted a drink. Something told me not to go, but I did anyway. I went to the side of the building with him. I should have listened to that little voice in my head and left." Carlos started to gasp for air as the memories began to flood back to him.

"He gave me a beer and after a while of us laughing and stuff he suddenly changed. He started yelling at me! He went crazy. He had this wild look in his eyes, like the eyes of a monster in rage. I got scared and started looking around the side of the building for somewhere to run, but I stumbled and went down hard on the ground. He then kicked me and kicked me until my head felt like it was on fire." Carlos took off his shades and removed the baseball cap that had been covering the bruise on the right side of his face.

Lynette gasped at the sight of his injuries.

"I heard screaming. It was loud at first; then eventually the screams seemed muffled. My body then went cold. I felt wet, and then I suddenly realized that the muffled screams were coming from me."

Jango handed him a Kleenex for the snot began to ooze out of his nose.

"This guy just beat me up for absolutely no reason other than the fact that I'm gay!" He searched fixed eyes for responses.

"How do you know that?" Lynette asked.

"Because he yelled it every time he kicked me! He kept yelling and saying how he hated faggots! He said that it was disgusting that men kiss all over each other in public!" Carlos tried to shake off the memory.

"Damn, man, I hope that going to see that guy was worth the ass whipping!" Keno stated.

"Nobody should ever treat anyone that way just because they are different!" Carlos replied.

"It's not about being different, man, it's about being gay! Two men banging each other! That is hard for anybody to take!"

"So you think that it's disgusting as well?" Carlos asked.

"I'm just keeping it real; the sight of two men having sex makes me want to throw up. But I always wanted to ask you, did fucking a woman turn you gay? Is that what turned you to? Was the sex that bad with a woman or that good with a man?" Keno asked.

"I have never had sex with anyone," he said softly.

"Damn, man! You a virgin? For real? You ain't never had sex with nobody?" Keno responded.

"I haven't had sex ever before!" Carlos tentatively admitted.

"And how old are you again?" Keno asked.

"Twenty-six."

"Wow, man, that is some crazy shit! So since you ain't been with a bitch or a dude, how do you know that you're gay? You ain't never had no pussy, so how you know?"

"You don't have to answer that if you don't want to, Carlos," Jango reassured him, noticing that he was becoming extremely uncomfortable with the questioning.

Carlos remained silent.

The others leaned forward in their seats, mouths agape in anticipation of his confession.

"Okay, then, just tell us what your responsibility was in that situation at the bar?" Keno asked.

"Well, I kind of knew that Pablo was not digging on me. He had stopped returning my calls and e-mails. I really shouldn't have gone to the bar. And I really should have never gone to the side of the building with that guy. I knew better. I was a fool! I need to learn to always listen to that inner voice. That guy should not have given me that ass whipping, but I shouldn't have allowed that vulnerable moment to hinder my common sense," Carlos confessed.

"Okay, man, good breakthrough. Good breakthrough." Keno turned to his right.

"And you, Lynette, what gives?"

Appearing to be lost in thought, her eyes slightly rose to meet Jango.

"Earth to Lynette! Earth to Lynette!" Keno joked.

"It's okay. You're in a safe space," Jango encouraged.

She faced Keno. "You asked us to be raw. I'm going to tell you what is exactly on my mind. I sit back and listen to all of you, and all I can think of is that I am not one of you. I don't have problems like you! I don't have money problems, I am not gay, I am not confused about my identity, I am not a lying criminal, and I don't need to fuck every man I see! So I just sit back and listen to everybody and count the minutes until this session is over! Now is that raw enough for ya?"

"What the fuck? You think that your shit don't stink? Let me tell you something, bit—" Keno fumed.

"Hold up, Keno!" Jango attempted to neutralize his brashness.

"Naw, man, she needs to look in the fucking mirror!" Keno continued.

"Do you *really* think that your shit is all perfect? Really now? You go out and spend thousands of dollars on injections for your lips, Botox, Lipo, and shit. Whatever it is you do to yourself, you fool yourself to believe that that is some normal shit. You come in here all high and mighty, like you're better than us, when the truth is that you are more fucked up than all of us put together. You talk about your father! Huh! You are really more like him than you think. You say that your father walks around like nobody else in the room matters. Hell, that is *you*!

"You walk into this room and don't even ask how anyone else is doing. And you have the nerve to say that you are not like any of us, and then start to call us out. Insulting us and shit! Hell, you need to check yourself, Lynette, 'cause the way I see it, out of all of us, you are the most fucked up! You really need to get it together before you lose your life on the operating table for an operation that you don't fucking need!" Keno spewed.

"Okay, that's enough, Keno." Turning to Lynette, Jango asked, "If you really feel that way, then why do you keep coming to the sessions, Lynette?"

"I don't know. I was thinking that maybe I should stop. I really don't feel like there is anything wrong with me! There is only one more operation that I need to have, and then after that I will be perfectly fine. Just because I want to look good for me doesn't mean that I have a problem," she said referring to her butt augmentation.

"If you think that nothing is wrong with you, then why the hell are you here? We all admit we need help. That's why we're here. If you don't really want to be here, then bounce!" Keno ordered.

"That's enough, Keno!" Turning to Lynette, Jango continued, "If your mind is closed, then we can't make any progress, Lynette. I understand that sometimes you may get more out of some sessions than others, but if you are telling me that you get nothing out of any of our group sessions, then that's something that we have to deal with!" Jango's brow furrowed.

"I am not saying that!" Lynette momentarily retreated.

"Then what *are* you saying?" Rockye questioned.

"I am saying that I just feel like I don't really belong here." Lynette, suddenly feeling trapped, abruptly stood to her full 6 foot height, grabbed her purse and coat, and stepped out of the group to leave. Before heading toward the door, she concluded, "I am *not* like any of you. I don't have problems like you! There are just a few things that I am trying to correct that nature messed up on, and that's all! After that I'll be fine. That's all I need! I am not like any of you! I am not like any of you at all!" She marched out of the front door.

"Wait, Lynette . . . Come sit back down. Please don't leave!" Jango pleaded, as he stood to his full 6 foot 3 frame.

"I don't belong here!" she yelled from out the door.

"Fuck her! Prima donna bitch! The air will smell better without her funky ass!" Keno said.

"Don't say things like that, Keno! You can really be such a dick sometimes. This is supposed to be a safe place! Don't talk about her like that! She needs our understanding not ridicule," Bailey said.

"Fuck her! Let's just move along." Keno turned to Rockye, holding an impatient edge in his voice.

"What happened fucked up in your week, Rockye?"

Rockye slowly inhaled before straightening in the folding chair, attempting to adjust her ample ass on the hard metal seat.

"Out the blue one day Andy asked me to have his babies," she answered with obvious embarrassment.

"And?" Keno responded.

"And the son of a bitch told me that he wasn't sure that he wanted to marry me! He had the audacity to ask me to have children, but tell me that I wasn't good enough to marry! I'm good enough to have babies with, but it's a whole 'notha thing to marry my black ass!" Rockye fumed as she recalled the conversation between her and Andy.

"I know that's right!" Keno said.

"What are you talking about? He probably didn't mean it the way you're taking it, Rockye!" Bailey explained.

Keno rebutted. "He said *exactly* what he meant! Dude knows the kind of woman that he's dealing with! He knows that he has a straight-up slut! Now I am not saying a slut doesn't have her place, but it is not next to a man as his wife. Let's face it, Rockye, some of the things that you have done or are capable of doing would make any man have major reservations about marrying you. But because you are one fine-ass thing, I can see how he would want to have babies with you!"

"Keno!" Bailey scolded.

"No! It's okay. That is one thing that I can respect about Keno. He may be an asshole, but at least he can call a spade a spade and not worry about what people think of him. Out there, he's a straight dog, but in here he keeps it real, and I appreciate that!"

"So, Keno, is that what you really think he's thinking? That I'm a slut and he doesn't want to marry a slut?" Rockye asked.

"I'm not a mind reader, but I am a man! And all I can tell you is what I would be thinking as a man.

"But you can fix it if you want. In order to do that, you got to show him that you can be trusted! And until you do and he believes it, he is not going to give you that level of respect or commitment!"

"Let me ask you something, Keno," Bailey said. "On a scale of 1 to 10, how would your girl Dee Dee rate? You know, as a woman worthy of marriage."

"An absolute 20! She was a ride-or-die chick! Always had my back! Always!"

"She was all of that, huh? But that still didn't stop you from cheating on her, did it? You didn't marry her, did you?" Bailey stabbed him with words.

Keno started to rile up, but he caught the look in Jango's face in his peripheral, signally for him to maintain his composure.

"True that! True that! It sure didn't, and for that I will forever kick my own ass for what I did. I have no one else to blame but myself."

He gave Bailey a cold glare. "Okay, Rockye, now tell us where your responsibility was in that situation."

"I can't blame anybody but me. I am 1,000 percent responsible! I alone conditioned my man to have those thoughts. I don't blame nobody but me! I guess that I would feel the same under those circumstances!" Rockye confessed.

"Fucking A! Now that you are being honest, what are you going to do about it to change his thinking?"

"As Michael Jackson said, I got to start with the man in the mirror! I gotta change me. I gotta change the way that I do things!" Rockye conceded.

"Change what exactly?" Keno encouraged.

"Like my clothing, being more accountable. And stop seeking things outside of my relationship! Stuff like that!"

"You got it, girl!" After a pregnant pause, Keno turned to Bailey.

"What about you, kiddo? What happened to you this week that was fucked up?"

"Don't call me kiddo! I'm a grown-ass woman!"

"My bad. Bailey—"

"My parents are ignoring my phone calls. They are doing to me what they did to my older brother, Edbart! They wrote me off just like they did him! My parents have decided that I no longer exist! I thought to myself that if it is so easy for my parents to write me off as though I don't matter, then what hope do I have for anybody else in this world to care about me?" Bailey explained.

"Why did they write off your brother?" Carlos asked.

"I don't know!"

"What does he say?"

"Who, my brother?"

"Yeah, what does he have to say about it?" Carlos tried to clarify.

"Don't know! Haven't seen or talked to him since he left!"

"Whaaatttttt?!" Keno exclaimed.

"You don't have any communication with your own brother?" Jango asked.

"Nope!"

"Damn! You got one cold-ass family! Their own kids just walk away, and they don't give a shit. That is some crazy-ass shit!" Keno stated.

"So how do you feel about that?" Rockye sheepishly asked.

"Angry as hell! I want to do something, something so big that it will make them pay attention to me! I-I am just so angry all the time, I find myself getting defensive with my employees and easy to be provoked. This thing with my parents has me really messed up!"

"So do you feel that you had a part in this beef with your parents? What part did you play in this craziness?" Keno asked.

"Yes, I did! I realize now that no matter how angry I am with my parents, I should have never disrespected them the way that I did. They are my parents, and I had no right to curse or talk to them the way I did! My fault was believing that I deserved respect from my parents. I want respect, but I have no right to feel like I deserve it!" Bailey explained.

"Are you fucking kidding me? You really believe that line of bull? I think parents should respect their children! They can't go around talking and treating their kids any ole kinda way because they fucked and a baby came out 9 months later! That doesn't give them the right to act an ass any time they want!" Keno added.

"I agree with Keno. My father treats me and my little brother like we have no rights or feelings just because he makes sacrifices to feed us and put a roof over our heads. Because he gets up and goes to work every day he feels like we are obligated to jump every time he says so! I think that is bull! He and my mom decided to have kids! Not me or my brother! They brought us into the world, so therefore it's their duty to care for us until we can care for ourselves. They wanted us. We didn't get a choice to choose to have parents!" Carlos, the 25-year-old virgin fumed.

"I used to get so angry with my mother because of her bad choices. Choices that affect me in my life today! I'm sorry, Bailey, but I agree with them. I think that parents should respect their children. I think that it was their decision to have children and that they should put their feelings and needs second to their kids. That is, until the children can take care of themselves, and then they need to respect the person that they created them to be. And your parents are just plain wrong with what they are doing to you!" Rockye commented.

"Fuck 'em! You don't need them!" Keno said.

Jango interjected, "Let's talk about anger for a moment. Anger is a response that you learn early in life to help you cope with pain. And while anger temporarily helps you overcome feelings of helplessness and lack of control, it disrupts relationships and makes you feel even more helpless and out of control. Like with Bailey, she learned to lash out when she was in pain as a result of her mother attacking her. And as a result of that action, the relationship is damaged." Jango stood up before continuing.

"Here are a few exercises I want you to practice when you start to feel angry. First, stop! Take a deep breath and don't say anything. Just observe but do not react. You are now at a crossroad here. You have the choice of how to respond to your anger or pain in a different way from your past. Second, watch what you say to yourself. Your self-talk can calm you down or feed the flames of your rage. Don't say things that will intensify your anger, but do say things that will help you get over that wave of anger. And lastly, act the opposite of how feel; smile, relax, lower your voice, and disengage rather than attack. Decide that you will deal with the situation later when you are calm. Let empathetic words come out of your mouth instead of judgmental and attacking words."

The bell signaling that the session was over sang in the background.

"Okay, everyone! Time is up for this session. How do you feel the session went today?" Jango asked.

"I think it was real!" Rockye answered.

"It made us see what the sources of our frustrations were for the last couple of weeks and how we played a part in it! It helped me get a little more clarity," Bailey replied.

"For me I guess I just felt like it was all about us today, not some story about a frog or something, but all of us identifying our own problems and the part we played in it!" Carlos added.

"What about you, Keno?" Jango asked.

"Sometimes we need change, Jango! It was good to have everybody get raw, but in the end, you always bring us back full circle with our shit. You help us get perspective and challenge us with another way to look at and handle things. I was sitting here thinking about it when you were talking, and I just feel like we were able to vent today. But in the end, you brought it back to anger and how to handle anger. You gave us some exercises on how to handle anger. And that is what we need, and you always give us that!"

Keno stood up and walked over to Jango, extending his hand.

"I respect what you do, man. It ain't easy! It was good for me to sit in your shoes for one time. I learned a different take! When you sit in someone else's shoes, it gives you more understanding. And I think only then can you really understand what it's like!" He gave Jango a firm handshake.

"What I did in this session was give everyone an opportunity to vent! What you do every time we come together is help us to peel away the shit layer by layer, look at it and get to the core of it so that we can identify it and handle it in the right context. That shit ain't easy! And I understand now that it will take time!" Keno concluded.

Jango stood up, surprised by Keno's comment.

Keno turned to everyone. "Today we vented, but this man is really helping us, and I can see now that it will take time! Nothing worthwhile happens overnight!"

"Keno made an excellent point just now! As you go throughout your week this week, try to walk in the shoes of the person you are having problems with. For you, Carlos, try to see things through your dad's eyes. He is old school, a hardworking, meat-and-potatoes man. If you try to look at things through his eyes, you may have a better relationship with him. Rockye, if you put yourself in your Andy's shoes, I think that you will find it easier to change some of your behavior. A man who sticks around after all he has been through with you, that man is a man who truly loves you. Be the change that you want to have in your relationship! And, Bailey, your parents raised an incredible woman. You truly are! You are smart, ambitious, and successful beyond your years, and you did it without having babies out of wedlock, doing drugs, or getting in trouble with the law. Hell, they must have done something right! Try to see things through the eyes of your mom."

"Keno, you made the decision to put you first, without consideration of your girlfriend. However, the bigger problem is not Sharon or your girlfriend, it is the fact that you don't have enough confidence in yourself to throw caution to the wind and take care of yourself without anyone there as a safety net. You need to realize that you are enough to do and be whatever you want. You ARE enough! Your girlfriend may or may not come back. You don't have control over that, but what you do have control over is you! You can have enough faith in your own ability to execute your own goals and dreams!" Jango concluded.

"I think that these are good points to focus on until we meet in 2 weeks. Put yourself in someone else's shoes. Bailey, try to really see your mom's point of view. Rockye, really try to put yourself in your guy's mind and see it the way he sees it! Carlos, do the same with your dad, and, Keno, I think you need to see things through the eyes of Sharon and Dee Dee." Jango held out his hand for Keno to shake once again.

"I'm proud of your contribution during this session, and I learned something myself. Good job!" Jango concluded, for he was satisfied with the outcome of tonight's session.

After everyone had left, Jango pulled out his calendar and noted to call Lynette in the morning. He needed to schedule a private appointment with her. He didn't want her slipping through the cracks. Everyone else was in different stages of psychological healing, he felt. All except Lynette, she was playing in dangerous territory, and prolonged absence from therapy could lead to irreversible damage, not only to her mind but more importantly her body from those unnecessary plastic surgeries.

Chapter Twenty-Nine

— Bailey Levine —

The faded sign that dangled in the wind on the remnants of a rusty, thin, frail wire read, "STANLEY STUBBS DETECTIVE AGENCY" in the older area of downtown Los Angeles. The office of the building was equally as dilapidated as the exterior, which carried a stench of mold that hung in the air, as well as dust and clutter as its sidekick. Directly across from her resembled a scruffy, disheveled "Columbo" look-alike. The chair that she rested on annoyed her because it wobbled back and forth when she moved on its two uneven legs.

"Miss Levine, what is it that I can do for you?" the older gentleman, sporting an afternoon shadow, inquired.

"I want to find out as much information as I can about my boyfriend. I mean, this guy I've been seeing for a while. I want to know where he lives, and what he does for a living. Is he married—things like that."

He scratched his neck and queried, "According to the information that you provided here, it says that you have been seeing this gentleman for about 3 years?" His eyes surveyed the file in front of him.

"Yes," Bailey answered, knowing exactly where his line of questioning was leading.

For the last 4 weeks, she had been unable to sleep. Every morning the questions would arise again with the day . . . the same nagging questions racing through her mind. *Where does Chance live? Does he really have a roommate that doesn't want people over or is he just lying to hide another woman? Does he have any love for me or is he just using me for money and kinky sex? What else is he hiding from me?* She desperately needed to know, for it was the reason for her insomnia.

Bailey finally decided after another sleepless night that she would hire a private investigator and once and for all get the answers to those nagging questions. She was tired of speculating. She needed to know the truth!

"I'm confused then as to why you don't know—"

Bailey completed the question. "—know the answers to these questions?"

"At least to where he lives or works."

"Mr. Stubbs, I—"

"Call me Stan," he corrected.

"Stan, I am truly ashamed to say that although I have been with this man for over 3 years, I don't know anything about him! I have never been to his house, nor his work, nor met any of his family. Nothing at all! I feel—I feel so—so disgusted with myself. It's like I'm under this spell when I'm with him. He has this hold over me. I really can't explain it. All I can say is that it is tearing me up inside, and I want it to stop!" Bailey fumbled over her words.

"Tell me something about him. How does he treat you?" he asked as he took out his legal pad.

"Well, Chance is attractive in an unconventional way. He has this look that draws you in, and he has this smile that melts me to my soul. He is also funny and, yeah, charming." She paused in thought before continuing. "He loves to talk to people. He would talk to people all the time when we were out, especially women. He had this gift to be able to strike up a conversation with anyone. He always seemed to find out things about people, things that he could use or things that would help him out at some point in time. I guess you could say that he has a way with people! He would strike up a conversation with anyone, anytime, and anywhere!"

"You said he did this when he was with you?"

"All the time! He would also be on the phone a lot. Yeah, he was always on the phone a lot!"

"Talking to whom?" Stan asked.

"I really don't know. He never told me. A lot of the times he would just walk away and finish his conversation. Sometimes it took as long as an hour before he came back!"

"And what would you do while he was on the phone?"

"I just waited until he came back!"

"You were not angry?"

"Of course I would be a lot of the times. But when I mentioned it to him, he would just tell me to stop nagging him. He told me that nobody was going to stop him from making his money, not even me!"

"What else would he do that you didn't like?"

"He would—" She held her head down in shame.

"He would what?" he prodded.

"He would take me to different places . . . to . . . to—"

"To what?"

"To have sex with strange men." Her voice trembled.

"And you didn't want to do this?"

"No! Never!"

"Then why did you do it?"

"He told me that this would make him happy! I wanted to make him happy!" She wept.

Stan handed her a Kleenex. "Did you ever say no?"

"Many times!"

"What did he do when you said no?"

"He didn't care how I felt about any of it! He just wanted what he wanted when he wanted it! My feelings didn't matter to him at all!"

"Tell me what you know about his childhood. Was there sexual abuse growing up?"

"He has never talked much about his childhood with me, but I did overhear him once talking about how his stepmother was the first woman he ever had oral sex with."

"His stepmother?"

"Yes. I believe he was young; under thirteen, I think."

"Was he abusive to you, I mean physical? Did he ever hit you?"

"He would get angry, but eventually he calmed down. He never beat me or anything, if that is what you are asking."

"What does he do for a living?"

"He just tells me that he is in the entertainment industry. He is always working on some big deal. One week it's this, and the next week it's another thing. I have never really seen anything that he has done. It always falls through, something always goes wrong."

"Does he have a criminal record?"

"I don't know. I only know that I gave him money for supposedly traffic ticket violation payments. He really didn't tell me what kind of tickets. He's very secretive."

"He would ask you for money, and you would give it to him without any questions?"

"I got tired of fighting him for the truth, and to tell you the truth, all I was looking for is for him to be nicer to me. When I gave him money, he would be nicer to me."

"You gave him money often?"

"Yes."

"For what?"

"Well, his cell phone got turned off one time, and his car got towed away because it was in the red zone. He lost his wallet at a car wash, stuff like that."

"So he is irresponsible?"

"I guess you can say that."

Stan scratched his head. "For the life of me, Miss Levine, I don't understand why a woman with so much going on for herself would want to be with a man like this. If you were my daughter, I would—" He stopped himself.

"I know this all sounds crazy. I don't understand it myself sometimes."

"Don't beat yourself up, for I have heard so much worse. But the question now is ... What do you want to do now?"

"I want to know what I am dealing with. I want you to tell me who I am dealing with."

"From what you have told me so far, I can tell you that this man fits the profile of a sociopath. And in my opinion, you are better off far the hell away from him, than trying to find out about him."

"Sociopath? What is a sociopath?"

"Well, for starters, sociopaths like this guy are very charming, manipulative, and cunning. They carry with them a feeling of entitlement. They feel like they have a right to certain things. They are also pathological liars. It's almost impossible for them to be truthful. They do not see others around them as people, but only as targets and opportunities to get what they want. They are outraged by insignificant matters, remaining cold and unmoved by other's feelings. These people do not perceive that anything is wrong with them, and this, Miss Levine, is what makes them so dangerous. They exercise control over every aspect of their victim's life when they can. Their ultimate goal is to create a willing victim. And, Ms. Levine, he has accomplished his goal with you!"

Bailey adjusted her behind in the chair; she was uncomfortable at how concise Stan was about Chance.

"By what you have told me today, the questions you should be asking yourself are not 'Where does he live? Or is he living with someone? Does he love you?' etc., but 'Why do I still want to be in this unhealthy, dangerous relationship that in no way can or does benefit me? And how the hell can I get out of it?'" Stan eyed her.

"I know that it does not make sense to you, Stan. It doesn't make sense to me either. But what I need from you is to find out for me who he really is. I need to know for myself if any of it was real. I desperately need to know if any of it was real or was it all a lie!" Bailey justified.

"And what if all of it was a lie, what then?" He shook his head in disbelief.

"I will move on with my life. I will move on. I promise I will!"

"And if there is truth?"

"As sad as it sounds I will find out how to make it work!"

"Are you *sure* about that?" the private detective asked.

"I'm not really sure about anything. I'm just doing the best that I can, the very best way that I can!"

"Very well then, I'll start working on it right away and will be in touch with you just as soon as I find out something." He stood up, signaling the conclusion of the meeting.

"Thank you, Stan." Bailey exited the dusty office, not feeling hopeful about her relationship with Chance. Yet, at the same time, she did feel optimistic about finding out the real truth because the worst thing about being lied to is feeling that you're not worthy of the truth.

Jango once told them that the truth that hurts is the same truth that heals.

Chapter Thirty

~ Rockye Haynes ~

"Who the hell is calling me at this hour?" she spit out as she reached across the bed to grab the handheld on the nightstand that held all too many things for the small tabletop.

She'd just bolted up out of bed at 5:45 a.m. from a sound sleep at the sound of the ringing telephone.

She knew that it couldn't have been Andy, for she left his house a little before midnight after yet another fight about her attire. When she stormed out the door, although already inebriated, he was reaching for yet another bottle of Jack Daniels. It couldn't be him because he was most likely passed out on the couch right about now.

The caller ID displayed Cyrus's number. She hadn't seen this producer since she had sex with him in the studio. She instantly became anxious. Last week she did yet another audition for one of three shows that he was producing. And although he wasn't present at the time, she was certain that he had viewed her tape by now.

Rockye had not been getting any callbacks lately, and due to her preoccupation in her personal life had not been giving the best performances on auditions.

"Oh my God, please don't let this be bad news." Her personal life had gone to hell, and she dreaded it spilling over to her career. Rockye spent her life and all the money she made on acting, dancing, and singing lessons to make sure that she was on point in all areas of her craft. But lately, her mind was just not present, and now she feared that all her hard work was going to be for nothing. *What bad news is Cyrus calling to give me?*

"Helloooooooooo?" she answered with trepidation.

"Rockye, it's me, Cyrus. We need to talk. Clear your schedule and meet me at Flemings at 7:00 this evening."

"Ummmm, what's going on?"

"Just be there!" he hung up before she could ask any additional questions.

At the sound of the dial tone, she instinctively started to worry. What was that all about? Her heart sank at the possibilities. She considered all the things that could be wrong.

She suddenly remembered what Jango said in group one day, "Worry is an illusion." He said that focusing on the worst-case scenarios won't keep bad things from happening; it only keeps you from enjoying the good things that you have in the present. So she decided right then and there that she would focus on the good things in her life.

But what good things would that be?

⁓

Cyrus slid his thick pink tongue over his super large bottom lip, a habit that he had taken to since he quit smoking cigarettes nearly 4 years ago as he sat across from her in the upscale restaurant. This nervous habit had since become his signature trademark amongst the ladies, as well as acting as a potent aphrodisiac. Rockye remembered the effect it had on her the first time she met him several years ago in a recording studio in Hollywood.

Cyrus Slade was one fine, sexy, hot-bodied writer/producer/director/actor with an extra helping of entrepreneur. He had had sex with a majority of all of the starlets in the industry that came across his path, including Rockye. Unfortunately, Rockye wasn't concerned with her reputation as a starlet sleeping her way to the top.

Even though she was nervous about the meeting, the thought of their prior sexual encounters turned her on immensely.

"Order anything that you like! The sky's the limit!" Cyrus stated, carrying a mystic air over him like an umbrella on a rainy day.

Rockye threw the menu she was holding down onto the table.

"What is going on? What's the bad news that you have to tell me? For as long as I have known you, you have never ever told me to order anything I wanted. Ever! You are too cheap for that! What the hell is up? Just go ahead and yank the bandage off quickly and get it over with!"

"Okay! Okay!" He slid his tongue across his lips again. "Don't get your panties in a wad. Calm your ass down! You act like I brought you here to give you some bad news or something."

"Well, didn't you?" Rockye sat on the edge of her seat.

"Slow your roll, girl. I got some damn straight-up news, and I just wanted to surprise you! I bet you are the kind of chick who opens Christmas gifts before Christmas."

"What is it, Cyrus?" Rockye demanded.

"Okay! Okay! Do you remember that play I've been working on?"

"There are so many of them. Which one?"

"The musical—the one about—"

"The girl who goes to sleep one night and wakes up as her alter ego!" Rockye finished.

"You remembered! I can't believe you remembered!" He smiled.

"Yeah, I remember. When you first told me about it I didn't like the story line, but after I read the manuscript, I really liked it!"

"You never told me that you liked it, Rockye," Cyrus said with a hint of surprise in his tone.

"I know, but you already have an ego as big as the Grand Canyon, and besides, we kind of got busy and never got around to talking about it again." The smirk on her face carried a rich perfume of sensuality as she briefly reminisced on that sexual encounter.

"Oh yeah, that was the shit! I remember that night like it was yesterday! Looking at you, a person would never even imagine that some kind of freak like that was living in there!" He licked his lips again.

"Yeah, whatever! So why am I here, and what has your play got to do with me and you letting me order anything that I want tonight? Spill it!" Rockye insisted.

"I got some investors that love it and are backing it 100 percent. We are going to Broadway, baby!" Cyrus beamed.

"What are you talking about?"

"I am taking the play to Broadway. We got a commitment and backing. It's a done deal!"

"Are you kidding me? That is so amazing! I'm so happy for you!"

"For me? No, not for me, for us! You've got the lead. I want you to play Monica!"

"What! Are you kidding me?" Rockye mouthed.

"Yeah, I didn't know you when I wrote it, but the part of Monica has your name all over it. We start rehearsal in 3 months, and hopefully, if everything goes as planned after New York, we should have a run for about 2 years. Three months should give you plenty of time to get your shit together."

"Hey, wait a minute. I can't go to New York! I have a life here and picking up and leaving is not an option!" Rockye insisted.

"Rockye, don't be crazy! This is an opportunity of a lifetime. Not many people get the chance that I'm giving you. To play the lead in a Cyrus Slade play, are ya kiddin' me? By the summer, Rockye Haynes will be a household name!"

Rockye thought about it as the waiter interrupted them to uncork and pour a bottle of champagne. She couldn't leave Andy. Or could she? Would he even care right about now if she was gone? After all, he didn't even love her enough to marry her. It would serve him right if she left to go to New York.

"How much will I be paid?" The wheels in her brain started turning.

"Scale but the per diem of $100 per day, and you will have your very own hotel room, car service at your disposal 24/7, and a supersized dressing room with a queen-size bed in it!"

"Scale, huh? I am not too happy about that!" Rockye cleared her throat. The bubbles in the champagne tickled her nose. She didn't like the idea of getting the industry's minimum wage when she felt she'd already paid her dues.

"Come on, Rockye! It's just to start!"

"I've always wanted to go to New York," Rockye said as she watched Cyrus licking his lips as his eyes perused the extensive menu. Although inappropriate timing, she found herself tingling with sexual tension. Her clit was throbbing, and her pussy was juicing up, flowing onto her G-string.

"May I take your order?" the waiter called from above.

"Yes, I will have the rib eye medium rare, with the garlic mashed potatoes, and Caesar salad with extra Parmesan cheese." Cyrus turned to Rockye.

"The rib eye here is off the chain!" he recommended.

"I will have the same thing except make my steak well done!" Rockye added as she handed the waiter the menu.

After the waiter disappeared, Rockye resumed the conversation.

"If I can remember correctly, Cyrus, Monica has a pretty demanding role. She sings, dances, acts, and her emotions range a pretty large gamut."

"It requires a real entertainer. Somebody like a female Sammy Davis Jr! I was watching one of his movies the other day, and I was just amazed at how talented he was. To me that is what a star really is! Somebody who does it all!" He flashed his pearly whites at her.

"Somebody like you! Not anybody can play the role of Monica. That's why nobody else can be Monica but you! You are a phenomenal actress! You can dance your ass off! Your voice is crazy off the hook, and when I look at you, you *are* Monica!"

"Flattering I must say! But, Cyrus, scale?"

"I'm operating with a small budget for now. The investors want to make sure that the play will do well. My up-front money is nominal, but after we get rolling and the audience comes in the way I expect them to, then we can negotiate a higher salary. I promise," he said.

"How much more?" Rockye probed.

"Look, Rockye, the only thing that I can promise you right now is scale and a chance at being a star!" Cyrus positioned the napkin in his lap as the waiter placed two thick pieces of meat in front of them.

"I'm putting everything that I have into this, and nobody wants it to be more successful than me. So trust that I'm doing everything in my power to have a hit on my hands. Okay?" He lifted a chunk of steak flavored with a portion of fat into his eagerly awaiting mouth.

Rockye watched Cyrus as his sexy, thick mouth moved side to side masticating the meat.

"Okay, then, Tyler Perry!" she joked.

"Whatever! You can call me what you want, but I'm going to make this happen!"

"I ain't mad at you! I believe you!" Rockye reaffirmed.

"Then you're with me?" Cyrus asked as his tongue slid across his lips once again.

Seconds before answering, the image of Andy crossed her mind. Was she really going to make a decision to leave L.A. without talking to him about it? How could she even consider leaving Los Angeles without even so much as a thought about the man that she loved? What about her group? She didn't want to leave her group or her friends. Everything that was familiar to her was right here in Los Angeles. But what had all of the acting lessons, singing lessons, and dance classes been about? Didn't she do all of that for a big break? This one big break?

"I got to talk it over with my man!" Rockye forced through the voices in her head.

"Your man? You mean that white boy that you been fucking?" Cyrus barked.

"Fuck you, Cyrus!" she retorted.

"Look, Rockye, it's okay to fool around with this white boy if you want, if you feel that is what you have to do, but don't start thinking that that shit is permanent. That shit ain't permanent! You think that white boy is going to marry you and take you off to some house in the country so you can have a whole bunch of his blond-headed babies?"

Rockye eyed him with contempt for he had hit close to home.

"Aww, shit! You really believe that shit, don't you? So you want to marry the white boy, huh? Fuck me! You think that that white boy is going to get down on one knee and propose to your black ass with some fat-ass diamond ring, huh?" Cyrus took a long sip of champagne, never repositioning his eyes from her.

Cyrus didn't know that he had hit a sore spot with her. Rockye was still having issues with the fact that Andy was not ready to marry her, a black woman! Could Cyrus be right? Was she a stupid bitch believing that eventually Andy would marry her?

"Come on, Rockye! If he really loves you, he'll be here when you get back! You have been waiting for an opportunity like this your whole life, and now that it's here, you do what? You're going to pass it up because of the *slight* chance that some white boy is going to want to marry your ass? What about YOUR dreams?"

Rockye remained silent. Not wanting to acknowledge that he could possibly be right, she just stared at the food in front of her.

"Besides, girl, we both know what you are *really* all about!" He winked at her as his pink tongue slid across his bottom lip.

"You are one stone-cold freak! And no one man can really satisfy you for a long period of time. How long have you been fucking around on this white boy that you say you love?"

"You don't know me," she retorted.

"Oh yeah, it sure didn't seem that way those times when you fucked my brains out like a wild animal! Do you remember the last time you fucked me, Rockye? I'll never forget that night! Do you know why I won't forget it?"

She didn't answer, just stared into his lusty eyes.

"I'll tell you why . . . because you fuck with the intensity of a man! You get yours, and you get yours hard! I felt like I was your joystick. When I pulled out my dick from my pants, you didn't see me anymore, you just saw the size, length, and width of my dick. You got off on it! After the first time we fucked, I said to myself that there was something different about you! I kept thinking about it with no real conclusion until the last time we got together; then it hit me!" He wiped his mouth with the cloth napkin.

"You suck dick like your life depends on it! Swallowing my whole dick was something that you had to do, and you didn't stop until you did. And then when we started fucking, I have never seen a woman come as much and as hard as you did over and over and over.

"It's like you go into a trance or some shit! I kept calling your name, but your body kept going into convulsions over and over. Damn, baby, you leave this planet when you are getting yours!"

"You, Rockye, are a come-whore! I understand that disease all too well because so am I."

He raised his glass. "To us! Two peas in a pod! For I too am a come-whore! I don't care who it is. If she can make me come and come hard, it is all good!

"So what do you say, baby? Are we going to New York?" Cyrus licked his lips again, and this time she lost all resolve. Rockye scooted closer to his side of the table, sliding her right hand up under it to find his penis which had already grown full size within his pants.

Rockye knew that what he said was the truth. She tried to fight it for a brief moment before finally surrendering to the overwhelming feelings burgeoning within her.

Relieving his massive erection from the confinement of his Jeans, Rockye pulled it out so that she could stroke it before suggesting they do what they both wanted to do ever since they sat down at the table. They ate quickly and hurried out to his waiting limo. After her sixth orgasm as she lay spent across the backseat of the limo, she heard Cyrus smugly say, "I take it that means you are going to New York?" as he looked across at the totally spent Rockye. He knew that he had the tool to get the job done, and he wanted her for his play. And when Cyrus Slade wanted something, he stopped at nothing until he got it—by any means necessary! He didn't worry about the cost. Fortunately for him, the price he had to pay benefited him as well. Cyrus looked forward to many more nights of stolen moments with his doppelgänger.

"Take a slow drive up Topanga Canyon to the beach. We're going for round two and don't want to be disturbed!" he instructed the limo driver as he rolled his tongue over his bottom lip.

Rockye giggled. "Are you sure you can handle round two?"

"What do you think?" he asked, cradling his erection firmly within his right hand.

Rockye, with no regard for her health or safety, eagerly enveloped his sex within her hungry mouth, chasing yet another orgasm. He exploded again as he rammed his rod deep down her hot slippery throat. The sense of shame didn't wash over her until much later—well after she had reached several more orgasms.

Chapter Thirty-One

⁓ Bailey Levine ⁓

Death never sends a notice to either the rich or the poor. The police found the late 85-year-old multimillionaire Dominica Aston dead; a paramour, 40 years her junior, had called 911. Although there were no sign of felonious activity, the case was still under investigation until the autopsy was completed.

It was strange to stand in the foyer of her deceased client's 8,000 square foot, lavish two-story, six-bedroom Mediterranean, knowing that less than a month ago she was found dead in the master bedroom. The once meticulously landscaped lot near the Palisades Village in Pacific Palisades sat on a little over an acre evidencing slight neglect.

Bailey recalled relaxing with the owner in the congenial atmosphere of the estate on many occasions. However, now she was in the company of the unsavory characters who just inherited it, Mary Helen and Charlton Aston. Charlton was the son of the late 85-year-old multimillionaire Dominica Aston who purchased the property just 5 years earlier—paying all cash, and Mary Helen was the sycophant wife of Charlton for over 10 years.

Apparently Dominica's death came unexpectedly as a result of a massive heart attack during a rigorous session of lovemaking with her 45-year-old lover, Laslow.

The house, although 8,000 square feet, seemed significantly smaller due to Dominica's extensive collection of original artwork, statues, and artifacts which she spent a lifetime collecting from her worldly travels. They hung on every available wall and lined the hallways and any available space in all the rooms. Each piece held a significant value of its own and was willed to one of her many different charities, which, of course, sent her surviving relatives into dramatic histrionics.

Her son, Charlton Aston, had been given the house and now he sat wavering on many aspects of the listing agreement for the recently inherited Pacific Palisades two-story Mediterranean. It was kissing one o'clock, and Bailey's patience was getting as short as their list of negotiable requests. Bailey shook her head in disgust as she dealt with the ignorance of her deceased client's progeny. She slid open the heavy sliding glass doors and followed them out to the backyard that overlooked the Zen stone waterfall.

"The walkway is in need of extensive repairs. Do you have someone in mind or would you like for my office to handle that for you?" Bailey asked with a huge lump of disdain lodged in her dry throat.

"We are not fixing anything!" Charlton stated.

Bailey took a deep breath. Even though this property was at a 6½ percent commission on a five-million-dollar price ticket, she was about 2 seconds away from telling him to fuck off!

"Just over there behind the rose garden, the gazebo is leaning slightly to one side. How would you like to handle that?" Bailey continued with a forced smile.

"As is!" Charlton stated. "They are buying it 'AS IS.'"

"I have to be blunt with you, Charlton. The current market will not allow for you to move this property quickly with so many obvious repairs needed. This house, if in perfect condition, is still 15 percent overpriced. If we do get a buyer for your asking price, they will have merit to negotiate us down after the home inspection. We are going to have to lower the price or repair and upgrade the areas I have pointed out for you on your recommendation sheet."

"I am not going to fix anything! So stop trying to force it down my throat!" Charlton turned around, surveying the back portion of the lot.

"I am going to go check out the garage," he said as he swiftly walked away.

After Charlton left, Mary Helen confided to Bailey, "His mother didn't leave him anything in the will but this house, and we just don't have the money to fix it up!"

Bailey smirked.

"Where is the guest house?" Mary Helen asked.

"On the other side of that wall of overgrown bushes, why?"

"Because Charlton and I will be living there until the house is sold."

"Oh! You are not going back to Seattle?" Bailey asked, annoyed at this new information.

"Well, Charlton lost his job, and our house is in foreclosure. We didn't know what we were going to do, that was, until we got the call that his mother died and left us her house. So we packed up everything and drove here from Tacoma," Mary Helen confided.

"How long do you think it will take for you to sell this house?" she continued.

"If you lowered the price by 20 percent, and fixed the items that are in dire need of repair, we should be closed within 60 days. I already have clients that have shown significant interest in this property." Bailey leaned forward to continue. "But you have to get Charlton to either do repairs or lower the price!"

Charlton marched back in.

"Do you know who owns the house directly across the street?"

"I believe it is a judge and entertainment lawyer." She walked over to the window to see what he was talking about and observed droppings in the windowsill which evidenced obvious termite damage.

"Are those blacks the owners?" He referred to the African American lady exiting a Jaguar parked in the driveway.

"Excuse me?" Bailey asked, wrinkles quickly forming on her forehead.

"I just want to know, are the owners black?"

"What difference does that make?"

"I don't want you to sell my house to anybody other than whites!"

"Charlton!" Mary Helen commented. "Why did you go and say that?"

"Hell, it's my damn house, and I don't want her selling it to nobody other than whites."

"What are you saying?" Bailey exclaimed.

"This is *my* house! And I don't want anybody in it except for another white person! No blacks, Mexicans, or them Chinese, Jews . . . none of them . . . just whites." He walked over to the counter and picked up the listing agreement.

"And put that down on the paperwork," he insisted.

Charlton handed Bailey the clipboard that held the listing agreement.

"Put it in the paperwork!" he demanded.

Her nostrils flared with anger at the demand.

Bailey took a deep breath and grabbed her calculator. Without saying a word, she divided 3 1.2 percent into $4,995,000. That would be her share of the commission.

$174,825.00! Bailey stared at the amount. She thought about the bonuses that she could give out to her much-deserving staff. She thought about Felicia, a devoted young lady who worked tirelessly for her, and how she could use a new car, some new clothes, and a much-deserving bonus would allow her the opportunity to catch up on bills.

Bailey took another deep breath.

"Charlton... even if morally I was okay with that, it is blatant discrimination for me to put such a thing in a contract. Legally, I can't put that into a contract!"

"Okay, so you can't put it in the contract. Just make sure that you only sell my house to somebody white!" he ordered.

What happened to this guy? Bailey thought to herself. He was so different from his mother. Or was he? Bailey never let on to Dominica that she was black. Maybe that sweet little old lady was a bigot as well!

"Do you realize what you are asking of me?" Bailey questioned.

"Look, I realize that you had a relationship with my mother. She must have liked you because she mentioned you over the years. But as for me, I just want to get rid of this white elephant and move on with my life. I could care less about this dump other than the money it will put in my pocket. That old broad didn't give a shit about me when she was alive! It fucking pisses me off that she only left me this house with all the damn money and stuff she had. All I want you to do is get rid of this damn house and get my money!"

"If all you care about is the money, then why do you care who I sell it to?"

"I don't have to explain myself to you. Don't *you* work for *me*? Just *do* it!"

Realizing that she was dealing with an ignorant bigot, Bailey just kept her mind on the $175,000 commission and not this ignorant excuse for a human being that was in front of her. Although it may have been wrong, she had to think of her business; so again, she swallowed her opinion with her saliva and didn't say a word!

Once Charlton and Mary Helen left the house after the last paper was signed and initialed, Bailey sat alone in the spacious kitchen feeling absolutely horrible. She took inventory of what she was feeling! She compromised her values for what? Money! Wow, she realized that she was no better than him! What had she become? She felt like a whore. She had become venal and therefore, easily bought!

Bailey felt herself sinking into that abyss of dispiritedness. She desperately needed to jolt herself from slipping into that debilitating state. She needed someone to make her laugh. She needed someone to make her feel, to feel anything other than what she was feeling now. And in the midst of her desperation, she picked up her cell phone and called Chance.

She had not heard a word from Stan since their meeting over a week ago and convinced herself that no news was good news. She held the phone in her hand wishing for what she knew to be a distant dream of them getting married and living happily ever after as the phone sang in her ear.

Deep down in her gut, though, she knew that Chance had no good intentions toward her but still she reasoned that regardless of her suspicions about him, he was the only person that made her feel alive, and she wasn't quite ready to give that up just yet!

On the fifth ring a perky-sounding young woman answered his phone.

"Helloooooooo."

"Uhhhhhh, can I speak to Chance?" she eked out, somewhat caught off guard.

"Who is calling?"

"Is he available?" Bailey was now angry. *Who is this bitch?*

"He's busy right now," she giggled. "You want to leave a message for hiiiimmmm?" the young girl teased.

"What ya doin', girl? Come on back in here," Bailey heard Chance yell in the distance.

Bailey pressed END on her cell phone. Bastard! Dirty bastard! She knew exactly what he was doing! He was freaking with that young girl. She wanted to cry, but she was too numb to cry! Why did she always do this to herself? What was wrong with her that he was the first person that she always turned to when she needed someone? Why was she so unlovable? What was wrong with her?

Suddenly, the deafening quiet of the house was beginning to close in on her. The creaking settling of the mansion was becoming eerie. She had to get out of there. But where would she go? She never felt so alone in all of her life.

Because of Charlton and Chance, she was sitting on the ledge of desperation, and if she didn't get off of it right away... She would probably do something that she would most assuredly regret. Suddenly, the sweet sleep of death sounded enticing... so enticing...

Chapter Thirty-Two

~ Keno Hunter ~

Lockup held a pungent stench of depravity. It carried a heaviness that instantly replaced his excitement of reunion with melancholia. He would never be so bold as to say this out loud but he sure was glad that it was Jimmy in this wretched place instead of him. His childhood friend had been incarcerated at the Twin Towers Correctional Facility on Bauchet Street in Los Angeles awaiting his arraignment.

Keno eased his body into the seat and placed the beat-up phone against his ear which held a faint scent of bad breath.

"I'm sorry, man!" The words quickly darted from out of Keno's mouth as his contrite eyes sought contact the moment his buddy sat down and placed the corresponding phone to his ear. The glass-meshed partitions made them painfully aware that their conversation was not at all private.

"At least I'm alive!" Jimmy managed a smile.

"I don't know what to say. I am just so sorry for everything. But I'm going to get you out of here as soon as possible."

"With what? You ain't got no money for my bail!" Jimmy joked.

"I don't, but Sharon's got a lawyer who has a grip of connections. We found out that you are going to court in less than 2 weeks. The lawyer is making a motion to do it sooner. Hopefully, by this time next week, you will be out of this hell hole."

"Are you fuckin' kiddin' me?" Jimmy sat up with excitement sparkling in his eyes.

"Real talk! Real talk!"

"Is Sharon that old broad you've been banging?" Jimmy asked.

"You ain't got to say it like that! She's in my camp! Real cool people!" Keno defended.

"Aw, it's like that! You got a thang for her now?"

"Look, man, all I'm saying is that she is cool people! Nothing more or nothing less!"

"It's all good then! I'm just glad that you are connected up like that! Anything to get my ass out of this fucking hell hole!" Jimmy's face held colors of hope.

"Hey, man, one more thing, you know that I fucked up. I wasn't thinkin'. I just panicked and—"

"Hold up, man. You forget Five-O got ears!" Jimmy looked around.

"That shit ain't even necessary. You my boy! I know what's up!"

Keno smiled with relief. He was satisfied that his friend was not angry for leaving him behind, leaving him to take the blame for the botched robbery. Jimmy was a true friend, and he would make sure that he did all that he could to get him out as soon as possible.

Jimmy mouthed the words, "Car. Radiator?"

Keno shrugged his shoulders. "Don't know," he mouthed back.

"Fuck!" Jimmy mouthed a response.

Keno had thought many a night about what had happened to the jewels in that radiator. The car had to be impounded and subsequently taken back to Rent-A-Wreck. But the risk of getting caught just to find out what happened to the jewels in the radiator was not one that he was willing to take. According to Jimmy's lawyer, they just charged him with evasion, not robbery!

So it appears that they never found the jewels, nor was he a suspect in the robbery. He also never ID'd Keno as the passenger that fled the scene.

"So what's going on out there in that big beautiful world?" Jimmy held a forced smile.

Disappointment coated Keno's face. "Dee Dee left me!"

"Say what?"

"She found out about Sharon, and she left," Keno confessed.

"Wow, man, that is some serious shit. Dee Dee was some kind of special! Hard to find women like her!" Jimmy exclaimed.

"Don't remind me!" He cleared his throat, trying to keep the tremble out of his voice.

"I can't get her on the phone at all! She won't return any of my calls or answer the door at her house. I've sent her flowers, candy, cards, teddy bears, sang her songs, begged forgiveness, and have left her so many messages on her phone that her voice mail is full."

"Fuck, that is some deep shit! She really don't wanna talk to your ass, does she?" Jimmy commented.

"I know I fucked up, Jimmy, but I was trying to get paid. A brother just can't catch a break! I really got myself in a hell of a fucked-up situation. But if it wasn't for Sharon I don't know what I would have done. She has pulled my ass out of the fire more times than I can count."

"I feel you, man! It's hard out there for a brotha!"

"But I feel like shit! I had a good woman and look at what I done gone and did! I don't know what to do now. I haven't been able to talk to her. How do I fix things with her?" Keno asked.

"I think Dee Dee is a sweet girl and all, and she loved your crazy ass for sure! I saw it in her eyes when she looked at you. I never told you this, but I used to be so jealous because you had a woman who loved you like that. The bitches that I laid up with was nothing like her. They was true sluts! I know that there are more women out there like Dee Dee but what the fuck, I never ran into any of them! I don't know how you gonna fix this shit, but that Dee Dee is one of the keepers!"

"Is that shit supposed to make me feel better?" Keno snapped.

"What I am trying to say is this! Ex-cons got it hard! We don't have many options! Our prison record is like a scarlet letter around our fucking neck! People realize that we done did some shit in the past and it's like we got the plague. The system is set up for us to end right back in this fuckin' place. Cons like us . . . our choices are fuckin' limited!" He leaned in closer to the partition in a gesture of sincerity.

"I understand that you love Dee Dee and all. She really is a good, decent woman. I wish you could have the happily-ever-after shit. Hell, in another time and place, you two could have had a couple of kids, a three-bedroom house, and two fly cars in the garage. But that ain't the real! The real is that you is an ex-con, and nobody is gonna give you a chance. Other than her love, a good meal, and a couple bucks for gas, Dee Dee can't help where it counts! You need somebody like this Sharon chick! She is gripped up with paper and likes your ass! If you play it right, you can catch the break that you need to get your ass out of this fuckin' bottomless pit; so in my opinion, just stay with the old broad!" Jimmy advised.

"That's the last thing that I would have expected you to say!" Keno stated with surprise in his voice.

"Why?" Jimmy asked.

"'Cause you all for love and shit. You a crazy-ass romantic! So it looks like you are telling me to stay with Sharon, is *that* what you're saying?" Keno clarified.

"Keno, I would give everything I have, which isn't much, but I would still give everything I had for a woman like Dee Dee. It's women like her that makes us better men. If I had a good woman by my side like her, I wouldn't be in this fuckin' place. I wouldn't be alone trying to raise my daughter to be a good woman! I guess you did what you had to do, but if it was me, I would have done all I could to keep a woman like Dee Dee by my side!"

Keno remained silent, mulling over his friend's advice.

"Fuck what I think, that is some ramblings of a man locked up in this fuckin' hell. Forget what I said. Look, I know that you love this girl, and it must hurt somethin' awful, but you got a chance to put some real shit together with the help of this old chick! Do it, and when you finally get something crackin' in your life, go back and try to get her back!"

"What if she is with somebody else by then?" Keno queried.

"That girl is really in love with you, and besides, from what you told me, she's not the kind of girl who bed-hops. How long did it take her to get with you after her last boyfriend?"

"Almost 3 years! And it took me over 6 months just to get a date!"

"See what I tell ya? She'll be there! In the meantime, just hook up with this old broad and stack your chips. Let her help you build some kind of business or something! You got a fuckin' good head on your shoulders. Put it to work and make some shit happen! Trust me, if I had myself an old rich broad in my life that was digging on me, you best believe I wouldn't be in here now!" Jimmy joked to ease the tension.

Jimmy's words replayed over and over in Keno's head as he drove back to Culver City. He truly missed Dee Dee, but he had to admit Jimmy had a point, and right now, all he needed to be concerned about was repositioning himself for success, and Sharon was just the person to help him do it.

She had been insisting that he move into her Wilshire penthouse condominium. He decided on his drive home from his visit with Jimmy that he would pack up his shit and move in with her right away. After all, the major reason why he didn't do it before was Dee Dee. And now that she was no longer in the picture, he could move forward without trepidation!

A business, huh?! He thought about what Jimmy said about starting a business.

Keno would have to put some thought to what his friend suggested. What type of business would he start? In the past, he tossed around the idea of owning his own business… but what indeed?

On second thought, the truth was that if he was really honest with himself, he would admit that he was desperately afraid of failure. Fear basically controlled him; it kept him living in his current desperate situation.

The raw truth that he would never speak out loud but intimately knew within his soul was that he didn't have enough confidence in his own ability to do anything outside of manipulating women to keep him awarded with that safety net to live and pay his bills.

The thought of owning his own business was nice in theory, but the truth was that he would never start his own business because he didn't believe in himself enough for that!

How ironic, he thought. Here he was selling a bill of goods to women that he himself didn't have confidence in! Yes, it looked good on paper, but the truth of the matter was, he didn't have the guts to stand on his own and start his own business. He was afraid. He was very afraid.

Chapter Thirty-Three

❦ *Bailey Levine* ❦

I don't think that I have the guts to actually kill myself, but I have these thoughts . . . strong thoughts of just going to sleep and never ever waking up again!

Bailey was still in her depressed funk. She had assessed that she was too much of a coward to end her life and too much of a coward to stand up for herself. So she just maneuvered throughout the days in a perpetual mediocre stage of existence. Today, she had left work at about six in the evening, which was abnormally early for her. Her intentions were to go do some therapy shopping, but when she hit the entrance to the Westside Pavilion, the mood left her so she decided to go home to her cocoon of comfort.

Bailey sat on her oversized couch drinking wine and languishingly searching through the channels of her 80-inch wall-mounted plasma, desperately looking for something that would relieve her of the intense loneliness that consumed her.

"*Will & Grace*. Nope. *Grey's Anatomy*. I've seen it. Some girly movie on Lifetime. Nope. *America's Next Top Model*. Nope. *Cosby Show*. Seen it. *Housewives of Atlanta*? *Everybody Loves Raymond*?" on and on. She flicked and dismissed each program.

After a long, slow-moving hour, she switched it off and turned on her Bose radio. The first song that dropped from the changer was a Prince song, "Darling Nikki." That was the song that Chance would play for her when that prurient spirit visited him. It didn't make sense, but when she heard the song, instantly, a desperate aching surged her heart, making it painfully obvious of his absence. She had an intense longing to hear his voice, be in his presence, feel his skin, and occupy his space, that space that enraptured her.

Stop it! Stop it! You can't do this to yourself now! Think about something else!

In efforts to uplift her mood, she put on one of Beyoncé's albums, *I Am*, and started dancing around the room. Unfortunately, as time proved, that didn't work either. Her mind kept drifting back to Chance's wide smile, the sexy dimple in his right cheek, and the smooth baritone voice.

The third glass of wine was beginning to loosen the reins she had placed on herself in reference to Chance. She began to delude herself with fantasies about their relationship. Everything that she wanted him to be was now a reality in her daydreams. He was attentive, loving, and cherished her. They were married and had two kids. She envisioned the four of them on Sunday, her cooking breakfast, him reading the Sunday paper, and the kids playing with their toys by the fireplace. It was a sweet dream, or could it maybe one day become a reality? Chance did love her—right? He cared for her—right? After all, he did tell her that he loved her many times—right? She longed for him now; maybe they could have the happy-ever-after, after all—right?

Desperately wanting to feel the thickness of his arms around her and the smoothness of his mocha skin, Bailey felt the veil of restraint quickly fall off.

And so the birth of the phone call that would send her spiraling back into her addiction: Chance.

Her finger quivered as she dialed his number.

He answered on the second ring, and the sound in his voice convinced her that he was feeling as nostalgic as she. At least that is what she told herself.

It had been weeks since she'd seen the private detective and still no word from him. Again, she convinced herself that no news was good news.

"Hello, beautiful. I was just thinking about you. I miss you!"
She rested in the sound of his words.

"I miss you too, Chance." Her words carried an intense longing.

"What are you doing, babe? I wanna see you! Can you make some time for me?"

"Why don't you come over to my place?"

"I'm house-sitting for a buddy of mine. Come over here. Daddy sure misses you!"

Bailey didn't remember the ride over to the address he had given some 22 miles south of her home because her heart was filled with anticipation for what was to come when she fell into his arms. She was happy again. She was hopeful again. She was on her way to see the only person in the world who made her *feel*.

The effect of his half-naked body and warm smile onsite as he eased opened the door caused her to give in to him fully. It was no longer important where he had been, nor why he hadn't called her in weeks, nor who that young girl was who answered his phone. No, it didn't matter anymore. The only thing that mattered was him, right there, right now!

She threw herself onto him and kissed him without reservation. His hands revisited her body with familiarity as Bailey got lost into the fantasy of old times, good times, better times to come. She lost herself within the *feeling* . . .

Snatching her up on impulse, Chance carried Bailey into the bedroom which housed an entirely too large sleigh bed for the room. In her peripheral she caught sight of things that had a feminine energy to them: candles, jewelry boxes, and pink-colored walls. Instead of the obvious, she chose to concentrate on how good Chance was making her feel as the smell of strong incense floated through the air, carrying with it a romantic allure.

Bailey breathed in happiness and breathed out distrust.

"Oh, Chance, I missed you so much!"

"I missed you too! Come here, girl, and let me show you how much."

She stroked his toned abs and wondered how a man could have such flawlessly clear skin. It was obvious that this man took really good care of his body, for he was well groomed.

She tried to kiss his chest, but he waved her away and commenced to make love to her with tenderness that was not commonplace. As he generously sucked and kissed her pulsating body, she expelled all reservations that she had about him.

Just maybe he had changed. Just maybe the old Chance was replaced by the Chance she had hope for all these years. His touch was gentle, it was soothing, and at the same time, it was passionate and satisfying.

For once she didn't have that nagging suspicion that he was going to introduce the involvement of other participants. It was just the two of them, what she had wanted all along!

And as Whitney Houston made reference to it in the *Waiting to Exhale* movie, she exhaled and succumbed to Chance fully!

"Damn, baby, your pussy tastes like honey! Scoot down here near the end of the bed so that I can really get at it!" he encouraged.

He had never spent so much time pleasing her orally ever before. Bailey quickly obliged.

"Ooooooooh yeah! How pretty and pink it is inside! Hold on, let me look at it!" His finger probed, pulling it open and carefully exploring it with his tongue. This was a technique that she had never experienced from him ever before. She really enjoyed it!

"Chance, what are you doing? That feels so good! Oh my . . ." She tried to pull her head up to see what he was doing.

"Lie back, baby; I just want to taste your beautiful pussy! I never took the time to enjoy it before." He tilted his head to the side and started to lick the other side.

Bailey couldn't believe that he was taking so much time to please her. Whatever had gotten into him was wonderful. Maybe now they could have the relationship that she always wanted, get married, have some kids, and finally be a real family!

Oh my goodness, he was hitting her spot! His tongue held on to her clit as she went buck wild, trying to get loose from the grip and hold on to the sensation all at the same time; the intensity bordered pain. Just when she thought she couldn't take it anymore, the explosion happened. The orgasm was so huge that she actually squirted liquid from her vagina into his awaiting mouth.

Lost in ecstasy, Bailey forgot about all of her suspicions regarding Chance. She totally surrendered to the feeling; it felt so damn good! She had wanted this all along!

"Oh, Chance, that was incredible!" She sat up, moved next to him, and started kissing the back of his neck.

"Okay, babe, I am not done with you yet. Come here!" Chance pulled her down to the edge of the bed again.

He scooted her near the edge facing the window and stuck his fully erect penis into her mouth.

"Suck it up! You know how you like to suck it up!" Chance vigorously gyrated his hips in a counterclockwise motion.

She followed his rhythm.

"Swallow it up! Come on, swallow it all up! I want to feel the back of your throat!" He thrust his penis in so far and rapidly into her throat that she began to gag.

"Hold up! You know that you are my dick sucker! Come on, do what you do best!"

That tone in his voice was familiar to her. Why was he talking to her like that again? Was he going back to his old habits? Bailey's body tightened up with reluctance.

"Oh, I see, you want some dick in you now!" he barked.

Chance flipped her over, and in the same movement, plunged his penis into her vagina.

She gasped at the discomfort.

"Awwww, shit, that's what you wanted all along, huh? Isn't that what you came over here for? You missed this dick, didn't you? I bet you go to bed every night thinking about this big dong, don't you?"

She increasingly became more disgusted at each stroke.

"Come on, Chance. You're hurting me! Stop! I don't want to do this anymore!"

"Stop, my ass! You and I both know that you miss this dick. And I'm going to give it all to you, every fucking inch of it!" Chance pounded and pounded, ignoring Bailey's pleas until he ejaculated a half hour later. She remembered turning her body off to the deleterious banging and penetrating jabs into her vagina. She didn't want to *feel* . . . She didn't want to *feel* anymore . . .

"That was helluva good!" He got up off the bed and went into the bathroom, oblivious to Bailey's sobs.

Bailey curled up into a fetal position at the head of the bed; her face salty from the tears, and her vagina sore from the injurious punishment.

Chance reentered the room, walked over to the television, picked up the remote control, giving no notice of Bailey whatsoever, and clicked it on.

After about 10 minutes, it was as though he suddenly remembered that there was someone else in the room with him.

"Hey, Bailey, can you get me something to drink?" he threw from over his shoulder.

After he didn't hear a response, he turned around to face her. "What's up with you?" he asked in a perfunctory tone.

"*What's the matter?* Are you fucking kidding me? You hurt me, Chance!" Bailey cried out.

"For real? I didn't know that you wasn't feelin' it!" His tone was cavalier.

Bailey cried.

Chance moved down to the side of the bed she was on and stroked her foot, an unctuous effort to appear concerned.

"Bailey, you have a pussy that makes a man lose his damn mind. Don't be mad! Okay?" He smiled at her, blowing her a kiss.

"It's your fault, babe. That pussy made me go nuts! Don't be mad." He kissed her fully on the lips. "Didn't you like how I made love to you earlier? I got caught up . . . that's all . . . don't be mad, babe . . . 'K?"

She relented and once again fell into his intoxicating spell; the addiction that caused her to lose all reason. Chance and those damn feelings.

"I love you, Chance! I just want us to be like it was before! Back in the day when we seemed so perfect for each other, you know, before the others, before the men, before the . . . the . . . issues!" she pleaded.

"Like before? Why can't it be better, babe?" He smiled his signature smile.

While stroking her foot, Bailey forgave Chance and fell into her delusions of love once again, the love that she never ever received from him but only dreamt about.

He got in bed with her. They spooned and within minutes fell asleep within each other's arms. Slightly before dawn, the alarm clock alerted them of a new day.

"Good morning, baby!" Bailey purred, as she kissed him passionately, ignoring his tart morning breath.

"What's up? You sure slept good! You called in so many hogs, you woke a brotha up several times!"

She giggled.

"Sorry! I haven't slept that good in a long time. I sleep really good next to you, Chance."

"Well, glad a brotha could help a sista out! Now, do you think that you can make me some breakfast? I would love some grits, eggs, bacon, and pancakes right about now!"

"Whatever you want, baby!" she sang. Pulling on his T-shirt, Bailey sauntered into the kitchen to start cooking the man she loved breakfast. She looked about the kitchen to get the necessary items to cook but noticed that the place held an obvious feminine flavor to it.

Noticing a magazine on the kitchen table, she picked it up to see it addressed to La Tasha Johnson. Oh no, he didn't! This was the home of some other woman. Bailey started to see red. The anger burned in her gut as her eyes continued to survey the rest of the place. Matching dishes, color-coordinated placement sets, and light blue curtains. It was clearly a woman's place.

Before she could storm off into the bedroom with an accusatory colloquy, she heard a familiar sound coming from the bedroom. It sounded like her! There is was again . . . She was screaming!

Bailey quickly raced into the bedroom.

Chance was sitting on the edge of bed masturbating.

"What the hell is that?" she hollered.

"That's us, baby!" He held his penis in his hand, moving it up and down in a fast rhythm.

"You *taped* us?" Bailey yelled in disbelief. "I can't believe you taped us!"

"Hold up, girl . . . hold up! . . . let me . . . .get . . . get . . . my...!" His hand moved at a rapid pace until he spilled forth his ejaculation.

"Damn, baby, that was the shit! You want to see?" He devilishly grinned up at her.

"Are you out of your fucking mind?" Bailey raced over to the television and pulled out the videotape.

"I never told you that you could tape me! You fucking sick bastard!" Bailey started pulling on her clothes.

"I should have known that you were still the same, sick, perverted bastard that you always were!" She bent down to look under the bed for her shoes. "Fucking pervert!"

"Pervert?" He laughed out loud. "You call *me* a pervert? What the fuck are you then?"

". . . a stupid bitch for believing that you were more than a sick, perverted bastard!"

"Fuck you too!" he retorted.

Bailey searched the house for the rest of her belongings, her purse, coat, and cell phone.

"I can't believe that you brought me to another woman's house. You are pure evil! How could you do this to me? What kind of a monster are you?"

"Look, bitch, *you* are the one who called *me*. You know what the game is! It has always been the same; ain't shit about us changed but the day!" Chance commented.

"I hate you! I fucking hate you! I'm sorry I ever met you!" Bailey cried.

"You hate me? Look, Bailey, you knew what I was about! I have never lied about who I was! You don't hate me; you hate yourself because you couldn't change me! Don't hate the player, hate the game!"

Bailey opened her mouth to respond, but on second thought, decided it would be in vain to comment to this lunatic, perverted asshole. Chance was never going to change. She finally realized that she was the one who desperately needed to change.

She grabbed her belongings and the tape, raced out the front door, and vowed to never return again—never to return to her addiction—Chance!

Chapter Thirty-Four

~ Andy Reynolds ~

"Women!" he grunted as his mind drifted to thoughts of his mother, his so-called baby's mom, his sisters, and his girlfriend. Women were always talking about how dirty and low-down men were, but in reality, they were just as wild, if not wilder, than men. Hell, women were cheaters just like men, except they were just clever with the shit! He saw his mother manipulating men to give her money, buy her clothes, and pay her bills without an ounce of feeling toward the man other than an income source. His sisters just used men as a way out of their indigent lifestyle. His baby's mama . . . well, that bitch just wanted a free ride through life and figured that she had found a sucker chump in him, and as for his girlfriend, Rockye . . . that bitch was just a slut; plain and simple!

Andy's arms felt shaky and tight as he increased the weight on the bench press machine by an extra 50 pounds. The burn in his arms pushed his body temperature up a few more degrees as the intensity of his workout always heightened when he was pissed off. And at that moment, he was extremely pissed off.

As he ended his eighth rep on the bench press he suddenly felt a familiar presence looming above him.

"Hey, buddy!" Campo, his childhood friend said, standing above him sporting a half-moon grin.

"Camp, I didn't think that you were gonna make it," Andy eked out as he let the bar slide down into its resting position.

"I know, man, work has been kickin' my butt!" Campo commented as he eased down on the bench next to Andy.

Holding a 75-pound weight in his right hand, he lifted it in an easy up-and-down motion.

"We got this big contract from Northrop. They are upgrading their network, so my butt got tons of work. I'm working double time, and it's kicking my ass."

Andy searched his buddy's face. "Yeah, man, you do look kinda wiped out!"

"I haven't been getting enough sleep! I don't see how people function with so little sleep."

"You up to working out?" Andy asked.

"Need to, man! I ain't got a choice! Can't have my body lookin' tore up!"

Campo turned to fully face Andy. "You look kinda messed up yourself with them suitcases under your eyes. What's up with you?" he asked.

"All bitches are evil! All they do is fuck around on you, finding every opportunity to squeeze every bit of life out of you. All women are sneaky! I will *never* trust another woman again!"

"Damn, man, where did all that come from?"

"I'm just tired of all the drama in dealing with females . . . That shit drives a man to constantly be looking for a drink!"

"Come on, dude, I know that you have been hurt before, but being hurt is just a part of love. You need to stop blaming your mom and every woman that you've been with in the past and just deal with the issues in your current relationship. You just wilding out right now!"

"Maybe so, but all I see is their devious, lying-ass activities. It's crazy how they are so damn scheming!"

"Dude, get serious! Put ya' damn pride aside and examine your own shit because you are not totally blameless here. I mean, I have trust issues too, but I won't say that based on my past bad relationships that I will never fully trust another woman . . .

ever again. Stop blaming all women based on a few. What's up is that men and women are so different. If you just think about it, it's a wonder why we even get along because we see things so differently!"

"What's that got to do with cheating, manipulative, and lying bitches?"

"Look, man, men and women react to things so differently. For example, a woman who has seen her mother struggle all her life to put food on the table will react differently to men compared to women who had a loving, supportive father in the house. How she interacts with men is based on how she perceived things earlier in her formative years."

"What the fuck is that supposed to mean?"

"Here, let me break it down for you this way. The reason men and women react differently is simple. Ask a boxer, what punch can you recover from faster? The one you are looking for, or the one you never saw coming? Simply put, women, in the back of their minds, always believe men will be men; they will always be chasing skirts, and inevitably end up cheating. But men, on the other hand, never think that a woman is out there doing her thing, you know, giving up some tail to get a bill paid or even just to get the attention that she wasn't getting at home, for that matter. It's all perspective, and every situation is different. Just don't lump everything together and judge all women based on the ones in your past."

Andy realized that he did make some sense, but he wasn't ready to acquiesce to the point just yet. He moved back over to the free weights.

"So what started all of this? Where did all of this come from?"

"Got problems with my girl!" Andy confessed.

Campo switched the free weight to his left hand. "What kind of problems?"

"We were talking the other day in bed, and I told her that I wanted to have some kids with her!"

"You *what*? Are you kiddin' me?" Campo responded.

"We were just lying around in bed one morning, and I was feelin' her and things just seemed right! She looked so beautiful and like somethin' out of the movie…I just got this feeling and the next thing I knew, the words just popped out of my mouth: *'I want to have a baby with you!'*"

"What did she say?"

"It didn't go the way that I thought." Andy moved over to the butterfly machine.

Campo followed behind him, seating himself on the leg press machine to his left.

"She started talking about getting married and shit! Camp, I ain't ready for no marriage. She got all bent out of shape and said that because I was white and she was black, that I only want to fuck her but not marry her. You should have heard her! She went so far as to call me a 'Mr. Charlie.' It was whack!"

"How the hell are you gonna ask a woman to have your kids and not know that she wouldn't bring up marriage?"

"Wasn't thinkin'!"

"You sure the hell wasn't! Have you told her about Marcella and your daughter?"

"Hell no! That bitch doesn't exist to me!" Andy said.

Campo cringed at the comment. Andy knew that his friend found his views on his baby's mama and so-called child agitating.

"What about your daughter? She doesn't exist either?" Campo said with cutting sarcasm.

"Look, Camp, I told that bitch that I didn't want to have any kids with her. She decided that she was going to have a baby when I told her that I didn't want any with her. She made that decision on her own, so she can raise that little bitch all by her damn self," Andy said with contempt.

"You don't think about your daughter? You don't miss her? After all, she is your own flesh and blood! You mean to tell me that you can just walk away like that and not look back?" Campo asked. Being left by his father when he was born, Campo had a huge resentment for men who walked away from their children. That's why he never had children and still lived at home with his mother.

"I don't really know 100 percent if she is not mine but I do send money every month for the kid!" Andy paused before pushing through a couple of additional reps.

"I just don't understand why you don't just go get tested and find out for sure."

Andy remained quiet. He knew why he never took a paternity test. It was because on the off chance that it was his, he didn't want to have to carry the burden of guilt around about how he treated the little girl thus far. It was by far easier to stay in denial, hoping that by paying Marcella money every month, it would award her the freedom to live her life and leave him the hell alone. His contempt for her outweighed the thoughts of having a relationship with the child.

"Marcella is trash, and I don't want anything to do with her!" he concluded his thought.

"You wasn't saying that when you had your dick deep inside her all those months. She wasn't a trash then, was she?"

"Look, man, what the fuck is your problem? That is *my* shit! Why you makin' it yours?"

"Because I feel sorry for the kid! She doesn't deserve to be treated like that by her own damn father!"

"Look, I told that bitch when she got pregnant to go have an abortion! She decided to have it all on her own. She told me that it was her damn body, and that she would do with it what she wanted. She told me that she always wanted a baby and that she was going to have it whether I liked it or not!" Andy moved over to the treadmill.

Campo followed in tow.

"When I found out that she was just a slut, at that point she became like the others . . . another piece of ass to me! Once I found that out, I was not going to invest anymore into that bitch. And besides, I don't want to be responsible for raising another whore in this fucked-up world!" Andy said, referring to his daughter.

"Hey, man, to this day you still don't know if she was lying to you!" Campo retorted, referring to a time when Marcella didn't come home one night when she was living with Andy.

"If a bitch stays out all night and doesn't come home, and she is not in jail or the hospital, then she is for sure fucking some other dude!"

"I remember how much you was into her back then. You wasn't calling her a slut then!"

"That was before I found out that she was a lying, cheating whore. But once I found out, fuck it! I was done! She was lucky I didn't put a bullet into her fucking head!"

"Not everybody is like your mother, Andy! You have to remember that!"

Andy bristled up.

"Hold up, Dre! You keep comparing all your women to your mom, and eventually they do something that resembles some shit your mom did, and then you go ape shit! You gotta get some fucking help. Go see somebody! We all got issues, Dre, but that shit you got resting on your heart is some serious shit. You need to get that shit in check!"

Andy remained silent, lips pressed together in defiance.

Moving into the stretching area, Andy and Campo positioned themselves on the floor adjacent to each other to do push-ups.

"So what you gonna do about your girl?" Campo referred to Rockye.

"I don't know!"

"Do you love her?"

"I love her ass like crazy, but I just don't trust her! I know that she is out fucking around on me!"

"You don't know that for sure. You have never caught her, have you?"

"No, I haven't but—"

"But nothing. If she makes you happy, then stay! If you are so damn unhappy, then leave her."

"I can't leave her!"

"Why?"

"I fucking love her, that's why!" Andy defended.

"Whatever, man!" Campo conceded. "Stay—leave—whatever! But whatever you do, just don't bring another baby into the situation until you know exactly what you want! That shit ain't fair to the kid!"

"Who says life is fair, Camp? Who says life is fair?" Andy concluded as he rolled over on his back to begin his 200 sit-ups.

Chapter Thirty-Five

⁓ Rockye Haynes ⁓

Should she go to New York for the part of a lifetime that she had been preparing for all of her life or stay in Los Angeles with the man she loved? How would she tell Andy if she decided to leave? What was more important—love or career? Would she be insane for not putting love first? Wasn't she preparing for an opportunity like this all of her life? So why was she even second-guessing herself? Wasn't the answer obvious—go to New York for the opportunity of a lifetime, the lead in a Broadway play? Why was this decision so difficult for her to make?

Where the hell is Bailey anyway? Rockye desperately needed a voice of reason! She'd been calling her best friend's cell for the past 2 hours. No answer. And at the present moment she needed someone who could make sense out of the myriad of questions going through her mind that demanded urgent answers.

She finally broke down and called her office. Bailey didn't like to be called at work, but, hell, this was an emergency!

Damn! She was in a meeting till late afternoon. Bailey worked too damn much! Fuck! What the hell was she going to do? She couldn't decide this kind of thing all by herself! And waiting until next week to discuss it in group would make her go insane. She needed someone to talk to right away! But who? She had no one! Her mother was dead, her best friend was unavailable in some damn meeting, and Andy was out of the question because he was the main source of her bone of contention.

"Fuck, what am I going to do now?" She felt like she was going to implode.

Whenever Rockye was in a quandary, she went running to get clarity. It was a beautiful Thursday late morning and a few hours ago she had just completed an invigorating Pilate's class. Running is what she needed so as not to go lose her damn mind.

It was an unusually warm fall morning, and the trail at Balboa Park was full of the normal slightly overweight housewives, Rollerblading teenagers, and the typical joggers. She fell in tow behind a very short Hispanic woman pushing a double baby stroller.

The smell of fresh cut grass filled her nostrils as she strutted pass the adjacent golf course to her left. Slowing her pace to observe a young couple kissing passionately under a tree, Rockye decided to plant herself on a bench nestled in the southeast corner of the trail and watch young love in its purist form. It reminded her of how things were with her and Andy in the beginning of their relationship, which seemed like ages ago.

The events of the past week flooded her mind as she turned her focus to a pair of hummingbirds moving about in the tree above her.

Rockye's thoughts drifted to Cyrus's proposal, which, for all intents and purposes, was the opportunity of a lifetime that she had been preparing for all these years—the lead in a Broadway production that held the potential to run for years. She would get the fame that she had hungered for, and hopefully, a movie role, or maybe even a television show. The lack of money would no longer be an issue, and she could really start mastering her craft. This was a dream come true!

But then there was Andy, a man whom she genuinely loved with every fiber of her being. She had never known such love as she had with him. She felt complete happiness when they were in sync together. However, his unwillingness to commit to marriage made her question the very essence of their relationship.

And then there was *her* problem; she couldn't stay faithful if her life depended on it. Her body craved the taste, the feel, and the smell of other men; it craved orgasms.

She folded her legs in the lotus position on the bench, angling for a clearer view of the billowy white clouds slowly rolling by as though they were taking a leisurely afternoon stroll.

Rockye desperately wanted to make the right decision, and although it really came down to one of two directions—go to New York with Cyrus for her career, or stay in Los Angeles with Andy for her relationship—it would be a struggle to decide.

True love is really hard to come by; the type of love that completes you to your soul was rare, but on the other hand, she had been working her entire life for an opportunity like this one. And should she *really* pass up an opportunity of a lifetime for a man who didn't want to marry her? Rockye didn't know what to do, and she had hoped that a midmorning run in the park would provide her with the much-needed clarity to make the right decision.

Suddenly she felt an odd presence. Then, as though out of nowhere, an older, heavyset African American woman fashioning long gray hair and a loose-fitting dashiki appeared by her side and eased onto the bench beside her. Her face, while warm and inviting, held many deep caverns of wrinkles of experience, and her massive eyes carried wisdom and mysticism.

"You are troubled," the older woman commented, her head slightly bent in Rockye's direction.

"Excuse me?" Rockye asked, her brow wrinkled with curiosity.

"I have been walking around the track, and your spirit pulled me over to you!"

Rockye locked eyes and held her gaze.

"You have a big decision to make, do you not?" the woman asked.

"Yes, I do! But how did you—?"

"You are anointed to dance and sing! You are gifted to entertain. You are also a free spirit! But no earthly vessel can domesticate that spirit!" She paused and spoke in some strange language that Rockye thought she had heard in some Christian church she'd visited a few times.

"You have been judging yourself too harshly! Your shortcomings are what you do, they are not who you are! You are more than your shortcomings!" A serious look washed over the older woman's face.

"However, it is time for you to stop dwelling on these shortcoming. Concentrate on your future from now on!" She spoke in that weird language again.

"Don't look back anymore. Stop holding others responsible for all the things that went wrong in your life. You are right where you are supposed to be! You need to move forward today as a new creature and release your past! Forgive yourself for the things you've done, and then free your mind! Free your heart! Free your spirit! Free yourself to live the life you are here to live! Move on to your purpose. You have a purpose here in this earthly realm. You were born to accomplish that purpose. Your purpose is bigger than these minuscule issues you stress over now. Release it now! Let it go, and then you will know exactly what to do!"

The older woman turned to face the sky. "And so it is."

"Don't turn to the right or to the left! Move from your past and into your future! Move into your destiny!"

The older woman stood up to leave.

"Wait! Can you help me decide what to do? I need help!"

"You have all you need within you! The only source you need to make any and all decisions is within you! Call on that source! No one else! Ask no one else their opinion on what you should do, but consult that inner source within you, and you will get your answers!" The older woman started to walk off.

"Wait! Who are you? What's your name?" Rockye shouted behind her.

"I am but a messenger!" The woman turned to answer Rockye.

"Remember, do what is right and good. I caution you to turn from your old ways. For when you turn from destructive behavior, only then will you have clarity about the direction you need to take. It will be as clear as the blue in today's sky!"

"Thank you so much!" Rockye uttered.

"Just remember to do what is right and good! When the time is right, you will know the right way to go!" She spoke in that strange language again. At that moment a strange chill went through Rockye's body.

"I warn you though—stop the deception! What you are doing with those men you meet is foul; you must cease it immediately, because if you don't, you will pay a very high price!"

Rockye watched the older woman disappear into the distance, wanting to run after her and ask more questions. But she didn't for she already knew what to do next.

A strong gust of wind carried with it a sense of urgency to see Andy. His eyes seem to be looking at her through the leaves of the tree that she was sitting under.

Rockye's Movado displayed 4:15, and she knew that in a matter of 30 minutes, Andy would be walking in his front door from work.

She had no idea what she was going to say, but she had a strong sense of urgency in her heart to go to him; for now she believed in her heart that when she looked in his eyes she would know instantly if she should leave or stay.

Chapter Thirty-Six

～ Andy Reynolds ～

"Where the hell are you?" Andy said to himself as he drove northbound on Crenshaw on his way to his girlfriend's house early from work. Crossing Adams, he took an abrupt left turn. His mind kept imagining her having sex with that guy from her voice mail. What kind of name is "Black" away? Vivid, graphic images of Rockye bent down on all fours while some dark, bald-headed dude slammed his stiffened appendage rhythmically into her as she screamed his name following each orgasm flitted around in his head and tormented him.

Hitting the accelerator, increasing the speed to an unlawful 55 miles down a residential street, he continuously dialed her cell phone. Voice mail. Then her home number. Answering machine. Cell phone. Voice mail. Home phone. Answering machine. Cell phone. Voice mail.

Why was he so obsessed with the thought of her having sex with this man named Black? Was this "Black" a black man? Deep down, did she really want a black man bedding her over him, over a white man? He remembered the saying, *"the blacker the berry, the sweeter the juice."* Was he enough for her sexually? The thoughts chased his sanity. He dialed her numbers again.

Cell phone. Voice mail. Home phone. Answering machine. Cell phone. Voice mail. Home phone. Answering machine.

He started pounding the steering wheel at each stoplight. "Turn green! Hurry the fuck up and turn green!" He dialed her numbers again and again and again.

Cell phone. Voice mail. Home phone. Answering machine.

He had been calling her all day. When he awoke that morning and didn't find any messages from her on his cell, he was annoyed but not upset. It wasn't until after lunch, when his several placed voice messages were not returned that he began to get angry. In the last conversation he had with her yesterday afternoon, she indicated that she had her "group" that night and would later hang out with her friend Bailey for a while before going home. He expected a call from her before going to bed as she did most days, but as indicated by his cell that morning... nada!

About 3 p.m. he got so worked up that he had to leave work early! He couldn't concentrate for shit! All he could think about was what Rockye was doing, or better yet, who was she doing? He knew in his heart of hearts that she was stepping out on him, but for the life of him, he couldn't prove it. His gut told him to go over to her house. He believed that what he was looking for he would find if he left now and went to her house. At each mile and unanswered dial, he got increasingly enraged.

"Fucking cheating bitch! When I catch you, you won't be able to cheat with another motherfucker ever again!" The images he manufactured got more vivid with each mile.

In his mind's eye, he pictured this "Black" guy, a muscular man with a voracious appetite slow stroking his woman... first in and out, then side to side. She groaned as the length teased her G-spot, his fingers pinching her nipples and occasionally his massive hands spanking her on the butt leaving a sensuous tingle and a red hue. Her face glowed with satisfaction and craving as the intensity of his strokes quickened. Her screams encouraged him to alternate positions, moving to her favorite sixty-nine position which allowed him to taste her and her swallow him. The self-manufactured image drove him insane, and by the time he reached her house, he burned with rage.

Wheeling his Range Rover up the narrow driveway, he slammed the gear into park and propelled himself from the driver's seat. He hurriedly surveyed her backyard and noticed her car wasn't there. Neither was any other car. Locating the spare key up under the display frog near the back door, he glanced around before inserting in and pushing the door gently open.

It didn't appear that she was home, so he felt at ease to look around to see what he could find to prove his theory that she was cheating on him. He was determined to get some proof about who she was stepping out on him with . . . whether it was this "Black" . . . or someone else!

Once inside he caught sight of the disarray. Rockye was definitely not a woman who believed in keeping a clean house. It was messier and more cluttered than filthy, like his mother's house was when he was growing up. If she kept her ass at home more and not in the street so much, just maybe she could keep a decent house.

Her granite countertop, stainless steel kitchen smelled of leftovers too long in the refrigerator and soiled dishes in the sink needing to be loaded in an already-overcrowded dishwasher.

The bathroom's pedestal sink carried remnants of days of spit-out toothpaste. Her toilet bowl looked as though it hadn't seen a toilet brush in months. Andy shuddered at the thought that his mouth touched what sat on that disgusting toilet seat.

Before entering her bedroom, he made a silent bet to himself that the bed wasn't made. Right again! All of the covers were in a pile at the foot of the bed. Each chest of drawers was wide opened with clothes brimming and spilling out of them. On top of the dressers was everything from magazines, shoes, jewelry, towels, clothes, and dirty dishes.

Who taught this woman how to keep house? Or rather, who *didn't* teach her? Andy shook his head in disgust.

He made his way to the laundry room which housed piles of clothes on the floor as well as on top of the washer and dryer. He walked over to a pile of underwear. Picking up a black pair of thongs with his thumb and index finger he looked on the inside. It held a snail trail stain that resembled caked semen. He abruptly flicked it on the floor, and then kicked the pile of clothes next to him to the other side of the room in frustration.

"Funky bitch!"

The living and dining room, however, not cluttered, did carry with it several layers of dust.

He rounded off his search by ending up at the front foyer table where her answering machine was sitting. No blinking lights! No messages!

He searched through her desk for her day planner and found nothing that would give him any indication of where she was or who she was with.

He riffled through her desk and adjacent file cabinets; still nothing!

Eventually he sat down and rested on her oversized, mauve couch. All of this snooping around was wearing him to a frazzle. As his size 13s rested on the matching ottoman, Andy searched his mind for possible places she could be. As the many thoughts spun around in his head he began to feel fatigued and drifted off to sleep.

He sprang up some 15 minutes later with the words of his friend, Campo, echoing in his mind.

"*Not everybody is like your mother, Andy! You have to remember that!*"

Could it be that he was presuming that the activities of his mother would transcend that relationship to every other relationship he would have with women? Was he really projecting his feelings of his mother onto his girlfriend?

Rockye wasn't all bad! Although most times she seemed self absorbed, at times she did show evidence of a compassionate heart. Andy's mind shifted from his thoughts of distrust and betrayal to a time early in their relationship where Rockye exhibited bounteous behavior to a homeless woman on the streets.

One chilly November evening, he was riding with Rockye to pick up some vegetables from the Valley Produce Market on Vanowen Street in the San Fernando Valley.

While cruising down the street, Rockye abruptly merged from lane 2 to lane 1 on Reseda Blvd. and pulled up on a sidewalk near a bus stop.

"What the hell are you doing?" Andy squeaked as he pulled himself off of the dashboard from the abrupt halt.

"Sorry, baby. Are you okay?" she asked, although her attention was diverted to a homeless woman slouched over at the bus stop.

"I guess, but what the hell—"

She didn't hear him for she had already jumped out of the car and was talking to the homeless lady. It all happened so fast. For in a matter of seconds, he saw his girlfriend reach down and remove her brown, fur-lined UGG boots and put them on the feet of the homeless woman. Next, she jetted back to her car and removed a blanket, her jacket, and a few bottles of water that she kept for emergencies, handing them to the woman, as well. Before leaving, she held the woman's hands and looked as though she prayed for her. Taking long strides back over to the passenger-side door she asked,

"Honey, you got a few bucks? I don't have any cash. I'll give it back to you later."

She took the forty bucks from Andy and handed it to the woman. Andy watched Rockye do something that he didn't even realize that she had the capacity to do; a random, unselfish act of kindness! It was at that moment, observing such compassion for another human being, that he discovered that he was in love with her. It was at *that moment, he believed she took possession of his heart. He never shared that revelation with her, but it was the turning point in their relationship. Not long after that incident he asked Rockye to be his girl and their relationship took on a new handle.*

As his mind meditated on that incident, his heart softened. Why did he always think the worst of her? She had done so many things for him over the years; loving and kind things. Every time he needed anything, she was there! She was his best friend, his confidante, his companion, and despite whatever bad times they were going through, if he picked up the telephone and needed her, she was always there! Wasn't that the most important thing? Isn't loyalty and devotion the most important thing? Was he expecting too much? Had he really labeled her in the same caliber as his mother?

The musical tone of his cell phone aroused him from his own verbal inquisition into the present.

He recognized the ring tone. It was Rockye.

"Hello!" His voice was deep and broody.

"Hi, babee! Where are you?" Her voice was sweet and sensuous.

"Taking care of a few things. Where are you?" he diverted.

"I have been sitting in your parking garage for almost an hour waiting for you! I was trying to surprise you! You can't be at work, I called there!"

"You are at my *house*?" he beamed.

"Sure am! I went to Trader Joe's and got something special to cook you for dinner tonight! I was going to surprise you, but with my luck, the one night that I decide to surprise you, you don't come home right from work!" she teased.

"Where are you?" she repeated.

"I'm on my way home, sweetie!" He felt like such a fool for doubting her and rummaging through her house looking for evidence of infidelity.

"Why didn't you just let yourself in? You know where the key is!"

"I would never enter your house without your permission! I wouldn't want it done to me, so I would never do it to you!"

"Why? You got something to hide from your man?" he teased.

"Just dirty dishes, piled up laundry, and tons of vacuuming!" she confessed.

No shit! Andy thought to himself. *No shit!*

"Get the key and go on in. I'll be there in a sec," Andy instructed.

"Okay, baby! I'll see you soon!" Rockye blew him a kiss.

"Rockye?"

"Yes, babe?" she responded sweetly.

"I love you! You know that, don't you?" Andy asked.

"I love you, too, babee!"

"No. I really love you—"

"I know, honey, me too."

"Don't ever forget that! No matter what, okay?"

"Is everything okay?"

"Everything is fine. I just need you to know that you are the most important person in my life, and I never want you to ever feel like I don't love you!"

"I know you love me, honey, and I love you too. Now hurry home. I miss my babe!"

Andy glanced at his cell phone as the dial tone provided an annoying backdrop.

He desperately loved Rockye, and the thought of her being with another man took him to a high level of insanity. He didn't even want to contemplate what he would do if he ever caught her in the act. But why did he always think the worst of her? Why couldn't he just trust her?

Why was there this nagging voice inside of him always telling him that she's cheating? Why? Why? Why was all that echoed in his head, as he hit the accelerator propelling his Range Rover many miles past the legal speed limit to get to his apartment?

As he scurried home to meet up with his girlfriend, Andy decided that he was going to trust her. He decided to exhibit some faith in their relationship! It was high time that he believed in her, believed in them! Yes, he needed to trust his woman if he wanted to have any peace.

Chapter Thirty-Seven

～ The Circle ～

The door flew open. He had had enough, and today was the day to confront his partner.

Tyler had sat quiet for far too long, burning with frustration, anxious to challenge Jango about the unconventional techniques he exercised in the Tuesday group sessions.

"We have to talk!" Tyler announced.

"I'm about to start group. Can this wait?" Jango looked peeved.

"No, this can't! I have waited long enough."

Tyler always fashioned a heavy scowl on his face every time he was deeply disturbed. In the last few weeks his partner was using The Circle more and more as a pulpit for his religious beliefs. The sessions were now more often than not taking on the flavor of a church sermon instead of a psychotherapy group.

"Have you thought about what we talked about last time?" Tyler asked, anticipating a negative response.

"I know what I am doing!" Jango continued to assemble the room for the Tuesday session by placing the chairs in a circle and setting up the coffee canister.

With a sternness bordering reprimand, Tyler continued. "This is not a church, Jango! And you are not a preacher! People do not come to hear about Jesus! They come here to get help, psychological help! You have to understand that!"

"These people need Jesus in their lives!" Jango insisted.

Tyler took a long deep breath before continuing. "I understand that you love God, and that you feel you need to tell everybody about Him, but, Jango, this is not the place for that! Every one of these people has serious issues that need to be dealt with, and preaching about Jesus and telling them these—these stories is not the answer! They need real coping tools to learn how to deal with their lives. This is not a Bible study!"

"Jesus is the only answer!" Jango insisted.

"What has happened to you over these last few months? I know that you are proud of being a—a Christian, but it seems lately that you are becoming rather obsessed! What happened to you, Jango?" Tyler asked.

"What happened is that I see what Jesus has done for me in my life! I am a walking, talking example of what the Word of God can do in a person's life. I no longer want to provide a forum for complaints! That is not what I want to do anymore."

"So you do what instead? You decide to teach your religious theology? You have no real seminary training. What you are doing in my book is just plain dangerous, Jango!"

"My spirit tells me that I am doing the right thing!" Jango insisted.

"How do you know that this so-called spirit is from God? And not—"

"Wait just a minute—" He looked at his watch before continuing. "I don't have to explain myself to you! God is telling me to do it, and that's all there is to it!"

"Just in case you forgot, we are *partners,* and you can't just change what we have as our doctrine without my consent. We must reach a unanimous vote on any major changes. Remember?"

"I am led by the Holy Spirit, not you!" Jango bristled up.

"Look, Jango, you can't keep preaching! Just simply follow the protocol of the organization. Get back on track right now! This is not open for discussion! If you want to preach, then I suggest that you go get yourself a church and not make this business your pulpit for Sunday services."

Tyler turned to leave.

"I am going to do what the Spirit of God tells me, and that is all I have to say about it!"

"*Excuse me?*" Tyler turned abruptly to face him.

"Look, Tyler, I am going to do what I feel is right and that is all I have to say about it!"

"Oh, are you really? So is lusting after one of its members the right thing to do?"

Jango turned to leave.

"I'm serious, Jango! You will not be conducting the session's free style anymore. It is done in the outlined format or nothing!" Tyler demanded.

Jango glared at his partner to determine the severity of his demands. "Okay, then, if you feel that strongly about it, you can do it yourself! I'm outta here!"

Tyler stood in the middle of the room, not entirely surprised at his partner's response. Jango had not been himself lately, and the transformation had been eking upon him for some time now, which drove him to become increasingly defiant with Tyler; nonetheless, he waited in anticipation, hoping that Jango would turn around and come to his senses.

But he didn't! Jango kept walking! It wasn't until Tyler heard his car speed off from the back of the building that he realized Jango would not be coming back. He would have to lead the session tonight all by himself.

As The Tuesday afternoon group started filtering in, Tyler went back to his office, grabbed Jango's notes from the previous sessions, and quickly familiarized himself with them. He would navigate The Circle back to its original protocol and hope that it wasn't too late.

After everyone settled in, Tyler moved deliberately into the room, taking his place at the helm. The confused looks displayed on the faces of the group held the obvious question as to Jango's whereabouts.

"Good evening, everyone!" Tyler called out, forming a pleasant smile on his face.

"Hello, Tyler!" they answered back in unison.

"Jango had something unexpected come up, so he will not be here tonight! That is the bad news! But the good news is that you have me, and I guarantee that I will do my best to help facilitate a night of breakthroughs.

"First, I want to tell you something about me. I am drawn to rivers. I have swum, canoed, and floated lazily in an inner tube down many rivers all my life. I have sat hours along the bank of a river, thinking, dreaming, and planning my life. I liken life to a river. We don't have a choice of whether or not we are in this river. What we do have a choice about is whether we struggle against it, try to push it along or surrender to its current and go downstream.

"We have a choice to approach our life with joy, with playfulness, with power, and with love. We can fight the river or turn and flow with the current. I urge you to see that you have a choice in your lives. You can view yourself paddling in the river, struggling to keep your head above water, or you can choose to be the navigator of your own boat. Either way, you are on the water, experiencing both the gentle flow of the river and rough water, rocks, and storms. To be in the river, caught up in the current and in danger of drowning, is to be a victim. As a navigator in life, we take back our power and make choices regardless of what the river throws at us."

Tyler paused briefly before continuing. "This group's intent is to help you take back your power to navigate through your life, making the right choices, and to flow in life instead of fight—regardless of what life throws at you!"

They all clapped in unison. If he didn't know better, he would have sworn that they were happy at the changing of the guard.

Or was that his ego talking?

Looking around, Tyler noticed a new face.

"I see that we have a new face here tonight!" He nodded in the direction of an attractive brunette sitting next to Lynette, who displayed a generous smile across her face.

"Yes!" Lynette stood up. "This is my stepmother. I mean—this is Pam, and I thought she could benefit from our little group—so I talked her into coming to check us out!" Lynette uncharacteristically displayed a full smile.

Pam stood up. "I hope that you don't mind! Lynette told me so much about you all, I just knew that this was a place that I should be!"

Lynette's father, Howard Castle, divorced Lynette's mother, Rebecca, 5 years ago, after meeting his current, much-younger wife by 30 years, Pamela Lee Bruster, during a business trip. Months following his abrupt divorce, Rebecca committed suicide from an overdose of sleeping pills. Lynette's mother was never spoken of ever again after the funeral.

The once tenuous, polite relationship that Lynette and Pamela started out with went from an undercurrent of tolerance for her stepmother to one of mutual respect, appreciation, and love after they both discovered that they had so much in common. The more time they shared together, the more they discovered how much alike they really were, and in the process, they discovered a true friendship; a true sisterhood!

"Welcome, Pam! We are certainly glad that you are here." Tyler went up to Pam and shook her hand.

"Before we get started, why don't you tell us about yourself," Tyler instructed.

"Oh, okay! Well, I am Lynette's stepmom. Up until a few weeks ago, I lived a seemingly perfect life that held all the trappings of success. A big house, expensive cars, designer clothes, and so forth. But it was all a lie! My husband didn't really love me, and he ended up cheating on me and kicking me out of the house on my ass with nothing!"

"Damn, that's messed up!" Keno blurted.

"NO, it's okay! Because while I may have lost the big house, designer clothes, the expensive car, and whatnot—what I gained was a wonderful new friend in Lynette and an introduction to the real me! I am finally okay with me and not trapped in fear of not pleasing my husband's unrealistic demands. I'm on a journey to find my way to the real me. And that is why I am excited about being here!" Pam confessed before sitting back down.

Everyone welcomed Pam, and the camaraderie was uncharacteristically festive.

Once the group settled, Tyler announced his intentions for the session that evening.

"This evening we will be talking about relationships. A lot of us have grown up in families that lack the skills for solid, wholesome relationships. In order to change so that we can learn to get along with one another, we must learn these skills. Developing healthy, working relationships require honesty, humility, courtesy, confidentiality, and frequency. We must learn to lovingly speak the truth to one another, and until we do, we will live with an undercurrent of frustration. This environment of secrets is lethal to healthy relationships. Until we care enough to confront and resolve the underlying barriers, we will never develop true authentic relationships. My hope is that we will all feel free to speak from our hearts, and free our minds from what imprisons us, and realize that this is a safe environment of acceptance and trust. Here is where we should share our deepest hurts, needs, and mistakes, and know that our idiosyncrasies will not be rubbed in our faces but rubbed out."

He turned to Bailey, who looked preoccupied.

"Our lives are meant to be shared with one another. It's really about experiencing life together. Really being unselfish, honest, and truly loving and giving without expectation. It's not thinking less of yourself but thinking of yourself less! It's very sacrificial, you know?"

Tyler then turned to Rockye.

"Rockye, I understand that you have a big decision to make between your boyfriend and your career. Have you come to a conclusion yet?" he asked.

Rockye smiled a bright Colgate smile.

"I have decided that although my career is important to me . . . my relationship with Andy, and my friendships, are more important. I don't want to leave the people that I love. I have always wanted a close family, something I never had growing up. In deciding between my career and my loved ones, I started to think about what would be important to me if I only had a short period of time to live. No career, car, or material possessions would be able to comfort me. My man and the people I love would be the only thing that would do that! And besides, I really love Andy. I want to marry him, and have tons of kids with him!" Rockye confessed.

"So, you are just going to give up on what you worked so hard for all of your life for some man?" Bailey fumed.

"I know this may sound crazy! Believe me, I never thought that something like that would ever come out of my mouth. But I thought long and hard about it, and what is really important at the end of the day is that I have love in my life. Nothing is more important to me than that! Andy knows me, and he still loves me! And in the end, that is all that I really want!"

"So you think that your man really knows who the hell you really are?" Bailey spewed.

"Don't be so hard on her, Bailey!" Carlos remarked.

"It's a safe place here. Let her speak her mind!" Tyler chided.

"He has *no* clue as to who he is dealing with! If he did, he would leave your ass so fast, it wouldn't be funny! Tell him about all the other men, Rockye! Tell him about all of them and see what he does then!" Bailey spat.

"People change, Bailey! Why do you fucking care about it so much anyway? Mad at me 'cause I got a man? Is *that* it?" Rockye challenged.

"I could care less about him! All I'm saying is that you can't build your life around a man! They will disappoint you every time!" Bailey responded in a sober tone.

"I agree with Bailey!" Pam added. "That is the main reason why I am in the position that I am in now! I built my entire life around my husband and men like him! Why? Because I was too afraid to do anything on my own! I didn't feel confident enough in my own ability to trust myself to accomplish anything on my own! So what did I do? I depended on my body and my looks instead of my mind!"

"I think that people can change! Look at me. *I* am changing!" Keno admitted.

"Living with Sharon has every benefit that I could have ever wanted. I don't have to worry about anything. Financially, that is! Every bill is paid for by her accountant! The cook prepares food for me three times a day! My wallet is always full of money, and the best job ever was created for me! Anybody in their right mind would be happy!"

"You're not happy?" Tyler asked.

"Naw, because it is not where I want to be! I'm with a woman that I do not love!"

"Yeah, but you love her money!" Bailey remarked.

Keno eyed her but continued. "She cares a lot for me, but every day when I look into her eyes I feel awful because I know that I am not there because I love her but because of what she can do for me!"

"Have you considered leaving?" Tyler questioned.

"I have so many times, but I look at my alternatives, and then I just sit my ass back down on the couch and chill! I have changed because before I wouldn't even have cared a damn about what I was doing to Sharon. I do feel bad that I am using her, but I am nothing without her! Absolutely nothing!" he confessed.

"I used to think that I was nothing without my husband and his money, that was until I was put out on my own and realized that it was not as bad as I thought it would be! Sure, it's hard, but with determination and hard work I know you can make it on your own!" Pam explained.

"Miss Mary Poppins, there is a huge difference between the two of us! You are a lily-white woman, and I am a black man. A black man with a prison record! Nobody will hire me for shit or give me a fucking chance!" Keno defended his position.

Pam's expression of hope deflated at his confession.

"Nobody will hire a black man with a record! I read somewhere that it is so much easier for a dog in America than it is for a black man with a prison record!"

"So, what you are telling us is that this woman is your only hope for a good life?" Rockye asked.

"I would be a fool if I said that! So no, that is *not* what I am saying. What I *am* saying is that while I could push through the bullshit and make some kind of life for myself, it would only be a fraction of how good I have it now! And to be honest, I'm not willing to give it up to be what—pooooooor?" Keno defended.

"I used to feel that way, until my husband traded me in for a younger version of myself! I would still be existing in that world had he not thrown me out! I had all of those things that you are talking about, and more! But what I didn't have was dignity and self-respect. I always felt so empty inside!" Pam admitted.

"Yes, my husband gave me all of the material things that I could ever want or need, but what I didn't get was respect, consideration, and true companionship. He always made me feel insignificant! I always felt like he tolerated me, not really loved me."

"I feel the same way about my father! He makes me feel like there's always something wrong with me. All of my life I felt like there was something wrong with me because of his put-downs and criticisms!" Lynette added.

"And now?" Tyler encouraged.

"And now I understand why I felt that way! I was a victim of emotional and mental abuse. I internalized his comments and dismissive acts towards me as though it was my truth." Lynette sat up straighter, a secure smile on her face.

"My father is a sick man, and his sickness no longer has to be my sickness!" Lynette confessed.

"What Lynette and I discovered is that we can heal from this! What we did was try to hide our hurts, faults, fears, and flaws from ourselves by burying them through the shopping, plastic surgery, clothing, and makeup! But now we know that we can grow past those limitations we put on ourselves," Pam added.

"So what are you saying?" Carlos asked.

"I'm saying that we need to understand where a person is coming from. We need to learn about their history and what their perspectives on things are! When you know what they've been through, you can be more understanding. Instead of thinking about how far they still have to go, think about how far they have come—in spite of their hurts and challenges!" Pam confessed.

"Compassion—" Tyler interjected.

"Yeah, when you understand another's feelings as your own and are able to put yourself in their place, you will almost surely become more compassionate toward that person. I realized that my husband's father did the same thing to his mother that he was doing to me and Lynette. He took the cruel things he learned from his father and transferred them to us. I understand who he is because of what he experienced, and I decided to break the transmission of negative behavior because of what I learned as a result of putting myself in a place of understanding who he is and what made him who he is," Pam concluded.

Rockye interjected, "I have often thought that if my father was present in my life that I would not be searching for his approval in every man that I meet. I read a magazine once that said the reason some woman have multiple sex partners is because at each sexual experience they are seeking approval from the man that they are with! These men represent their absentee fathers, and the nurturing they never got and crave so badly! I dismissed it at the time, but now it makes perfect sense to me."

"You're right! It's not the sex act that you crave, but the interaction and anticipated approval from these men that you are yearning for. You are yearning for empathy. You have a deep need to be understood and to have your feelings validated. People are often in such a hurry to solve the problem that they don't have time to really understand what it is the other person is going through. Oftentimes, the mutual connection to the feeling is all that's required by the victim as validation! In your case, casual sex keeps you at a comfortable distance, which in your mind offers protections from pain, grief, disappointment, and abandonment. In Pam's husband's case, he protected himself by putting distance between them by picking fights and constantly criticizing," Tyler added.

"Lynette, your father may have been there physically, but he certainly was not there emotionally. He was an absentee father who left a trail of destruction from his abusive words."

"What about me, because my father is very much in my life, so I can't use the absentee father excuse for my own situation!" Carlos said.

"Your father was there physically, Carlos, but emotionally, he checked out a long time ago," Rockye reminded him.

"So in a way, we both had absentee fathers!" Lynette confirmed.

"The way I look at it is that his father paid the bills and put food on the table!" Keno said.

Carlos nodded his head.

"It takes more than putting food on the table and paying the bills to be a good father!" Bailey commented.

"Bailey, have you spoken to your parents lately?" Tyler asked.

She hung her head low. "They don't exist to me anymore! They are dead to me!"

"She's trippin', she doesn't mean that!" Rockye said.

"How the hell do you know what I mean? Nobody knows what I'm feeling!" Bailey vented.

"Then why don't you tell us how you feel, Bailey? We want to know what's going on!" Tyler said.

"Sometimes I wonder why the hell I was ever born! For what? To work hard all day long and come home to an empty house? To love a man that treats me like I'm worthless! To have parents that discard their children like yesterday's trash? I was born in a body that is the opposite of how I feel inside! Why do I feel so bad all of the time? I feel like an alien on this planet. I feel like I don't really belong here!" Bailey confessed.

"I can relate to that! I don't feel like I belong here either sometimes! I thought I was the only person that felt like an alien!" Carlos commiserated.

Bailey remained silent as she played nervously with the flower design on her left thumbnail.

"My mother came to me the other day and told me that she knew that I was gay!" Carlos interjected.

"Oh, snap!" Keno remarked.

"What happened? How did she find out?" Tyler asked.

"She said that she knew that I was gay since childhood! Isn't that crazy?"

"What made her tell you this now?" Rockye asked.

"I've been pretty depressed lately after what happened with me and Pablo, and getting beat up and stuff! She kind of got tired of seeing me sulk around the house. You know, being pathetic and all! So she just came up to me and started talking about it."

"Is she going to tell your father?" Lynette asked.

"No! My mom said that she is going to leave that up to me! But I'm afraid that when he does find out that he is going to beat me within an inch of my life, and then throw my ass out of the house!"

"How does that make you feel, Carlos?" Tyler asked.

"Scared! Scared for me, and then scared for my mom and brother! Once I tell my dad, I will for sure not be able to come back in his house ever again, that is, if he doesn't kill me first! And then what will my little brother do without me to buffer my father's brutality? I just can't leave him or my mother alone!"

"You can't keep living a lie either!" Lynette said.

"Easier said than done! There are other people involved that will get hurt! I don't want anybody else dealing with the fallout of my being gay!" Carlos said.

"What does that mean? You are held prisoner within your own lie?" Bailey asked.

"Forget all that bullshit! Just move the hell out of that house now!" Keno said.

"And that is coming from a man who is being held hostage by a woman he doesn't love!" Bailey added.

"Fuck you!" Keno yelled.

"Fuck you back! Ahhhhhhh!" Bailey screamed at the top of her lungs. "I hate this shit!"

"Hold up now, both of you!" Tyler turned to Bailey. "What are you feeling right now, Bailey?"

Bailey replied, "Hate! I hate all people who dismiss another human being because they don't fit into the neat little box of their expectations. I hate my parents for treating me like I don't matter! I hate Chance for what he has done to me! I am just damn angry and fucking hurt!"

"Whenever you are hurt by someone, you have a choice to make. You have to ask yourself, 'Will I use my energy and emotions for retaliation or resolution?' If you decide on resolution, you must first forgive the person, and then allow a clean slate to build trust. Forgiveness is about letting go of the past, and it must be immediate once you have determined that you will forgive them. Trust, on the other hand, has to do with the future behavior. Trust is rebuilt over time and requires a positive track record. You've got to give them time to prove that they have changed." Tyler took a sip of water before continuing.

"On the other hand, if you decide to retaliate, you must be aware that this type of behavior just keeps you on the roller coaster of anger, and eventually, you lose even more than you had before. Bitterness and resentment will destroy you! It's a lose-lose situation!

"What we have to do is find a solution. And the solution is communication. Eventually, we will have to heal all of our relationships, and we must use all of our skills to do this, especially empathy, compassion, nonviolence, and love. Communication is the key to every relationship. Love and openness are vital to the process, but so is safety; because if you don't feel safe you will not communicate. So the question becomes, 'How do you make the environment safe for communication?' You must detach yourself from the outcome. It is your sole objective at this point to just express the truth that is inside of you—that something that is fighting to bust out. Don't think about how they will reply but just allow your truth to be heard in its entirety." Tyler crossed his legs, and then continued.

"There was a case of a woman who was horrified to think that a codependent relationship she had with an abusive man was not over; she realized that the man might try to pursue her again. That fear paralyzed her. She was encouraged to express her truth to him and move on. Because once you have expressed your truth, it is up to you to live in that truth. However, if after expressing your truth, you discover that you want out of that relationship, then you must make sure that there are no hooks in you that will pull you back to that relationship. No anger. No violence. Nothing negative at all. If you can leave a relationship with love, empathy, and compassion, without any thoughts of revenge, hatred, or fear, that is how you can truly let go!"

Tyler concluded the session by instructing Carlos with specific skills on how to relate to his father; Keno on how to handle the cougar he was living with; Lynette, Pam, and Rockye on how much they had grown and the next steps in their healing process; but when he got to Bailey he noticed that she exhibited signs of disenfranchisement. Physically, she was there, but mentally, it was obvious that she had checked out.

Eventually the movement as the group dispersed roused her back to the moment. Tyler watched her languishing in her chair, staring at everyone as they lined their chairs up against the wall.

Tyler glided over to her in four quick steps, his hands casually tucked into his back pockets.

"Hasn't been going too well for you lately, huh?" His face held concern.

"What can I say? Life sucks for me right now!" Bailey replied.

"How about a private session tomorrow? We can take time to sort it out and put it in perspective!"

Bailey fashioned a cynical grin. "What's to sort out? My parents have decided to disown me and not answer any of my phone calls. My ex-boyfriend has broken my heart so many times that I don't think that it will ever be whole again, and almost everywhere I go, people think that I am white! Do you know how it feels to be in a room full of white people, people who feel so comfortable around you that they talk about your race like animals?"

Tyler shook his head. "I know that it seems bad right now, but we can sit down and talk it through! Sometimes when we are in the midst of the chaos, it seems much worse than it really is."

He pulled out his Smartphone which was nestled within his back left pocket of his jeans, and pushed the calendar button.

"What does your afternoon look like tomorrow?" He glanced up from over his glasses.

"No offense, Tyler, but I really don't feel like talking anymore. I am all talked out right now! All I really want to do is forget about all the things that are messed up in my life at this moment! I don't want to deal with, talk about, or investigate why I feel what I feel." Bailey grabbed her Louis Vuitton, throwing it over her shoulder.

"I just don't want to feel anything right now!" Bailey said, storming out, leaving Tyler alone in the middle of the room.

In the foyer was Rockye propped up against the wall deep in discussion with Lynette and Pam. Once Rockye noticed Bailey, she quickly broke away, catching her before she hit the front door.

"So what's up with that hostility today, girl? What's going on with you? You wanna go grab a cup of coffee and talk about it?" Rockye placed her right hand on Bailey's left shoulder.

"NO! I don't want to talk about it! I don't want to talk about anything! I don't want to feel shit! I just want to go home and be left alone!"

Bailey marched out the front door with Rockye and Tyler in tow calling out her name in the distance. She didn't care about anybody right now. She was tired of being angry, tired of being disappointed and feeling alone. All she wanted to do was go home, have a few drinks, go to sleep and turn off the audio track that was repeatedly playing in her mind that she was worthless and unlovable.

Chapter Thirty-Eight

～ *Bailey Levine* ～

She had turned into a raging bitch from hell, looking for any and every opportunity to tear someone a new asshole! Bailey sat at the helm of her 30-seat conference room, filled with the top producers of her real estate agency. As she looked at their eager, anxious faces she couldn't help but feel the anger that bubbled deep within her. She had been quick-tempered, unreasonable, and impatient ever since her last encounter with Chance. No matter what happened, she was combative and angry.

"They are looking for lofts in the downtown area, right in the heart of where everything is happening—near the Staples Center! Something rather large, over 3,500 sq. feet! I have pulled several listings on what is available within their price range, but I found nothing that fits exactly what they are looking for," Bryan said, one of the broker associates, as he updated all at the round table on a recent client looking for available condominiums in the downtown area.

Bailey got up and walked over to Bryan's side of the table.

"Last year, Bryan, how much did your 1099 read?" Bailey questioned.

"Uhhhh—the exact amount?" He nervously looked around the room at the others.

"I believe that was the question." Her tone was biting.

"One thirty-five," Bryan eked out.

"That would be one hundred and thirty-five thousand dollars, right?"

"Yes!" he confirmed in a tone slightly above a whisper, his brows furrowed with embarrassment.

"Bryan, do you think that most real estate agents make that in their first year?" Bailey asked, circling the table like a hawk.

"I don't believe so!" His voice shook.

"You don't *believe* so? Well, Bryan, let me help you out so that you WILL know! Most first-year real estate agents, if they make it that long in the business, average about $25,000 . . . or less!" She picked up the listings that he had pushed toward the head of the table for her to review.

"*This* is twenty-five-thousand-a-year work! How much again did you earn last year?"

"One thirty-five." His voice was faint.

"That again is one hundred and thirty-five thousand dollars, right?"

"Yes, ma'am!" Bryan confirmed.

She pushed the listings toward him. "Anyone can go on the MLS and pull listings. An agent who earns how much again—?"

"One hundred and thirty-five thousand dollars," he finished.

"One hundred and thirty-five thousand dollars does more! *Much* more! They don't stop until they find what the client wants, no matter what! They don't make excuses. They find exactly what the client wants, no matter who they have to talk to, where they have to go, what they have to do, and how often they have to do it!"

Bailey turned her attention toward the other top agents in the conference room.

"How many of you earned less than one hundred and thirty-five, as Bryan put it last year?" Her eyes surveyed the room.

"That's what I thought! Not a single one of you! And with that in mind, I don't expect any more substandard work from any of you! Do I make myself clear?"

Everyone agreed in unison.

"Very well then. Bryan, when can I expect to have some suitable properties to show the Gilroys?"

"Within 24 hours!" he said with confidence.

"Perfect!" she announced feeling victorious.

She turned to Felicia who had been eyeing her in disbelief throughout the meeting and said, "Is there anything else on our agenda that we have not yet covered?"

"The merger update." Felicia got up and quickly handed Bailey a thick manila envelope.

"Ah yes! Many of you have been asking the status of the Shultz acquisition, and it appears that as of this morning, Robert Mercer met with Mr. Shultz and reached a mutual agreement. Within 60 days, that is, after all the legalities are finalized, we will be adding all of Shultz Realty to Levine Reality! Our mission is finally accomplished."

Everyone stood up cheering, clapping their hands, and taking turns congratulating Bailey.

Bailey reminded her agents that there would be promotions and transfers occurring for those who displayed exemplary work and the desire to move into management.

"After all, I am only as good as my team!" she concluded as she suddenly softened.

How could she come into her office and take out her anxieties on her staff? After all, that was all she had, her amazing employees and her business. She didn't have a man, and her parents had abandoned her. Other than Levine Realty, she had nothing!

Felicia handed Bailey a Chai latte after everyone left the room. "Is everything all right, Miss Bailey?"

Bailey eyed her employee with a squinted eye of disapproval.

"I am not trying to get into your business, but I have noticed that you have been on edge lately. Is there anything that I can do?" Felicia apprehensively voiced.

"Everything is fine!" Bailey addressed Felicia's concern with dismissal.

Bailey felt Felicia study her before speaking. "Okay then, but I am here if you need an ear or a shoulder to lean on." She smiled.

"I'm fine! Let's get back to work," Bailey threw from behind the documents she was pretending to read. She really wished that she could open up to Felicia, but she knew that if she did, the dam of desolation would break, and she would not be able to stop the endless flow of tears that was stored deep within the reservoir of her soul.

Felicia paused a moment before giving in. "Very well then, if you do need me, just buzz."

Felicia turned to leave but stopped abruptly.

"Oh, this came for you a few moments ago." Felicia handed Bailey an unmarked, oversized brown envelope.

Instinctively, Bailey knew who it was from. It was from Stan Stubbs, the private detective.

"You can just leave it on the table. And, Felicia, close the door behind you!" she said, not once raising her head to meet the inquisitive eyes of her employee.

Bailey leaned back within her lambskin black leather executive chair, feeling a huge sense of dread.

She had single-handedly accomplished more things in the last 90 days than most people did in 10 years. Hell, than in a lifetime, for that matter! Sitting in the plush conference room of her two-story real estate firm, Bailey looked around and realized that not one person was there for her. No parents, no man, no friends, no nothing! She had spent her entire lifetime only to end up alone, and lonely. Success means nothing if you don't have someone to share it with! She felt that she had no one that she could call and share her fabulous news with! Nobody! She finally accomplished what she had been working so hard for all of these years. With the acquisition of Schultz Realty she was now the #1 independent real estate company on the West Coast. She should be celebrating, elated from the conquest, but instead, she sat alone . . . feeling extremely vulnerable and lonely!

Bailey was suddenly overcome within an abyss of despair. An overwhelming feeling of aloneness hovered over her like a thunderous Atlanta winter rain cloud. And she knew that it was about to get worse soon, she thought to herself, as she eyed the envelope that seemed to be screaming her name from the middle of the conference table.

The tears began to fall effortlessly down the face that hadn't held a genuine smile in months. Never in her life had Bailey felt so alienated and detached from the world. If it weren't for her business, she would have felt that her entire life was worthless. She reached for the envelope that held the answers that she knew would change her life forever.

Chapter Thirty-Nine

~ Keno Hunter ~

"Why are women so damn unreasonable?" Keno shouted as he slammed his cell phone onto the coffee table with a fiery temperament. Her home telephone had been disconnected last week, and now her cell phone was no longer in service! Damn! Last week, after discovering that Dee Dee's home phone had been disconnected, he drove over to her apartment to find it completely empty, without any evidence that anyone had lived there just weeks ago! *Everything is gone like it never existed,* he thought to himself as his eyes scanned the empty rooms where they had once made love, watched television, and shared countless laughs. His heart sank at the thought of never seeing her again. Standing in her apartment last week, his nostalgia quickly turned to rage as he realized that he had been abandoned by the one woman he believed would always be there for him!

"Fuck you, bitch! If you don't want me, then I don't want you!" he said out loud as he sat on the plush couch of Sharon's condo. If she could give up so easily, then so could he! The insensitive bitch had not returned any of his calls, nor could he get any cooperation from her friends, family members, or coworkers! And up until today the only avenue he had to reach her was her cell phone. Now he no longer had that as an option.

What was he going to do now? Keno vacillated between resentment and disappointment. He was well aware that he had messed up severely. He marveled at how one single act could bring about such excruciating pain and depression. He knew how important Dee Dee was to him; he intellectualized it within the gray matter of his male brain, but it wasn't until that very moment when he stood in the empty domicile that once was a refuge of love for the two of them that he fully understood the devastation that it brought to his heart. Dee Dee was gone, and she wasn't coming back!

So now he tried to force it out of his mind and continued playing WII on the 60-inch wall-mounted, Bose surround sound Mitsubishi home entertainment system. Earlier, the cook had completed and served him a sumptuous five-course meal of smothered pork chops and apple sauce, followed by a delicious dessert of cherries jubilee, and a glass of fine cognac. The fireplace was roaring in the background, and he was stretched out on the overstuffed ottoman wearing a soft, fluffy, handmade French bathrobe, enjoying the benefits of cohabitating with his paramour.

Earlier when he emptied out the contents of his slacks to place them in the valet on the dresser before stepping into the five-jet, marbled, heated floor shower, he took inventory of its contents; at least 10 $100 bills, his Mercedes-Benz key, a wallet full of platinum credit cards, and a 24-karat gold pocket watch Sharon had given him on the day he moved in.

Keno enjoyed every imaginable creature comfort in Sharon's home without any guilt; as a matter of fact, he felt a tremendous sense of entitlement. But as his ass rested comfortably on the folds of the ottoman, his heart ached for his girlfriend, Dee Dee, no matter how he tried to suppress it. He cringed at the thought of Sharon coming home in less than half an hour. He didn't feel like faking nice when his heart ached for the woman that he loved.

Watching the embers of the fireplace crackle, he allowed his mind to wander over his plight for what seemed like the one-hundredth time that evening. Was this all really worth it? Was what he had worth what he lost? He had every material possession that he could have ever dreamt of, and yet, he felt such lack, such loneliness, such emptiness in the deepest pit of his gut! The ache seemed at times debilitating. He breathed a heavy breath, allowing the pressure to release slowly from his lungs.

If he could only turn back time as a youth to the exact moment when he was going to commit his first crime as a juvenile, he would! If it were only possible to rewind time! He would walk—no—run away from all those idiotic thugs, most of whom now were either dead or drugged out somewhere. He would run his ass back to high school, study hard, and graduate!

Who knows, he may have even gone to college, played pro ball or become CEO of some Fortune 500 company! It was possible! Wasn't it? He certainly had the innate talent and personality! Keno had been told on all too many occasions that he had all the qualities of a leader. But was he really a leader? He felt so unsure of himself.

He reflected on something Jango once said. *"How do you know that you are a leader? Answer—Turn around, and if you have no one following you, then you are simply just out for a walk!"* He thought about it, and it didn't look so good at all!

A person sure can fuck up their life in an instant! A stupid act done on impulse can follow you around, screwing up your life forever! Keno thought about himself as a father. He contemplated about what kind of parent he would be if he had kids. He thought about his own dad. What would it have been like if he had a father in his life while growing up?

What would my life be like now if I had my dad around to teach me things, and keep me from hanging out with the wrong people? he thought to himself.

What would his life be like if his father had lived long enough to take him fishing, hunting, or bowling?

Hell, just to have a dad who would come home at night would have been huge!

No use in crying over what you never had! Fuck his father for dying and leaving him alone!

Look at how difficult my life is now because you were not around when I was growing up! He entertained the thought of him being a father one day.

If I ever have kids one day, I will always make sure that I am there for them every step of the way, Keno convinced himself.

Keno once believed that he and his beloved Dee Dee would have had kids someday. He would have been an attentive, devoted father, and she would have been a nurturing, old-fashioned, doting mother. What he wouldn't give right now for the ability to turn back time!

The click from the release of the dead bolt on the front door lock prompted him to sit up straighter in the ottoman. He scanned the clock; it was Sharon coming home for the evening. It was time for him to put his game face on.

Showtime!

"Hey, babe! How was your day?" he managed to say through a forced smile as she slung her belongings down on the couch adjacent to him.

"It was a fucking day like any other day!" she expressed with obvious sarcasm falling out of her mouth, along with the spittle from the harsh delivery.

Oh shit, this bitch is in one of her funky moods. It was not quite 9 p.m., so he couldn't give her the excuse that he was tired and wanted to go to sleep. He had been using the excuse that he was tired from a hard day of work lately, and it seemed to have kept her at bay from the overtime of pleasing her oversized body for hours.

"Sorry, you had a bad day! Are you hungry? I'll get Pascale to bring you dinner! You wanna take a bath before you eat?" He sang the last word, allowing a softer tone to inhabit the question.

"I'm not hungry! Get me a rum and Coke!" Sharon snapped as she pulled off her periwinkle blue pumps, dropping them in the middle of the floor, as usual. Keno hated when she did that because he found himself always tripping over them.

"Why don't ya eat something before you start drinkin'? I'll go get you a plate!" he insisted.

"I don't need a fucking daddy! Just get me the damn drink!"

While he maneuvered over to the bar to get her drink, angry at her tone, he envisioned himself choking the ever-loving shit out that turkey-necked bitch!

"Look, Sharon, you ain't got to go there! I just think that you should eat before you start drinking. But if you want to drink, then hell—drink! Drink the whole fucking bottle if you want!"

He poured her a large rum and Coke. Pulling out a coaster from the drawer of the table in front of her, he placed the glass down and walked back over to the ottoman to sit down.

She lifted the heavy crystal glass to her lips and gulped down a mouthful of the dark beverage, leaving remnants of the mauve lipstick applied over 2 hours earlier on the rim. Ten minutes and two drinks passed before she uttered a reply.

"What did you do today?" she barked.

"I was at the office until about 5:00, and then I went to the gym and ummmmm—yeah, then to the Fox Hills Mall to pick up a few white shirts for work. Then I came home and voilà, here I am!" He managed to produce a playful smile.

"What did *you* do today?" he asked with a forced air of concern.

"Earned the money to pay for those shirts you bought today, that's what I did!"

"What the hell is that supposed to mean?" Keno bristled up.

"Look, Keno, I had a very long day, and I am really tired!" Sharon backed down.

"You act like I just lay up around here all day long and watch TV doing absolutely nothing! I get up every morning and go to work," Keno defended, knowing that his job was just a token position in the project planning department as a result of a favor called in from Sharon to the CEO of Microtech, a gaming software company.

Sharon poured another drink. "I will not have an argument with you! I'm exhausted from a very busy day!"

"Why don't you sit down next to me and I'll rub your feet." He retreated while patting the area next to him, indicating for her to sit down.

"No, I don't want a foot rub. I just want to take a shower and go to bed!" Sharon refilled her rum and Coke.

"Sharon, don't you think that you have had too many of those?"

"Did you go to sleep and wake up this morning as my fucking father?" she commented.

Keno thought to himself, *Sharon knows that she has the upper hand.* He had nowhere else to go, and she was well aware that she was the one holding all of the cards. If he was the one in the power position, he would have told her to go fuck herself! But he was in no position to take a stand on anything. Keno was ashamed to say, but he simply had to suck it up and deal with it. He had no place else to go!

"Can I fix you a plate for when you get out of the shower?" he politely asked.

"No! I told you that I am *not* hungry!" Sharon snapped.

"Okay, then, I'll meet you in bed after your shower. I'll bring you some of that chamomile tea that you like so much." He got up to go to the kitchen.

"Keno, that won't be necessary! I'm tired! After my shower I'll be heading straight to bed." She turned to leave.

"Okay then, I'll join you in a minute. Just as soon as I find out if the Lakers won." He forced his signature grin.

"It would be a good idea, Keno, if you sleep in the guest bedroom tonight. I need to get my rest." The door closed behind her so fast that he didn't even have enough time to respond to the dismissal.

Keno knew that the Sharon of today was far removed from the Sharon several months ago. He had heard that this day would come; the day when the cougar would tire of the younger man! Unless the younger man kept things new and exciting, on the edge, so to speak, the cougar would eventually grow bored, and then an obvious display of contempt would replace the once-amorous behavior.

Sharon had become a cold, distant bitch who rarely smiled and showed Keno at every opportunity that his presence had become a burden. It would be just a matter of time before everything came to a head and she would want him gone—out of her bed, out of her house, and out of her life!

Keno looked around and realized what his alternative would be if he was no longer there with Sharon. Quite frankly, he had none! Nothing. Nada! He had to quickly figure something out. Going back to struggling and hustling was not an option that he wanted to remotely consider.

He flicked off the television and eased into their bedroom. He would not sleep in the guest bedroom tonight. He wasn't about to be dismissed like some servant. Sure, she had the taste of disdain swirling around in her mouth now, but Keno knew exactly what it took to lure her back over to "Camp Keno." He was a master at bringing her body to a thunderous orgasm. He may not have been able to do much else, but this one thing he mastered.

He untied the robe he was wearing, allowing it to fall to the floor from off of his muscular, recently moistened body of almond butter. He knelt down by the bed. He opened his mouth wide and started his tongue exercises. This was going to be a long night; a long, laborious night, and, although he dreaded it, he fixed his mind on his objective and continued his tongue exercises.

Chapter Forty

~ Bailey Levine ~

Who was Chance Lewis *really*? She desperately wanted to know ... Or did she?

The answers lay right in front of her in an envelope emitting an innocuous energy! It looked harmless enough; however, she knew that it contained the answers to the many questions that had caused her many sleepless nights; many anxious moments and many mean-spirited interactions with her employees. Emotionally, she was a wreck, but now she had the ability to extinguish the cause of those injurious feelings. It was finally the time to get the answers that she so desperately needed.

Bailey reared back into the security of the conference room's leather chair and stared at the oversized manila envelope as her heart raced wildly within her tight chest in anticipation of its contents. She realized that she was procrastinating; nevertheless, she still couldn't quite muster up the courage to open the envelope. Bailey gingerly eased her body up out of the chair, heavy from anxiety, and slowly paced the floor back and forth thinking about Chance and the effect he had on her life up to that point. Were there any good times, or was it all a figment of her imagination? She tried to reason.

They had been together for a little over 3 years and in that small amount of time, he had managed to destroy whatever self-esteem she had, stress her out to the point of deep depression, and if at all possible, made her feel even more unworthy than her parents had.

It was primarily because of her parents that she never felt good enough, smart enough, pretty enough, or capable enough, and this attributed to her deep ingrained inferiority complex. She was now convinced that when Chance came along he recognized a prime opportunity because of her obvious low self-esteem. He therefore took advantage of a ripe situation. As she deduced, it was because of her parents and Chance that she was the mess pacing that room there right now.

She edged up to a rectangular mirror that hung on the wall, cocked her head sideways, and studied herself. Bailey barely recognized the woman looking back at her. She had dark circles under her eyes from lack of sleep, numerous gray hairs jetting from her scalp due to the stress, as well as the obvious fatigue that coated her face like a cheap generic brand of makeup. This was a far cry from the exquisite Bailey of a few years ago.

Lowering her body back down into the confines of the chair, she put her elbows on the table, sheltered her face within her hands, and let the tears of anguish held imprisoned within her burdened soul pour forth.

She felt discouraged, depressed, tired, lonely, guilty, and overcome with despair. Bailey's soul ached for solace. Allowing the tears to gush forth, she cried for the lost and wasted years that she could not reclaim. She wailed for the countless degrading, demeaning experiences that she had in the name of love. She sobbed at the reality that the thought of having a happy future with Chance was that of a manufactured fantasy on her behalf.

The pain was so overwhelming; Bailey thought she would pass out from the weight of it.

Eventually she released her tear-stained face from the clench of her hands and eyed the envelope. She glared at it as an angry dog before striking its target. However, this time, it was with an anger that bordered detonation.

Suddenly, Bailey no longer wanted to be a pathetic, blubbering, weak excuse of a woman. She desperately wanted the old Bailey back. The one that started a company on her own and drove it to immense success! And with that reality, in that moment, she reclaimed her power!

Grabbing the envelope with conviction, she yanked it open with such force that the contents spilled forth across the table. Shifting her derrière within the Christian Dior Pencil Skirt, she took a deep breath and submerged herself into its contents.

He had nine kids. Six baby mamas. Bad credit. Bad health. Several overdrawn bank accounts. Unemployed. In deep debt. In trouble with the IRS and living with several women around town. He was separated from a wife of 7 years, and his driver's license was revoked because of back child support.

The envelope was filled with copies of his bank statements, cell phone bills, credit reports, as well as countless photos of him with various women and children.

Her heart sank as she realized that everything he had ever said to her was a lie. There would be no marriage, no babies, and no happily-ever-after! It was all a lie—all part of his manipulation! He never really loved her at all! Its confirmation hit her like a ton of bricks.

She scanned through all of the photos of various women and stair step children ranging from the cradle to teenagers. Damn him! He was even having babies while they were together! Bailey slid the photos back into the envelope. She felt nauseated at the sight of all of those other children. It was finally confirmation that they would never have any children together. She would never have with him the family that she always wanted. He stole her dream. It all made her sick to her stomach. What a bastard! What a lying bastard!

As she concluded reading the last document, Bailey finally got it! This wasn't his fault! She was the one who allowed herself to be navigated into this sick, toxic relationship. That small voice inside of her told her to abort the relationship at the onset, but she didn't listen. She should have yielded and run in the opposite direction from him right from the very beginning. But because of her desperate need for acceptance, approval, and love, she disregarded all the obvious warning signs and became a willing victim to his pernicious schemes. She shouldn't be mad at him, for she did this to herself. She allowed him to run havoc in her life. Yes, this was all her fault, and it was high time that she stopped blaming Chance and took responsibility for her part in this debacle!

Bailey decided to accept that this was the moment for her to stop playing *victim*. She needed to acknowledge her part in the fiasco of this relationship, forgive herself, and start taking back her life. It was time to take the steps toward healing and victory. What Bailey ascertained through perusing the incriminating documentation about Chance was that she had dodged a lethal bullet.

So she determined from that moment on, that instead of crying for what she lost, she would rejoice for what she escaped!

Kiss my ass, Chance! You are fucking dead to me!

She took the envelope over to the shredder and shredded each document, bill, picture, and evidence of that lying asshole.

She had dodged a bullet, and she was DONE with that son of a bitch! Forever.

Chapter Forty-One

~ Andy Reynolds ~

There was nothing more beautiful than the sight of her smooth cocoa-brown skin intertwined with his ruddy paleness. He marveled at the dichotomy.

Bending down, Andy ran his tongue lightly against Rockye's naked back, tasting its salty, sweet ambrosia. Her breathing was now laced with a peaceful hum. She fancied sleeping on her right side, and as always, when she was in REM sleep, her right hand cupped her vagina. It never failed, a little over an hour into her sleep; Rockye's right hand would find its way to her vagina and lock onto it. She held it like a child holds its favorite blanket as she slept. A contended smile graced her face as her left hand rested lightly on his left leg.

He lay perfectly still listening to the tune of the automatic sprinklers outside his bedroom window. They came on every morning at 4:30. One of the automatic sprinkler heads was busted from the constant abuse of the gardener's electric mower, and it sent a steady stream of water straight into the air streaming against his bedroom window.

Andy and Rockye had been inseparable for the past few weeks. Outside of work and the usual errands, they were always together. Andy noticed that his temper had become almost nonexistent due to the constancy of her loving, nurturing presence. As for Rockye, she had also changed as well; there was no longer that air of confusion or secrecy between them. Becoming an open book, disclosing every detail of her whereabouts, had become like second nature to Rockye. This was the behavior that Andy needed in order to establish the trust essential for him to feel secure within the relationship.

The woman he loved had become the woman he had always wanted her to be.

A cool breeze rushed in through the slightly opened window, causing Rockye to unconsciously tussle, exposing her bare ass to the early-morning air. As he enjoyed its round fullness, his mind traveled back in time to hours ago when her beautiful cocoa ass was high in the air as he methodically stroked her again and again to repeated orgasms.

Sex had been so fucking hot for the last few weeks. It was now common for them to have sex at least 2–3 times a day. Rockye brought him lunch almost every day, and dessert was usually her fucking the shit out of him in her car, his car, his office storeroom, or the communal bathroom. Her appetite was insatiable, and Andy dined on her delectable menu, requesting seconds.

Andy's thoughts revisited last night as Rockye experimented with a new technique in her skills of fellatio. While in the middle of swallowing his entire member into the deep cave of her hot throat, she started to simultaneously stroke it with her tongue as his penis careened deeper into her waiting throat in a rhythmic up-and-down motion, her tongue sliding up and down it upon entry and exit. Occasionally, she would pull it out and insert the tip of her tongue into the slit of his penis head. This was something that she had never done before and the feeling drove him to screams of rapturous delight. He loved the new Rockye!

Outside of the bedroom, they were in sync in every way. They craved the same foods, agreed on the same television programs, got each other's jokes, and harmoniously reveled in each other's company.

As Andy lay there reminiscing on the weeks that had gone by in comparison to the last few years of their relationship, the negative thoughts of doubt started to creep in.

He wondered how long it would be before it all fell apart. In the back of Andy's mind, he really felt that Rockye would wake up one day and realize that he was not good enough for her. He felt that one day when she finally discovered that he was not worthy, she would bolt to the nearest exit for good. Andy harbored the thought that if his own mother couldn't find him lovable, then how could any other female? He truly felt that when given the opportunity, women could replace you at any moment for a man with a bigger bank account, a man who had a better stroke, a better body, a better sense of humor, a better line; it didn't really matter because there was always another man; a better man! He felt that when the true Andy was exposed, fully exposed, she would leave him and never look back!

He needed a drink; he started getting agitated! Sliding gently from his woman's grasp, Andy removed himself from the bed, put on his robe, and went into the living room. The picture window had been left slightly ajar and the room was filled with the dense coldness of the winter morning. He pulled the thick robe closer to his body, seeking warmth.

After clicking the thermostat on, he heard the unit kick on, indicating that sufficient heat would soon be pouring in. Looking around for his bottle of Jack Daniels, he located it on top of the refrigerator. How did it get there? Rockye must have put it there for he remembered having left it on the coffee table. Grabbing a glass from the cupboard, he poured a full glass and sat down on one of the hard, wooden, dinette chairs.

He wanted to drown out the thoughts, but as he drank, his mother's face appeared in front of him as clear as day!

Ma? He reached out to the mirage. *Ma, is that you?*

He desperately needed to talk to his mother! Maybe he could kill some of the demons that haunted him if he addressed his issues with his mother. Then, hopefully, he would finally feel free to love his woman without that old baggage from his past.

The numbers on the telephone were fuzzy as he tried to focus long enough to dial the eleven digits that would get him back east to his mother's house.

The phone rang six times before his mother's voice, raspy and deep, answered.

"It's your dime—talk!"

"Ma? It's me, Andy!" Andy's chest thumped with anxiety.

"Ain't this about a bitch! A voice from the past! Why you calling?" Her voice seemed muffled and detached, not at all the resemblance of a mother who had not spoken to her son in over a year.

"I was thinking about you and thought I'd call and see how you and the girls were doing."

"Shit, it is cold as hell down here, and we running low on firewood. The damn pipes almost froze up on us last week. Cynthia's food stamps went to that stupid bitch across the street, and she took her own sweet time to walk her fat ass over here to give it to us! We was eating hot dogs on day ole bread 'cause of that fucking bitch!"

"How are the girls doing, Ma?"

"Cynthia's pregnant again! Ain't seen her ass for 2 days now. She must be with that Carter boy! I don't know what she sees in that one-eyed, crooked-toothed, bowlegged boy. He ain't got two nickels to rub together!"

She hawked up and spit before continuing.

"The Dodge broke down, and we take to walking to get around when we can't get rides! The man at the station said something about a trans—a trans something!"

"A transmission?" Andy clarified.

"Yeah, whatever the hell it is. He wants thirteen hundred dollars! I told him to stick it up his ass! I ain't got that kind of money. I'll just get me a ride! As long as I got a twat I can get some man to give me a ride somewhere!"

"Ma, I need to ask you something important!" He took a swig of Jack before continuing.

"Aw, hell! You in trouble? Fuck, Andy, I ain't heard from you all this time, and you call me 'cause you in some damn trouble! I got no damn money for ya!"

Andy interrupted, "Ma, I ain't in trouble! I just want to ask you something, that's all!" He took another drink anticipating courage from the liquid.

"Well, go ahead, I ain't got all day!" she barked.

"Do you ever think about that night in Charleston, you know, me being locked in that outhouse and all? I mean, do you ever feel bad about what happened to me?" Andy's heart was thumping right through his chest so loud that he feared his mother could hear it.

Silence was her response.

"Ma? Are you there?" Andy probed.

He heard the phone drop to the floor and footsteps in the distance.

"HELLO! HELLO! HELLO—MA, ARE YOU THERE?" He kept yelling into the receiver.

"Who is this?" asked a younger male voice after some time had passed.

"This is Andy! Where's my mother?" Andy yelled. "Is she all right? And who are you?"

"Name's Dirk. I'm your ma's friend! You her boy in California? Well, I be damned! I thought you was made up in her head!" Dirk replied.

"Yes! Dirk, I'm her son. But what happened to my mother? I was just talking to her and—"

"—that crazy broad ran outside with only them damn red lace panties on I done brought her yesterday. That is one crazy-ass bitch!"

"Can you go get her? And make sure that she's all right?" Andy pleaded.

"It's cold as a son of a bitch out there! I ain't gonna catch my death of cold 'cause she wanna do some crazy-ass shit like run outside in the cold in her damn drawers!" Dirk stated.

"Look, Dirk, just go and look for her, for goodness' sake!"

"Fuck—Shit—Damn—I didn't come over here for all of this bull. Sure didn't!"

"Hello! Hello! Hello!" After about 5 minutes a female answered as he continuously hollered for his mother through the phone. The voice sounded like his sister Patricia.

"Patricia?"

"Is this you, Andy? Oh, Andy, it is so good to hear your voice! I really miss you!" Patricia, his younger sister said.

"Pat, what's wrong with Ma? I was talking to her, and she just ran out of the house in her underwear! What's going on around there?" Andy insisted.

"I guess she didn't tell you, huh?"

"Tell me what?" Andy said with trepidation.

"She went to the clinic some 6 months ago, and them doctors told her that she got lung cancer. All that cigarette smoking, he said. It's pretty bad, and she won't take them treatments the doctor told her about! She's been acting crazy ever since. She been throwing fits all the time," Patricia explained.

"Why didn't you call me?" Andy asked.

"She told me not to! She told me if I did she would kick my ass outta the house!"

"Where is she? Did that Dirk guy find her?" Andy asked.

"No! And he won't 'cause he left! He ain't coming back, Andy! I think that he's fed up with her craziness, and besides, there ain't nothing else left for him to take. We ain't got shit else!" Patricia admitted.

"What can I do? I'll send some money!"

"NO! Whatever you do, don't send any money, Andy! Ma will just give it to a man or drink it up. It's bad, Andy, and it will only get better when she's under the dirt!"

"Don't say that, Patricia!"

"You and I know it. Ma is straight Ratchet! I have accepted it, and you need to as well. Do yourself a favor and forget about us and just live your life and be happy. You are the only one that did something with your life, and I don't want this shit of a family to mess up your life any more than it already has! It'll be better if you just forgot about all of us and go on and live your life!"

Andy remained silent, taking it all in.

"Andy?"

"Yes, Patricia."

"You need to know something! Ma talks about you all the time! She tells everybody about you and all the thangs you do! But the guilt still fucks her up."

"I didn't even think it ever crossed her mind, much less bothered her!"

"Believe me, it bothers her! I sometimes hear her talking to herself about it."

"That surprises me. I didn't think that she even cared!"

"She's a lousy mother; I am living proof of that, but she does feel bad about what happened to you; especially that night!"

"I still keep asking myself what kind of woman lets someone lock her kid out in the freezing cold night in an outhouse just because some drunk-ass man didn't want them around."

"We didn't even think that you was gonna live! I see you still think about that night, huh?" his sister asked.

"Hell yeah! I remember thinking to myself what was worse, the smell of the outhouse or the freezing cold of the night through my pajamas. I kept hoping that eventually she would remember that I was outside and come and get me. I kept yelling for her and hoped that she would tell that jerk she was with who had locked me in the outhouse to come get me. But she never did! She never came."

"Do you remember being in the hospital?"

"I remember waking up one night and looking around a big room and feeling so scared and lonely! I cried out, and nobody came. I kept crying out for her, and eventually, I guess, I fell asleep!"

"It wasn't until weeks later that we could come visit you in the hospital. You looked so little in that funny-looking bed, and you was so angry! You wouldn't even talk to nobody for a long time. Ever since then you was always so angry!"

"Well, hell, wouldn't you be if your mother let some nasty, strange man lock her only son in a stinky outhouse at night in the cold winter just so he could fuck undisturbed. She literally forgot all about my ass in the freezing cold night air and only remembered me when the police knocked on the door and asked about me. I still wonder to this day who called the police. When the bitch finally saw me, she was angry because she got in trouble. Imagine that, the bitch was mad at *me*!"

"Why did you call, Andy? What do you want from her?"

"I don't know what I was looking for. Maybe just for her to admit what she did and show some type of remorse for treating me, treating us, like we were an inconvenience! I want her to say that she's sorry! I want to know why she didn't love us more than she loved the men."

"That's not going to happen, Andy, so just do yourself a favor and forget about it. Move on with your life! You got to let it go!"

"I can't. I have to know why! I need to know why she didn't love me. Why did she choose all those men over me—why she—"

"—let it go, Andy! Sometimes there ain't no answers. It's just what it is!"

"But—" Andy was getting angry again.

"Go live your life; forget about it and just live your life!" Patricia hung up the telephone, and the echo of the dial tone filled the room.

"Patricia! Patricia!" He redialed. Busy tone! He redialed again. Busy tone.

Andy slammed the receiver in its cradle, grabbed his Jack Daniels, and drank until he fell into an alcoholic coma. He didn't want to feel anymore. He didn't want to have to look at the fact that his own mother could care less if he lived or died!

Chapter Forty-Two

≈ Rockye Haynes ≈

W*eeping may endure for a night, but joy comes in the morning."*

The sun came streaming through the mini blinds, announcing the arrival of morning. Rockye sat up looking around the bedroom for Andy. She called his name. No answer. She called it again. Still no answer.

He must have gone to the corner Starbucks to get their coffee as he had every morning she'd slept over. Swinging her long legs off the mattress onto the floor, she lifted her arms high into the air giving her back a good stretching. She yawned and rubbed her eyes. As her eyes focused, she caught sight of the Hallmark card she had given Andy earlier in the week.

After her encounter with the old lady in the park, while driving over to Andy's place, Rockye gave her life some serious thought. *How did that old lady know all that about me? Who was she? Was she a messenger from God?*

"Remember, do what is right and good. I caution you to turn from your old ways. For when you turn from destructive behavior, only then will you have clarity as to the direction you need to take. It will be as clear as the blue in today's sky!

"Just remember to do what is right and good! When the time is right, you will know the right way to go! I warn you though—stop the deception! What you are doing with those men you meet is foul; you must cease it immediately, because if you don't, you will pay a very high price!"

What the old lady said began to resonate to her very core. As she thought about what she said; weighing her career options and the possible loss of her relationship with Andy, she began to collapse into a waterfall of tears.

It all came to a head that afternoon when she was walking down the aisle of a neighborhood Hallmark card store. Rockye caught sight of the store as she turned on Jefferson just a few blocks from Andy's house. Deciding to get him a card, she perused the aisles. Her eyes caught sight of this magnificent birthday card which read, "My Husband, My Life," and for whatever reason, she just lost it. She wailed uncontrollable heart-grieving sobs right there in the aisle of that Hallmark store.

One of the employees touched her shoulder in efforts to calm her down, but that just made the sobbing intensify. It didn't matter if the entire store had stopped to gawk at her; the only thing that mattered at that moment was the overwhelming feeling of loss and desperation that had crept up into her heart and soul at the very thought of losing Andy.

The young girl working at Hallmark didn't know what to do with the hysterically crying woman making a scene in the birthday section of the card shop.

Rockye finally managed to collect herself, whimpered out an apology, rushed out the front door, raced to her vehicle, climbed inside, and locked the door. Once safe inside the confines of her vehicle, the waterfall erupted once again. With her cupped hands pressed firmly over her eyes, tears spraying through the clasped fingers, Rockye emptied herself through the flow of tears.

An overwhelming pain and sadness came with the sudden realization that Andy could possibly no longer be in her life. When you finally realize that the person you really love the most could be really gone from your life, something changes within you. At that moment in the Hallmark store was when Rockye realized that losing Andy was not one of the changes that she wanted to happen in her life.

She didn't want to lose the man that made her feel secure, loved, and valued. She realized that nothing else mattered to her but Andy. In that moment, Rockye had a paradigm shift, as Jango would say. Right then and there, she decided to dedicate 100 percent of herself to her man and make him happy. The old narcissistic Rockye, her inconsiderate behavior, was over. She was done with other men, dressing inappropriately, and conducting herself in a manner that was inappropriate for a married woman. Someone once told her that you should act like a wife long before you become a wife. And she really wanted to be Andy's wife. She desperately wanted to change!

Checking herself in the rearview mirror after she regained composure, Rockye marched back into the Hallmark shop and bought that birthday card. It wasn't Andy's birthday, nor was he her husband. That didn't matter! What mattered was her love for Andy and her decision that nobody would ever come before the man that she loved ever again! Nobody!

She had made her decision, right there in the birthday aisle of the Hallmark store. She would not be going to New York for the opportunity of a lifetime; she would be staying in Los Angeles with her man!

Rockye smiled at the birthday card now perched on Andy's dresser as she extended her arms for yet another stretch before glancing over at the clock; it was 7:45 a.m. She would wait and see if Andy would go with her on her daily morning run when he returned with the coffee. The tickle in her throat called attention to its dryness. She got up to grab a glass of orange juice from the refrigerator before getting dressed for her run.

Approaching the living room, she noticed Andy straddling the couch asleep.

"Andy! Andy, honey!" She lightly shook him.

"Baby, wake up! Andy! Andy!"

He lightly stirred but didn't awake.

"Andy, wake up!" Noticing the empty Jack Daniels bottle on the floor in front of him, Rockye finally understood why there was difficulty in waking him. He was stone-drunk! Rockye had seen Andy drunk like this before, and by the emptiness of the Jack Daniels bottle, she knew that he was indeed inebriated. Nothing could wake him when he was dead drunk like this. Only time!

Rockye hated it when Andy got drunk because it was always an indication that something was really bothering him. She knew that there were things in his past that he didn't share with her; those undisclosed secrets were most likely the source of his dismal mood swings. Although she inquired repeatedly, he never shared with her the source that caused those changes in his disposition and therefore drove him to the bottle. So after getting her feelings hurt all too many times upon inquiry, she just stopped asking.

Rockye covered him up with a blanket, walked back into the bedroom, put on her jogging suit, and headed out the door for a long morning run.

Before she closed the door behind her, she glanced lovingly at her man. He was drunk, he was passed out, he was a mess, but she loved him and didn't regret for a moment making the decision to pass up her career for his love.

He was her reason for living, and she would stick by him, no matter what!

Chapter Forty-Three

~ Andy Reynolds ~

"First, you take a drink, then the drink takes a drink, then the drink takes you." *F. Scott Fitzgerald.*

Andy felt dehydrated, his head pounded in succession with each heartbeat, and his mouth held a sour, bitter taste. When he awoke he realized he lay sprawled on the couch, too disjointed to move. The light assaulted his eyes but not as much as trying to focus on things did.

After pulling himself off the couch as he fought the heaviness of his body, he called out for Rockye. When he didn't get a response after many attempts, he deduced that she most likely had gone for her morning run. Moving to the bathroom and climbing into the shower likened to shouldering a barrel of cement, however, the water from the shower invigorated him. It was as if he got a second wind from it as it slowly knitted him back together.

Finally, Andy retreated into the kitchen to prepare a late breakfast for when Rockye returned from her morning run. Almost two hours later he'd completed the task of straightening up the living room as well as cooking a couple of mushroom, onion, and sausage omelets. The delicious fragrance permeated the house. His hangover headache had subsided somewhat since his third cup of coffee. From the looks of the empty bottles he had deposited in the trash, he had consumed at least two 25-ounce bottles of whiskey.

Although he knew that he desperately needed to quit drinking, he pacified himself by telling himself that *he could stop whenever he wanted*, but that he needed it right now to mask the tremendous pain he was carrying around inside of him.

Rockye eased in un-expectantly and hopped up on top of the counter behind him sporting a peevish temperament.

"So how ya' feeling?" Sarcasm laced her voice.

Andy was startled. "You trying to give me a heart attack?" He hated when she snuck up behind him.

"No, I'm not, but what's up with last night? I thought that I had hid the bottles from you, but I see that you found them! What's up with you getting drunk?" Rockye said, getting to the point.

"My mother's got lung cancer!" Andy got to the point as well.

"What? You talked to her? Did she call you? Did you call her? What happened? How did you find out? What—"

"—hold up with the questions!" He walked over and sat down at the breakfast table. "We need to talk!"

She followed him in tow.

"I have been having a hard time sleeping lately. I know that I haven't said anything to you about it, but I've been having nightmares, and when I wake up I'm drenched in sweat. I start drinking because I can't get back to sleep," Andy confessed.

"How long has this been happening?" Rockye asked, sitting uncomfortably close to him.

"About 2 or 3 months now."

"Oh, baby, why didn't you tell me?" Her look of genuine concern touched him.

"I just dealt with it!" His eyes settled on a crack in the ceiling as he tried to form the words to explain.

"What kind of nightmares?"

"Mostly about my mother and stuff that happened to me growing up."

"Did you have one last night?"

"Not so much. I just had stuff on my mind and couldn't sleep last night, so I came into the living room to get a drink and while sitting there thinking I just decided to call her." Andy stared into the distance.

"—you called her?"

He nodded.

"What happened?"

"She answered the phone in all her blazing glory! Nothing had changed; she was still the same cold, hateful, selfish bitch that I had known growing up."

Rockye leaned forward and tenderly rubbed his forearm.

"I asked her about a few things that happened when I was growing up," Andy confessed.

"What did she say?"

"She threw the phone down and ran out of the house in her damn underwear!"

"Are you serious?"

"She didn't even want to talk to me. Can you believe that shit? What could I have possibly done to her for her to hate me so? Why doesn't she love me?"

"Oh, honey, it's not you! I'm sure that your mother loves you. She just doesn't know how to express herself, that's all! How could she not love such an incredible man?"

He pondered the question briefly before continuing. "How can anyone ever truly know what love looks like or feels like if they have never truly experienced it from their own mother? After all, isn't that supposed to be your first real experience of love?"

Rockye shook her head. "You can't look at it like that, sweetheart! Your mother has her own demons that she's dealing with. It has nothing to do with you or how she feels about you. Your mother loves you!"

"How can you say that? She doesn't love me! You have no right to say such a thing because you were never there. You didn't see how she treated me or my sisters!" he barked.

Andy jumped up from the table and slammed his fist into the refrigerator. "I hate her! I hate the fucking bitch! I hate her! I hate her! I hate her!"

Rockye's face once painted with empathy was now replaced with fear. The angry Andy was back!

"Honey, calm down!" she whispered.

"All my life she has put someone else before me! She never had any time for me! But you let some man come over—she'd come alive! Always some new man climbing up in her ass, and for what? A fucking dollar, *that's* for what! Fucking whore! No wonder she got cancer! It serves her right for all the fucked-up shit she did to me and my sisters! I don't understand how God let a bitch like that have children. Ignorant tramp bitch!" Andy fumed.

"And just to think that for a minute I actually missed the fucking cow! I had been thinking about going down there to see her and tell her how much I missed her! Missed *what*? I hate her! I hate what she did to me. I hate what she did to me and my sisters—" He slammed his fist into the refrigerator.

"All those nights I slept in the closet so that I wouldn't hear some piece of shit drifter tossing her ass around the room to get his nuts off! How can a mother let her children witness such perversity? I think the only reason that she had children was to be able to have an extra hold on the poor bastard she was fucking just to get some damn money!" Andy felt the hatred burgeoning inside of him.

"I hate her! I hate her!" he screamed.

"I hope that bitch suffers a long time before she dies! I'm glad that she got cancer, and I pray that she suffers as much as she has made me suffer!" Andy walked around the kitchen with his fists balled up, anxious to slam them into something, anxious to destroy anything. His eyes scanned the kitchen for something to destroy.

"Andy, honey, you shouldn't say things like that about your mother! She *is* your mother, good or bad. That should count for something!" Rockye tried to reason with him.

"Are you taking up for that bitch?" His thin lips pursed as his eyes blazed red from anger.

"No, baby! I just want you to understand—"

Andy cut her off. "—understand *what*? You making a case for that tramp? Is that what you're trying to do?" He picked up the toaster and hurled it across the room exposing the drywall from the hole he just created upon the impact.

"You don't get it do you? My mother would rather lie in bed with some fucking cock passing through town than spend any time with her kids. I was her only son, and the bitch had made up her mind that any man that could fuck her or give her money was worth more than me! If she wasn't up under some man, she was asleep or drunk in her room, or on the telephone running up the phone bill with some asshole. It never failed; time and time again she let me know that I was an inconvenience in her life. I *hate* the bitch!" He twirled around to face Rockye.

"And *you* are going to take up for the whore?"

"I am not taking up for her, baby; I'm just trying to calm you down!"

"Why were all the men more important than me? Why didn't she ever choose me?"

"Those men were not more important than you. Your mother is just sick. It has nothing to do with your value or how much she loved you. You are such an amazing man, honey! No man could ever walk in your shoes. I love you so much, and I'm sure that your mother loves you more than you know; more than any of those men she was with!"

"What about the men, Rockye? Do you love me more than all the other men?" His eyes bulged with rage.

"What are you talking about? What men?"

Shaking with trepidation, she backed up into the refrigerator.

He galloped in front of her, his hand closing around her neck. "You think that I don't know about you and all the men? You think that I'm some stupid-ass punk? I know what you've been doing behind my back! I know that you have been fucking men all over town! You think I'm some damn idiot? Bitch, I'll kill you! I'll be damned if I let another woman fuck over me! You and that cunt of a mother of mine can burn in hell for all I care. I hate all of you tramp, cheating, slut-ass bitches! I hate you all!" He hands squeezed her neck until her body became limp and slid to the floor.

As the oxygen left her brain, she dropped like a ton of bricks, her face flushed from a lack of blood.

"I have spent my entire life wanting you to love me—praying that one day you would wake up and show me some type of attention—some affection—any kind of affection! Hell, I didn't even need that much, a fucking hug—to put a bandage on my knee when I fell off my bike. Was it too much to ask you to sit down and have dinner with us every now and then? But what the fuck did you do? Or *who* did you do is the better question?" Andy found a fresh bottle of Jack Daniels. After opening it, he tilted it, downing about one-fourth of the bottle in a single swig as Rockye lay motionless on the floor, fear etched across her face.

"All the other kids had mothers who showed up at school when they had plays, bake sales, and shit, but what was my mother doing? She was at home fucking the janitor! I was the laughingstock at the school. Everybody knew that my mother was the town slut, but hell, I still took up for your nasty ass! I got my ass beat up all of the time taking up for you! For what? So that you could show me that I'm nothing? What the fuck is wrong with you, bitch?"

Semiconscious, Rockye pulled herself to her feet. "Andy—listen to me. It's me—Rockye! I am *not* your mother, honey! Look at me—please!" she pleaded.

He started hyperventilating. "I loved you, Ma—why didn't you ever love me? What's wrong with me? Why didn't you love me?"

"Honey, look at me! Please just look at me!" Rockye yelled, attempting to pull him from the trance he was in.

"You have nothing to say, do you, bitch? You have no explanation for your ass! Well, fuck you, then! I don't care about you either!" He hurled the half-empty bottle of Jack toward her, missing by inches, and crashing into the stove sending fragments of glass all over the kitchen.

"Ahhhhhhhhh!" Rockye hollered as she maneuvered out of the way of the spraying shrapnel.

"Get out! Get the fuck out of my damn house! I hate you, and I'm glad that you have cancer—I want you to die—die, bitch, die!"

Rockye scooted herself up against the wall, aiming for the front door, hollering for dear life as fear held her eyes wide in terror.

"Stop that crying, bitch! You think that that shit is going to make a difference to me now? Get your ass up and get the hell out of my house! You don't want me! You never wanted me! Why didn't you just get an abortion? Why didn't you just kill me when you found out you were pregnant with my ass?" He grabbed his face beet red with anger within his large open palms. His stringy hair limp and wet from perspiration was disheveled about his head.

"Why didn't you just kill me when you found out you were pregnant with me instead of torturing me slowly throughout my entire life?"

He glared at her. "You have nothing to say, bitch?"

Rockye kept calling his name, however, he didn't see her—he just saw his mother, the pain and scarring that she had left behind.

"Why did you always choose them over me? Why didn't you ever love me? Why didn't you ever love me?" he yelled at Rockye.

Rockye slowly maneuvered herself toward the front door; her eyes never leaving him until her hands found the doorknob.

"Every other man was more important to you! Let's just see if those bastards will be there when the cancer starts eating up your ass so bad that you can't fuck them anymore! I hope that cancer has you feeling the pain that you caused me, bitch! Get out! Get out!" Andy yelled through the door as Rockye escaped and hauled ass down the street with an Olympic quickness.

"Fine—just leave then. Why would I want anyone around me that doesn't care about my ass anyway? Go! Just get the hell out—get the hell out!"

He searched the kitchen until he found another bottle of Jack Daniels. The reality was that his own mother never cared about him; it was a pain so formidable that only significant amounts of whiskey would allow the fact to be bearable.

He tilted the bottle again, guzzling the fermented beverage until the pain subsided and he slipped into narcosis.

Chapter Forty-Four

~ Bailey Levine ~

"*The victim mind-set dilutes the human potential. By not accepting personal responsibility for our circumstances, we greatly reduce our power to change them.*" Steve Maraboli

Bailey decided to no longer blame other people and circumstances for the kind of life that she had. Blaming others only served one purpose: It made her feel like a victim. And victims didn't have power over their own lives.

"I am no longer going to allow my past to control my life. I am taking back my life. I am the only one responsible for the type of life I lead. I am taking control over my own thoughts, as well as my actions. Today, I have decided to stop being a victim!" Bailey stated.

"What the hell happened to you—invasion of the body snatchers?"

"No invasion of the body snatchers! I just decided that I no longer want to be victim. I decided to no longer blame my mother, my father, or even Chance. Perhaps maybe they did play a part in my brokenness, but I can make it stop with me now—right now!"

Bailey caught Rockye up to date on the outcome of the investigator's report on Chance.

"Damn, Bailey, discovering that Chance was the son of a bitch I always said he was caused all of this—this drastic change in you? But why now? You had to know that somewhere deep down inside of you all of this time that he was a cheating, lying, conniving, disgusting piece of shit. It was so freaking obvious!!!"

"That's enough, Rockye! It's not about Chance or my mother or my father or anything external. No, that would make it all about them when it has nothing to do with anybody else but me. As for Chance, I'm the one who opened up my heart, my legs, and my purse to a man who was not worthy of me. I convinced myself to believe what I wanted to believe. I can't imagine that you would understand how you could want someone to love you so bad that you would brainwash yourself to see something that was not there."

"I knew that Chance didn't love me. I knew it! But I hoped that one day he would look at me—I mean *really* look at me, and then something would click in him and he would see in me all the things that I couldn't see in myself. I know that it sounds silly, but I just thought that one day he would love the real me right out of me."

"Love the real you right out of you—what the hell does *that* mean?" Rockye's face held an expression of confusion.

The two girls met for coffee at Starbucks in Westwood. It was a gloomy Saturday afternoon when Bailey got the phone call from Rockye to meet. Bailey could tell by the tone in Rockye's voice that she had something on her mind.

Initially upon the discovery of the real truth about Chance, Bailey went through half a dozen emotions: rage, anger, sadness, depression, loss, and hopelessness, but subsequently she settled on relief . . . relief from a heavy weight being lifted from her soul. The discovery of Chance's lies liberated her, allowing her to break out of the thick shell of self-deprecation. She felt literally born-again when the reality finally settled in her brain that she had been freed from her self-imposed prison. She was finally set free!

In the 1956 American black-and-white science fiction film, *Invasion of the Body Snatchers*, extraterrestrials took over a small town in California. The invaders replaced human beings with duplicates that appeared identical on the surface but were devoid of any emotion or original individuality. This was the visible change that Rockye was referring to.

They agreed to meet at Bailey's favorite Starbucks because of its oversized stuffed chairs and the authentic wood burning fireplace. Fortunately, they had just heaped on several new logs when Bailey arrived, allowing the crackling of the wood to provide a tranquil, soothing ambiance to the room.

The warmth of the fire provided a relief from the potent chill in the air. After placing her bag and jacket on the chair next to the one she was saving for Rockye, Bailey ordered a chai latte, paying for her as well as Rockye's beverage, and then settled in to watch the fire excitedly dance around on the wood.

What was it about the jetting flames of a fire that made people become introspective? It somehow calls one to invite the whys, how comes, and what happens to into your mind! It carries you into a deeper part of yourself—the self that only fire and the ocean can navigate you to. Bailey pondered on the prospects of her future. She was coming from a place of limited possibilities before, but now her perspective was that of limitless possibilities. Where would life take her now? What would the man of her dreams be like? Where would life take her now that she no longer was weighed down with low self-esteem or low self-worth? She felt that no matter what came her way she would be able to conquer it. As the aphorism states, "As a man thinketh in his heart so is he." Bailey realized that she was literally what she thought about herself, her character being the complete sum of all of her thoughts.

As she stared at the fire, she realized that just days ago the sight of something so beautiful would have caused her to feel hopeless, but now, the fire was magical; it held with it a sense of unclaimed possibilities for her; it held high expectations for her future. As the song says, what a difference a day makes.

Bailey got so lost in the myriad of possibilities that she was no longer aware of her surroundings until Rockye's presence propelled her back to the present.

"Beautiful fire," Rockye commented, settling in with a coffee mug holding a steaming beverage.

"Do you know that there are almost 11 million people here in Los Angeles city alone? Where in some countries like Jamaica, Armenia, or Uruguay they don't even have 4 million people! The whole country doesn't even have 4 million people!" Bailey commented.

"Wow, I didn't know that!" Rockye raised the cup of extra sweet ambrosia to her full lips and pulled the liquid slowly into her mouth.

"With so many people in L.A., why does this place feel so disconnected? What is it about this place that makes you feel like you are on an island? Like you are all by yourself?" Bailey asked, not expecting an answer as she continued to stare into the now-roaring fire.

"Hmm, I don't know. It's probably because people are just trying to make it through another day in this fucking crazy-ass world! I don't think that when they wake up in the morning and get dressed to go out into the world that they even think about other people. I think that people think about the stuff that is going on it their lives; you know, like bills, getting to work on time, how to pay for health insurance, whether their husband or wife is cheating on them, what they are going to eat for lunch, cook for dinner, or watch on TV that night! I think people are so far removed from really important stuff like global warming, the effects of methane gas, the growth of AIDS, cancers, our contaminated drinking water, or even the well-being of their neighbors and coworkers. People just don't stop and look around to see if anyone is in need of any help! They are too busy just trying to get through the day as best as they can!" Rockye replied.

"We as a human race need to be more conscious of each other around us. It's sad that people are literally dying around us; emotionally, spiritually, as well as physically, and people don't even notice a thing!" Bailey said with her eyes transfixed on the crackling fire as though she didn't even hear Rockye's comment.

"Easier said than done! We all got too much shit going on in our lives. It just seems like we don't have enough time to take care of our own lives, much less to really look around and care about our neighbor. It's funny 'cause the other night I had this dream where I was lying in bed one morning, and I had a stroke. It was like five or six o'clock in the morning, and I couldn't even move. I could feel it happening to me, but I couldn't do a damn thing about it. I couldn't even yell or nothin'. I lay there and died all alone, and nobody ever came to see about me!"

"Hey, I thought I was the only person who thought weird shit like that." She lifted her cup in Rockye's direction. "Glad to know that I'm not alone in crazy thinking."

"Nobody should die alone! It's just too sad! People really need to be more present with each other. We need to be more caring and observant!"

"I know, Rockye, I don't want to die alone with nothing to show for my life but a bunch of money in the bank that the IRS will take. That's why things had to change! If I want something different for myself I have to do things differently. It's really all up to us—to me. I must make the change. I must make it happen—me—only me!"

"I think that after everything that I have done, Bailey—you know, with all the other men, that maybe I don't deserve to live this life with the love of a good man!" Rockye reflected.

"Rockye, we are our best selves when we are in healthy relationships. We are our best selves when we find a core group of people we can communicate with, share with, and depend on! It's a sad, lonely life when we isolate ourselves from one another!"

"—relationships can be so hard!"

"It all boils down to a mind-set. Just make up your mind to do it, and then just do it!"

"How can that be so easy for you to say? What the hell has come over you? Just the other day you were a monologue of doom and gloom. What the fuck happened?" Rockye retorted.

"I should be asking you that question. It appears that the role of the person of reason has shifted. What the hell happened to *you*? Is this pessimism the reason you wanted to talk to me?"

"Andy and I had a big fight a few weeks ago! I haven't seen or talked to him since. And I don't know what's going to happen when we do finally talk! I felt that all I knew that was right with the world—my rock—my constant—is gone! Our relationship may be over because of me and my bad Karma," Rockye confessed.

"What happened?" Bailey asked, anticipating the reason. "He went bipolar again?"

"Come on, Bailey, that was uncalled for! Why do you always have to say shit like that about him?"

"Okay! Okay! I shouldn't have said that! But did he catch you with somebody?" Bailey questioned.

"No! He didn't catch me with somebody! I haven't seen you in a while, but, Bailey, I have changed! Something happened to me, and I'm a new person. I see things as though I'm looking through new eyes. I am no longer that same person that felt it necessary to satisfy every personal desire that I had just because I could. I am *not* that person who feels the need to satisfy my flesh on a whim. That's not me anymore. Now I want something deeper and more lasting. In spite of the problems that Andy and

I have, he really is the man for me! I love him like crazy, and I decided to stop all the craziness and give myself to him 100 percent," Rockye explained.

"Okay, so if he didn't catch you with somebody, then what happened?" Bailey asked.

"Well, it happened after he called his mother. He fucking snapped! I have never seen him like that ever before. He actually thought I was his mother and tried to choke me out! I was so fucking scared!" Rockye started to tear up.

"Did he hurt you?"

"Not really! But I'm so afraid for him, and I don't know whether I should call him or just give him some space. What should I do?" Rockye pleaded.

"Lose that asshole's phone number and move on with your life! You are a beautiful girl, and there are so many other men out there that will love and appreciate you without any of his crazy-ass issues. Do what I did—get rid of the trash in your life and liberate yourself from it. Besides, maybe you should consider going back black anyway!"

"I *know* that you just didn't go there, Miss Half and Half!" Rockye defended.

"*That* comment wasn't necessary! All I'm saying is that it has been too long already; it's just time to give up and move on. Get in a relationship with a man that doesn't have so much baggage! A man that can love you like the queen that you are! You deserve a happily-ever-after, and the proverbial white picket fence with the knight in shining armor!"

"Are you kidding me? Are you trying to tell me that you think that there *is* such a thing as a perfect relationship? Are you *serious*? Every relationship has its issues! Ain't shit perfect, Bailey!" Rockye said.

"Maybe not, but you won't have to deal with a mental case! That man is a fucking nut!"

"Be careful, Bailey, you're talking about the man that I love! He may not be perfect, but he is perfect for me! Your problem is that you've been in such a dysfunctional relationship with that pervert Chance for so long that you've lost touch with reality on what a healthy, loving relationship looks like!"

"I may not have had a healthy, loving relationship, but I do know dysfunction when I see it. I messed up a lot in my life, but God knows that I'm reclaiming myself back from that abyss of destruction. I deserve better, and so do you! I've accepted reality, and all I'm saying is that you should too! You should run as fast as you can away from that situation and don't look back!" Bailey concluded.

"I can't give up, Bailey! I remember one thing that my grandmother told me before she died. I was just a little girl, but I can remember it like it was yesterday. She said that no matter what you are going through you can choose to get out of it by running from it, or you can choose to hang in there. It's easy to run; however, it's not easy to put on your killer shoes and fight. It's your choice to rule or rest! So with that in mind, I decided to fight for my relationship! I will not give up!"

"Whatever! All I know is that in the end you will be the one that ends up getting hurt! That man is a fucking lunatic! In my opinion, that relationship is a waste of time! You have set yourself up for one gigantic disappointment. You can convince yourself that you are in love with him if you want, but all I know is that his behavior scares the shit out of me. Rockye, I just want you to get out of it before you get hurt!" Bailey stated.

"Bailey, I'm glad that you have found strength and courage. I'm glad that you feel optimistic about your future, but that doesn't give you the right to tear mine all apart! Andy and I may have had our problems, but we really love each other. What happened to you is your story—it is not *my* story!"

"What happened to me is that the reason nobody cared about me was because I didn't care about myself! Now that I do, I will *never* let others take advantage of me or mistreat me ever again. I have the power—not them—*me*! And that is all I want for you! That is all I want for you!" Bailey repeated.

Rockye eased up close into her friend.

"Your story is not my story, Bailey! Andy and I love each other, and we will get through this with flying colors. And in the end, we will be better off than ever before—watch—you'll see!"

Rockye's words fell on deaf ears because Bailey was crying inside, tears from a huge abyss of concern for her friend. Rockye was a stunningly beautiful woman on the outside, but in Bailey's opinion, on the inside, she was an open sore of disease and had not even realized it yet!

"I'm afraid for you!" Bailey cried. "I feel something bad is going to happen."

Rockye cradled her friend's hand within hers while looking deep into her glassy eyes before replying.

"Don't worry about me, I'll be fine! Andy and I will work it all out; trust and believe we will be better than ever! You will see—you will definitely see!"

"Rockye, I read in an article once that said, *'Life should be understood looking backward and lived moving forward!'* Had I taken that to heart a long time ago I would not have wasted most of my life feeling so torn up because of other people's actions or opinions of me. All I want for you is what I want for myself—the best of everything that life has to offer!"

"Well, then, you can stop wanting that for me because I already have it!" Rockye chimed in.

Fear slithered up Bailey's spine. She shook her head, trying to cast off the sense of foreboding. "I hope so," she whispered.

Chapter Forty-Five

Rockye Haynes

*S*ometimes you have to be strong all by yourself. What ultimately is meant to be will end being just as it is supposed to be and what's not—won't!"

Love is worth fighting for! But Rockye didn't want to be the only one fighting. She remembered the countless times when Andy was fighting for them, and now she was the one doing the fighting. This fighting thing was uncomfortable—it was really hard! Is this what he felt all those times when he was fighting for them all alone?

On the drive home, Rockye thought about Andy and the way things once were between the two of them. Some of her earliest memories were of them finishing each other's sentences, laughing at the same things, holding hands, and eating off each other's plate. She thought about how his voice always gave her comfort.

Without knowing it, their relationship had changed. She hadn't realized how much she had grown accustomed to Andy's presence until he was no longer around. And now all she could think about were the good things about their relationship.

There was this huge hole in her heart at his absence. When you really love someone, there is nothing else but the yearning to be close to them that haunts you when they are absent. Hearts do not have calendars, nor do they understand the notion of time or distance. They only know how it feels to be without each other. This is the reason why you miss someone so much when they are not there. Your heart only feels their absence, even though the separation may be temporary.

For some strange reason, Rockye began to crave Andy. She craved his good night kisses, the way he always made her feel adored. She wanted to be with him, next to him, listening to him breathe; she missed his smell; she missed his energy.

She hoped desperately that things would turn around sooner than later. She wanted her man back; she ached for the way things used to be between the two of them.

She got so lost in thought that she had not realized she was now parked in her driveway. Gathering her belongings from the passenger seat, she hurried out of the car and to her front door for the night air held a chill that she was not prepared for in her thin blazer.

After Rockye managed to get through her front door, the first thing she did was check her answering machine. Since Andy hadn't called her cell phone, the only hope she had left was her home answering machine.

Damn! No blinking lights! No messages!

"Damn, where was he?"

Worry started to grip her stomach. The somersaults it was doing in her belly made her feel queasy. She decided to take a long, hot bath, for the hot water always made her feel better.

After brushing her teeth to remove the tangy flavor of the hot wing sauce she ate earlier for dinner on her tongue, she ran a bath laced with a Casablanca Lily fragrance. Stripping from her clothes, Rockye slowly lowered her naked body into the soothing heat of the water. Letting out a rather audible sigh of satisfaction, she allowed her body to succumb to the inviting water, melting away the tensions and frustrations of the day. She sat there taking in the silence of the house while the heat from the water relaxed her body. It did feel good, but regardless of how hard she tried, she ached for Andy.

Why hasn't he called? Could it mean that we are really over? No! Couldn't be! It was just a silly argument! He couldn't possibly throw away everything that we had together just because of one fight—could he?

A sinking feeling welled up within the pit of her stomach! It ached for an answer! She longed to hear his baritone voice, she hungered to be in his arms, feel his lips dancing on her neck as the tender kisses he planted gave her chills. It was funny how she even missed him chastising her about her clothing!

"Where in the hell could he be? And why hasn't he called?" Rockye called out loud into the bathroom's heavy silence.

Questions and more questions darted in and out of her head. She thought that she knew this man, but come to find out she didn't really know him at all! The man she loved so much would not have let her walk out of his life without a fight! She thought about the argument that night.

How could it be that a man who loved her so much could hate his mother so much? He *really* hated that woman! From the few stories that he told her, she understood why. She now tossed around the idea that maybe that was the reason he always suspected her of the same behavior as his mother. Did he really believe that she was cheating on him, or was it him projecting about his mother onto her?

Her body experienced a wicked shiver as she replayed the words he spewed at her when he was choking the shit out of her that day in his kitchen.

"You and that cunt of a mother of mine can burn in hell for all I care. I hate you! I hate her."

She remembered when his eyes glazed over as though he no longer was in the room with her, but with his mother instead.

"You never wanted me! Why didn't you just get an abortion? Why didn't you just kill me when you found out that you were pregnant with me instead of torturing me my entire life?"

Rockye knew at that point that she was in danger, for the man she loved was not the man she loved at that moment but the boy who was hurt by his mother. He was not in the room with her, but in the house of pain with his mother.

"*Why did you always choose all the men over me? Why didn't you ever love me?*"

Rockye kept calling his name, but he was lost in that dark, deep hole—that hole that only his mother could pull him into. At that moment, she realized that if she didn't get out of that apartment, he would have killed her, thinking that it was his mother!

Bailey's words crept into her thoughts. She always said that he was crazy—a lunatic—not quite right in the head!

"Was Bailey right? Is Andy really crazy?" She had always convinced herself that he just had a bad childhood, you know, like most people! He wasn't crazy . . . or was he? She vacillated back and forth.

She was tired of speculating. She wanted answers. She was no longer going to be a passive woman sitting and waiting for her man to resurface, waiting for him to validate her with a phone call. She would get the fucking answers she wanted. She would get the answers she deserved!

A fire started to burn rapidly in her belly! It got hotter and hotter until her entire body was heated with curiosity. Rockye propelled herself out of the water; quickly towel dried her body, and threw on her pink Juicy Couture sweat suit. She was going to Andy's to get answers!

Pushing through each amber signal light, she arrived at Andy's house in record-breaking time. After circling the walkway, she hit his front door and knew instantly that he wasn't home.

Several weeks' worth of *L.A. Times* was sitting at his front door! Rockye walked to his parking stall and saw that his car was gone!

Where could he be? Frantic for an answer, she retrieved her cell phone from the passenger seat of her car and called his cell phone. It went right to voice mail, then she called his house and the answering machine was full. She now had become desperate, so regardless of the lateness of the hour she called one of his coworkers. He had no clue where he had gone! He was taking a leave of absence was all he had told them.

Rockye's heart sank! Something was definitely wrong! Could he have just had enough of her antics? Why would he leave and not tell her he had gone? Was their fight really *that* bad? Did this relationship mean more to her than to him? Was he with another woman? Had he been seeing other women when she was out doing her dirt?

Maybe Bailey was right; he finally had enough of her shit and moved on!

She once heard someone say, "There are the haves and the have-nots!" And right now, she was for sure a have-not! A career on Broadway—NOT! A man who loved her—NOT! A happily-ever-after—NOT!

Rockye sat on the stoop in front of his house. She didn't know what to do next! They say when you don't know what to do, just do nothing!

She sat on his step doing nothing!

Absolutely nothing but watching the traffic pass by . . . feeling like she had really screwed up her entire life. Why didn't she recognize that she had a good thing with Andy? Why had she been so careless with her man's love? When Andy was feeling her, actually loving her, she had been too busy running behind the elusive orgasm with strange men. Now, Andy had disappeared, to God knows where, and she didn't know if she'd ever see him again. Just the thought made her stomach plummet into the depths of despair.

Chapter Forty-Six

~ The Circle ~

I alone cannot change the world, but I can cast a stone across the waters to create many ripples." Tyler pondered the quote of Mother Teresa as he surveyed the pleasant faces sitting in front of him. He fashioned a satisfied smile as he took the helm in front of the group.

"So, by the look of you all, I can tell that there's a lot going on!" he commented as he carefully surveyed the room, allowing his attention to land on Carlos.

"Carlos, it seems you've been out in the sun. What's going on with you?" Tyler questioned.

"I met somebody." He smiled a wide smile. "—and I am so incredibly happy!"

"Who is he, and how did you meet him?" Rockye asked.

"He's Marissa's, my coworker's, brother. She had been telling me about her brother for the longest and finally we went out." He scanned eyes for reactions.

"I tell you guys that I have never met anyone like him before in my life! It's like we were made for each other," Carlos beamed.

"Tell us about him!" Tyler urged.

"There is so much to tell! He's gorgeous, funny, and smart, and umm—sensitive, loving, and patient. But the most important thing is that he really gets me! I tell him how I feel about things, and he really understands me! I can really be myself with him, without being afraid." He tilted his head to the side.

"I never had a person who understood me so much like David does." His soft eyes looked around the room with the naiveté of someone in young love.

"He sounds very special Carlos," Pam, the newest member of the group, expressed.

"He is! But what I love about him the most is that he makes me laugh. We are always laughing! It feels soooooooo good to laugh! David has me in stitches all the time!"

"Okay, so you laugh, but have you guys got busy yet? You know, knocking boots?" Keno asked.

"Don't be so crass, Keno!" Bailey barked.

Carlos twisted around in his seat, noticeably nervous from the question, for his glances darted around the room like flitting fireflies. He cleared his throat before answering.

"Our relationship is more than physical; it is mental and emotional."

"Oh, I see, so you still a virgin then?" Keno egged.

"What the hell is wrong with you?" Bailey voiced. "Show some couth sometimes!"

"Carlos, it's okay to exercise some restraint until you feel comfortable enough to take it to the next level. Things come to us when we're ready. It's not good to rush anything. I'm glad that you are taking your time," Tyler added.

"Yeah, just be patient like I am with Andy. I know in my heart that things will eventually work out!" Rockye added.

"I agree with Rockye. The element of patience allows the unfolding of destiny to proceed at its own unhurried pace. When we are impatient, we create misery for ourselves and for everybody around us. We rush to rash judgments and act without considering the consequences of what we are doing. Rushed choices are forced and often incorrect, and we are most assuredly going to pay a steep price for this rush to action," Tyler instructed.

"Yeah, I don't think you should rush into sex before you really get to know him," Lynette commented.

"When you are patient, you will inevitably gain understanding. The more you understand a person, the less likely you are to have a knee-jerk reaction and do something harmful to yourself or the other person," Tyler finished.

"Believe me, I'll be patient because I don't want to mess this up at all! It feels so right!" Carlos stated.

"I miss Dee Dee. She was the only person that could just look at me and tell what I was feeling." Keno's face carried deep sadness.

"I could call her on the phone and within a few sentences, she could pretty much tell what was on my mind and what kind of day I was having. She always knew what to say to me—always!"

"It sounds like you really miss her a lot," Pam said.

Keno nodded. "I really do! I fucked up really bad! And the worst part about it is that I can't reach her to tell her how sorry I am. She doesn't even know that I'm willing to do whatever it takes to fix things!" He nervously picked at his fingers.

"I would give anything to have her back!" Keno concluded.

"It serves you right if you never see her again!" Bailey barked.

"That was pretty harsh!" Lynette commented.

"Yeah, after all, he *is* sorry!" Pam added.

"Like you have never made a mistake before in your perfect little life?" Keno defended.

"I have never cheated on anyone before! I think that shit is foul! In my opinion, you got what you deserved! You had a good woman, and what did you do? You cheated on her with someone for the sake of money! She should have left your cheating ass!" Bailey barked.

"Bailey—take it easy now!" Tyler directed.

"That's okay, Tyler, Bailey's right! I got what I deserved! I had the most incredible woman in the world in my corner, and I just fucked over her! I deserve to be miserable!" Keno conceded.

"I don't believe that! Just because you make a mistake doesn't mean that you should be doomed forever. You were simply trying to survive the best way you knew how," Lynette sympathized.

"Yeah, from what you've told us, trying to get a job with a prison record and getting turned down again and again had to be really hard on you! And I have found that we can do some really bad things even though our intentions are good. So don't beat yourself up so bad, Keno. Even though you cheated on your girlfriend it wasn't done maliciously!" Carlos reasoned.

"Oh, hell, no! I don't believe that you said that shit! Put yourself in her shoes. You have a man that you love the hell out of. You do everything within your power to make him happy—at the point of denying yourself sometimes. You do things that in your heart you do not want to do. You put your feelings and needs and wants on the shelf to satisfy his requests, and what happens in the end? He hurts you so bad that it's almost impossible for you to go on each day without thinking about it, without it tearing at your insides. It hurts you so bad that you feel like you are literally going to die! A person like that doesn't deserve to ever feel good again in life!" Bailey retorted.

Everyone in the room stared at Bailey in disbelief, for they knew that she was not talking about Keno and Dee Dee; she was talking about her and Chance. It was painfully obvious that that wound was far from healing over.

"While it is not good to lie or ever mislead anyone that you are in a relationship with, sometimes we can justify what we do because we are so immersed within the situation. I am not excusing what Keno did! Not at all! But he made the choices he made based on the extreme set of circumstances that he was dealing with!" Tyler reasoned.

"Keno, it is commendable that you have come to terms with what you did to your girlfriend. I think that if she were here today and heard how remorseful you are, from what you have told us about her, I believe that she would forgive you because she sounds like a very compassionate woman. So if Dee Dee would forgive you, then you must forgive yourself! And after you forgive yourself, then you must make amends to those you have hurt, and that includes the woman that you are living with now. She is as much a victim as your girlfriend," Tyler concluded.

"I don't know how you are going to do it, Keno, but you got to move out of that woman's house and out of that situation as soon as possible. You are for sure using her, and she is for sure pimping you!" Rockye said.

"And from the looks of it, you don't look like you're very happy there anyway!" Lynette added.

"I'm not, and it's getting worse every day! I feel like I'm sinking so far deep into my own mess." His eyes surveyed the group. "What do you do when you don't know what to do or where to start?"

"I'll tell you what I'd do. I'd do a quick assessment of what I really want in my life at that point, and then I'd ask myself, what am I willing to give up to get it, and then I'd brace myself and make the decision to do whatever it takes to accomplish it! And then I'd just put my total focus into it and not look back until it's done!" Rockye advised.

All eyes stared at Rockye because they had never heard such conviction in her voice.

"One thing you must consider when you're making a decision is what you want the outcome to be. Ask yourself what's your objective. And when you determine what your objective is, then you work backward to accomplish that objective. Ask yourself, Keno, what you want your life to look like in 6 months, in 1 year, in 3 years, and then work backward to make that happen." Tyler then turned to Rockye.

"Rockye, it's so good to hear you speak with such confidence. Did you decide to take that part in the production that would move you to New York?" he asked.

"You know, I realized something the other day. I realized that for me, the only thing that matters to me is having real love in my life. Having someone that in this crazy world we live in that has eyes only for me! I realize that all of the money in the world is worth nothing if you don't have at least one person who really knows who you are and still loves your ass anyway!" She smiled a knowing smile before continuing.

"I've been taking Andy for granted. And in my brokenness I was looking for something, looking for someone else to quench the emptiness I was feeling inside. I was a hot mess, and now I'm so grateful that I have finally had an epiphany and am no longer in that thunder cloud of delusion and confusion," Rockye explained.

"Wow! What a change!" Lynette commented.

"How does Andy feel about this new you?" Tyler asked.

"I'll tell you when he comes home. I don't know where he is! He's MIA," Rockye said.

Tyler's eyes raised in query. "MIA?"

"We had a fight, and I haven't seen or heard from him in weeks," she confessed.

"Tell them what happened," Bailey prodded her. "He put his hands on her! Choked her and threw her out in the street!" she concluded without allowing Rockye time to respond.

"Did he hurt you?" Carlos asked with concern.

"NO!" Rockye shot Bailey an angry look.

"Yes, he did! She just doesn't want to say, but the son of a bitch choked her and threw her out of his house like she was a dog!"

"It didn't happen like that! He just had a really hard time dealing with something. That's all! Sometimes he gets a little—"

"—bipolar! That bipolar asshole is crazy!" Bailey stated.

"Come on, Bailey—"

"Come on, my ass, Rockye! That white boy is crazy! And you need to leave his crazy ass alone before he kills you!" Bailey said.

"Do you feel like you're in danger, Rockye?" Tyler asked with a wrinkled brow.

"Absolutely not! Andy loves me and would never lay a hand to hurt me! Ever! He was just having a bad night because of something that happened with his mother, that's all!" She turned to Bailey.

"—and no matter what happens, I'm never going to leave my man! When you love somebody you fight for them! You don't leave when the going gets bad! That's what's wrong with people today; they walk away when things get a little bad! I'm going to stick it out and stay with my man until the end!" Rockye defended.

"Until the end all right! You're going to mess around with that lunatic, and he's going to put your ass in the hospital! Hey, but YOU are going to stand by your man. Yeah ... *right*! Whatever!" Bailey's tone held sarcasm as she rolled her eyes into the air.

"Well, I think that it's admirable! If people felt more like that we would have fewer divorces and less broken homes," Pam commented.

Before Tyler turned to address Pam he concluded with Rockye. "I know that you love Andy, Rockye, but make sure that you are not putting yourself in any danger. Look at the situation objectively and make a decision based on the facts not feelings. Will you do that?"

Rockye smiled an acknowledgment. "I have, Tyler! Don't worry, I'm in no danger! No danger at all!"

"Okay then." He turned to Pam. "So, Pam, how are things with you and your husband? You look happy! Did the two of you reconcile?"

"Oh no! He has moved on with a younger version of me, and the only thing that we have in common now is the specifics of the divorce settlement." She flashed Tyler a wide smile.

"Okay, then, I give. What has you so utterly beaming? As a matter of fact, what has the two of you looking so radiant?" Tyler asked Lynette and Pam.

Lynette said, "I just want everyone to know that this lady next to me has one of the most incredible business minds around. She single-handedly put together a business plan for an Internet Web-based fashion and design company.

"This business is going to make us millionaires in our own right! And to top it off, she has set aside enough money for all of the startup costs, and then some. Because of her we'll be independent of my father and his money!" She winked at her new business partner.

"That sounds exciting! Congratulations, Ladies!" Tyler said. "I wish you two the best of luck in your new business venture!"

"Listening to you guys today, it seems to me that most of you have had a paradigm shift."

"What's that again?" Keno queried.

"A paradigm shift is when a significant change happens; usually from one fundamental view to another. I want to share with you guys the BE—DO—HAVE PARADIGM," Tyler started.

"Huh?" Rockye said.

"Most people believe that if they 'have' a thing, more time, money, or love, for example, then they can finally 'do' a thing, write a book, take up a hobby, go on a vacation, buy a home, start a relationship, which will allow them to 'be' a thing, be happy, peaceful, content, or in love. In actuality, they are reversing the Be Do Have Paradigm. In the world as it really is, as opposed to how you think it is, 'having-ness' does not produce 'being-ness,' but the other way around.

"First, you be the thing called happy, or knowing, wise, or compassionate, then you start doing things from this place of being and soon you discover that what you are doing winds up bringing you the things that you always wanted to have.

"The way to set this creative process in motion is to look at what it is that you want to 'have,' ask yourself what you think you would 'be' if you 'had' that, then go right into being it.

"In this way, you reverse the way you've been using the BE DO HAVE PARADIGM. In other words, in life, you do not have to *do* anything. It's all a question of what you are being!"

Tyler got up and started pacing. "Things just don't happen. They are driven by agents of change! Things happen in our lives because of something that changed. Can you give me an example of something that happened in your life recently that has caused you to change?" Tyler's eyes surveyed the room.

Carlos spoke up. "Well, for me, it happened when my little brother ran away from home, for when we didn't know where he was, I saw my father crumble and turn into a broken man. It was at that point that I then realized that he was just a regular man, not the Superman that I had made him out to be in my mind! From that point on, my father became human, subject to human strengths as well as human weaknesses. Shortly after that is when I started accepting my own differences. I started accepting my sexuality, and because of that, I became open enough to allow someone into my life and into my heart!" Carlos said.

The silence provided the nudge Rockye needed to contribute.

"For me, my life changed when I got the job offer of a lifetime. I thought that if I took that job I would for sure lose my man. I didn't like that thought at all! At that point I got clarity in my life about what I really wanted. I realized that I wanted love in my life more than money, validation, or fame. I want a family to come home to. I want children and a husband that rubs my back at night. I want a house that I can complain about keeping clean, dishes in the sink, trash that has to be taken out, and grass that needs to be mowed. I realized that I want *all* of that! What happened to me was I discovered what I really wanted in my life, and as a result, I no longer feel lost or empty. One day I'm going to marry Andy, start my own dance school for inner-city kids, and have a whole lot of babies!" Rockye concluded.

"That's wonderful, Rockye!" Tyler acknowledged before turning to Pam to share.

"Even though my husband threw me away for a younger woman and abandoned his commitment to our marriage, I discovered that I am pretty terrific just as I am, not to mention one hell of a businesswoman. I'm starting a business with my stepdaughter, and for once, I truly love who I am!" Pam added.

"That's fabulous, Pam," Tyler responded; he then turned to Lynette.

"When they told me that I couldn't have more plastic surgery, I started to spiral down into a very dark place. But then, my stepmother came to my house needing a place to stay after my father put her out of his house, and for whatever reason, I guess pride and ego, I couldn't let her see me in those dark places, so I pulled my ass together, and in the process, we found out that we were not what my father had been saying that we were all this time. We discovered that his opinion of us, our value, and worth as women did not have to be our opinion and value we have of ourselves. What happened to me is that I discovered that I was more than what I looked like or what others thought of me. I discovered that I have value and I have a lot more to offer the world just as I am and not how I look physically!" Lynette added.

"I'm so proud of you, Lynette!" Tyler smiled a smile of satisfaction before his eyes landed on Keno.

"So many things have changed for me. When my girlfriend found out that I was fooling around on her and left my ass, I talked my friend into doing a crime, and now he's in jail doing time instead of me. The guilt is fucking me up! The woman that I was cheating on my girl with is now treating me like I'm an inconvenience and a burden. Every day I feel as though the rug could be pulled out from underneath me at any time! I lost the best thing that had ever happened to me in this crummy life, and for the life of me, I have no fucking clue what to do to get myself out of this damn mess I created! I get it now! For when you do fucked-up shit, that shit will eventually catch up with you! Wrong always catches up to you!"

Tyler didn't comment on Keno's remarks but turned instead to Bailey, who had been watching everybody with a look of disdain on her hardened face.

"Bailey, what has changed for you?" Tyler questioned.

"What has changed for me? I have learned that if you count on people, you set yourself up for a for-sure disappointment. If people can't do what they are supposed to do for God, what makes you think that they are going to do things for you?

"So I don't allow people to be a deciding factor for altering my life any longer." She paused before continuing.

"I have successfully purchased one of the largest independent real estate brokerage firms in Southern California. My competitor was getting old and losing his edge. I found an opportunity to capitalize on it and bought him out! I am now the largest, most successful independent brokerage firm not only in Southern California but on the West Coast! What happened to me is that I discovered true independence, and I discovered it by my own POWER! I don't need anybody! I only need ME!" Bailey concluded.

Tyler looked at Bailey. He knew that she was speaking from a place of significant pain and hurt. Her parents had been a constant sore spot in her life, and their abandonment was hitting her very hard.

Tyler looked at his watch. They had gone over the session by 25 minutes. He brought conclusion to the session by giving them an assignment for the next meeting.

"Write down what you want your life to look like in 1 year, 5 years, and 10 years from now," he instructed. "Give me details, about a paragraph or two, for each year, and make it as detailed as you can." And with that he dismissed the Tuesday afternoon group.

Tyler replaced the folding chairs neatly up against the wall after the group dispersed. After straightening up the room he then collected his briefcase and coat to leave, anxiously anticipating going home to relax in his oversized La-Z-Boy recliner, drink a beer, and eat the leftover chili he made 2 days prior. The seasoning would be perfect, and his mouth started salivating at the thought.

"Not bad!" a voice startled him in the distance.

He turned around to see Jango in the corner. Tyler smiled at his friend.

"Jango, how long have you been here?" he asked.

"Long enough! That was pretty impressive!" Jango fist pounded his friend and business partner.

"I do my best, but I am not you!" Tyler complimented.

"Stop being modest, buddy! In my book, you give me a run for the money," Jango admitted.

They proceeded to walk to the front door together.

"Have you decided to come back and lead The Circle sessions yet? Without the religion this time?" Tyler added.

"I prayed about it, and now I'm waiting on God's answer." Jango slapped Tyler on the back, and then continued.

"But, Tyler, I have to admit that you are really good at this. I could learn a few things from you."

"Are you saying the man with the double major in psychology can learn something from *me*?" Tyler joked.

"Okay, you got me! I'm sorry that I said that I was more qualified than you at this! I was really trippin'!" he retorted as he watched Tyler lock up.

"You forgive me?" Jango asked.

"No need! We boys!" Tyler reassured him.

Jango smiled and fell in tow beside Tyler as they walked out to the parking lot.

"You hungry?" Tyler asked.

Jango nodded his head. "I can always eat!"

"There's some leftover chili at my house, and last I looked there were three beers in the frig. We can fight for the last one!"

"Right behind you, buddy! Right behind you!"

As the two college buddies walked to their cars in the parking lot, Jango shot Tyler a proud smile. "'Paradigm shift, huh?"

"Paradigm shift—" Tyler echoed.

"Impressive. Didn't know you knew—"

"—not bad for a man with a minor in psychology, huh?" Tyler baited.

"Not bad," Jango conceded. "Not bad at all—"

"—they miss you, you know? Especially *her*," Tyler interrupted.

Jango grunted.

"There is one benefit if you don't come back, you know. The two of you can date each other!"

"I don't know about that."

"She needs you, man, and truth be told, you need her. I see the way the two of you look at each other. Do you love her?"

Jango cleared his throat.

"Be honest!"

"I do. I really do!"

"Then you need to think long and hard about your next move, don't you?"

"I'll take it to God in prayer."

"You are nothing if not consistent, my friend."

"I will always wait on God before making a move. It's how I roll."

"I ain't mad at you! If a brother can't stand for something, he will fall for anything."

"Now did you say that you got some chili at home?" Jango asked.

"—and beer."

Jango thought about it. He wanted Bailey, but he wondered what was holding him back from making the first move…

Chapter Forty-Seven

~ Bailey Levine ~

Who says a passionate impulse can't be a rational decision? Bailey envisioned herself behind the wheel of a white GT Bentley convertible ever since she saw that caption on a Bentley Motors Web site, her long tresses blowing in the wind, and her favorite black Bvlgari shades shielding her eyes, confirming her status of eminence.

She decided that today was the day to make that concept a reality! She had finally accomplished the acquisition of Shultz Realty and within months she would see a drastic increase in her profit margin. Money would be rolling in as a result of the merger.

Along with her successful real estate firm, Bailey desperately wanted to possess a confidence in herself. She wanted to feel empowered! Deserving! Worthy! Entitled! She wanted to feel worthy of love, happiness, and a great life, because when you know your worth, no one can make you feel worthless. And now she was ready to operate in that sovereignty. And today would be the start of operating in that fact by indulging in that passionate impulse; buying that white convertible Bentley! CASH!

"The W12 engine's ability to make 9 percent more power and 15 percent more torque is due to much more than tweaking the boost output of its twin, low-inertia turbo. Nearly all engine internals have been reengineered to reduce mass, including the pistons, connecting rods, and even the timing chain. The fuel economy and carbon-dioxide emissions are both improved by 3.5 percent." The words jetted from the salesman's mouth as his eyes scanned the promo sheet in his hands.

"Is that so?" Bailey responded although she had tuned out his droning.

"The standard GTC has a kind of incongruous acceleration, and it feels a bit like a locomotive with a resolute, unstoppable urgency. Before you might expect it, the tachometer needle swings in a blur up to the 6,500-rpm redline and the six-speed automatic gently supplies yet another ratio and even more speed." He revved the engine for effect.

"I see!" Bailey said, half-listening. As she sat next to pitchman in the passenger seat, her body melting into the fine Italian leather upholstery, she mentally took ownership of the car and her new life.

"The Bentley Continental GTC Speed is more powerful, more poised, and more controlled than ever before. The exquisite Continental GTC now has a sharper, more assertive disposition that still doesn't compromise the car's effortless ability as a grand touring machine," the salesman continued.

"Uh-huh!" Bailey responded.

Bailey wasn't paying too much attention to the novice young salesman's pitch. She had decided earlier that after all the papers were signed on one of the biggest mergers of the largest independent real estate firms in Southern California with hers, making her now the largest independent real estate firm in the West, that she wanted to do something extremely lavish for herself. Something that when she looked at it, it would scream that she was successful. She was accomplished! A winner! It would be evidence; it would be her trophy; the symbol of her worthiness!

And after the destruction of her happily-ever-after fantasy with Chance, she needed something to make her feel better, and a brand-new convertible Bentley would just be the ticket!

Weeks ago, while surfing the 'net, an ad popped up on the screen for the Bentley Continental GT Speed. At that very moment, she decided that she had to have it. And ever since then, she started anticipating the close of the merger and thereby the purchase of this magnificent piece of machinery.

Now today, after all was said and done and the last legal document was finalized for the merger, she dragged her exhausted but elated body out of her quiet office, emptied of bustling, eager employees, to head home for the weekend. Bailey had decided that she would make two trips before retiring home. One to Applebee's for an Asian chicken salad, and two, the Bentley dealership in Beverly Hills. And not necessarily in that order.

"Do you have any questions, ma'am?" the young salesman interrupted her thoughts.

"Yes, how long have you been working here?" Bailey asked.

"This is my second week!" the young salesman announced proudly.

"Let me give you a piece of advice—uh—" Bailey searched the badge on his shirt for his name.

"Adam Pope."

"Adam, you are very good at reciting all of the facts about this vehicle. However, people do not buy because of the facts. They buy because of the benefits that they will receive as a result of obtaining the thing that they want to buy."

Bailey walked around the car, eyeing its sexy details.

"Do you even have a clue about why I want to buy this car?" she asked as her hands caressed the hood of the car.

"I guess it's because you want one?" A stupid look washed over his face.

"Because it's sexy—it's exclusive—it screams success—it differentiates the driver from most people. It's because it's a status symbol!" She positioned herself behind the wheel.

"Because when you own one of these fine vehicles, it shows the world that you are now playing with the big boys! It shows that you are extraordinary!" Bailey concluded.

Adam eyed her with a look screaming confusion as what to say next.

"I don't care about torque and the recalibrated management engine system whatever—all I care about is the look on people's faces when they see me drive up in a car worth almost $300,000!"

Bailey turned to fully face Adam.

"Do you understand?"

"Yes, ma'am!" he timidly responded.

"Good! Now let's get to the paperwork! I want to be out of here as soon as possible!" Bailey turned and started walking back to the office with the eager young salesman following closely in tow.

Bailey felt that out of all the things that had gone wrong in her life, this was tangible evidence of one thing that she had done right: a successful career!

This would show the world, her parents, and Chance that she was indeed worthy!

What more did she need? Wasn't she on top of the world? Didn't she have it all?

... Or did she?

She paused. Something in the pit of her stomach bothered her. She knew the truth. Underneath all of her accomplishments, she knew she still felt empty.

Chapter Forty-Eight

⁓ Keno Hunter ⁓

"Anxiety's like a rocking chair. It gives you something to do, but it doesn't get you very far."
Keno's heart knotted within his tight chest as he sat on the couch, anxiously awaiting Sharon's arrival. The embers in the travertine fireplace crackled noisily, announcing the settlement of the recently added log. The house was uncharacteristically quiet and dark. Keno had turned off all of the lights except the one lamp that hung above the couch where he sat. Sharon had been nagging profusely about the rising electric bill, amongst others, and to circumvent any more verbal altercations, he simply turned off everything except for sufficient light necessary to ward off blinding darkness.

The clock was kissing eleven, which normally was characteristically late for Sharon, but ever since she had made it abundantly clear that his presence was unwanted, she had been hitting the door closer and closer to midnight for the last 2 weeks. It was painfully obvious to Keno that she was avoiding him. So tonight, Keno decided that he would confront Sharon and see if, by any means necessary, he could restore the harmonious symbioses their relationship once shared.

Five minutes to twelve, Keno heard keys unlatching the lock at the front door. He straightened up from the languishing position he had settled in on the couch. Startled by his presence sheltered in the darkness, Sharon let out a small yelp as her eyes adjusted to take in his shadowy figure. She pulled up the knob on a wall, bringing illumination to the room.

"What the hell? You scared the shit out of me!" She walked over to the chair adjacent to him and switched on another lamp.

"What the hell's the matter with you? Why are you sitting here in the dark?" An obvious aggravated attitude leaped from every word.

Keno ignored the question. "Sharon, we need to talk." His voice was barely above a whisper.

"I'm tired, Keno! I have an early-morning meeting, and all I want to do right now is take a hot bath, have a drink, and go to bed." She hastened her step to the bedroom before Keno could respond.

Keno eventually got up and followed Sharon into the bedroom. She had removed her dress, her undergarment Spanx, and pulled her shoulder-length hair up within a black scrunchie. He eased up behind her.

"Do you love me, Sharon?" Keno asked.

"This is not a talk that you want to have!" Sharon warned.

"As a matter of fact, this *is* a talk that is long overdue." He stood in front of her, tall and erect, as though positioning himself for battle. He asked her again. "Sharon, do you love me?"

Sharon gazed at him with an expression of disgust. "Love?" She chuckled. "I once loved the representative."

"Excuse me?" Keno asked with wrinkled brow.

"The person that you presented yourself to be in the beginning of this relationship is the person that I once loved. You had this cavalier cockiness, a brazen boldness about you that held a sexy arrogance." She held an expression of reflection for several moments before continuing. "There was this something about you, something that I admired and resented about you all at the same time. There was this strong maleness that you carried around with you like—like a badge." Her eyes then caught his, and her countenance softened.

"I looked at you, and all I could think of was that I had to have you at any cost. I resolved that I would do whatever it took to own you. You had become my obsession!" Her eyes caressed him from across the room as she voiced her feelings.

"There was something in the scent of your sweat, something in the taste of your semen, something about you that I couldn't quite define, but it possessed the very essence of me!" She abruptly went into the bathroom and squatted down on the toilet to take a piss. A tiny fart pushed through.

She had an uncanny way of extricating herself from a situation at the most inopportune times, he thought. And in this case he was very disturbed by the timing and the audacity of the act. *How fucking disrespectful!*

Keno watched her as she peed, then got up, removed the electric toothbrush from its cradle, and brushed her teeth; all of this without washing her hands. *Nasty bitch!* he thought.

"There was a time when I couldn't wait to get back in your presence once again. I couldn't go an entire day without thinking about you and missing you! I would even think up excuses to call you just so that I could hear your voice." She continued through a mouth full of toothpaste.

"The way you made love to me made my body implode! I have never had so many orgasms at one time in my life!"

Sharon pulled out her multicolored satin head scarf and pink foam curlers from underneath the sink and started to roll up her hair; something she never did in front of him during the earlier part of their relationship.

"Everywhere I went, I saw something that I wanted to buy for you! I just wanted to see you happy—to see you smiling!" She stopped rolling up her hair for a moment and glanced at him through the reflection in the mirror.

"You were everything to me, and I couldn't imagine my life without you in it!" She sighed to herself.

"You never answered my question," Keno insisted.

Sharon looked up at him blankly.

"Do you love me?" he repeated.

"How can you love someone you don't respect?" she coldly stated.

Keno eyed her without comment.

"You are a weak man, Keno! You honestly didn't think that sooner or later that line of bullshit that you sell people wasn't going to backfire on you?" She finished rolling her hair and carefully tied the satin scarf around her head.

"You blame your failure in life on your prison record or your bad breaks! You blame this situation or that person! You toss the blame on everybody else *but* you!" She paused before continuing. "Once I took off my rose-colored glasses and saw beyond that wide, sexy smile, your captivating charm, your timely wit, and your relentless skills in bed, I saw what you really are! You are a NOBODY masquerading to be a SOMEBODY. You are a user, a liar, and a coward!"

Sharon walked up so close to him that he could smell the Crest toothpaste of her breath.

"Do you, for a moment, think that I didn't know about that little bitch you were sleeping with? What was her name—Dee Dee?"

Keno's heart sank as he heard Dee Dee's name jet from her now-twisted lips. What did she know about Dee Dee? The room started to spin. "Sharon—what did you do?"

"Shut up! I'm talking! You shut the fuck up! I once told you that I am not a woman to be fucked with! I don't like weak, bitch-ass men. I used to admire you; now I pity you! You think that you could fuck around on me and I would never find out about it?" She padded over to her walk-in closet, went in, and came out with a brown, oversized envelope.

"I know where you go, who you see, what you spend, where you spend what you spend, and even when you take a shit!" She threw the envelope on the floor in front of him. As it hit the floor, its contents spilled out.

It seemed as if he stopped breathing. Everything appeared to be happening in slow motion. Pictures of him and Dee Dee kissing slid forward amongst many pages of his personal information, such as cell phone bills, credit card statements, bank statements, and the like.

"I know that you spent many nights wondering why she disappeared so quickly." A sinister smirk covered her face.

"What did you do to her?" Keno reared up.

"You'd better lower your fucking voice and take a few steps back off of me before you find your black ass shot in the fucking head right here in the middle of this fucking floor!" Sharon threatened as her body positioned to execute her threat.

Keno stepped back; he remembered the gun in her wall safe.

"Just what I thought! Ain't got no balls, muthafucka!"

He slowly bent down and picked up the envelope and all of its contents off the floor.

"I knew how you felt about her! Loved her, didn't you? Hurt your ass like crazy to lose her, didn't it?" She went back to the closet and returned with a videotape and held it out for him to take.

Keno was lost for words. Was this really happening? No, it couldn't be. He had to be dreaming. This had to be a horrific dream. Yes—yes—this had to be a dream! However, he pinched himself and realized that he wasn't dreaming. He was indeed awake and living this fucking nightmare!

"Go ahead and take it! You might as well see what I showed your precious little girlfriend!" Sharon let out a wicked laugh.

"What is this?" Keno asked as he scanned the tape for a label.

"Just a little movie of you and me enjoying ourselves in bed!" She replicated the wicked laughter, but this time it seemed to come from deep within her soul. It sent chills up his spine; thousands of tiny needles on attack alarming him of his impending fate.

"What the fuck? What did you tell her? What did you say to her?" He shook himself from the trance.

"We had a nice little talk, Dee Dee and I!" She smirked. "I really see why you cared for her and why you were so heartbroken. She is really a sweet little thing! Not much to look at but sweet!"

Keno held his head in his hands as he yelled out, "Why—Why—Why did you do this?"

"Go ahead take a look at the video," Sharon provoked. "Should I get you some popcorn?"

Keno hurried to the VCR and inserted the tape. Within seconds nauseating visions of him inserting his tongue into Sharon's rectum while she deliriously screamed in pleasure played in front of him on the oversized plasma flat screen. He sat there in utter shock as he noticed that his body felt abnormally foreign.

When did she tape this? Keno had no idea that he was ever being taped. No idea whatsoever!

"What did she say when she saw this?" Keno asked in a frantic voice, his heart still racing at the shock.

"You know, I got to say that she is one class act! I could tell that it shook her to the very core, but she behaved like a real lady. She watched it all the way through without so much as a tear. It didn't matter how she tried to control herself, though. I could tell that it really fucked her up!" Sharon recalled.

"What did she say?" Keno asked, his face etched with defeat at the query.

"She asked me why I found it necessary to come show her that tape."

Keno hung on her response.

"I told her that I wanted her to know the type of bastard that she was dealing with!"

Sharon bent down and pulled out a stack of Hallmark cards from the manila envelope on the floor.

"She may have been cool and calm in the beginning, but it wasn't until after she saw these loving cards that you had given me did she lose it! I think she felt that you really loved me. Poor little thing rushed into the bathroom, and as much as she tried to hide it, I heard the sobs loud and clear through the door!"

Keno held his hand to his head, shaking it back and forth. "Why—Why—Why did you do this?"

"Why did I do this, you ask? It's simple. Revenge! I told you to never fuck over me! You thought that you could come in here and use me, spend my money, lie to me, all the while professing love to some other woman!" She laughed another wicked laugh.

"You fucked with the wrong woman, Keno!"

Keno threw his head back and yelled, "How could you do this? Oh my God! Ohhhhh myyyyyy God!"

"There is a saying that goes like this, 'When you play with matches you may get burnt.' In your case, Mr. Badass, you decided to play with dynamite and you got yourself blown the fuck up!"

Sharon marched out of the bathroom and to the front door.

"Keno!" she called.

He walked out into the hallway.

"Get the hell out of MY house!" She held the door wide open for him.

He looked at her, and then his watch. *What the fuck is she talking about? Does she want me to leave this very moment? Does the bitch know what time it is?* His mind inventoried the many lies he could spin at her to get her to change her mind. Although his mind was reeling with what she had just confessed, he knew that he had to quickly come up with a plan to calm the bitch down. He wasn't about to let her kick him out.

"Come on, Sharon—let's calm down here! Let's just sit down and talk about this. We can work it out—we can work this all out!" he pleaded.

She held her stance.

The wall clock shifted loudly at each second as he became painfully aware that she was standing her ground. It appeared that she really wanted him to leave. He could find no soft spot in her eyes for him. So he began to take the first step from abundance to fucked!

Slowly Keno walked over to the table in the foyer and picked up his car keys.

"Leave with what you came with!" Her eyes demanded him to replace those keys.

"Sharon, you can't be serious. What am I going to use to get around with?" he asked.

Sharon looked at his feet.

Shaking his head, he picked up his cell phone.

"I said leave with what you came with!"

He stared at Sharon's face which was hard and cold, and then replaced the cell phone back on the table next to the car keys.

"Also leave all my credit cards and any cash in your pocket!"

He pulled out his wallet and emptied its contents on the table.

Keno eyed his jacket hanging from the coat stand. *Come on, bitch! You can't be that damn heartless, can you?*

"What the hell, I'm feeling generous. Take it!" Sharon spewed as she held the door open wider.

Keno pulled his jacket close to his body, inserted his hands in his pockets, and walked out the front door. As soon as his body entered the hallway, the weight of the door as it slammed behind him shook the wall.

Keno moved listlessly toward the elevator, his head tucked into his neck. His world, the world and life he had had with Sharon, had just come to a rapid end.

He never saw this coming, he thought; losing Dee Dee was a formidable blow, but now he had lost his job, his car, his clothes, his money, and the holder of the purse—his paramour, Sharon Faraday. His life was fucked. Now there was no one who really gave a shit about him. The only person who really cared about him in this miserable world was gone—Dee Dee was gone! He had no one to turn to. He was alone, lonely, broke, and homeless. He had really fucked up his life this time!

What a mess! What was going to be his next move? He had no idea.

Chapter Forty-Nine

~ Bailey Levine ~

Who owns a million-dollar home, was the sole owner of a multimillion-dollar business, and just bought a three hundred thousand-dollar GT Bentley, cash? Bailey Levine, that's who! Bailey felt on top of the world and kept reciting in her mind, *nothing can bring me down now!* She'd beaten back her feelings of emptiness, and started focusing on her accomplishments. For the moment, she felt fine.

Bailey stood at her kitchen sink staring out of the double-paned windows at her newly purchased Bentley which rested proudly in her long, manicured driveway. The events of the day swam around in her mind. At the strike of the four o'clock hour that day, Levine Realty officially celebrated the acquisition of Sid Shultz's real estate firm, making Levine Realty the largest, privately held independent real estate company on the West Coast. It had been an arduous acquisition due to the fact that Sid vacillated on the terms of the agreement at least half a dozen times.

One of Sid's main concerns was honoring the contracts for his agents, especially the veterans. He had been known for the generous benefit packages with his seasoned agents: no desk fees, generous commissions, no office administration fees, extensive marketing and advertising support, etc. While these items were a bone of contention for Bailey, she finally realized that in the long run she would be getting much more than she was giving up, so she conceded to most of the terms.

So minutes after four p.m., as her office celebrated the growth of her real estate firm, Bailey reminisced on how far she had come, the many challenges and roadblocks that she had managed to overcome in her business. The most challenging was sitting amongst her white clients muffling her voice of disapproval as she ignored their racist jokes about minorities.

Because of her Anglo-Saxon features, she was mistaken for white 100 percent of the time. Her keen features, light skin, and silky straight mane allowed Bailey to be welcomed into the club of the "pale people," as one of her college friends called it, and ostracized by the "people with pigment," as the same college friend referred to all people of color.

Sitting across the table from those racist clients made her sick to her stomach and often so angry that the encounter generated intense migraine headaches. But no matter how angry she got the majority of the time she just sat there and said nothing—all in the interest of a dollar. The burden of carrying around the shame and guilt became so overpowering sometimes that it caused her to be often overwrought. That was why she had developed a habit of acquiring an evening drink to dull of the pain.

So at that very moment as she looked out into the yard at her newest symbol of success, she reviewed her accomplishments; owning a home valued at over one million dollars, a tremendously successful real estate firm, and a vehicle worth almost $300,000 sitting in her driveway! Anyone looking in from the outside would say that Bailey had it going on!

Although Bailey kept telling herself that she was on top of the world as she looked at the showpiece in the driveway, it was not at all the case.

On the contrary, as she sat sipping her wine, she acknowledged that she felt anything but successful. Bailey still felt empty, alone, and lonely. Material possessions in and of itself didn't make her as happy as she once thought. She thought to herself, things and accomplishments are not worth a damn thing without someone to share them with! And right now, right there in her kitchen, Bailey realized that she had absolutely no one in her life to share her good fortune with!

Her only friend, Rockye, was off on some journey to find her man. It was impossible to have any type of conversation with her because Andy was all that came out of her mouth, and to be frank, Bailey was quite sick of hearing about it.

Bailey hated the fact that she didn't have a man in her life with whom to share her accomplishments. She quickly emptied the contents of her third glass of wine and continued to ponder her desolation.

And then her mind traveled to her parents! Bailey felt her heart sink and the pit of her stomach churn as she dwelt on the fact that they had not returned any of her calls nor tried to contact her for months. What hurt the most was her father's ambivalence! Bailey could understand her mother's dismissive behavior; after all, their relationship had always been strained, combative, and filled with hurtful recriminations most of her life, but the one thing that she thought she could always count on was her father's love and adoration. She felt comfort in the fact that she was Daddy's little girl, and no matter what hurtful things her mother may have said to her or about her, she knew that her father loved and supported her. Bailey felt that she could always count on her father, in spite of what was going on between her and her mother.

Bailey never imagined in a million years that her father would have turned out to be such a spineless coward!

"Look at me! I have all of this and nobody to share it with!" Bailey cried out loud into the spacious kitchen.

"What good is having success in your life if you have no one to share it with?" she asked herself.

After pouring yet another glass of wine, Bailey moved over to the couch and curled up with her Chardonnay. It took tremendous resolve not to break down in a flood of pity tears. She had never felt as insignificant in all of her life as she did at that very moment. Bailey wondered to herself how many more nights her life would be filled with such emptiness and loneliness.

The wine was taking its toll on her, and she drifted off into a wine-induced sleep. An infomercial for the Tread Climber was on her television when her cell phone startled her back to consciousness.

It was the hospital! There had been a terrible car accident. They had Bailey as the emergency contact. It was serious, she was told by the attending nurse.

"Is she alive?"

She held her breath awaiting the answer ...

Chapter Fifty

⁓ Rockye Haynes ⁓

*S**ex is not the answer. Sex is the question. 'Yes' is the answer."*
"I can't take this anymore. I'm about to explode!" Rockye screamed.

Rockye raised her head above her overstuffed pillows for the fifth time since retiring for bed just after midnight to glance at the clock which ticked 10 minutes past four a.m. The night air was pleasantly warm for a spring morning, as a slight breeze played her wind chimes which decorated her bedroom window. She was extremely restless and desperately horny. Even after pleasuring herself about four times, her clitoris continued to throb and pulsate.

As her eyes remained transfixed on the ceiling, her mind played back film from a prior indiscretion.

One fall morning a Time Warner cable man appeared at her door to replace a malfunctioning cable box. His name was Maurice. Nothing exceptional about Maurice other than his full mouth and pink tongue that continued to make annoying sucking noises through his teeth.

As he moved deliberately in front of her, installing a new cable box, Rockye zeroed in on his lips and his tongue. Eventually, he became aware of her fixation on his mouth.

"You see something you like?" he asked with a newfound sexiness.

"That depends," Rockye teased.

"On?"

"How well you can use what God gave you."

Maurice moved closer to her and dragged his heavy pink tongue slowly over his upper, then bottom lip. A sexy smile drew her deeper in.

"How about this?" He pressed up against her and eased his tongue into her waiting mouth, allowing it to dance slowly within hers. She moaned from pleasure. He was a phenomenal kisser, leaving her unnerved and wanting more.

"So you can kiss! But can you lick and suck?" Rockye boldly asked.

"Better than a bitch!" he confidently stated.

"Oh really?" Anxious to find out, Rockye moved to the other side of the room and sat down on the edge of the couch, holding her legs slightly apart, enough to expose the fact that she was without panties.

"Oh really, my ass!" He rushed over to the couch. She allowed his hands to maneuver off her clothes and position her in an optimum position for oral copulation.

From the moment he placed his hot mouth on her vagina, Rockye knew that she was in for an amazing treat. This man owned her pussy from the moment he slid his tongue up and down her clit. He suckled, nipped, licked, lapped, and literally buried his entire face within her wet mound for at least an hour before she cried out for him to stop. Around her sixth orgasm as the juices ran down her ass, she let out a scream that was sure to wake the dead.

"Oh, pleeeeeeease stop! I can't take it! Pleeeeeeease stop!" Rockye cried as she stiffened her body for yet another explosive orgasm.

"Come on, girrrrrl, you can give me another!" Maurice urged as his tongue never left her bobbing and weaving vagina.

"Stop—Stop! I cannot taaaaaa—ke it any—mooooorrrrrre!" She expelled as she gushed a release of hot, wet, bodily fluids for the seventh and final time.

"So, what's the verdict?" Maurice asked, displaying her sexual juices all over his face.

"Oh yea—a bitch has nothing on you! You can kill a pussy!" she exclaimed.

He moved in closer. "Now that you know that I can lick it, I'm going to show you how well I can stick it!" He mounted her and proceeded to fuck her like a rabbit for 2 hours.

Now as she lay alone in her bedroom, boyfriend MIA, she couldn't sleep due to the throbbing in her groin.

She picked up the phone and dialed Andy's number yet again. And once again, she got voice mail immediately. Where the hell was he? she asked herself for what seemed like the hundredth time that day.

Her efforts to be a patient, understanding girlfriend were beginning to wane.

"Fuck this shit, I need some dick! I need some lovin'! I need Maurice!"

Throwing caution to the wind, Rockye got up and found his phone number under "Cable Man" in her cell phone contacts and called him.

He answered on the first ring.

"It took you long enough!" he announced through the phone.

"Hello, Maurice! This is Rockye!"

"I know *exactly* who this is! I've been expecting your call!"

"Excuse me?" She wasn't really sure if he knew who he was talking to.

"Rockye, I've been waiting for your call ever since that morning. I knew that sooner or later you would call." His cockiness was transparent.

Whatever! she thought to herself. He could think whatever he wanted. She just needed him to come over and serve her up. She was climbing the walls and couldn't take it another hour.

"How quick can you get over here?" she asked with a sense of urgency.

"Where's your man?" Maurice asked.

"That is none of your business!" she stiffened up.

"It's all of my business if I don't want to take a bullet in the back of my head!"

"My man is out of town! He's not the concern here! My pussy is!"

He laughed a knowing laugh. "I'll be there in less than an hour."

The phone went dead. Rockye rolled over and played with her pussy until she climaxed yet again! Her body was jonesing for sexual release, and she didn't have time to wait for Andy to resurface. She felt her body about to implode if she couldn't explode and climax over and over! She needed the feel of a man inside of her, and she needed it right away!

She leaned her head back and got lost in the thought of hot-gushing, butt-cramping, gut-hosing orgasms. *Hurry the fuck up, Maurice. Hurry the hell up!*

I need my nut! Times like this a vibrator won't do. I need some straight-up thug loving!

Chapter Fifty-One

☞ Bailey Levine ☜

One thing about tragedy, it takes the focus off of self! Apparently, a drunk driver had run a red light and struck the 1980 Honda Civic at 75 miles an hour, forcing the vehicle head-on into an intersection. It took the Jaws of Life over an hour to extricate the driver from the vehicle which had collided with a Metro transit bus.

"She has no family!" she answered when the nurse asked her about immediate family.

They needed authorization for surgery, and since Bailey was listed as the "in case of" emergency person in her wallet, Bailey's urgent presence at the hospital was required.

"I should be there in less than twenty minutes!" Bailey grabbed her keys and rushed out the door. She was no longer thinking about herself but the welfare of her devoted employee, Felicia, who had been in a terrible car accident.

Once at Cedar Sinai Hospital Bailey anxiously paced the waiting room for the emergency room staff to inform her of the condition of her assistant, Felicia. The cramped waiting room was jam-packed with a horde of injured victims and anxious, concerned families.

Eventually, she heard her name called over the PA system and rushed to enter the door that was held open slightly by a stoic, slightly overweight nurse holding a manila folder in her left hand.

"Are you Bailey Levine?"

She nodded and quickly secured herself within the confines of the narrow hallway that she had just entered.

"Come with me then," she added as she moved swiftly down the corridors of the hospital to a back office near an elevator.

"Have a seat in here. Doctor McClendon will be with you shortly." And with that she was gone, leaving Bailey alone, terrified and anticipating the worst.

The doctor entered in shortly afterward, his furrowed brow indicating the seriousness of the situation.

"Good evening—uh—" He searched his paperwork for her name.

"Bailey Levine. Just call me Bailey! How is she, Doctor?"

"I'm afraid it's very serious, Bailey. She has sustained many internal injuries. She has massive internal bleeding, broken ribs, and a ruptured lung. Her left leg is broken in so many places our best hope is to just save it. We won't really know the full extent of her internal injuries until we go in!"

"What is her condition now, Doctor?" Bailey's voice cracked with foreboding.

"She needs surgery immediately; time is of the essence." He looked at the paperwork in the folder he was holding. "Are you a relative?"

"She has no family that I know of. I'm her employer. She works for me."

He rubbed his short beard before continuing. "Apparently we have two issues here, Bailey. First, we need an authorization for surgery. It looks as though you are the person she listed as the emergency contact, and second, it appears that she does not have any medical insurance!" He looked at her, fully expecting her to clarify the issue one way or another.

"I was not aware that she didn't have insurance because it's available to all of my employees, but what has that got to do with anything?"

"If we cannot verify medical insurance, then we will have to transfer her to the county hospital," he coldly reported.

"County? Are you fucking kidding me! She could die in the process!"

"I understand your concern, but we would not let her die; however, protocol calls for us to—"

Bailey cut him off. "—to hell with protocol! She will *not* be going to county. I will pay for whatever she needs! Just take care of her! Do whatever needs to be done to make her well. I will take care of all the costs!"

"I must warn you that her injuries are quite extensive and the expenses will be rather costly."

"Doctor, don't worry about money. It will not be a problem! I will take care of it!" Bailey declared.

Bailey eyed the doctor. "She will not be moved to county! The surgery will be done here!"

"Miss Bailey, do you have any idea how much this will cost?" the doctor asked.

"I don't care how much it will cost; I just want her to get better! I have the money. Don't worry, her bill will be paid!" Bailey proclaimed.

"By the time it's all over, it could be close to several hundred thousand dollars!" the doctor boldly confirmed.

Bailey instantly thought of her Bentley. Returning the Bentley should do it!

"I got it covered. I don't want Felicia to die! That is all I care about!"

"Very well then, come with me. I'll take you to Admissions." The doctor closed up the folder and swiftly maneuvered Bailey over to Admissions.

After the paperwork was completed, she asked the nurse if she could see Felicia.

"She is being prepped for surgery, but I guess you could see her for a few moments. Follow me." The nurse waddled over to pre-op with Bailey closely in tow.

"I'll give you a moment. I need to go check on her blood work and test results before she goes into surgery." She disappeared.

Bailey eased up to her bed. Felicia's tiny braid-framed face looked childlike, sunken deep within the folds of the hospital bed. Her face, severely bruised, displayed smears of dried blood in her hair and on her neck and face. There was a huge tube coming out of her mouth, and many smaller tubes extending from all other parts of her petite body. The sight terrified Bailey and confirmed the seriousness of the situation.

Doctor McClendon emerged. "It's time to take her to surgery now."

"When will I know something, Doctor?"

"Just as soon as I know what we are dealing with." His answer lacked a modicum of bedside manner. "You will be informed just as soon as we know more."

The doctor turned and walked out of the room.

Bailey stroked Felicia's hand as she was wheeled out of the room.

"I'll be here when you wake up, Felicia!" Bailey called out to her assistant as she exited the room. On the off chance that she could hear what was going on around her, Bailey wanted to let Felicia know that somebody was there for her!

"I'll be right here when you get back!" Bailey said to her employee and friend as the door pulled shut.

For once in a very long time, Bailey was not thinking about herself but of the welfare of someone else! She planted herself in the hard chair that faced the clock in the room Felicia was just wheeled from.

It would be a long night! A very long night! Hopefully, the news of death would not come with the morning.

Chapter Fifty-Two

~ Keno Hunter ~

"*If things get bad, they'll most likely get worse.*"

The cold breeze racing in the night air chased him, matching his hurried steps as he moved fervently down Wilshire Blvd. The thickness of it numbed his face, making way through his leather jacket to the thin material of his shirt, and finally resting on his flesh. It was a bitter cold, a cold that belonged exclusively to the lateness of the night.

Traversing down Wilshire Blvd., Keno hadn't a clue about what he would do next, where he would lay his head, or how he would be able to provide for himself now that his benefactor had excommunicated him from her bed, her life, her house, her pocketbook! What the hell was he going to do now! He was now homeless, jobless, and womanless! And as his grandmother would say, "He didn't have a pot to piss in or a window to throw it out of!"

How the hell did it all go so wrong? Keno asked himself.

He couldn't believe how much he underestimated Sharon. He had always believed in the powers of his male prowess. His ego allowed him to believe that it was impenetrable! But was it? Dee Dee left him, and now Sharon! Her diabolical plan to disenfranchise him from his Dee Dee while stripping away his dignity, as well as his belongings, was far more than he thought she was capable of. What kind of woman would throw a man out into the cold night with only the clothes on his back, no money in his pocket, no car, and no place to go? A heartless bitch, that's who! Fucking dried up old ass, bad breath skank! She would never be able to keep a man if it wasn't for her money!

Keno cursed her as he advanced eastbound on a somewhat abandoned Wilshire Blvd. Quickly, his emotions turned from anger to worry to panic! Where would he go? What would he do for money? This was the first time in his life that he didn't have some female that he could depend on to help him out of a bad situation! He could not think of one woman that he could turn to for a hot meal, a warm bed, the use of her vehicle, a few dollars for his pocket, or endless hot pussy! Dee Dee, sweet Dee Dee was long gone! That bitch Sharon put him out and snatched his whole world right out from underneath him. Keno had never been without a variety of resources, and he started to panic. A sudden sinking feeling erupted within his chest, one similar to riding on a sudden drop roller coaster. It was hard for him to catch his breath as his heart did what seemed like massive somersaults. He suddenly felt dizzy and off balance.

As the cold breeze kicked his ass with each hurried step, his eyes scanned the street for a clue about what he should do next or what direction he should take! There across the street was a bus bench with a steel partition surrounding it. He would rest there for a while, sheltering himself from the night hawk as he gathered his thoughts. Scanning the deserted streets, he jaywalked over to the other side, stuffing his hands deeper into his jacket pocket to escape the penetrating headwind.

After searching the night sky as though expecting a clue for direction, Keno folded his arms across his chest, and as he leaned up against the steel grate, he prayed, something he had not done in such a long time. A bright star in the night sky glistened. It pulled at him, bringing the thought of his grandma to his mind. Granny Ann was his sweet, loving grandmother, who was his only source of authentic love in his life as a child. She always knew the right thing to say to him when he had gotten himself in a *"pile of trouble,"* as she would always say. She was the only woman he believed loved him unconditionally and without an agenda. The star twinkling brightly above him somehow stirred up a sense of her presence in that moment.

He lifted his glassy brown eyes in efforts to connect to her in the heavens above and spoke softly to her into the distance.

"Granny Ann, it's me, Keno. I really miss you so much. Boy, did I go and get myself into a 'pile of trouble' this time. I need your help, Granny! I don't know where to turn. I really messed up this time. Not only with Dee Dee and Sharon but with my whole life! I ain't done nothin' with my life but screw it up! I got this criminal record that holds me back from getting a good job. I ain't got no real skills but my hustle and game." He chuckled. *"At least I thought I had hustle and game! I really should have listened to you, Granny. If only I had listened to you instead of ditching classes and hanging out with the wrong people, I would have graduated high school and went to college. If I did I would be something right now instead of wandering the street in the middle of the night with no place to go!*

"Just to think of what my life would be like right now if I would have only listened to you! I would not be out here on the street, homeless, broke, alone, and cold as fuck—sorry, Granny—cold as a fish!

"Granny Ann, please help me and show me a way out of this horrible mess! Please help me." Keno prayed until he felt calm in his body and a slow rhythm in his breathing.

When Keno was done, he opened up his eyes and looked to the right and left of him as if expecting an immediate answer. The streets were empty and still. He rocked back and forth in an effort to generate a little heat from the penetrating cold. Moving deeper into the enclosure of the bus seating area, he thought about how it was that the homeless could sleep in such unbearably freezing cold conditions. Pulling his jacket closer to him provided no relief; it only reminded him that he was not equipped for his present situation.

Closing his eyes once again Keno resumed the dialogue with his deceased grandmother.

"Granny Ann, I really had such a wonderful girl in my life. You would have really loved her. She was so sweet, and you know, Granny, my Dee Dee really loved me. But what did I go and do? I cheated on her with another woman. I remember you telling me so many times that it's hard enough to find a great love, but if you find a good one, then you are for sure blessed. I found a great love, a woman that always had my back and looked out for me no matter what. I didn't deserve her, truly I didn't! She was so perfect for me though. But what did I go and do? I went and totally messed it all up by dealing with Sharon. I got caught up with the money and all the stuff that she could do for me. I knew what I was doing to Dee Dee was wrong, but I didn't care! All I thought about was my own self. I didn't think about her and how she would feel! I just thought about the money, my car—oh, do I miss my Benz right now—the clothes, the jewelry, and the food—oh my goodness, Granny, I ate so good! I thought I had it all under control. Huh! I can see now that I didn't because the player got played this time!

"Granny Ann, can you reach down from heaven and show me what to do now? I don't want to do another crime! I really don't want to break into some person's house, or rob a man on the street, or steal someone's car! I really don't want to do to another woman what I did to Sharon. Even though Sharon was a piece of work, she didn't deserve for me to treat her like I did and use her. She really didn't!" Keno had a moment of remorse for his actions.

"What I really would like to do, Granny Ann, is maybe start my own business and earn my own money! I just want to pay my own way from now on! I did what I did because I didn't know any other way! I really didn't know any other way! Granny, can you show me what to do now? Please, Granny, help me!"

Keno leaned his head to the side of the steel cage and continued talking to his grandmother until he fell asleep, his jacket pulled up tight against his body and the collar attempting to fend off the rushes of wind.

As the temperature dropped, a few buses pulled in and out, and a steady stream of night travelers cruised down the street. Keno nestled up against the enclosure and drifted into a foggy sleep on the very street he once called home; a penthouse suite in one of the most exclusive condominiums on the Wilshire Corridor. Due to the night weather, he'd wake up every half hour or so to make sure he didn't die from exposure. *Dang!* Contrary to popular belief, it was cold in California at night! He would stand up and would also look around to make sure no one tried to attack him. He felt like a cornered animal, and knew if he had to he'd kill anyone who even tried to bother him.

Suddenly he heard some rustling. He looked down . . . and saw it was a rat. He let out a little yelp! He stomped his feet. "Get away! Scat!" The rat scurried off into a hole.

Feeling bereft, Keno shook his head. Oh, how far he had fallen!

Chapter Fifty-Three

~ Bailey Levine ~

How is it that the lack of sleep always made her feel like she was coming down off of a medicinal high? Felicia's surgery lasted 12 hours, and after 4 hours in recovery she was eventually transferred to ICU. As Bailey waited for the prognosis of the surgery, she took inventory of her myriad of feelings. Her life had taken an abrupt turn in under 24 hours. To think that just yesterday she was celebrating the acquisition of Levine Realty and the cash purchase of her symbol of success, a brand-new GT white convertible Bentley.

Now she was sitting in the hospital awaiting the outcome of Felicia's surgery. Would she live? Did they save her leg? The reality hit her as the day's light filtered in through the narrow hospital window that her trusted employee may not live to see another day, or possibly live without a leg.

Bailey felt small as she realized how unimportant the things that she felt were so important just hours ago. She felt guilty as she revisited the insignificant issues that plagued her before the phone call from the hospital. Life is so precious, and the health of your loved ones even more so.

Suddenly, she felt a huge desire to see her parents. She longed to talk to her father and make up with her mother. It didn't matter who was right or wrong. All that mattered was that they were alive and they had each other. For where there is life, there is hope.

Doctor McClendon appeared red-eyed and haggard in the doorway. His face carried no evidence of a successful surgery. The prognosis was still uncertain; the next 48 hours would determine Felicia's fate. Because of the severity of her internal injuries, it could go either way; she could die or make a total recovery. Only time would tell.

She sat in the waiting room after hearing the news, uncertain about what to feel. If she was a praying woman, she would pray right now. But because she wasn't particularly a religious person, she felt that her prayers would fall on deaf ears, so she sat and rocked back and forth on the seat as the weight of her exhaustion covered her like a blanket.

"May I get you a cup of coffee?" a friendly, round-faced nurse inquired.

The afternoon staff was considerably more attentive and compassionate than that of the morning. They reassured Bailey that they would take great care of Felicia and that she should go home and get some rest. If any changes occurred they would notify her immediately. Laura, Felicia's shift nurse, was a lanky, curly-headed woman from Atlanta. Her Southern accent and maternal nature afforded Bailey with enough reassurance that her assistant would be okay for a few hours of her absence to indeed go home, shower, and rest. So she collected her tired body and exited the waiting room, carrying the weight of her exhaustion and anxiety with each step.

Her plan was to go home, take a long, hot shower, grab a quick nap, and return, hopefully, refreshed to some good news! At least that's what she told herself.

As she hit the nurses' station, she reiterated to one of many uniformed women milling around the center station, "Nurse, if there are any changes—" Bailey said, pointing to Felicia's room, "please give me a call!" Bailey handed the nurse her business card.

The nurse seated on a stool closest to her looked up from behind a mountain stack of patient files and acknowledged Bailey with a smile and a nod.

Bailey trudged to the elevator, got in, her feet feeling cement heavy, and with the dwindling energy she had left, pushed the down button marked *L* for lobby.

Resting up against the right side of the elevator, Bailey surveyed the hallway in front of her as she waited for the doors to close. In the distance she observed a man that oddly resembled her father. As she strained to focus, her tired eyes confirmed that it was indeed her father.

"Dad?" she said with a question of uncertainty as she jetted out of the elevator and scampered up to the man holding his head in his hands.

He lifted his head to the familiar voice.

It *was* her dad!!!

He looked so old and fragile; she made the mental note as she caught full sight of his face.

"Bailey!" Relief washed over his sunken pale face. He rose quickly to fall into her embrace and wept uncontrollably.

"Dad! What's going on? Why are you here?"

"It's your mother! She's slipped into a diabetic coma!"

"Dad, what are you talking about? Mom doesn't have diabetes!"

"She does, honey!" He fell back into his seat as Bailey looked down at him, fully witnessing her father's frailness. "I'm sorry to tell you, but she does, Bailey. She has for some time now."

"For how long? How could you have kept something like this from me?"

"It is a long story, honey! Your mom didn't want me to tell you! She didn't want you to know. You know how prideful your mother is." He grabbed her hand. "She begged me not to tell you! I tried to convince her, but she refused to listen. You know how stubborn your mother can be."

"Dad, I'm confused! I don't understand. How long has Mom had diabetes, and why is she here in the hospital in a coma? What does that mean?" Bailey was becoming frantic.

"Your mother has had diabetes for some years, but lately, her body began to reject the insulin. And a few days ago she slipped into a coma. The doctors say that she has renal failure now!" Her father looked up with a helpless expression on his face.

"Who told you that that your mother was in the hospital?"

"Nobody! I was here visiting a friend when I saw you sitting here, Dad! Is that why you haven't returned any of my calls?" Bailey asked.

"It's a long story, sweetie! I'll tell you all about it later." He grabbed her hand.

"She hates me, doesn't she? Why does she hate me? How can she not tell me that she was sick? I don't understand any of this!" Bailey started to cry.

"Your mother doesn't hate you, sweetie! It's complicated. So many times I wanted to talk to you about it but—"

"—but what?" Bailey searched her father's eyes for clues.

"Let's talk about that another time." Her father lowered his head and started to cry. "It doesn't look so good, sweetie!"

"Dad, what are you saying?"

"The doctors think that she may not make it!"

"What? Mom is going to die?" Bailey cried out.

Douglas got up and hugged his daughter as she cried out in anguish.

"She can't die, Dad!"

"Honey, all we can do is hope for the best!"

"I need to see her, Dad! I need to see her!" Bailey pleaded.

"Shhhhh! It's going to be okay, honey! Shhhhhhh!" Her father consoled her.

"I need to see Mom! I need to see Mom!" Bailey cried as her father stroked her head as he had so many times when she was in distress as a child.

"Bailey, there is nothing we can do now but wait."

Bailey didn't hear anything her father said through her own sobs. She felt so utterly consumed with grief. First, she lost the illusion of the love of her life with Chance, then Felicia gets into an accident and her life is hanging in the balance, and now her mom—so much loss—so much taken away from her in such a short amount of time.

At that moment a strong sensation of dread washed over her, causing the short hairs on her arm to stand up. It was the strong feeling of impending death in the hallway of that hospital floor.

The question was . . . Who was going to die . . . her mom or Felicia?

Chapter Fifty-Four

⁓ Rockye Haynes ⁓

Sex has a smell. It has a taste. It has its own energy. It's alive. From the moment Maurice walked in the front door, Rockye knew that she had made a horrible mistake. He carried with him a perfunctory energy. His swagger was overconfident, his attitude cocky, his once-clean-shaven face was hairy and scraggly, his breath stale, and his eyes cold and unfamiliar.

Unlike before, his kisses were rushed and unsatisfactory, and his touch slimy and invasive. While she lay on the bed flinching from the discomfort of his bites in her pubic area, she realized that she had made a terrible mistake. While her man was off dealing with his own issues, instead of her praying and preparing herself for his return, she opened up her body to this man and succumbed to her sexual urges instead of controlling them.

The Maurice that she remembered long ago was long gone. And instead of lying there until it was over so as not to make a scene, Rockye decided that she was quickly going to end this wrong.

She slid up on the bed.

"Ummmmm—Maurice! I'm not feeling this anymore!" Rockye swung her legs to the edge of the bed.

"What?" He seemed riled up.

"I want to stop! I am not feeling this anymore!" Rockye explained.

"Oh no, bitch! You gonna give me what I came over here for!" He moved over to where she was sitting and thrust his erect penis into her mouth. She gagged and pushed back.

"What the hell is wrong with you? I said that I was *not* feeling this anymore!"

"Ain't you 'bout a nothing-ass bitch!"

"Excuse me?!" Rockye pulled the sheet up on her naked body.

"You heard me! I called you a nothing-ass bitch! Any female who has a man and calls another man over to fuck her is a nothing-ass bitch!" He spit on her.

"Bitches like you disgust me!"

"Get out of my house!" She grabbed the cordless telephone and raised it in his direction.

"Oh—" He laughed out loud. "You think that you can scare me with a telephone call?"

He raised his hand and slapped her across the face so hard that the impact threw her up against the headboard and knocked the phone out of her hand.

Rockye screamed at impact.

"Your man thinks that he has a woman that is into him, and here you are fucking the cable guy. Letting him run all up in your pussy and your mouth! You are *trash*!" he insulted her.

"Why are you backing up like I'm going to rape you or something? Right now, I wouldn't fuck you with someone else's dick! You ain't even worth it, bitch! You disgust the hell out of me and—" He laughed out loud. "—and for the record, I decided that I am not feeling YOU anymore!" He picked up his jacket.

"You think that you got off easy? Trust this, you filthy whore! Tramp-ass bitches like you get *exactly* what they got coming to them sooner or later!" Maurice laughed a bone-chilling laugh as he strolled out of her front door.

Rockye remained still, shaking with fear at the head of her bed, sheets held up against her naked body as she waited for the sound of his car to disappear into the distance. Her face stung from the impact of his slap, and as she held her hand to her face, she cried at the thought of what could have happened to her. He left, but it could have turned severely ugly. He could have raped her. Moreover, he could have killed her like in the movie, *Looking for Mr. Goodbar,* where the sex-addicted female character met a tragic demise.

For the first time she felt afraid of this demon taking up residence inside of her. Finally, Rockye realized that the more she pushed the envelope in search of this physical release, the closer she might come to her own death.

Chapter Fifty-Five

～ Keno Hunter ～

Where the hell am I?

His eyes popped open with quickness as the smell of bus fumes, the sound of traffic, and the sudden awareness of the presence of bodies around him jolted him to the morning. His body was stiff, and his nose was crusted from dried mucus. His mouth tasted of something rank and probably smelled as rancid as it tasted. As he stood to exit the bus enclosure, the reality of what happened last night stirred up a sudden sense of trepidation. He remembered his plight, he remembered once again that he was homeless, jobless, and without any prospects of a rich paramour to provide for him. He began to feel the weight of the enormity of it all. His heart sank, and he felt like everything was irretrievable. A sudden cloud of doom hovered over him. It swallowed him up into its dark puffiness and wrestled him deeper into its condensation.

Sometimes things just seem so big that the prospect of having a fighting chance is remote. He searched his pockets for his cell phone. Oh shit! Bitch took it! Shit! Shit! Shit! How did people navigate through life without a cell phone? It had all of his contacts, calendars, addresses, etc., in it. Wow, he felt so fucking lost without his cell phone. His stomach growled. He searched his pockets for some money. Bitch took his wallet too! Fucking old-ass, bad-breath bitch! Anger replaced hopelessness and started to seethe within him, rising up like acid reflux as he thought about what she had done. She didn't have to leave a brother broke like this!

Or did she?

He was wrong. He was dead wrong! He knew he should just take the consequences of his actions and move the hell on by making the best of the situation.

Shouldn't he?

But the anger kept tapping him on the shoulders, reminding him of how conniving bitches really are! He thought about all the women that had disappointed him in his life. He thought about every one of them leaving him, even his grandmother. She may have left him because she died, but she left him, nonetheless! *Women always leave!* he thought.

His stomach continued to rumble, and the fact that he was hungry suddenly began to take precedence over his other thoughts. Getting sustenance was now the priority. He remembered that there was a Denny's only blocks away from where he was. He would walk over there and get something to eat. Having gone to Denny's in Westwood many times before, he remembered how lax the waitresses were and knew that it would be a piece of cake to accomplish a dine-and-dash there. He was once again in survival mode and would do whatever it took to provide for himself—whatever!

The restaurant was somewhat full, and he eased in without particular notice. The bathroom was vacant, and he did a basic wash down before returning to his table and eyeing the rather extensive menu. The waitress came, he ordered, sitting quietly and rather reserved, not wanting to call attention to himself because he knew that after his meal he was leaving without paying the bill.

After gobbling down a sumptuous breakfast of blueberry pancakes, hash browns, three eggs, sausage, bacon, and ham, he felt a newfound strength and an inner confidence that was temporarily lost the night before. Fuck doing the right thing!

Fuck other people's feelings! Fuck love and happy endings. That shit doesn't happen for people like him! He told himself that he was strong, that he would survive. It was now time for him to stop feeling sorry for himself and formulate a plan to get the hell out of this fucked-up situation and back on top in a winning position. He was a king, he was a winner; he was a prize to any bitch that he decided that he wanted. If he got a rich, vulnerable bitch once, he could for sure do it again! *Pull your head out of your ass, Keno, and do what you do best! Pounce and conquer!*

He ate his belly full, waited for his waitress to go back into the kitchen and the register attendee to disappear, then he grabbed his bill and sauntered out the front door like the king that he was. Keno was back; the man that could do anything that he put his mind to was BACK!

The next item on the agenda was a hot bath, a good sound sleep, and a comfortable place to map out his next plan. Although he just ate in a Denny's, he had decided to move forward, embracing his once-sense of entitlement. He would no longer move about like a vagabond. He was royalty, and he would operate as one.

Beverly Wilshire Hotel (a Four Seasons Hotel) was not too far away. He had decided to spend the day and night there. Anybody could sleep on a bus bench, a Motel 6, or the lobby of some unguarded hotel, but Keno was not anybody. He was somebody, and this somebody wanted to lay his ass on the fine sheets of a plush bed in the Beverly Wilshire Hotel. The how didn't matter. It never did with Keno. When he set a plan to do something, his mind took to formulating the actions to making it happen. Wherever there were women and weak men, he would prevail. So he set out to the Beverly Wilshire Hotel and knew that when he got there the how would manifest itself before him in a countless number of ways. And like a true sycophant that he was, he would use his smooth flattery to get him a room and all of its 5-star amenities without paying a single dime.

Within minutes of entering the hotel he found his victim.

Her name was Lola. She was a 22-year-old Nigerian maid who fashioned pimply skin and an obvious overbite. She giggled when he flirted with her. She fingered her twists, a natural hairstyle that he found rather unflattering to most who wore them. Her body language displayed his effects on her, and within 30 minutes from eyeballing her, they were having hot, uninhibited sex in one of the rooms on her designated floors. Afterward, she gave him a key to a room that was hardly ever assigned due to its lack of view and proximity to the trash shoot *and* every dollar that she had in her pocket. She promised to return tomorrow with more money, more giggles, and sweet, young pussy! Keno was back! The king was back! She left, and he fell back onto the opulence of the mattress and its coverings, allowing himself to drift into an abysmal slumber.

The next morning Keno pulled himself together and started making phone calls. He called everyone he could think of until someone volunteered enough money for him to get a new cell phone, toiletries, and some fresh clothes. He was bound and determined to remedy his situation within the next 24 hours. Keno knew that he was not a loser and therefore decided to make it a point to get back on top as quickly as possible.

With his obvious good looks, his swagger, and the extra-large man-tool that he carried below his belt, Keno had all that he needed to regain a position of favor rapidly.

After a good night's sleep and a sumptuous meal, Keno started the plans to immediately propel himself back on top. Lola had entered his room early that morning and serviced him for several hours. He had to admit that having sex with someone that young had him working harder than he had with Sharon.

This sweet young thing had a voracious appetite and absolutely no inhibitions. Initially, he was a little rusty, but it didn't take him long to turn up the dial and crack open his repertoire of skills to turn the 22-year-old out, leaving her utterly spent and intensely enamored by his skills and the essence that is "Keno." When he emerged from the shower after their sex session, he noticed a love note on the dresser and $100. He smiled at the thought! It probably was a lot of money to her, and while he should have not taken it from the kid, he reasoned that if she was fool enough to leave it, he would fucking take it!

Stupid bitch, he thought as he slid it into his pocket before leaving the room.

He stood calmly in the lobby surveying the foot traffic. Once securing a *Wall Street Journal* from the lounge area, Keno settled in and planted himself with an optimum bird's-eye view of the main entrance. He watched individuals representing millions of dollars check in and out of the hotel; all exhibiting various degrees of wealth and success with trappings obvious to his trained eyes. He carefully assessed each prospect, analyzing all the factors that would determine their viability to his plan. His plan was that he needed to find another Sharon. He needed to find another rich woman that had an entryway of vulnerability that he could take advantage of, pure and simple. He had come to realize that he was a master manipulator of women. His extensive man-tool, his charisma and keen mental skills, could ingratiate women into his web and pull them into his world. He was handsome, smart, sexy, charming, and single. He could portray whatever character he needed to in order to get what he wanted. He was an artful chess player. And yes, maybe he lost the game with Sharon and even Dee Dee, but didn't all masters lose games sometimes? He told himself that it didn't matter that he lost, it just mattered that he learned from his loss and got better at playing the game. He was a winner, and he was a king!

❧

It took several hours before the answers to his problems graced the lobby.

She was about 5 foot 7 inches tall with a very small build, wore thick-framed glasses, flats, and a simple Anne Klein-belted sheath dress. She had wide set eyes, a sculptured nose, ears a little too small for her head, and a disproportionate lower extremity. Regardless of her plain looks, this woman walked with the air of someone of considerable means.

Keno eyed her discretely from behind a newspaper. He noticed that decorating her petite arm was a Hermès Birkin bag. Keno recognized it because Sharon had a similar bag, and he knew it to be worth over $10,000.

As she checked in, he made his way over to the guest elevators and pretended to be on a business phone call. When the elevator bell sang, indicating that the elevator had arrived, he maneuvered his way next to her and started a fake conversation for her benefit.

"I will not be able to fly there this week. Send Phillip instead. He will be a better match for our Tokyo investors because he studied there as an undergrad. Very well then, I'll call you when I return from Seattle next week." He paused as though he was listening to a response.

"No, I don't have a date yet but secure me an extra ticket if it will make you happy. I have a week to find Mrs. Right!" He chuckled, before hanging up.

He glanced over at her and smiled.

"How hard is it to find a date here in Los Angeles?" he asked.

"I wouldn't know. I am not from here." She spoke with a blue blood air.

"So you wouldn't be able to recommend some L.A. hot spots then?"

"Not really. When I do come to town I don't do much socializing."

"Well, it sounds like you could really use a night out then! Would you do me the honor of accompanying this lonely bachelor to dinner this evening?" he asked, sporting a pervasive smile.

She blushed.

"I don't know—" She started to twirl her hair as the elevator hummed to the penthouse.

"Don't worry, I won't bite! We can eat here in the hotel if you like. It has been such an arduous day, and I would simply love some company."

"Well, I guess dinner in the hotel would be okay." She smiled as she unconsciously leaned into him.

Once the elevator closed, in those brief few moments, Keno worked his magic. As he complimented her and worked his Keno charm, he could tell by her body movements that he had found his next victim. The bell dinged, signaling the arrival of the penthouse floor! The woman beside him was now leaning into him and still twirling her hair. Her smile was relaxed and had turned warm and inviting.

"Allow me the honor of helping you to your room," Keno said as he gallantly secured her luggage, then placing his hand in between the elevator doors to hold it open, he continued.

"By the way, my name is Keno Hunter." He extended his hand toward her.

She quickly met his with hers. "Juliet Foxworthy."

Keno trailed behind her. His plan would be to infuse himself into her evening, charm her with his gregarious personality, and draw her in with mental gymnastics, and finally win her over with his sexual prowess. This woman looked as though she was sexually backed up anyway.

Once he laid the pipe on her, she would be sprung! And by the end of the evening, his problems would be over! And this time he would not mess this one up!

"I'm meeting a colleague later for a quick meeting. Why don't we have dinner together afterward? Say about seven?"

"I look forward to it, Keno!"

He smiled his signature smile and touched her hand. She appeared to swoon. Easing in to him slightly, she slid her card to open the door. He pushed opened the door for her and held the weight of it open with his body as she pushed past him inside.

He placed her bags just inside the room of the massive foyer. She sensuously held his gaze, obviously enamored by his essence. Her eyebrows rose, and her lips pursed as her eyes followed him. The chemistry was there, the temperature rising, and the attraction obvious.

After completing the task of placing her luggage inside of the foyer, he gazed down into her curious eyes. She coyly smiled. He licked his lips; kind of like LL Cool J's signature move. She leaned in to him.

His eyes burrowed into hers, and hers drinking in the essence that is pure Keno. In that instant the room seemed to shrink and their breathing became labored. He knew that she wanted him, and he knew that once he fully sexed her up, she would be his; mind, body, and pocketbook!

He moved closer to her and asked, "Would you like me to stay?"

She nodded, and he eased in to her penthouse suite, allowing the door to close behind him.

Women are so predictable! So vulnerable! Was it really this easy, or was he really that good?

Chapter Fifty-Six
～ The Circle ～

"Worrying is like sitting in a rocking chair. It gives you something to do, but it doesn't get you anywhere."

Tyler scratched his head in worry as his eyes scanned the notes from the Tuesday evening sessions. He had to admit that he was not at all pleased with Bailey's progress. Her life was spiraling out of control and as indicated by the furrow of his brow, Tyler was extremely concerned for her.

She desperately needed more than what the confines of The Circle counseling sessions provided. However, he had a devil of a time trying to convince her to see him privately. Bailey insisted that she had everything under control, and the current sessions were all that she needed. There was a formidable stronghold of stubbornness on her part that seemed impossible to break.

Tyler was lost in thought, pondering possible strategies for her when a familiar voice roused him.

"I know that look all too well!"

He raised his eyes to observe Jango leaning in the doorway. He sported dark blue jeans, a black cashmere sweater, and a mischievous smile.

"Ah, man, you late!" Tyler, carrying slight annoyance on his face, nodded in his direction.

A comfortable silence hung in the air for a few minutes after Jango plopped down in the chair adjacent to the big oak desk where Tyler was working.

Tyler allowed his eyes to return to his notes, his right leg jiggling from agitation because of Jango's tardiness. Earlier in the week they had set a summary disposition meeting for the Tuesday group at one o'clock today to go over specifics and strategies of each patient, and as his eyes quickly surveyed the desk clock, he deduced that his partner was well over 45 minutes late.

"Do you remember what we talked about a couple of weeks ago?" Jango finally broke the silence.

Tyler raised his eyes up slightly from over his reading glasses. He felt the heat rising from under the collar of his polo shirt at the question. *What? No apology for his blatant disregard for my time?* Tyler thought.

"It could be a number of things." He carried an edge in his voice.

"—about me coming back to lead The Circle sessions," Jango reminded him.

"You mean about you *praying* to come back to lead the sessions!" Tyler corrected.

"Yes, that's what I want to talk to you about! I was sitting in church last week, and it just hit me! I got this incredible knowing within my soul. It was amazing, Tyler! It was like nothing I have ever felt in my life before. In that moment I knew what it was all about!"

"What—what was all about? You're not making any sense, dude!"

"What my life purpose is, Tyler! I understand now what my purpose is. It's not about me! It's not about me at all! It is truly about Him! I get it now! It is all about God's plan for me!" Jango said as his eyes danced about in excitement. He cleared his throat before continuing.

"I love Jesus! I believe He is the answer for every human problem. With Jesus in my corner, no matter what is going on in my life, I know in my soul that everything will be fine. I now realize that it is my duty to tell everybody that He is the only way to their wholeness.

"I watch these people come in here week after week, all broken up and confused! All fragile and in pain, and I just want them to know that with Jesus they don't have to feel any of that anymore. They can have such peace! They don't have to feel so hopeless. I just want them to have what I have! I want them to know that they may feel lonely, but they are not alone. You know?" Jango explained.

"Jango, I feel you, man. Truly, I do! I admire your relationship with God and how it fills you. However, we are here to help our patients figure out what makes them do what they do, and then show them how to navigate through it. People come here because they need help with their day-to-day lives, and they look to us for sound strategies on how to deal with them. This is psychology and not religion, Jango! The two are like oil and water—they do *not* mix! We are *not* a church, Jango," Tyler rebutted.

"That's the point! I understand that now! This is not my forum, Tyler! I have a calling on my life to be an evangelist! My mission in life is to tell people about Jesus. Tell them that He is the way, the truth, and the life! I need to show people the way to a personal relationship with Jesus, because, Tyler, it is really all about Him!" Jango's signature smile illuminated his round face.

"So, exactly what are you saying?" An edge became more apparent in Tyler's voice.

"I'm saying that I am now going to go preach the Gospel and tell people about Jesus!"

"What? Are you sure?"

"Like nothing else ever before in my life!" Jango confirmed.

"So what does that mean for The Circle—this organization that we started together?"

"You are doing just fine! Nothing needs to change. Nothing at all!"

"It is *not* fine! Because I am doing everything now Jango! I am doing all of the sessions, all the office work—everything!

And now you are telling me that you are walking away!" Tyler's voice had become a few decibels louder in frustration.

"It may seem like I'm walking away, but I just really need to do this right now! I am not abandoning you or our organization."

"Really?! What do you call it then? You walk away into the sunset and what, pray? And I'm left to do everything all by myself? What exactly does *this* mean?"

"We can hire another therapist to help you. That will take a lot of the extra work off you. It means that you continue to stay at the helm, and I stay in the background and advise you, then I pray!" Jango clarified.

"Advise me and pray, huh? Are you fucking kidding me? What kind of bull is that?"

"That is what God has called me to do!"

"That sounds like a cop-out to me! No matter how you rationalize it, you are walking away from your responsibilities in this organization and leaving it all in my hands!" Tyler fumed.

Jango took a deep breath and ran his recently manicured fingers though his prickly hair before responding to Tyler's concern.

"I know that this does not make sense to you. It didn't to me at first, but God spoke to me, and I must be obedient to His call. Let me ask you something. You have known me for a long time, right? Have you ever known me to do anything as radical as this before?"

Tyler shook his head.

"Okay, then, I've never been a person who walked away from responsibilities, right?"

Again, Tyler shook his head.

"So, my friend, this must tell you something about how strongly I believe in what I'm doing! This must tell you that this is bigger than you or me! Bigger than what we are doing here." He got up and sat on the desk in front of Tyler.

"I need you to trust me on this one. I need your support!" Jango's glassy eyes were wide with sincerity.

Tyler had never seen his friend so passionately convinced about anything before. He knew at that moment that this was larger than life, and he had one of two choices: continue to fight or support his longtime friend.

He allowed a wide smile to dress his face. "So what do things look like going forward?"

"For now, you continue to stay at the helm, and I will remain in the background—advise and pray!"

"Advise and pray, huh? I don't totally agree with it, but I support you, and that's all I got!" And with that Tyler reached from a pile-high stack of files on his desk and pulled open the first file.

"Now let's get to work or are you abandoning me all the way—"

"I know that this must be a hard pill to swallow, Tyler, but trust me, this is God's will and in the end, you will see for yourself."

Tyler grunted.

"And for the record, I am here to advise and pray—so let's get started."

Tyler held his tongue. The words that wanted to erupt would have been vile and anger-laced. In all the years that he had known Jango, this was the most committed that he had seen him about anything. Although it was going to be an extreme inconvenience to him, he decided to push past his preconceived notions and support his friend 100 percent.

"Carlos—" Tyler announced, deciding to move on with the meeting's agenda.

"Ah, Carlos. Has he been able to come out yet?" Jango asked as he sat back down in the chair across from Tyler.

"He came out all right! He told his family!"

"What did his father do?" Jango asked, his mouth agape from surprise.

"Not at all what we thought would happen! Let's just say that his family is closer than ever."

"You got to be kidding."

"It appears that his father already knew. His father admitted that it was the primary reason for his being extra rough on the younger son, Miguel. He didn't want him turning gay as well!" Tyler explained.

"He acts like being gay is contagious or something—" Jango voiced.

"I know! Go figure."

"How did Miguel handle the news about Carlos being gay?" Jango asked.

"Miguel ran away when he found out about it. It seems that he really believed that their father was going to really hurt Carlos when he found out. So he wanted to divert the attention away from his brother to him. So he ran away."

"What was he thinking?" Jango asked.

"He wanted to come up with a plan to help his big brother!"

"What a kid!"

"Yeah, pretty brave young man!" Tyler commented.

"How about Carlos's inability to connect sexually?"

"Well, it looks like everything is okay on that front as well!" Tyler then frowned. "He met someone and fell head over heels in love. However, I'm concerned that he's moving entirely too fast with this guy. He has no sense of pacing. As a matter of fact, they are getting ready to move in together."

"We all know how strong of a hold your first love has on you!"

"And we all know the statistics of longevity of first loves as well!"

"True!" Jango commented. "We just have to keep an eye on him!"

"—and wait for the crash! Because just as sure as the sun will set in the evening, it will for sure happen!" Tyler predicted.

"You are the eternal pessimist!" Jango replied.

"No, realist!" Tyler corrected.

"So what's your next step with him?" Jango asked.

"While he's riding on this natural high of his first love there isn't much I can do but monitor him and try to keep him as grounded as I can."

"I'll keep him lifted up in prayer," Jango replied.

Tyler winced at the comment as Jango picked up the next file. This *"lifted up in prayer"* stuff would take some getting used to. Although he professed to support his college friend, he still carried resentment in his heart and felt extremely abandoned.

"What about Lynette? She concerned me the most. Her attitude about her body and the severity of her lack of self-esteem worried me—not to mention the surgeries."

"Well, things have taken a turn for the better. No more surgeries and I am pleased to say that out of them all, she has exhibited the most improvement. She has come to terms with her body issues and has partnered up with her stepmother on a Web-based design company called U DESIGN IT. Such a fabulous idea! They created this software that allows you to upload photos of your body with actual measurements, and then design outfits specifically for your body type. The software is interactive and guides through the colors and styles complimentary to various body shapes and sizes! It's pretty cool," Tyler explained.

"And you say she partnered up with her stepmother? Are you talking about her father's wife? The one that is just a few years younger than her?" Jango asked.

"The very one! That lady is one smart cookie. The two of them have a winner with this business! But the best part of all is the relationship that the two of them have developed. They get each other, and the irony is that Lynette's father was the catalyst."

"So you say she has come to terms with the surgeries?" Jango asked.

"I honestly believe that she has come to terms with it. She now talks about what she is going to do with her life instead of her body! She even mentioned creating a foundation for girls with eating disorders."

"Wow! What about the stepmother? What's her story?" Jango asked.

"Pam is quite delightful. Very wholesome and sweet! She has helped our Lynette successfully deal with so many issues about her father as well as her insecurities about her body," Tyler continued.

"What's this? You have a file on her?" Jango asked as he noticed Tyler reading from a folder with the name PAMELA CASTLE on it.

"Yes. She recently joined The Circle and everybody really took to her!" Tyler beamed.

"Yeah, I can tell!" Jango joked.

"Nothing like that!" Tyler shrugged off the insinuation.

"I'm just happy when I see people reclaim themselves back from an abusive relationship or situation."

"What's the situation with her and her husband like now?"

"Even though they are going through a divorce they have managed to stay civil with each other. Pam attributes it to the strength she gained within therapy to stand up for herself."

"So what's the next step for her?" Jango queried.

"Since things are going really well, I guess you just pray and I'll monitor their progress!" Tyler sarcastically replied.

"Praise God! So what about Rockye?" Jango asked, oblivious to the sarcasm.

"That is another big change! She decided that she would totally commit herself to Andy and stop all of the running around. Just like that! And get this—she was offered the lead in a Broadway play in New York and turned it down flat because she didn't want to leave Andy. She said that she was now ready for something different for herself. And that would require for her to be different, so she just changed! Just like that!"

"So when is the wedding?" Jango joked.

"Well, there lies the problem! Andy is MIA, and she has not heard from him in weeks. Regardless of his disappearance though, she hasn't lost hope! She is committed to waiting patiently for his return. She has done a 180, and the change is quite remarkable."

"Now that *is* amazing! I never thought that I would hear that about her, at least not this early in therapy! Good job, Tyler!" Jango said with a tinge of obvious envy.

"I can't take the credit for that one. I really don't know what happened, to tell you the truth! She's a different person, and I think that out of all of them, I am most surprised! She just overcame that addiction all on her own! She truly developed some tremendous resolve!"

"I guess the cause has to be bigger than you!" Jango stated.

"You got that right!" Tyler confirmed.

"Just keep an eye on her. Make sure that she does not relapse into her old ways, especially if Andy doesn't resurface soon," Jango advised.

"Got it covered." Tyler finished writing his notes in Rockye's file before closing it and replacing it back on the desk.

Jango pulled out the Keno Hunter file. "What about him?"

"Well, that is another story altogether. After his girlfriend found out that he was cheating on her with Sharon, she left. Then Sharon revealed to Keno that she knew about Dee Dee all along, and then threw him out on his ass late one night penniless! She took everything that she had given him all away."

"What did he do?" Jango asked.

"He called me a couple of times, asking me if he could stay with me."

"Did he?"

"No, but I gave him some money for food and a hotel room. He didn't come to group for a few weeks, and then one day I saw him drive into the parking lot in a silver Jaguar. He marched in and informed everyone that he just moved into a downtown high-rise loft."

"What's the deal with him?" Jango inquired.

"I asked him what was going on, and he told me that he was a true Mack. And with his skills, he would never ever be poor again!" Tyler explained.

"What do you think that meant?"

"Who knows? I heard him telling somebody on the phone that he loved them. Probably was the woman who owned the silver Jag."

"When will he ever learn?"

"I guess we have our work cut out with him," Tyler concluded.

"How are you going to handle him now?"

"He's too cocky now—too full of himself. He needs to be in a vulnerable place in order to be receptive to anything we have to say. He's not looking for what he can do for himself. He is looking for what others can do for him. This will take time and a lot of patience to turn that behavior around."

"For sure. I'll keep him lifted up in prayer!"

Tyler winced at the comment.

"What about her?" Jango's lips turned a sheepish smile as he pulled out Bailey's file.

"Her mother is in a diabetic coma at Cedars-Sinai. It doesn't look like she will ever regain consciousness."

"Did she get a chance to make amends with her mother before the coma?"

"No! That's a long story in itself. Just suffice it to say that there are still tons of unresolved issues there. But in spite of it all, her business is flourishing, and she continues to come to group no matter what! I know that she misses you! Every time she hits that door, I can see her looking for you. And when she sees my face, she tries not to show her disappointment. You connected with her, Jango! You may need to personally circumvent me on this one.

"—she also has never resolved her feelings about her ex-boyfriend. That relationship really did a number on her. Bailey has so much rage buried so deep within her; she is a walking time bomb! You really need to talk to her. She listens to you. Talk to her, man."

"I'll think about it. You know that I got feelings for her! Don't want to complicate things and hinder her progress," he confessed.

"Well, don't take too long. She needs more than I can give her right now. I don't want her to fall off of that high-ass tightrope she's walking on." Tyler paused before asking, "Will you at least call her this week?"

"I'll pra—"

"I know—I know—you'll pray about it!" Tyler finished his sentence.

"You know, Jango, tomorrow is not promised to us. You love that girl, and I know that she has strong feelings for you. Seize the moment! Go and see her, talk to her. She really needs a friend right now. She needs to stand next to someone who cares for her and will support her during this very difficult time in her life. You are in love with her. And if truth be told, she is in love with you! Go to her and show her what real love looks like."

Regardless of the fact that Tyler offered his college friend some words of encouragement on love, he was not happy at all about Jango's new revelation and his abandoning the business. He was so displeased that he could have reached across the table and socked him every time he heard him say he would *pray* about it.

He felt abandoned, and although he knew he was perfectly equipped to step in and run the business, he resented Jango for moving on ... for what? A better cause—to fill his life purpose.

But was Tyler angry that Jango was leaving or jealous because he had clarity of his life's purpose? Only time would tell, but for now he had to keep his focus on his patients because that was for him his life's purpose!

Tyler remembered something he had heard years ago. "*The purpose of life is not to be happy. It is to be useful, to be honorable, and to be compassionate. To make enough of a difference in as many lives as possible to justify that you have lived and lived well.*"

Tyler didn't have a clue what his future might bring, but he did know that he was responsible for lives; he was responsible for the emotional healing of the patients that came to him.

Jango had a mission to preach the Gospel, but Tyler's was to provide an environment to make positive and lasting changes in people's lives. Upon second thought, he realized that both he and Jango had similar missions; although they took different avenues, both were vital to people's health and well-being; one was spiritual and one was secular. God or science? Who was to say which was the right one...

Chapter Fifty-Seven
~ Bailey Levine ~

How is it that God answers some prayers but not others? Felicia's surgery went tremendously well! The doctors were able to repair her leg and after a few months of rehabilitation she would be walking normally. The week following the accident, Bailey spent most of her time at the hospital between her mother's room and Felicia's. Her mother was still in a diabetic coma, so all she could do was sit by her bedside and speculate on the dozens of questions floating around in her head and pray that she would have an opportunity to talk to her mother once again. Her father was an emaciated wreck, so questioning him on anything just seemed to add undue stress to him. Therefore, they just sat most of the time in silence.

But conversely, while visiting Felicia it allowed her the opportunity to learn so much more about her employee during that recuperative period. Bailey learned that Felicia had an undeniable faith in God, reverence for the Bible, and an unstoppable determination to accomplish whatever it was that she set out to do.

During one of their heartfelt conversations, Bailey found out that Felicia was abandoned by her unwed 17-year-old mother when she was 2 months old, had lived with seven different foster parents, was severely beaten regularly by the last one, and still managed to graduate high school with honors. Felicia was an amazing young woman in spite of the adversities she experienced growing up.

"How did you do it, Felicia? I don't know that I would have been able to make it with all of the challenges that you had to face growing up. What was your secret?"

"My secret was and still is Philippians 4:13, 'I can do all things through Christ who strengthens me.' That is my secret. Christ in me is the hope of glory. When I stopped trying to figure out things on my own and turned my life over to Him—well, things changed—my feelings about things changed. I was able to forgive and have compassion for those people who hurt me. I was able to see it with a different heart—a heart of love!"

"It was just that simple?"

"Oh no, nothing is that simple. It's a process that I daily work toward perfecting. You see, Bailey, life gives us no guarantees, but the Lord Jesus guarantees that He will never leave us or forsake us. He is with us every moment of each day because He lives in us. That is my strength! That is my *secret*, as you called it."

Bailey wanted what Felicia had. She wanted that confident joy and security. She wanted to believe and experience what Felicia was talking about. She knew that she could no longer do things on her own, and maybe it was time to give up trying and turn to this Jesus Felicia referred to. She wanted to be able to see things with a different heart.

They talked hours on end about Felicia's faith, and it was utterly gratifying being around her as she answered her myriad of questions about this Christ that she talked about. Bailey saw in Felicia the woman she always wanted to be!

By the end of the week, Felicia's prayers had been answered.

"So the doctor says that I will probably be able to go home by the end of next week!" Her bright smile preceded the news.

"Oh, that's wonderful, Felicia!" Bailey leaped up from the edge of the bed and hugged her, careful not to lean on the leg that had been cast from toe to thigh.

"We'll have to celebrate big time!" Bailey continued as she gingerly sat back down at the edge of the bed.

"I can't wait to lie down in my own bed! You know, Bailey, you really don't realize how much you miss your routine until you can't do it anymore." She struggled to sit up straighter in the bed. "Every morning I would get up and read my Bible, eat my morning breakfast cereal, pack my lunch, and take the same route to the office." Felicia paused before continuing. "On my way to work, I would always talk to this homeless man sitting on a bench next to the Winchell's Donut Shop where I picked up donuts for the office. Most people looked at him and felt pity because he smelled and slept in the streets. I didn't feel bad for him though. I talked to him all the time. You know, Bailey, he is one of the smartest, kindest, most grounded people I have ever known! He would tell me all the time, *'Don't feel bad for me. It's all of you I feel bad for. I am not rushing around frantically to some job just to pay bills. I enjoy the sun on my face and calm in my spirit, so don't worry about me. I'm good, really good!'*" She smiled to herself as she reminisced.

She looked up at Bailey. "I miss him! I miss my routine! There is something about having a routine that gives me so much comfort. You know what I mean?"

Bailey glanced at her friend. "I never thought about it, but I guess that you're right! I think that we take those things for granted. But now that I think about it, there are things that I do on a regular that gives me comfort as well."

"Like what?" Felicia asked.

"Ummmmm—like sitting on the stool in my kitchen and reading the paper in the morning before I get dressed for work; like the smell of my wintergreen jojoba body wash that I have used since I was 17 years old; like the way that my favorite pillow smells as I bury my face in it every night before I sleep; like leaving my office every night, and looking back to see my company name displayed on the building; like going to my parents' house for Sunday breakfast."

Felicia detected that all-too-familiar tone in Bailey's voice that she had become intimate with since her hospitalization.

"So how is your mother today?"

"No change." Despair quickly reflected in Bailey's eyes.

"I have faith that your mother will wake up real soon. You can't give up!" Felicia squeezed her friend's quivering hand.

"Do you really think so?" Bailey got up and walked over to the window which overlooked the parking lot of the hospital. "I have so many questions that I need to ask her. I just want to find out why—why she was always so angry with me! I want to know why it seemed like she hated me!"

"I believe that you will get your answers!" Felicia encouraged.

A stubby day nurse walked in and interrupted.

"They want you downstairs for tests, young lady."

Bailey gathered her purse and jacket. "I'll be back later! You behave yourself!"

"Bailey?" Felicia called as she positioned herself on the bed to get into the wheelchair.

Bailey turned around to face her new friend.

"Thank you for everything that you have done for me! I know that you paid my hospital bill. I promise that if it takes the rest of my life, I will pay you back. I thank you from the bottom of my heart. Nobody ever cared for me enough to do anything like this. I am just so grateful beyond words for everything that you have done. I just wanted to make sure that I said, 'Thank you!'" Felicia began to tear up.

Bailey smiled to herself. She knew that she had given up her Bentley in order for Felicia to remain in Cedars-Sinai hospital and get the best care instead of going to the county hospital.

Bailey realized that it didn't matter what she lost because the most important thing was that she was able to really help somebody who needed it, and as a result, she gained a new friend, and a new perspective on life. She had done something selfless for someone else for a change!

"You are welcome, Felicia. And the only payback I want is for you to get better and get back to work."

It was sad that it took Felicia almost losing her life for Bailey to see what an incredible human being she was. She had found a friend, a good friend, and Bailey was the better for the experience!

As she made her way down the hallway from Felicia's room to her mother's, she remembered that she needed to call Rockye again. She hadn't spoken to her in over a week. Their last conversation wasn't the best because she expressed her disdain toward Andy. Rockye was insistent on waiting for him to resurface, and Bailey's opinion was the contrary, "Leave his ass!"

Bailey realized how much she missed her friend and decided to not let the day end without telling her so.

She reached into her oversized Louis Vuitton satchel and pulled out her cell phone, saying under her breath, *"Why put off later what you can do now?"* Bailey hit speed dial #5, which was Rockye's number.

It went straight to voice mail. She called her cell phone again. It went straight to voice mail yet again. She called her home number—voice mail full. She called her cell phone again, and again it went straight to voice mail.

That was unusual for Rockye because no matter what she was doing, Rockye always answered her phone or at least returned a missed call within minutes! In the pit of her stomach Bailey knew something was very, very wrong!

Chapter Fifty-Eight

Rockye Haynes

All the most powerful emotions come from fear, anger, and love—especially love. Love is chaos itself. Love makes no sense at all sometimes. It shakes you up and spins you around. And then, eventually, it either falls apart or falls together.

Andy finally resurfaced. Apparently, he had taken a trip to his small hometown outside of Chicago to visit his mother. At his absence her heart ached for him. She couldn't sleep, eat, or think clearly. All she wanted was for him to come home so that she could love him and show him that she was a changed woman.

Now that he was home, it was literally a nightmare come to life. Rockye was finding it increasingly difficult to communicate with him. He was mean, distant, and withdrawn. His bouts of rage and anger had intensified so much since his return that she walked in a constant state of anxiety when around him. It seemed that every little thing set him off.

Curious about what happened with his mother, Rockye continued to press him for the outcome of his visit; a topic that sent him into greater fits of fury.

"I don't want to talk about it! Why don't you ever fucking listen?"

"What is *wrong* with you, Andy?" Rockye glared at him from the kitchen island as she poured herself a glass of lemonade.

"YOU are what's wrong with me!" he snapped.

Rockye took a deep breath. Deciding not let Andy set the tone for the evening, she changed the subject.

"Okay, we don't have to talk about that! What do you want to do tonight? I have really missed you, sweetheart, and I think that we should do something fun tonight," she said pressing forward, not allowing his disgruntled attitude to dissuade her. She continued as her heart ached for the Andy of yesterday.

Andy stretched out on the couch and lifted a can of Budweiser beer to his mouth. "I just want to chill!" he threw from over his shoulders.

"Okay, then, let's go get a movie and we can pig out on junk food right here!"

He let out a loud fart.

"Come on, Andy! That was disgusting! You're not even tryin' to get along!"

"Look, if you don't want to be here, you can step!" he barked.

Rockye took another deep breath to calm her nerves before walking over and sitting next to him on the couch. Most people would have given up at this point, but she refused to. She was prepared to fight for her man and would continue to take his funky attitude for as long as it took.

Andy immediately pulled back. It was obvious that her presence was not welcomed.

"Baby, I don't want to fight! I am so just so glad that you're back home. All I want is to be with you. I missed you so much when you were gone. And now that you are home, I'm just—just so happy. I don't want to fight, baby. I just want to crawl up next to you and make love all night long!" she leaned in to whisper in his ear.

"Come on, Rockye. I told you that I just want to chill!" He pulled away from her.

She searched his face for the man that she loved. He was long, long gone!

She eased her long body onto the floor in front of him, using the back of the couch as a support. He was drinking heavily, and at each emptied can of beer, he emotionally moved miles and miles away from her.

Would the Andy of yesterday ever return? Was he gone for good? Was this a payback for all the dirt that she had done to him? Payback is a bitch! And she didn't have a clue what to do to turn things around.

He was angry, he was mean, and he was distant. She felt unwanted and alone. It suddenly dawned on her that she no longer had options. She had screwed herself. Rockye had made the wrong choice. She should have gone to New York with Cyrus. She should have made the choice to go after her career instead of love! But she chose love. She chose Andy. She chose WRONG!

As Andy farted again, she made up her mind that at the first opportunity she had she would call Cyrus and beg to get back what she had so stupidly thrown away! If there was a chance in hell to get that lead part back, she would bust her ass to do whatever she needed to do to get the hell out of this situation and go to New York. Forget about being the perfect woman. If Andy didn't want her, she would do the one thing that she was really good at! Her career!

Fuck relationships—fuck men—fuck love! How many men would put a woman before their career? Women were the only ones who threw their life on the burning pyres of love—just as she had done. Now here she was left with nothing. No love and no career. She had truly fucked herself! She threw her life away… all in the interest of love! What the hell would she do now?

Chapter Fifty-Nine
~ Bailey Levine ~

Was death something that you could feel coming? Would its presence hang in the air like the aroma of sautéed onions? Bailey hovered in the doorway, watching her parents, wondering if her mother would ever return to the land of the living. Her father's head nestled on her mom's left arm as his slightly curled body hung over the hospital chair onto the reclined bed of his comatose wife. Although as dysfunctional as it may have been, she so desperately longed for those times gone by when her mother nagged as she cooked Sunday breakfast and her father passively read his newspaper.

She missed her mother's voice. Why did it seem so hard now to remember it? Please don't let her die! Her heart did somersaults as she ruminated.

Noticing her mother's hair at a disarray on top of her head, Bailey moved over to the bed, set her purse on the nightstand, and pulled open the drawer to retrieve the comb and brush she had placed in there only days earlier. She gently pulled it through the graying strands. The sound of the brush sliding through her mother's dry hair caused her father to stir but not awaken. She glanced down at him as she smiled at his sleeping noises.

Turning back to her mother, she gasped when she saw her eyes looking up at her.

"Mom!"

Marjorie opened her mouth to talk but words got caught in the dryness of her throat. Bailey quickly eased a little water into her mother's mouth from a paper cup on the bed stand.

Marjorie softly cleared her throat before managing a faint smile at her daughter.

"Oh my God, Mom—I can't believe you're awake. How do you feel?" Her face was painted with concern.

"Like—like I have been hit by a Mack truck!" Marjorie forced out.

Bailey held the straw for her mother to pull in more water to her dehydrated throat.

"Thank God that you're awake. We have been so worried!"

Marjorie scanned her environment looking as if she was trying to ascertain her whereabouts.

"You're in the hospital, Mom. You slipped into a diabetic coma and—"

Marjorie glanced down at her sleeping husband and interrupted. "—how is he?"

"Dad?" Bailey choked back the tears trying to emerge. "You know Dad!"

Marjorie gave him a knowing look that only a wife of over 30 years could.

"Let me wake him." Bailey moved toward her father.

"Don't!" Marjorie demanded.

Bailey's eyes asked why.

"I need to talk to you!" Her eyes fell onto the corner of the bed. "Please sit down, Bailey."

Bailey obeyed.

"We need this time together. There is not much of it left!"

"Don't say that, Mom! You're going to be just fine," Bailey encouraged.

"No! I don't have much longer. I am going *home* tonight!" She gazed off into the distance and a tranquil look of peace radiated on her face. "They are waiting for me. I was given this time because I need to talk to you." Marjorie's face held a maternal expression that Bailey had only seen intermittently throughout her formative years.

"I need to tell you something." Tears started to form in the corner of her eyes which had turned gray from the illness.

Bailey grabbed her mother's hand.

"I have to apologize to you, honey."

"For what, Mom?" Bailey knew what she had to apologize for. This was something that she had been yearning to hear so desperately all of her life. She asked the question, but it was merely rhetorical.

"I was an awful mother to you and your brother. If you only knew the demons that I lived with honey—you would understand..."

"What are you talking about, Mom? What demons?"

"I have never known real love in my life until your father—if you only knew!"

"Talk to me, Mom. I have so many questions, Mom. Please talk to me!"

Bailey gave her mother another sip of water as she struggled to get the words out.

"Your grandmother—your grandmother—she gave me away when I was 9 years old to her sister, my aunt Evelyn. I came home from school one day to find that I had to leave and go live with my aunt Evelyn. Your grandmother never explained why or what happened. My clothes were already packed and sitting by the door when I walked in from school. Mister Edwards from the corner drugstore drove me to my aunt's. When we got there he just put my things on the porch and left. Nobody ever explained anything to me. I was just sent away!"

"Why did Grandma send you away?"

"I never really understood until I was grown why she gave me away like some puppy dog or something! My mother was jealous of me! She was jealous of my youth—my innocence. I got the attention that she once got, and she hated it!

"I stayed with my aunt until I turned 13. I was such a badass that I had to go back to my mother's house because Auntie Evelyn could no longer take my sass. I had such a bad attitude. My mother let me come back begrudgingly. But truth be told, she didn't want me there at all. My life after I moved back was filled with endless chores and criticisms. My mother would go off to the neighborhood pool hall in the afternoon and come back home the next morning very drunk. I spent a lot of my time alone and lonely.

"I can't remember your grandmother ever telling me that she loved me. She just called me a lot of bad names! She was a mean woman—real mean!" Marjorie began coughing after the declaration. Bailey attempted to get up to get her mother more water.

"No—no—I'm okay!" She paused moments before continuing.

"And my dad was illiterate. He never even finished third grade. I remember him always drinking beer and watching baseball. Sometimes he would pick me up and tickle me until my giggling got on my mother's nerves and she hollered for him to stop. He stopped and either sat back down to watch television or just simply left to go somewhere else to drink.

"I don't remember much conversation in my house, only the thick air of indifference." Marjorie held an impenetrable gaze with her daughter.

"I remember always asking myself, 'Why does she hate me so much?'

"Regardless of all that chaos in my house, I graduated high school and got accepted to college. When I got accepted to college, I went to my mother and asked her to give me the money I had been saving since I was old enough to work. I had been working since about 10 or 11 years old. I would always give my money to my mother to put in a savings account for me so that I could collect interest. I read about it in some magazine and told her about it. She said that she would open up a savings account for me because I was too young at the time.

"I didn't know that she took the money that I had given her all that time and spent it on herself!" Marjorie paused.

Bailey could tell that it was getting increasingly difficult for her mother to speak.

"I got accepted to Albany State College, and the day that I was ready to leave, I asked her to go to the bank and get my money for me."

Bailey anxiously awaited her mother to continue.

"She—she laughed—right in my face! Then she told me that she used the money to feed my stupid ass!"

Bailey got up to hug her mother.

"No—no—sit down! I want you to hear this!" Marjorie insisted. "I stood there just looking at her. I didn't know whether I should scream or cry! I just looked at her in shock!"

Marjorie attempted to reach for the cup of water on the dresser. Bailey quickly assisted her.

Marjorie continued, "I just picked up my suitcase and walked out the door without saying a word!

"As I left the house, I could hear her whistling! *Whistling!* Can you imagine that? Her only child was going off to college with no money, no good-bye, no nothing, and my mother was whistling!"

Bailey watched her mother's face contort from the memory.

"You see, Bailey, when I left there, I tried to forget her, my father, and that whole damn nightmare, but I still had so much anger and resentment inside of me.

"After finishing college, I came to Los Angeles and started sleeping around with any man that gave me the slightest bit of attention. I think I did it because I just wanted somebody to hold me, you know, love me!"

Her mother looked deeply into her eyes.

"The reason why I blew up on you that morning when you came to the house for breakfast was because I thought that you were pregnant! It reminded me of the many abortions I had before I met your father. I'm ashamed to say that I lost count at about eight. The guilt of killing over eight of my own children haunted me daily. What kind of woman can kill her own flesh and blood so easily? It took a piece of my soul every time I thought about it.

"I wasn't really angry with you! You see, this condemnation lives inside of me, eating at me; the memory of it—of all the babies that I killed, it tortures me. When I looked at you and your brother it would torment me so much!"

"You always acted like you hated me. Why?"

"I didn't hate you, Bailey. I hated myself. I hated that I had a good husband and healthy, wonderful children in spite of what I deserved. I hated that I killed innocent children—my children! That is what I hated, not you or your brother!"

"Mom, I am so sorry for you!" Bailey's face was stained from tears.

"I know that I was wrong! I know that I was so mean to you and your brother! So many times I wanted to just hold you in my arms and tell you what an amazing kid, person, and woman you had become. I look at you and am so proud at the things that you can do, have done, and are doing!"

She reached for her daughter's hand.

"Your mother is not proud of this, but that guilt, grief, and anger stopped me from being a good mother to you and your brother. I had so much guilt and anger in me that I couldn't control it. I just couldn't control it! It literally controlled me!"

Marjorie looked down at her husband.

"Your father put up with a lot from me. He tried to protect you children from my demons." She reached out and lightly stroked his hair.

"Your dad is an angel! He was always by my side to help me through the despair, the breakdowns, the serious bouts of depression and the rage. Your father kept most of it from you children."

She eyed her daughter.

"Don't be angry at your dad! I know that you resent him for how he handled things, but your father was doing the best he could to keep our family together. Dealing with my demons was a full-time job!" She stroked his head softly before continuing. "I never felt like I deserved such a wonderful man or any more children after what I did. Those feelings consumed my life to the point that it affected you kids and your father!" She looked over at him.

"But he never gave up on me! He never left me! He was always by my side! I will always love your father for the way he loved me." She looked back at her daughter.

"I wish for you that type of love, sweetheart! I wish for you that type of love!"

"Mom, I am so sorry! I didn't know! I didn't understand! Please forgive me for the things that I thought and said—" Bailey softly sobbed.

"No, honey, it is I that asks your forgiveness. I couldn't have asked for a better daughter! You and your brother have been my pride and joy. I am so sorry that I allowed those demons inside of me to take over. I am so sorry that I wasn't a better mother! Please forgive me, Bailey! Please forgive me! I am truly sorr—"

Bailey noticed that her mother's breathing had become severely labored.

"Take it easy, Mom! Try to relax!" Bailey encouraged.

The monitors in the room suddenly began to vigorously beep.

As the nurses rushed in, her father suddenly sprang up from his long overdue slumber.

"Marjorie!" He jumped up.

"Daddy, she was just talking to me!" Bailey cried.

"Stand back!" the doctor demanded as he rushed into the room.

Bailey embraced her father as they watched the nurses injecting her IV and the doctor taking her vitals.

"Please move aside!" the nurses ordered Bailey and her father.

Minutes later the doctor pulled her father aside and with a hushed voice informed him of his wife's plight. It was obvious that life was slowly leaving her body. Her eyes got cloudy, and she just stared into space, like she was looking at something intently. Bailey glanced down at her mother's hands and noticed that the nail beds were getting white. Her heart raced at the sight for she had heard that white nail beds were evidence that death was imminent.

Her mother was dying right in front of her.

Bailey moved up close to her mother and whispered, "I love you, Mom. I love you!" She smothered her mother's bloated face with desperate kisses.

As Bailey's lips rested on her mother's forehead, she inhaled her deteriorating scent.

"Ba—Bail—"

"Yes, Mother, I'm here. Don't try to talk. I'm here!"

"Take care of your fa—father! He—he is a good man! Look after himmm! Prom—promi—promise me!" Marjorie pleaded.

"I will, Mom. I will!" Bailey reassured her.

"—love you, Bailey. So prou—proud of yoooou both! Tell your brother wha—what I said. Ask him to for—for—forgive me! Ask him—" She labored to speak.

"Yes, Mom, I will!"

"—and Ba—Bai—Baiiley. Don't let my de—demonnnns be your de—demmmmons! Plea—Please don't—"

"Yes, Mother. Yes, I promise I won't. I love you. I lov—" The machines starting violently beeping!

"Mom! Mom! Mom!" Bailey cried out. But she had taken her last breath. She was gone.

Her mother had died and was now finally free from her demons.

Instantly, Bailey felt an immense void. Her mother was dead…gone forever! She started crying, she felt bereft at such a primitive level, and at that moment no one could fathom the depths of her pain.

For everything in life there is always a beginning and an end. This is the tough part, the most difficult thing when you see it coming—death.

Maybe she would finally meet the eight-plus children that she had aborted, and it would give her the much-deserved peace that she never got on this earth.

Good bye Mom. May you rest in peace…finally!

Chapter Sixty

✎ *Andy Reynolds* ✎

*S**ilence is the safest course of action when one holds massive distrust for another within the confines of his heart.*

Andy felt like a different man since his return from Chicago. He likened it to the time he climbed a tree to retrieve a neighbor's cat and twisted his body in an awkward position in attempts to reach the cat huddled deep within its leafy confines. Reaching up high above his head to secure the cat he felt something in his body snap. The audible sound afforded him no noticeable pain to speak of at the moment, but he felt a physical shift within his body that would change the way he operated in it forever. To this day, because of that injury, he had limitations on the movement of his upper torso.

Similarly, he felt the same thing emotionally after his return from seeing his mother. Something snapped within him at that encounter, and he hadn't felt the same since. He felt broken, like pieces of him had slipped from its fixtures. He felt utterly disjointed.

Not understanding the emotional tug-of-war within his own consciousness, he just preferred to be left the hell alone and Rockye's exuberant disposition sent him into fits of fury and rage. He just wanted her away from him, away from sucking up the air that he so desperately needed to breathe in efforts to just find some type of normalcy once again. But he couldn't do that because she was always there, always talking, and always asking dumb-ass questions.

"Why won't you talk to me, Andy? You act like you hate me or something."

"I just want to be left the hell alone, Rockye. Can a man get some peace and quiet in his own damn house?"

"You know I don't have to be here! I can walk out that door just like I walked my ass in—"

"—what's stopping you then?"

"Come on, Andy, I don't know what's going on with you, but please know that I love you, and I just want to help. Just tell me, baby, how I can help you. I love you. Please just talk to me!" She attempted to put her arms around him as she sat beside him on the couch.

He pulled away.

"*Really?* Is that how it is? You don't even want me to touch you? What the hell is wrong with you? You haven't been the same person since you came back. What happened at your mom's? Why won't you talk to me?"

He remained silent.

"Talk to me! Talk to me, damn it!" she pleaded.

He continued to stare at the television.

"Okay, so *I* am the enemy now? You can turn me off just like that?"

Andy's eyes remained transfixed as he glared at the television.

"Say something to me. Fucking talk to me!!!!! What the hell is going on with you?"

"I want you to leave me the hell alone! I want you to get the hell out of my house! You really don't want to be here, and I don't want you here. Sooner or later you are going to leave me anyway, so do us both a favor and just get it over with. Just go!"

"What the fuck are you talking about? What happened to you down there with your mother? What did she do to you, Andy?"

"I said get the hell out of my house!" He stood up and glared at her. "Get the fuck out now!!!!!"

Rockye fashioned a look of disbelief, exhibiting a piercing hurt within her wide eyes. She opened her mouth to speak but instead shot him a look of surrender, then grabbed her purse and scurried out the door.

Finally, he could get some damn peace and quiet!

He heard her heels clicking on the steps as she raced down them two at a time in haste.

Relieved that she was finally out of his apartment, he secured another beer and replanted himself on the couch, thumbing through the cable channels as the lingering scent of Rockye's perfume still hung in the air.

What had he hoped he would feel once she was gone? Peace? Calm? What had he hoped the presence of sweet solitude would bring him? He sat there waiting for the blanket of relief to envelop him. But nothing—nothing had changed since her departure because he still felt violently angry!

The ball of anger had continued to grow since his return from visiting his sorry excuse of a mother in Chicago. It had intensified so much that he found it increasingly difficult to contain it within himself.

Images of that visit continued to replay over and over in his mind.

Once he had decided to visit his mother, he severed all communication with Rockye, his job, and the few friends that he had so that he could mentally prepare himself for the encounter. Ever since he was informed of his mother's cancer, he felt compelled to confront her, to question her, to look her in the eyes in hopes of understanding why he always felt such a disconnect with women, with his sisters, and with his girlfriend, Rockye.

After he updated his job that he would be using some of his vacation time, he took off to Chicago in hopes of getting some understanding, answers to questions, and hopefully some much-needed closure. Unfortunately, his arrival was met with repugnance from his mother.

The trailer she lived in was so dilapidated that it seemed like a good wind would disintegrate it to a pile of rubble. He took the four stairs to the front porch with apprehension, the beat of his heart muffled by the heaviness of his breath. He didn't know what awaited him on the other side of the door. He knocked, but it was met with no answer. He eased the door open after the second knock was not met with a response. His heart raced with anxiety.

Once inside his eyes caught sight of an image that he felt would be burned into his memory forever.

After navigating through the trailer searching for someone, his eyes fastened in on his mother tea bagging some old dude on the kitchen floor.

Their eyes met. His widened in shock and hers squinted with aggravation.

"What the hell are you doin' here?" were hardly the words he expected to hear from a mother that had not seen her son in almost 5 years. Begrudgingly, she removed herself from between the old dude's legs and pushed past both of them to the bathroom.

Eventually, the half-naked old dude got so uncomfortable with his presence that he picked up his clothes, which were strewn about the floor, and strolled out the front door of the trailer.

When his mother finally emerged from the bathroom, she looked around for the old dude.

"What the hell happened to Bert?" Anger was evident in her gravelly voice.

After she determined that he had indeed left she said, "He left? Fuck! You just cost me $40! Damn, you always did have the worst fucking timing! What are you doing here anyway?" she said as she lifted a cigarette to her lips and took a long pull.

"I came to see about you, Ma." His eyes filled with concern.

"You came to see about me?" She roared in laughter. "What the fuck for?"

"'Cause—'cause you are sick and all!" he managed to get out.

She yelled at the top of her lungs. "What did those lazy cows tell you? It ain't nobody's damn business! Nobody but mine!"

"Look, Ma, I came all this way to see you and talk to you!" His eyes searched hers for a maternal connection.

"What the fuck do you want to talk to me about?" She blew a thick cloud of smoke in his direction. "I ain't got shit to say!"

"Okay, then, then, I want you to just listen—listen to what I have to say!" Andy felt his heart pounding in his chest so hard that he was certain that his mother heard it as well.

His mother sat on the edge of the kitchen chair; her legs opened wide enough that her bush peeked out from underneath her tattered dressing gown.

Although Andy was repulsed, he continued. "Ma, I came all this way because I want you to know that if you need anything, you know, during this—this time—that I am here for you! I want you to know that I will help—I am willing to help! I just want you to know that you are not alone." Andy stumbled over his words.

His eyes searched hers for a response.

His mother got up and walked over to him and sat down next to him on the stained ottoman. Her breath was so stale that it made his eyes water.

"Out of all my kids, you was always the soft one!" She looked him up and down.

"You come down here, wearing an expensive suit, to what—to tell me that you is here for me? Why? What kind of jackass keeps going up on a dog that bites 'em?" She reached her hand in between her gown and scratched around the aureole of her left breast; a habit that Andy found extremely distasteful.

"I don't want nothin' from you!" She got up and stood over him.

"Let me ask you something," his mother continued. "What was the real reason that you came down here? What are you looking to get from me?" She lit up another cigarette.

"Answers—" He eyed her with boldness.

"Answers?" She laughed a wicked laugh. "You want to know why yo' mama is like she is? You want to know why yo' mama likes to drink Beam and Daniels and get fucked morning, noon, and night? You want to know why yo' mama didn't amount to shit? You want to know if I'm scared to die from this damn sickness that's inside my body?"

Andy followed his mother's lips with his eyes. It took every bit of strength that he had to hold back the tears of anger that were quickly forming.

She noticed the glassy look in his eyes. "You was always soft, Andy! That's your fucking problem!"

He wiped the tears with the back of his sleeve that started to fall down his cheeks.

"I know what you came here for! You came here to give forgiveness and make amends as them damn alcoholics are always talking about. Making a fucking amends! You want to tell me that you forgive me for being a no-good mama? You want to make up with this old bitch before I die so you can feel good about yourself?

"Look, Andy! I am just gonna tell you like it is! I was born the daughter of a whore, a woman that all she cared about was fucking. She didn't care about if her kids was hungry, healthy, sad, happy—whatever! All she wanted was a drink and a dick up inside her! I grew up with that shit, and that is what I am!

"I didn't want no damn kids. You kids was what happened 'cause I was too fucking drunk or high to have the trick put on a condom." She paused.

"I ain't nobody's mama. I am a whore who likes money and plenty of dick! And as quiet as it is kept, most all women is like that too.

"I heard you have been laying up with some colored girl back there in L.A.!" She lit up another cigarette.

"You be a fool if you trust any bitch! All bitches care about is some money and who has the biggest Johnson." Her eyes traveled down to his crotch. "And if my memory serves me right, you ain't got the biggest Johnson. You took after yo' no-good daddy! His shit was long and skinny. Didn't really have no fullness to it. Couldn't keep a bitch if he tried!" She laughed.

"So what you need to do now is take your long skinny dick, your expensive suit, and all your fucking questions and just go back where the fuck you came from—that is what you need to do!"

In the distance, a car pulled into the driveway and its occupant slowly moved up to the door; the gait favored a person who sported a limp.

"Hey, babe, where you at? I brought everything we need to party with." A semi bald middle-aged man holding two brown paper bags in his hand entered his mother's trailer.

She lit up another cigarette, discarding the previous half-smoked one in an overflowing ashtray when she saw him enter.

"Big Daddy! You just in time." She moved over to him and simultaneously grabbed his crotch while pushing her nicotine-coated tongue down his throat.

Afterward, the man turned to face Andy. "Who this?"

"Nobody; besides, he was just leaving!" She pushed the man into the bedroom. "I'll be in by the time you finish taking yo cloths off."

His mother turned back to Andy. "This is who I am! This is who I have always been! I ain't shit, and give most women half the chance, they will show you that they ain't shit either! Now go on back to where you came from and leave me the hell alone!"

Andy stood up to leave. He didn't know what to say. The rage that held a home in his belly had spread throughout his whole body. He had an anger that was lethal. All he wanted to do was hurt somebody.

He wanted somebody to feel the unbearable pain that he was feeling right now!

Anger is a paralyzing emotion. You find it difficult to move, to think, to rationalize. Anger makes you helpless; it's absence of control.

Andy hated his mother so much at that moment. He imagined her body curled up on the floor, knees to chin, and the blood of her futile heart seeping out over her chest, arms, and legs, flooding the floor of the dilapidated trailer, down the four stairs and out into the dusty dry ground of the front yard.

As he sat alone in his apartment consuming massive amounts of alcohol to dull the pain from the thoughts; thoughts of his mother's scandalous behavior, his girlfriend's promiscuity, and his baby mama's acts of opportunism, he ruminated about killing all of them. He smiled as he imagined their bodies twisted in a crumpled heap from his brutal retaliation while the blood drained slowly out from their lifeless bodies – Die, bitches, die!

Epilogue

The burgeoning rage inside of Andy was about to explode. It had been hours since Rockye left his apartment. Andy switched from beer and was now guzzling whisky. As he lifted his fourth glass of Beam to his lips and swallowed its entire contents, his thoughts drifted back to his mother's last words.

"*This is who I am! This is who I have always been! I ain't shit, and give most women half the chance; they will show you that they ain't shit either!*"

He picked up the telephone to call Rockye. He dialed her cell and got voice mail. He dialed her home and got the answering machine. He looked at the clock. It was 12:50 a.m. Where the fuck was she?

Decent women are at home at this time of night! He dialed her cell again. It went straight to voice mail. He dialed her home number and the answering machine came on after a few rings.

This time instead of hanging up he left a drunken message.

"You are a no-good bitch! You fucking whore! I know that you are out fucking around. Who is he? A black one like you? So I guess you are tired of this skinny-dick white boy! If you think that I am just going to let you fuck over me just like that, you got another think coming to you, you whore! You cheating whore!" When he finished he slammed the phone into its cradle.

He attempted to stand up but stumbled back onto the couch. He cursed again and on his second attempt to erect himself managed to propel himself upward.

His anger had now become uncontainable; his mission was now to exact revenge. He was tired of being the victim; he was ready to get justice for himself. He was ready to finally get justice!

Andy slipped on his suede loafers, grabbed his cell phone, keys, and wallet from the table by the front door, and stumbled to his car, the half-empty bottle of whiskey in one hand and a determination for justice as his intent.

After hearing Andy kick the door in, panicking, Rockye instantly sprinted toward the wall-mounted telephone near the dishwasher and yanked it off its cradle. Sinking onto the floor near the refrigerator, she dialed 911. It rang once, and then a baritone-voiced female answered, but before she could respond, there Andy was standing over her, holding a metal pipe high in the air in his right hand.

"Put the damn phone down, bitch—NOW!"

She let it slip from her tight grip, allowing it to tumble to the marble floor.

"You cheating bitch! Where is he?" His eyes darted wildly around the room.

"Where is he? Come out you coward!" he roared. "You can have sex with her, but you can't fight for the bitch?" His wild eyes continued to survey the room.

Rockye didn't know what Andy was in a rage about, but she knew that she was often careless in her indiscretions and it was entirely possible that Andy had discovered or uncovered one of the many. She said a quick prayer and hoped that his anger was a result of too much alcohol, but nonetheless, her gut confirmed that it was far more serious than that!

Rockye remained motionless, fearfully balled up on the floor in utter panic; the telephone which had slipped from her hands lay inches from her on the floor. Although her eyes continued to search for a way out, deep down in her belly she knew that she was in big trouble!

All of a sudden their eyes met, and for a brief moment, Rockye identified with the man who loved and adored her; the man that not long ago was sitting across the table expressing his love for her as they ate a dinner that he had just prepared. Then just as quickly as it came upon him, it vanished! *Violent* Andy returned!

"People told me that you were no-good! But did I listen? Hell no! I loved you and was foolish enough to think that my love was enough!" He paused. "What a damn fool I was!" His faced softened momentarily. "I loved you, Rockye! With all of my heart I loved you! Why couldn't you just do right? Why? Why couldn't I be enough? Why all the men? WHY?"

She remained motionless and stiff from fear, her wide eyes pleading for mercy.

"Answer me, bitch!" Andy shouted a few decibels below a thunderous roar.

"Baby, please calm down! I love you! Just listen to me! Baby, please! Andy, please just calm down!" Rockye desperately pleaded.

"You are trash—always have been—always will be! You will never hurt me again," Andy yelled out loud. He spit on her body, kicked her, and lifted the metal pipe high above his head, then hurled it down with full force on the right side of her head.

Rockye let out a bloodcurdling scream in anticipation of the metal pipe slamming into her body.

The force of the blow sent her spiraling into semi consciousness. Her body fell heavily to the floor as a pool of blood quickly formed beneath her.

Rockye briefly focused on Andy standing over her, his face holding the expression of pleasure. Her whole body felt numb, and she felt wet and sticky. It appeared as though the temperature had dropped considerably for she was extremely cold. Things were getting blurry and the bright yellow colors of her kitchen were beginning to fade to a dismal gray.

"Why were the men always more important than me? You always put them first! Where are they now, huh? You will *never* hurt me or anyone ever again!" Rockye heard Andy say as she focused on a smile of satisfaction on his face.

As Rockye lost the fight with consciousness, she faintly heard Andy's last words: "Ma, you will never ever be able to hurt me again. You finally got what you deserved!

"Die, bitch, die …"

About the Author

R. Ceci Dymally was born and raised in Southern California. She discovered her passion for writing during her childhood. She honed her skills in high school and wrote her first manuscript in her freshman year at UCLA, studying Journalism. She further persued her passion for writing into the arena of Children's literature with her first book, *Affirmations for Children*, published in 2004.

Ceci's talent for creating colorful, sexy, and poignant characters coupled with relative, relatable, and controversial subjects brings the novel to life. Each page has the reader thirsting to know what happens next. *Twisted Circle* is her debut novel and the first of a trilogy.

www.ingramcontent.com/pod-product-compliance
Lightning Source LLC
Chambersburg PA
CBHW031400290426
44110CB00011B/217